D1193115

A NOTICE TO THE READER

The prices of all products listed in this book have been omitted primarily because they are subject to frequent change. This would make the book outdated before the next edition could be printed. The publisher does, however, maintain a printed list of current prices. This may be obtained by sending two (2) first class stamps along with your name and address to: The Great Outdoors Trading Company, 24759 Shoreline Highway, Marshall, California 94940

WE NEED YOUR HELP

It is the intention of the publisher to stay abreast of the developments in this sport by printing new editions of this book on a regular basis. We ask, then, that all readers, organizations, dealers and manufacturers join in the effort to keep this book up-to-date by sending us any corrections, additions, revisions or deletions they may have. This information, concerning any of the subjects covered herein, will be gratefully appreciated. We ask that this data follow the general format of our present listings and be mailed to: The Great Outdoors Trading Company, 24759 Shoreline Highway, Marshall, CA 94940.

The Complete Outfitting & Source Book for
SPORT DIVING

DEDICATION

To Mame
for keeping the faith

The Complete Outfitting & Source Book for
SPORT DIVING

Compiled By
The Staff of the Great Outdoors Trading Company

Written and Edited By
Larry Clinton, Jr.

Published By
The Great Outdoors Trading Company

Printed in the United States of America

First Printing: December 1978

Published by the Great Outdoors Trading Company,
24759 Shoreline Highway, Marshall, CA 94940.

Distributed to the book trade by Holt, Rinehart and Winston,
383 Madison Avenue, New York 10017.

Art Director: Marja Wicker

Cover Photography: John Clark

Typography: Graffic Jam

Library of Congress Cataloging in Publication Data

Clinton, Larry, Jr.

   The complete outfitting & source book for sport
diving.

   (A Holt Great Outdoors book)

   1. Skin diving. 2. Skin diving — Equipment
and supplies. I. Great Outdoors Trading Company.
II. Title. III. Title: Sport Diving.

GV840.S78C53   797.2'3   78-56573

ISBN title number: 0-03-045606-1

Table of Contents

Introduction

As soon as he mastered the challenge of surviving in his environment, man began devising ways to utilize the four basic elements as his playthings. The earth's slopes and hollows were there to be climbed and explored, its flatlands manicured into sporting greens. Air became something to soar through, with various mechanical aids. Even fire has been harnessed to power our pleasure-machines.

Water, in its liquid and solid forms, also stirred man's playful imagination. But until very recently, our enjoyment of water had been limited to its surface, in recreations like boating, swimming, skiing, skating. As the following section documents, man has been plunging beneath the seas since the beginning of history for profit, science, and warfare . . . but only in this century for pure pleasure.

"Innerspace" —that exotic megacosm beneath the sea, offers divers an overwhelming sensory experience. Taste and smell are muzzled, opening the other senses to a rush of new perceptions. Most obvious is the exhileration of weightlessness. It is no coincidence that so many aviators have also been underwater enthusiastists. The fishman and the birdman share the thrill of freedom in an alien medium. The phantasmagoria of undersea life also offers a incomparable visual experience with its kaliedoscopic array of beautiful and bizarre colors, shapes, and textures.

And yet there are even more subtle sensations awaiting the alert diver. Between mechanical rasps from his regulator, he can hear small shrimp crunching their way through a coral reef. With gentle fingers he can learn the texture of sponges and other marine growths, or feel the friendly

frenzy of reef fish feeding from his hand. The novelty and variety of underwater sensations keeps divers returning again and again to the underwater world.

These and other enticements are luring more and more diving recruits. Today there are some 4,000,000 certified divers, with close to a quarter million more being trained each year in the U.S. alone. The major international certifying agencies report that the number of certifications issued has risen 35% a year for each of the past five years, making sport diving one of the fastest-growing recreations in the world.

Preserving the Underwater World

All this increased activity has unfortunately taken its toll on the underwater environment. Many reefs have been decimated by collectors and careless divers. In some areas, entire species of gamefish and shellfish have been threatened, and intricate marine food chains have been drastically disrupted. Sport divers have also encountered shocking evidence of man's pollution of the seas, and in some cases have contributed to that pollution through their own carelessness and neglect.

Those who know and love the sea well enough to dive in it must recognize the vulnerability of this delicate ecosystem. "Innerspace" is truly the last frontier on earth, but it is a fragile frontier, and must be approached with great respect and care by all who venture there.

Responsible divers know that exercising such care is generally a simple matter of observing local regulations and a few basic rules of common sense. Among them:

•*Leave each dive site the way you'd like to see it again.* If you find litter, clean it up; don't add to it. Don't bring anything with you you don't plan to bring back. Before collecting any plant or animal life, ask yourself whether you'll enjoy seeing it on your coffee table or in your garden as much as you do undersea. Bring home memories, or pictures if you can, not souvenirs.

•*Only take game you can use.* Trophy-hunting has become an outmoded concept. So has over-harvesting. It's nice to "share the wealth," but be sure there's plenty left for next time. If you dive for game frequently, vary your locations. Don't pick a site clean.

•*Swim lightly on the reef.* Careless hands,

elbows, knees, and feet can do untold damage to living corals and plant life. Adjust your buoyancy so you can hover over or next to the reef without touching it. Swim slowly and take care not to kick up sand—otherwise you could drown coral polyps and scare away the fish you've come to see.

•*Take responsibility for your fellow divers.* Help those less experienced when ever possible. If you spot divers breaking the rules, bring it to their attention—suggesting alternatives, if you can. Patronize dive shops, charter boats, resorts, and tour operators who demonstrate respect for the underwater environment.

How to Use this Book

There are many good sport diving how-to guides. This book is not one of them. Instead, it has been compiled and written for the person who has already made a commitment to the sport and wants to deepen that commitment—and for those beginners who wish to become more involved in the sport and want to know how.

In a sense, no book dealing with such a varied and fast-changing subject can ever be "finished." The technology of diving, the choice of sites, the nature of the diving industry and consumer groups, are all constantly evolving.

The listings and other information in each section reflect the most complete and accurate information available to us at press time. In a few cases there will be products, services, sites, or organizations left out because our inquiries went unanswered, because changes occurred after our deadline, or because they had somehow escaped our attention. Since the concept of this book calls for it to be updated on a regular basis, we hope to rectify any such omissions in future editions. Your help in bringing any oversights to our attention would be sincerely appreciated.

We have not "test-rated" products or services in this book. Rather, we have tried to present buying tips and objective comparative information from manufacturers and suppliers so the reader can make his or her own decisions. We are unable to take responsibility for any inaccuracies or omissions or for any failure of products or services to perform as described. Since costs of goods and services are subject to change without notice, we have not included prices in this book. For the most up-to-date price information, see the notice on the inside front cover.

History

Who can say what first lured early man to struggle forth from his native land and plunge himself into the sea?

Was it hunger for the gleaming fish he'd seen the seabirds feasting on? Was it lust for the untold treasures he imagined beneath the waves? Mystic fascination with the ocean's vastness and might? Or could it have been a primal instinct drawing him back through eons of evolution to his original home?

Unfortunately, no accounts exist of that first manfish and the compulsion that drove him to brave the depths. Instead, our earliest evidence of man's undersea exploits consists of the stuffs he wrested from the ocean floor. Architectural findings dating as far back as 4500 B.C. in Mesopotamia include mother-of-pearl ornamentation. Even more extensive use of mother-of-pearl appears in pieces from the Theban sixth dynasty (c. 3200 B.C.).

Greek divers were supplying sponges for household use as early as 2000 B.C. The divers even utilized sponges in their work. They carried oil-soaked sponges in their mouths and bit them, sending the oil to the surface to still choppy waters and steady the beams of sunlight that danced on the bottom. The robes of Grecian noblemen and women were often colored with Tyrian Purple dye extracted from shellfish. Red coral was a regular item of trade between the Greeks and the ancient Chinese mandarins, who probably bartered for it with pearls brought up by their own divers.

Ancient mythology affirms man's fascination with the underwater world. The Sumerians believed in the demigod Gilgamesh who dove in search of magical seaweed.

In the classical Greek pantheon, Poseidon (renamed Neptune by the Romans) was one of the 12 great Olympians, brother of Zeus and ruler of the Sea. Poseidon lived in a luxurious undersea palace and was usually depicted with trident in

Antique bust of Vulcan, blacksmith of the deep, from the Vatican Museum in Rome.

Ancient depiction of Dionysus at sea, surrounded by playful dolphins.

hand. Poseidon's son Triton was the trumpeter of the Sea, playing his music on a great shell. Nereus, the original Old Man of the Sea, had 50 lovely daughters called Nereids, the sea nymphs.

Hephaestus, the God of Fire, was cast from Olympus in a dispute between Zeus and Hera, and fell into the sea where he set up his black-smith works in an underwater cave. He married Aphrodite, said to spring from the foam of the sea. The Romans knew this immortal pair as Vulcan and Venus.

The genetic link between mankind and sea creatures was recognized by the writer Oppian, who recalled the legend of Dionysus' capture by pirates. The handsome God of the Vine frighten-

end his captors overboard and turned them into dolphins. "Diviner than the dolphin is nothing yet created," wrote Oppian, "for indeed they were aforetime men and lived in cities along with mortals, but by the devising of Dionysus they exchanged the land for the sea and put on the form of fishes."

While the classical civilizations believed in the sea as a playground of the gods, they ironically turned it into a battleground for the settling of their own disputes, these battles occasionally taking place beneath the surface. In the first recorded undersea attack, Thucydides tells of Greek divers destroying defenses at the harbor of Syracuse in 415 B.C.

14

Aristotle wrote an account of Alexander the Great employing divers for similar demolition work during the siege of Tyre nearly a century later. He also detailed Alexander's personal journey below the surface in a diving bell—history's first record of this invention.

Herodotus, a later Greek historian, recounted the legend of the famous diver Scyllis and his daughter Cyane (or Hydra) who destroyed the invading Persian fleet of King Xerxes by swimming out to the anchored ships with hollow reeds for snorkels and cutting the anchor lines. Modern day salvage divers such as Robert Marx are still attempting to recover the treasure that went down with the Persian galleys.

Warfare, it seems, provided ancient divers with double employment: first in underwater demolition, and then in reaping the spoils of sunken vessels. The divers of the Levant were famous for their wreck-diving skills. Rhodian salvors received rewards based on the depths at which they worked: one-tenth of the value of goods retrieved down to 12 feet; one-third between 12 and 22 feet, and half of everything brought up from below 22 feet.

Most of the early diving was done by naked men or women, aided only by an armload of stones to help them reach bottom. But there are indications of early attempts to stretch man's brief incursions into the silent world. Assyrian bas-reliefs dated about 900 B.C. depict early aquanauts with goatskin bladders, which were supplied by air drawn through long tubes from the

13th century French manuscript depicting Alexander the Great's descent in diving bell. In background is a legendary sea monster which, according to myth, took three days to pass Alexander's bell.

15

Syrian sponge divers operating half-blind before the invention of tortoise-shell goggles.

Assyrian bas-relief from British Museum shows underwater warrior breathing from air bag.

surface. Alexander's frogmen also used goatskin breathing bladders. The Greeks lowered inverted vases so sponge divers could get an extra breath or two of the trapped air.

Writing in the first century A.D., Pliny told of military divers breathing through float-supported tubes. In the treatise *De Re Militari,* written in 375 A.D., military expert Flavius Vegetius Renatus described the first design of a full diving suit ever found in print. Vegetius' diving dress even included a hood which tapered into an air pipe. Roger Bacon postulated air reservoirs for wreck divers in this *Novum Organum* in the year 1250.

The first known attempts to clarify man's vision underwater were made by pearl divers in the Persian Gulf as late as the 14th century. Their crude masks were fashioned from polished tortoiseshell and were augmented with tortoiseshell nose clips. Halfway around the world, the Polynesians were probably using similar devices at the same time.

During the Renaissance, scientists made dramatic advances in diving dress and in underwater vehicles—specifically diving bells and submarines. One of the first was a Venetian named Roberto Valturio, who in 1472 designed a hand-propelled wooden sub that could be portaged in sections.

Leonardo da Vinci turned his fertile imagination to the sea toward the end of the 15th century, and sketched designs for simple breathing tubes in his *Codex Atlanticus*. Later his efforts became even more visionary, including leather diving lungs, hand and foot fins, and a full suit with sandbag weights and a face mask. Leonardo also envisioned a submarine with its own periscope, but withheld specific details from his journals "as the wicked nature of men might tempt them to bore holes into the bottoms of other vessels, thus sinking them with their crews."

In 1505 Swedish historian Olaf Magnus reported spotting submersible kayaks covered with sealskin off Greenland. In the 1530s, an Italian named Guglielmo de Lorena used a diving bell while trying to raise Caligula's pleasure galley from the floor of Lake Nemi. In the earliest reliable record of an operating diving bell, it is claimed that de Lorena was able to stay submerged up to an hour with his device.

A few years later, Holy Roman Emperor Charles V and 10,000 other spectators on the banks of the River Tagus at Toledo, Spain watched two Greek stalwarts step into a contraption resembling an upended vase, holding burning candles. The "bell" and its passengers were lowered into the river, and when they were hoisted out the men were dry and the candles still burning. Word of this remarkable demonstration swept Europe.

On his third voyage of exploration to the New World, in 1498, Columbus described Indians wearing pearls brought up from the Caribbean. As trade routes began opening up in the West Indies after the conquest of Mexico, the native divers proved so effective that they were either worked to death or sold into slavery to European salvors. Eventually, entire races such as the Lucayo tribe of the Bahamas became extinct. The industrious Spanish solved this manpower shortage by importing African slaves as pearl and salvage divers.

In the 1680s Captain William Phips of Bristol, Maine talked England's Duke of Abermarle out of

Vegetius' diving suit probably looked like this illustration from an anonymous 15th century manuscript.

two ships and enough cash to mount a treasure-hunting expedition among the shoals south of the Bahamas. After one unsuccessful voyage, Phips located a sunken galleon. Using a salvage bell with trapped air which allowed his Bahamian divers up to 45 minutes on the bottom, Phips took £300,000 worth of jewels, pieces of eight, silver bars, and gold objects d'art from the wreck, valued over $1,500,000 today. This discovery kicked off a treasure-hunting binge that returned more than 100 million ducats from the waters of the Caribbean to the coffers of Europe from the 16th to 19th centuries.

Meanwhile, Englishman William Bourne drew up blueprints in 1578 for an undersea boat which included such advances as ballast tanks and a snorkel. But it was in the 1620s that the first truly workable submarine was built, by a Dutch emigre to England named Cornelius van Drebbel. Van

*European traders quickly learned to utilize the skills of West Indian divers,
such as these Cuban sponge-fishers.*

Drebbel's submersible galley, with 12 rowers, toured up and down the Thames for 10 years carrying such illustrious passengers as King James I, and became a famous novelty of Jacobean times. According to Ben Jonson's description, it looked like "an invisible eel . . . an automa (that) runs under water with a snub nose and . . . a nimble tail made like an auger, with which tail she wriggles betwixt the costs of a ship and sinks it straight. . ." Unfortunately for van Drebbel, the British Admiralty took his invention less seriously than did Jonson.

Other governments, such as Russia's, were quicker to adapt to submarine warfare. During the Russo-Turkish War in the mid-17th century, Cossacks rowing greased cowhide submersibles attacked Turkish shipping.

In 1679 Giovanni Alfonso Borelli experimented with a conical breathing bell, but, more importantly, he also sketched the first concepts for a self-contained recirculating breathing apparatus. One Borelli design consisted of a large air bag over the diver's head with a glass viewing port; there are no reports of its ever being fabricated, which is just as well since Borelli mistakenly presumed the recirculated air could be purified by water-cooling. Another Borelli design, however, introduced the concepts of webbed shoes and a metal head-ball with glass window, both of which foreshadowed later—if unconnected—developments.

The idea of sending pressurized air from the surface to a diving bell was first proposed by a Huguenot scientist named Denis Papin in 1689. Papin realized that his method would alleviate the problems of purifying recycled air, and would also

19

This method of raising wrecks with pontoon ships, pioneered in 16th century Italy, is still used today. (facing page, top) Not all early diving efforts were taken seriously. This 19th century George Cruikshank caricature, "Going Down in a Diving Machine", lampoons some of the imagined hazards of undersea exploration. (facing page, bottom) Diagrammatic view of a diving bell similar to Halley's. Weighted barrels of fresh air were lowered to the bell.

allow the air pressure to be regulated according to the depth of the bell.

Sir Edmund Halley, the astronomer who gave his name to a comet, designed and built a diving bell in 1690 which has been called the forerunner of present day bells. He described it this way:

> The Bell I made use of was of Wood, containing about 60 Cubick Foot in its concavity, and was of the form of a Truncate-Cone, whose Diameter at the Top was three Foot, and at the Bottom, five. This I coated with Lead so heavy that it would sink empty, and I distributed the weight so about its bottom, that it would go down in a perpendicular situation and no other. In the Top I fixed a strong but clear glass, as a Window to let in the Light from above, and likewise a Cock to let out the hot Air that had been Breathed; and below, about a Yard under the Bell, I placed a Stage which hung by three Ropes, each of which was charged with about one Hundred Weight, to keep it steddy. . .

Fresh air was supplied to the bell via lead-lined barrels which were raised and lowered to it in turns. Water pressure forced the air from the barrels into the bell, and Halley claimed this system allowed him and four other men to stay in the bell for 90 minutes at 10 fathoms, with a diver working outside breathing through a tube from the bell.

Various inventors were attempting to increase man's underwater mobility at this time. After studying da Vinci's notebooks, young Benjamin Franklin constructed hand and foot fins. Later, he recalled:

> I made two oval palettes each about ten inches long and six broad, with a hole for the thumb, in order to retain it fast in the palm of my hand. They much resembled a painter's palette. In swimming I pushed the edges of these forward, and struck the water with their flat surfaces as I drew them back. I remember I swam faster by means of these palettes, but they fatigued my wrists. I also fitted to the soles of my feet a kind of sandals: but I was not satisfied with them, because I observed that the stroke is partly given by the inside of the feet and ankles and not entirely with the soles of the feet.

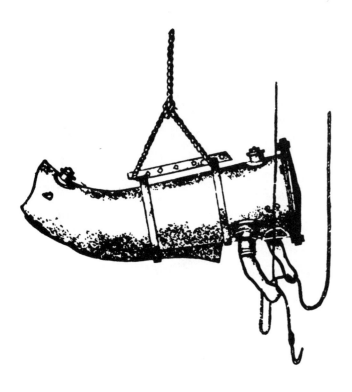

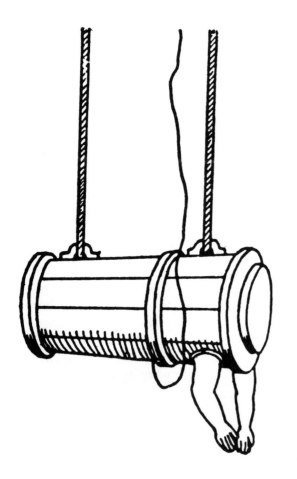

Diving machines designed by John Lethbridge and Captain Rowe both allowed free use of arms.

By 1715, John Lethbridge of Devonshire had designed a leather suit which worked successfully in dives to 60 feet. Then the idea of "diving armor" emerged. In 1728, an English captain named Rowe built a "diving machine" which enclosed diver and air supply with a glass window and air-tight arm holes. Lethbridge came back in 1749 with the first rigid diving suit, a barrel with arm holes and a windowed metal globe for his head. Here's how it worked, according to Lethbridge's own account in *The Gentlemen's Magazine*:

> I lie straight upon my breast, all the time I am in the engine, which hath many times been more than 6 hours, being, frequently, re-freshed upon the surface, by a pair of bellows. I can move on about 12 square, at the bottom, where I have stayed, many times, 34 minutes. I have been ten fathom deep many times, and have been 12 fathom, but with great difficulty. . .

Five years later helmet suits supplied with pumped air were used on a salvage job at Yarmouth. And in 1772, a Dr. Freminet demonstrated the first self-contained helmet dress to the French *Académie des Sciences*. Carrying a tank of compressed air with him, Freminet descended to 50 feet for an hour at Le Havre.

During the American Revolution, a young Yale student named David Bushnell worked up plans for a submersible made of barrel staves and iron. He presented his plans to George Washington, who later described Bushnell to Thomas Jefferson as "a man of great mechanical powers, fertile in invention and master of execution." Washington funded Bushnell's project, and the young man built a one-man sub called the Turtle because it looked like two turtle shells clamped together. It carried a mine attached to a screw which was to be bored into an enemy ship's hull. A time fuse would allow the Turtle to escape before the mine exploded.

The first authenticated attack by a military submarine began on the evening of September 5, 1776 at New York. The Turtle was towed from New Rochelle and cut afloat. Sergent Ezra Lee hand-cranked the screw prop until the Turtle nuzzled up against the stern of Admiral Howe's flagship H.M.S. Eagle. Then he submerged the Turtle and began trying to drive the screw into

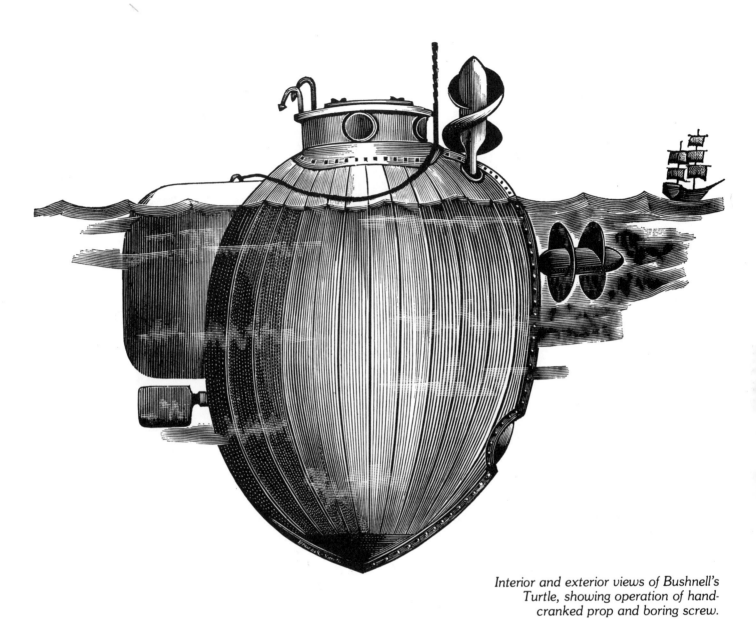

Interior and exterior views of Bushnell's Turtle, showing operation of hand-cranked prop and boring screw.

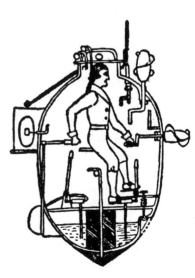

the Eagle's hull, only to feel it bounce off repeatedly. Unbeknownst to the Americans, the Eagle's bottom was sheathed in copper, which the Turtle's screw could not penetrate.

Lee worked valiantly all night but finally lost his trim and, drifting to the surface, realized it was now daylight. He was spotted and cranked off furiously, dropping his mine as a diversionary action. The Turtle made it back to American lines safely and attempted two more unsuccessful attacks before Bushnell lost his enthusiasm for manned vehicles and turned his attention to floating mines.

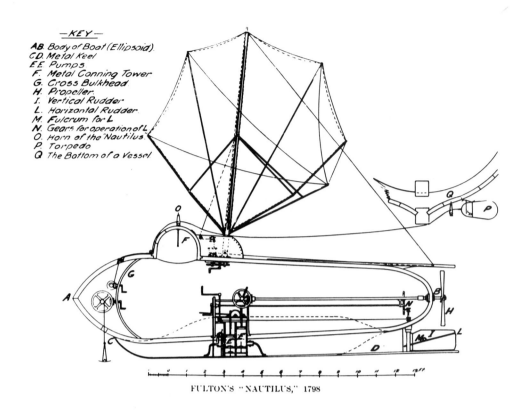

FULTON'S "NAUTILUS," 1798

Plan for Fulton's Nautilus showing horizontal rudder (at rear) and sail for surface navigation.

After the American Revolution, the political upheaval in France attracted Bushnell and his innovative countryman, Robert Fulton. In 1800 Fulton tried to sell a 21-foot submarine prototype called the Nautilus to Napoleon Bonaparte. Although the Nautilus is now regarded as the first truly practical submarine, negotiations between Fulton and Bonaparte broke down, and the sale was never made. In 1807 Fulton tried to interest U.S. President Jefferson in the Nautilus, but was again rebuffed. Finally, the discouraged young inventor turned his interests toward steamboats.

Fulton did, however, make two significant contributions to undersea history. First was the use of a horizontal rudder which, in modified form, is still in use today. Second was the choice of the name "Nautilus," which has since been handed down to a long line of underwater vessels, including Captain Nemo's ship and the U.S. Navy's first nuclear sub.

In 1819 Augustus Siebe introduced the open diving dress, with a helmet that, like a diving bell, allowed water to enter and exhalations to escape through its loose bottom. Compressed air pumped from the surface kept the water from reaching the diver's face. Its usage was limited because the diver couldn't bend over without flooding the helmet.

During the 1820s, W. H. Taylor designed the first metal dress with articulated joints. Englishman W. H. James made an unsuccessful attempt at a closed-circuit rig, employing a metal air chamber worn around his waist with a pipe leading to his mouth. Unfortunately, the air "girdle" held too small a supply to be practical.

Brooklyn machinist Charles Condert devised a working self-contained rig in 1831. Condert wrapped a six-inch copper pipe around his waist with compressed air fed into a closed dress through a tube. He made several dives into the East River, but drowned when the breathing tube broke.

Seeing the limitations of his open dress, Augustus Siebe brought out a "closed" diving

The steamboat wasn't Fulton's only folly, in the view of many. This 1811 caricature of a fierce-looking warfish satirized the design of the Nautilus. (bottom photo) An experimental scuba design from Condert's time, showing a compressed-air tank and an underarm bladder to regulate the flow of air into the helmet.

suit in 1837 which allowed full freedom of movement in any position. Then, in 1839, Siebe introduced the first really practical closed dress, with a helmet that could be screwed onto the breastplate of a waterproof suit. The design also included a practical surface pump and valves which allowed the diver to regulate his air supply. The "hard hat" outfit had evolved into the basic form it would retain for the next 100-plus years.

Biologists began to look into the sea, literally and figuratively, in the 1840s. Edward Forges, working on the Isle of Man, was one of the first to specialize in deep-sea research. Another early diving scientist was zoologist Henri Milne-Edwards, who was later mentioned in Jules Verne's *Twenty Thousand Leagues Under the Sea.*

Submarines were back in the news in 1850 when German Corporal Wilhelm Bauer used his porpoise-design Sea Diver to break a Danish blockade at Kiel. Reportedly, the Danish fleet scattered at the sight of the 25-foot warfish.

Sie Siebe's improved closed dress.

On a subsequent try the following year, the Sea Diver nosed down into a 60-foot pothole, trapping Bauer and two crewmen. Coolly opening the seacocks to let water in and compress the remaining air, Bauer and his men successfully executed history's first submarine escape. Undaunted, Bauer continued to promote the concept of submarine warfare, and to develop new models. On a demonstration dive in Russia in 1855, he set up a camera to shoot photos through his sub's portholes—the first known attempt at underwater photography.

Submarine warfare was given another try during the U.S. Civil War. The Confederates launched five different undersea attacks on Union ships, and the last one, against the ironclad Housatonic in Charleston Harbor, succeeded. However, Confederate enthusiasm was dimmed when the sub, christened the H.L. Hunley after her designer, sank alongside her victim, shattered by the mine she had detonated against the Housatonic's well- armored flank.

The evolution of the modern manfish took a giant leap forward with the 1865 introduction of the "aérophore" system by a French engineer, Benoit Rouquayrol, and naval lieutenant, Auguste Denayrouze. The "aérophore" consisted of a reserve air tank on the diver's back which could be detached from a surface-fed line to allow

The first submarine to complete a successful undersea attack was christened the H.L. Hunley, after her designer.

Underwater salvage scene of the type described by Charles Dickens and Robert Louis Stevenson.

The Rouquayrol-Denayrouze "aerophore"— grandfather of the modern Aqua-Lung— intrigued Jules Verne and other undersea visionaries of the late 1800s.

the diver complete independence for a limited time. The diver breathed from the tank at the hydrostatic pressure of any given depth through a valve he regulated. Thus was born the first satisfactory demand regulator for an open-circuit breathing apparatus. In a short while, it was in wide use throughout Europe.

By this time man's underwater exploits were stirring the imaginations of the British literati. In his *Uncommercial Traveller*, Charles Dickens described the scene of an 1859 salvage operation off Anglesey, England:

> . . . a diver in his grotesque dress dipped heavily over the side of the boat alongside the lighter, and dropped to the bottom . . . The divers were down then, and busy. They were 'lifting' today the gold found yester-day—some five and twenty pounds. . . .

Jules Verne's *Twenty Thousand Leagues Under the Sea*, published in 1869, was thought to be a work of science fiction, but it actually chronicled many of the underwater developments of the day, such as the previously noted mention of diving zoologist Henri Milne-Edwards. At one point, in discussing the desire to free aquanauts from the confines of air hoses, Verne had Captain Nemo tell the French Professor Arronax the solution "is to use the Rouquayrol apparatus, invented by two of your countrymen."

But the Scottish adventurer-novelist Robert Louis Stevenson went Dickens and Verne one better by actually donning diving dress and venturing beneath the surface. He described his first dive, in Wick Bay, Scotland, during the late 1860s, in his *Random Memories*:

> Looking up, I saw a low green heaven mottled with vanishing bells of white; look-ing around . . . nothing but a green gloaming, somewhat opaque but very restful and deli-cious. . . Bob (Bain, his diving partner) motioned me to leap upon a stone; I looked to see if he were possibly in earnest . . . With the breast and back weights, and the twenty pounds upon each foot, and the staggering load of the helmet, the thing was out of reason. I laughed aloud in my tomb; and to prove to Bob how far he was astray, I gave a little impulse from my toes. Up I soared like a bird, my companion soaring at my side. . . .

Yet the experience wasn't entirely euphoric for Stevenson:

The air . . . as it is supplied to you by the busy millers on the platform, closes the Eustachian tubes and keeps the neophyte perpetually swallowing till the throat is grown so dry that he can swallow no longer . . . although I had a fine, dizzy, muddle-headed joy in my surroundings, and longed and tried, and always failed to lay my hands on the fish that darted here and there about me, swift as hummingbirds—yet I fancy I was rather relieved when Bain brought me back to the ladder and signed me to mount.

With all this undersea activity, men were learning diving physics largely by trial and error. The first medical man who actually dived to study the effects of depth and pressure, starting in 1866, was the French physician Alphonse Gal.

A few years later Gal's countryman Paul Bert, whose 1878 treatise *La Pression Barométrique* had earned him the title of "The Father of Aviation Medicine," began to study the reasons for the deaths and injuries Gal had reported. Working with bridge builders suffering from what was then known as "caisson disease" or "diver's palsy," Bert developed the first decompression tables and recompression chamber. He was greatly indebted to the Englishman Robert Boyle, who had experimented with compressed air two centuries earlier. Bert's findings laid the foundation for modern medicine's knowledge of the effects of pressure on the human body.

In the late 1870s H.A. Fleuss, an employee of the Siebe-Gorman firm that had grown from Augustus Siebe's early helmet-diving experiments, designed the first workable closed-circuit rebreathing unit. The self-contained rig used caustic potash to remove carbon dioxide from exhaled air.

At the same time, an American named John Philip Holland built a steam submarine which dived on an incline using movable hydroplanes. He continued to produce different submarine models for the next 40 years.

Zoologist Charles Wyville Thomson launched the greatest oceanographic expedition in history in 1876. His findings established that life exists at all ocean depths.

In 1893, diving scientist Louis Boutan made the

John E. Williamson's "photosphere" off the Bahamas. Cameramen in chamber focus on diver working Andros Reef.

first photographic exposures underwater, at Banyuls-sur-Mer, France. He had experimented with a "drowned" camera, but found that the shutter movement caused ripples in the water, so he switched to watertight cases pressurized by external balloons. Boutan developed a system of artificial lighting which was later revived as the flash bulb. He wrote the first book on the subject, *La Photographie Sous-Marine et Le Progrès de la Photographie,* in 1900.

During the late 1800s many independent tests were made of submarines powered by gasoline, steam, and electricity. By the turn of the century, subs were taking an important role in naval strategy. The U.S. Navy commissioned its first submersible (J. P. Holland's Plunger) in 1900, the same year the British Royal Navy announced its first submarine flotilla of five Holland boats built by Vickers. The Germans founded their own U-boat flotilla in 1905.

In 1902, Sir Robert Davis of England and H. A. Fleuss collaborated on an updated version of Fleuss' original rebreather. The result was the first submarine escape lung.

On a more peaceable note, marine archaeology got its start about this time, when Greek sponge divers brought up various pieces of statuary from a wreck off the island of Antikythera.

A great medical advance occurred in 1906 when the British Admiralty Deep-Diving Com-

mittee, under the direction of John Scott Haldane, established systematic decompression tables good to 200 feet, which allowed for staged ascents faster than those Paul Bert had computed. Haldane also made important improvements to the compressed-air pumps of the day.

However, protecting divers from the pressures of the depths was still an important consideration. Two German engineers, Neufeldt and Kuhnke, introduced the first practical armored diving dress in 1913. Reportedly safe down to 500 feet, the suit included ball-and-socket joints for the artificial limbs and a telescoping tail which could

Holland-designed submarine being inspected by members of the Naval Academy's Class of 1902.

Bouton's massive camera housing was buoyed by a floating barrel.

be extended by compressed air to regulate buoyancy. Seven years later the pair produced an advanced version which became the true modern armored suit.

The Williamson Expedition, which premiered in 1914, was the first underwater movie. Virginian John E. Williamson shot the film from a camera chamber he called a "photosphere" 30 feet down, off Nassau. The film includes footage of Williamson killing a shark with a knife. Following the movie's instant success, Williamson made a series of underwater features including a silent *Twenty Thousand Leagues Under the Sea* 40 years before Walt Disney shot his remake.

By 1914 war had erupted in Europe, and German U-boats began registering their first kills. In 1917 the Germans declared unrestricted submarine warfare and sank six million tons of

were three close friends—Philippe Tailliez, Frédéric Dumas, and Jacques-Yves Cousteau.

Dr. W. H. Longley, an ichthyologist, made the first underwater color photos in the Dry Tortugas in 1923. Three years later he pioneered underwater artificial lighting for color photography, firing magnesium charges in the surf and reflecting them down to illuminate his scenes. By 1925 an American engineer named Hartman was conducting underwater television experiments off Capri.

In 1925 Yves Le Prieur developed a manually valved independent compressed air lung. The air flowed from a cylinder worn on the chest into the diver's mask. "We had our first grand moments of leisure in the sea with Le Prieur's lung," Cousteau later recalled.

About this time the American scientist William Beebe began his experiments in helmet walking and underwater photography. Then he met a New England engineer named Otis Barton and they collaborated on the first bathysphere, a tethered two-man ball with steel walls one and one-half inches thick. In their first test dive, near Bermuda in 1930, they achieved a depth of 800 feet despite a leaking hatch.

Breakthroughs were also being made in diving physiology. Sir Robert Davis, head of Siebe-Gorman, previewed plans for a submersible decompression chamber. The British Admiralty

British shipping. The following year, two Italian officers rode a 23-foot seagoing chariot into the Adriatic port of Pola to attack the Austrian fleet.

Navigating with their heads just above the waterline, the charioteers attached a TNT warhead to the bottom of the superdreadnought Viribus Unitis. They were taken prisoner before they could escape and were actually aboard the huge vessel when their charge went off and she began to sink. It was then they discovered that the warship had been captured by revolutionary Yugoslav seamen and that they had destroyed an Allied ship.

After the war, scientists were able to turn back to peacetime underwater pursuits. In 1919 Massachusetts Professor Elihu Thomson first suggested using helium instead of oxygen for breathing in mines. The Navy began experimenting with helium for underwater work in 1925.

During the '20s, a band of hearty fanatics took up free diving in the Mediterranean. They were led by Guy Gilpatric, who sealed flying goggles with putty to help him see underwater. Gilpatric also fashioned a hand spear from a curtain rod and embarked on the adventures he was to chronicle in his 1938 classic, *The Compleat Goggler*. Among Gilpatric's later diving confreres

World War II-vintage UDT action. Frogmen are snagged with a rubber loop and flipped aboard a rubber raft lashed alongside a speeding PT boat.

Bathyscaphe Trieste, originally designed by Auguste Piccard in the 1940s, safely carried his son Jacques to the bottom of the sea in 1960.

Committee established diving tables to 300 feet in 1930.

Sport diving came of age rapidly in the '30s. The spear gun was introduced in France in 1931. The first sport diving club, the Bottom Scratchers, was formed in California in 1933. Also in '33 Louis de Corlieu produced the prototype of his patented foot fins. The *Club des Sous-l'Eau* was founded in 1934 by Yves Le Prieur and film producer Jean Painlevé.

Two years later a French diver named Fernez modernized the design of centuries-old Japanese and Polynesian goggles, fitting them with a water-tight rubber frame. Cousteau made his first dive with Fernez goggles later that year. In 1938 a Frenchman named Forjot took out a patent on a mask covering the eyes and nose.

During the early '30s U. V. Bogaerde tested his own underwater camera design and reflecting lights in Falmouth Harbor. Underwater cinema-tographer J. D. Craig, filming with a stationary camera off Baja California, accomplished a grisly "first." One of his divers literally disappeared underwater—his air hose came up separated from his suit and an underwater search of several days turned up no clues to his whereabouts. Finally Craig developed the film that had been in the camera that day and was astounded to see a giant manta attack the diver and carry him away—the first and hopefully last actual footage of a fatal confrontation with a creature of the deep.

In 1935, Mussolini invaded Ethiopia. As a defense against possible intervention by the British Mediterranean Fleet, two Italian lieutenants devised an electronic underwater torpedo which two men could ride, reminiscent of the surface chariot used at Pola in 1918. However, the later model could submerge, and its passengers were equipped with Davis rebreathers. After a few unsuccessful attempts, the charioteers scored their first kill when they sank the British tanker Denbydale in Gibraltar's Grand Harbour in 1941. A later underwater attack that year sunk the H.M.S. Queen Elizabeth and the Valiant in the same harbor, obliterating the last remnants of the Royal Navy's Mediterranean Fleet. The potential of underwater warfare was clearly demonstrated.

The U.S. office of Strategic Services quickly formed an underwater combat team equipped with oxygen rebreathers developed in 1940 by Christian J. Lambertsen. The British began training "underwater working parties" for primarily defensive purposes. On the Pacific front, the Japanese used midget submarines in their assault on Pearl Harbor.

Many of the lessons learned in war have peaceful applications too. In 1943, Professor J. B. S. Haldane, son of the man who established the first systematic decompression tables, began a series of experiments which further shortened decompression time. He also experimented with oxygen poisoning and cold-water survival, frequently serving as his own guinea pig.

It was in 1943 that the modern self-contained underwater breathing apparatus was born. Georges Comheines used a semiautomatic regulator to dive to 166 feet off Marseilles, but his achievement was to be overshadowed by the development of the Cousteau-Gagnan Aqua-Lung. Cousteau was now a French naval lieutenant and Gagnan a Parisian engineer, very much like their forebears, Denayrouze and Rouquayrol. Cousteau sought a fully automatic demand regulator, without any of the hand controls on the current models. Gagnan had developed an automatic valve for feeding cooking gas into automobile engines which the pair adapted for underwater use.

After a few tests in the river Marne, Cousteau and Gagnan made some minor adjustments. Then Cousteau, Tailliez and Dumas undertook some 500 experimental dives as deep as 203 feet off Marseilles, right under the noses of the German occupation forces.

By 1944 underwater warfare had begun to escalate. The U.S. had formed its first Underwater Demolition Teams, and a Nazi underwater unit attacked the Nijmegen Bridge in Holland. American frogmen, as the UDT came to be called, saw their first action at Kwajalein Island. Then they cleared the way for amphibious land-

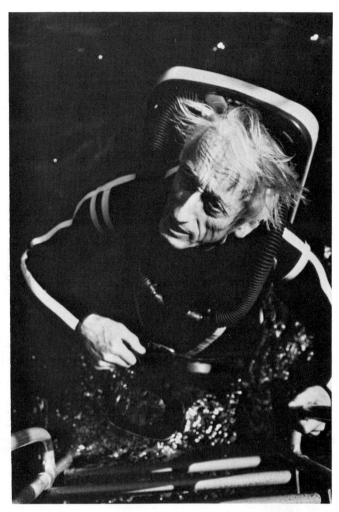

Jacques-Yves Cousteau, co-inventor of the Aqua-Lung and father of sport diving.

ings on Guam, Leyte, and Iwo Jima before moving to the Atlantic to participate in the D-Day landings.

In 1945 Cousteau, Tailliez and Dumas founded the French Navy Undersea Group, the forerunner of Cousteau's present organization. They continued to experiment quietly in underwater technology, physiology, and photography throughout the '40s.

Auguste Piccard began testing his bathyscaphe (Greek for "deep boat") in 1948 off West Africa. Unlike the tethered bathysphere, Piccard's invention was a free submarine vehicle, with a steel ball suspended from a metal buoyancy chamber filled with gasoline, which is lighter than water and practically incompressible.

The following year Tailliez et al. published *La Plongée en Scaphandre*, with tables for successive Aqua-Lung dives. By 1953 the Aqua-Lung was being marketed in the U.S., and Cousteau's

Double-domed Tektite habitat, which housed four aquanauts for two months in 1969.

A topside view of Sealab I, first of four Sealab experiments in underwater habitation.

Diver leaves submersible decompression chamber "elevator" to enter Sealab I undersea laboratory.

lyric account of his group's early diving exploits, *The Silent World,* was published. The sport of diving was beginning to flourish.

Since that time Cousteau and his engineers have continued to pioneer many of the major advances in free diving, including mixed-gas lungs for deep dives. They and others have also made great progress in the field of submersibles.

In 1960 Auguste Piccard's son Jacques and U.S. Navy Lieutenant Don Walsh piloted the bathyscaphe Trieste to the very bottom of the ocean floor, 35,800 feet into the Challenger Deep of the Mariana Trench. Piccard later recalled his sensations during the deepest descent of all time:

> Like a free balloon on a windless day, indifferent to the almost 200,000 tons of water pressing on the cabin from all sides . . . slowly, surely, in the name of science and humanity, the Trieste took possession of the abyss, the last extreme on our earth that remained to be conquered.

The 1960s were also the decade of the undersea habitat. In September, 1962 Cousteau and Edwin A. Link, inventor of the Link Trainer for aviation cadets, launched separate but cooperative experiments in underwater living just 100 miles from each other in the Mediterranean.

In these initial trials, two men stayed 169 hours at 33 feet in Cousteau's Conshelf One. Link's initial Man-In-Sea test called for a diver to remain in a submersible portable inflatable dwelling at 200 feet for 48 hours. The experiment had to be aborted when a mistral capsized a support ship bringing needed helium. A subsequent attempt, in 1964, was extremely successful.

Also in 1964, the U.S. Navy instituted its first Sealab project, with four divers spending 11 days 193 feet down off Bermuda. Five years later, four aquanaut-scientists completed a 60-day mission in 50 feet of water in the Virgin Islands. Since then many other underwater habitats, including a few private ones, have been constructed.

Another innovation of the '60s was the development of submarinos or "taxis of the deep," in the phrase of underwater historian James Dugan. This new generation of highly maneuverable, pressure-resistant undersea vehicles opened broad new vistas of submarine exploration. Among them are Cousteau's famous diving saucer; the Alvin and Aluminaut which teamed in 1966 to recover the H-bomb that fell to sea from a wrecked B-52 off Palomares, Spain; and other well-known models such as Deep Diver, Deepstar, and Deep Quest.

In the '70s we have developed a growing awareness of the delicate ecology of the sea, and of our responsibility to preserve the food chains and other vital interrelationships of the marine environment. No longer is the sea a challenge to be conquered. Today it is a vital resource of great wealth and abundance, the original source of life for the entire planet, which must be cherished and nurtured so mankind can continue to enjoy its unique gifts for all the generations to come.

Basic Equipment

Technologically, sport diving is in its adolescence. Reliable scuba gear, for instance, has been around less than forty years. As a result, diving equipment is still evolving rapidly, and the market place is crammed with a dizzying proliferation of products, models, styles, and prices. Some older equipment, even if still in working order, has been obsoleted by new products and diving techniques. The choices open to the equipment-buying diver can seem overwhelming. But with a little common sense and some general guidelines, you can make intelligent and economical buying decisions suited to your own individual needs.

In this chapter we will present the basic gear needed for both skin and scuba diving in the normal range of diving conditions. First, of course, are the basic diving items. Mask, snorkel, and fins are vital to the diver's vision, respiration, and propulsion. Under the heading of personal buoyancy devices we have included weights, safety vests, and buoyancy compensators which may be needed by the free diver and are mandatory when using scuba. Another essential ingredient is the underwater knife. Exposure suits are necessary for anyone diving in water colder than 78°F. This represents the basic skin diver's equipment package.

Scuba divers must add a compressed air tank and harness (or backpack), demand regulator with submersible pressure gauge, plus a depth gauge, to be properly outfitted. Beyond these basics there is a wide range of accessory products which are described in the following chapter.

We have chosen to review only products readily available to sport divers, and have not included esoteric equipment used primarily in commercial, scientific, or military diving.

Each type of diving equipment comes in a variety of models which offer unique features, many highly specialized. When possible, try to develop a clear picture of the type of diving you plan to be doing before you begin buying equipment. If, for example, you have no intention of diving in cold water, or deeper than 33 feet, your needs will be far different from someone planning to pursue more diverse diving experiences.

On the other hand, some gear is designed with flexibility in mind. If you don't want to limit yourself, look for adaptability and versatility in your gear, so it can be used in a variety of underwater situations.

Each equipment category in this chapter is introduced by a discussion of the major designs and features available, with specific buying tips. This information is presented to help you narrow your choice.

There are, however, some general shopping hints which relate to all types of gear. Number one: comfort is paramount. Diving can be as rigorous or as leisurely as you wish, but there's no point fighting uncomfortable equipment no matter how great a challenge you seek. Unfortunately, comfort is not easily measured. What looks or feels great on dry land may turn into a torture device underwater.

So, underwater is where the ultimate buying decision should be made. Try to rent or borrow as many different models of each piece of equipment as possible before buying. Talk to your diving buddies or fellow students for their impressions. There's another good reason for this strategy: the more gear you're familiar with, the better diver you are. You never know when you may rent strange equipment on a diving vacation, or buddy up with someone who's outfitted differently than you are. Don't become dependent on a single system. Your confidence in the water will increase with your knowledgeability.

Most diving certification courses will require you to provide some of your own gear — usually mask, snorkel, and fins. If you can borrow a comfortable set from a friend, fine. Otherwise, buy only the minimum required for the course until you complete your certification and you're sure you want to continue in the sport. Anyone who's seen the numerous want ads for "Full set of scuba gear — used once — best offer," can appreciate this strategy.

Once you've decided to buy and narrowed your choices, talk to the pros. Your certification instructor will recommend specific brands and models. Since most instructors are also sales-people, double check their recommendations to be sure you're not simply being steered toward big-ticket or high-margin merchandise. If the instructor listens to your needs and doesn't recommend one manufacturer exclusively, you're probably getting sound advice.

Have an expert check each piece of gear to be sure it's functioning properly before you take it out of the store. Be sure the salesperson shows you the proper way to put on and use each piece of equipment before you buy it. If anything seems uncomfortable or unweildy, keep trying other models until you're satisfied.

Make sure that all the individual pieces of equipment you buy are compatible with each other. For instance, be sure you can strap your depth gauge on over your gloves, that the straps of your buoyancy compensator don't interfere with the quick-release mechanisms of your weight belt or tank harness, and that your mask is just as comfortable with a regulator mouthpiece in place. Beginning divers have a great advantage in this regard, if they can afford to buy a complete outfit all at once. But even if you buy on a piecemeal basis, try out each piece of gear in conjunction with your other equipment.

Dive shops often pre-select several pieces of gear — even an entire diving outfit — and market them as a package. If you buy this type of package, remember that each item must fit your body and diving needs. Don't compromise just for the sake of a package price.

Pay particular attention to the materials used in all gear. Fittings and housings should be strong and corrosion-resistant, either stainless steel or high-impact plastic, depending on their use. While colorful equipment aids underwater visibility, some pigments can weaken rubber products. If you buy black rubber equipment and find that visibility is a problem, you can add brightly-colored stripping later. Ask about maintenance. Some materials require more care than others.

Closures should be durable, secure, and easy to work underwater with gloves on. Many fasteners are now being made of Velcro, which consists of opposing strips of nylon material, one side woven into hundreds of tiny loops, the other side with an equal number of hooks. These closures resist moisture and salt corrosion and have the added advantage of being adjustable.

The more expensive equipment may contain features and niceties you don't need. If you're concerned about cost, shop sales (which most dive shops promote, especially in off-seasons), and look for last year's models which may still be on dealer's shelves. If you buy used equipment, have a qualified equipment specialist inspect its condition, even if it costs you a few dollars more.

Check into warranties. Be sure to determine exactly what the warranty does and does not cover. And, lastly, save your sales slips. If you do happen to bring home a lemon, you can return it to the shop.

For the following equipment listings, the editors of The Great Outdoors Trading Company contacted the major diving equipment manufacturers marketing in North America. Unless otherwise noted, all products are available through diving retailers. We are grateful to the manufacturers for their cooperation in bringing this body of information together. Any manufacturers whose equipment is not included in this section are invited to forward product literature to the editors for inclusion in our next edition.

We have not necessarily tested each piece of equipment presented — we'll leave the fun of that up to you. If you wish to contact any of these manufacturers, refer to Appendix H for their addresses.

Mask Buying Guide

Face masks serve a variety of functions. They improve underwater vision and alleviate the sting of salt water by creating a space of air between the water and your eyes. They keep water from inadvertantly entering your nose. And they help prevent "squeeze" on your eyeballs.

Goggles are unsuitable for diving below the shallowest depths. First of all, they tend to leak more than masks. And because they do not cover the nose, they cannot be cleared of water without returning to the surface. Also, there is no way to equalize the pressure inside the goggles with the water pressure outside, so the edges of the goggles can be squeezed uncomfortably against the facial tissue, occasionally into the eye sockets themselves.

You should never wear goggles with scuba, since scuba regulators distribute air throughout the body (including the sinuses) at ambient pressure (the same pressure as the water around the diver). Therefore, the pressure in the sinuses behind the eyes can become so much greater than the pressure inside the goggles that "eye squeeze" can result. The effects can range from discomfort to bleeding to actual eye damage. With a mask, the diver can exhale through his nose to equalize the pressure on either side of his eyes.

All other requirements being equal, your first mask should combine the greatest field of vision with the smallest internal volume of air. The less air trapped inside the mask, the easier it is to clear. You should particulary avoid larger volume masks for snorkeling, since you may not be able to clear them with one breath. The closer the faceplate fits to your face, the better your upward, downward, and peripheral vision and the less resistance in the water. Some masks are particularly designed for this kind of low displacement.

To be sure a mask fits properly, hold it to your face without the strap secured. Inhale gently, and the mask should stay in place through suction. Try holding the mask this way for 15 seconds or so. If it stays in place with no other support, and if you cannot feel any air seeping in, you can be sure of a watertight seal. If there is a slight leak, check in a mirror to be sure the skirt isn't doubled over or your skin isn't wrinkled (especially at the base of the nose and the hairline, two major points of leakage). Men with moustaches often experience leaks, which may be sealed off with an application of petroleum jelly. If you can find no other cause for the leak, the design of the mask may just be too wide for your face.

Masks can also fit too tightly. After the initial test, don the mask again, this time with the strap in place. Inhale again. If the face plate touches your nose, the volume is too low for you. Also be sure that the bottom skirt doesn't press uncomfortably against your nostrils. Wear the mask for a few moments. When you take it off, check for deep red lines or signs of chafing. If you can't relieve the discomfort by loosening the strap, try a larger-volume mask.

Be sure the mask fits comfortably and seals properly with your exposure suit hood, if you plan to use one.

Soft rubber, neoprene, and — occasionally — soft plastic, are the most common mask materials. Hypo-allergenic masks are made of silicone, without the organic chemicals usually added to rubber for strength and corrosion resistance. The silicone is long-lasting and translucent, so it allows additional light to enter the mask. It is also more expensive than rubber, so expect to pay more for a hypo-allergenic mask.

While mask construction may be rigid around the face plate, the skirt should be soft and pliable for greatest comfort and surest seal. Broader skirts are generally more comfortable, but narrower skirts tend to fit better with exposure suit hoods. Feathered (tapered) edges comform easily to your facial planes. Many masks feature a double-edge seal, with an interior skirt to trap any water that might seep through the outer skirt.

The face plate is usually held in place by a stainless steel or plastic retainer band. An adjustable band can be handy for changing the face plate if it should be damaged.

Look for a tempered safety glass face plate. It's shatter-resistant, practically scratchproof, and perfectly clear. Plastic lenses fog up more frequently, scratch more easily, and are less clear than safety glass. Tinted faceplates (glass or plastic) cut the light coming into your eyes, particularly in murky water when you'll want all the light you can get.

The head strap should be easily adjustable, especially if you're going to be using the mask with and without a hood. But make sure the adjusting mechanism is slip-proof. Strap retainers can keep loose ends from flapping or snagging. A split band, with portions fitting above and below the natural protrusion at the back of your head, provides extra comfort and a more secure fit.

Avoid masks with built-in snorkels. These are rarely seen in reputable dive shops because they leak easily and are incompatible with most sophisticated diving gear and techniques.

Here are some special features you might want to consider:

A "wrap-around" face plate will increase your field of vision, but will add internal volume and increase drag. Curved one-piece lenses will cause some distortion. Other models have "side windows," so each lens remains flat; multi-lens masks with flexible posts separating the lenses allow the mask to bend to individual face sizes.

Some masks can be ordered with ground-in or bonded-on prescription lenses, or with lens frames that fit inside the mask. These are available in most of the common mask styles.

One-way purge valves built into the face plate or mask skirt can aid in clearing water. Large purge valves work faster than smaller ones, but may increase drag or block downward vision.

If, like most divers, you need to pinch off your nostrils and blow to clear your eustachian tubes, you may want to consider the variety of systems which help you do this. One is the soft nose pocket. Another type has finger wells in the bottom skirt of the mask; try them out to be sure squeezing your nose through the wells doesn't break the seal of the mask around the nose and lips. You'll find these features especially helpful if you intend to carry something in one hand.

Masks

AMF Voit

Swimaster Wide View

Large purge valve. Neoprene sponge seal. Minimum displacement. Adaptable to corrective lenses.

D 1001. Black.

Swimaster Full View

Three lenses with relatively low volume. Double seal, purge valve, nose pocket equalizer.

D 1002. Black.

Swimaster Balboa

Double seal, low profile, approximately 7 cu. in. interior volume. Non-slip split head strap. Two lenses, nose pocket.

D 1003. Black with red trim.

Swimaster Baja

Single lens placed close to face for low displacement, wide field of distortion-free vision. Nose pocket, double-edge skirt, split head strap.

D 1004. Black with red trim.

Competition

Positive double seal. Purge valve, nose pocket. Close-to-face rectangular tempered lens. Stainless steel band, neoprene rubber body.

D 1005. Black with black, red, white, or yellow lens rim.

Wide Vision

Positive double seal. Finger wells. Rectangular tempered lens. Neoprene rubber body, split strap.

D 1006. Black with black, red, white, or yellow lens rim.

Custom

Contoured short skirt especially designed for narrow faces. Oval tempered lens, stainless steel fittings, split head strap.

D 1007. Black.

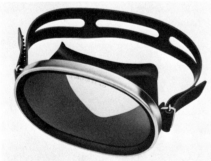

Scuba Diver Mask

Soft flared edge, finger wells, purge valve, oval tempered glass lens, stainless steel band, rubber body, split head band.

D 1008. Blue.

Special Mask

Soft flared skirt, tempered oval lens, purge valve, stainless steel fittings. Non-slip strap locks.

D 1009. Blue.

B90S

Economy model for skin and scuba diving. Tempered glass lens, stainless steel fittings. Split strap with non-slip locks.

D 1010. Orange.

B10NB

Plastic lens, patented purge valve, strap locks.

D 1011. Blue.

Surf King

Beginner's model. Thermoplastic body, plastic lens, strap locks.

D 1012. Black.

B50 Junior

Designed for youngsters aged 5-10. Flared skirt, plastic lens, non-slip strap.

D 1013. Blue.

B40Y Junior

Designed for children aged 2-8. Flared skirt, round plastic lens, non-slip strap.

D 1014. Orange.

Sport Diver

Designed for narrow face. Rectangular lens, purge valve, nose pocket.

D 1015. Black with blue lens rim.

Cressi-Sub

Pinocchio

Original nose pocket mask. Soft rubber skirt, split head band.

D 1016. Black with black, blue, or yellow lens rim.

Pinocchio De Luxe

Wide vision. Soft rubber skirt with nose pocket. Chromed metal lens ring.

D 1017. Black.

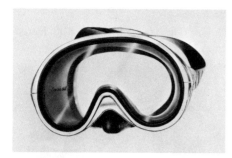

Pinova

Shaped nose. Low volume, wide angle. Plastic lens rim, split head strap, nose pocket.

D 1018. Black with rim in choice of colors. Sizes: regular and Pinobaby for smaller faces.

Pinova Optical

Expanded side and bottom view with reduced volume. Single lens can be ground for assosimetric and negative astigmatic corrections. Nose pocket.

D 1019. Black rubber with choice of colored rims.

Quarzo

Rectangular wide vision lens with plastic rim. Nose pocket, split head strap.

D 1020. Black rubber with yellow or orange rim.

Superlince

Two lenses, nose pocket, split head strap. Available with prescription lenses (assosimetric or negative astigmatic corrections).

D 1021. Black rubber with choice of colored rims.

Piuma

Low profile rubber skirt, easy adjusting strap locks. Available with single or double lens.

D 1022. Blue and black. Sizes: regular and Piuma Jr.

Alfa

Soft rubber with ABS lens rim. Partially shaped nose.

D 1023. Black with black, yellow or orange rim. Sizes: regular and Alfa Jr.

Lince Optical

Holds two prescription-ground lenses (up to -6 correction).

D 1024.

Lince

Two lenses to minimize inner volume and provide wide view. Nose pocket.

D 1025. Black and black, yellow, or orange rim.

Dacor

Professional

Minimum air space. Heavy duty construction with large purge valve. Purge valve optional.

D 1027. Black. Sizes: regular or Mini-pro.

Trivue

Nose pocket, three tempered lenses for 180° peripheral and downward vision. Double feather edge seal, flex corner posts for snug fit. Purge valve may be kept sealed or cut open at diver's option.

D 1028. Black.

Vedo

Designed to hold diver's own prescription lenses in rubber inserts.

D 1029. Black.

Universal

Slanted design to maximize visibility.

D 1030. Black or blue. Sizes: regular or Mini-Universal.

Equaleye

Tempered dual lenses, nose pocket.

D 1031.

Equalizer

Finger wells, optional purge valve.

D 1032. Black or blue. Sizes: regular or Mini-Equalizer (20% smaller).

Nautilus

Nose pocket, purge valve (may be kept sealed).

D 1033. Black.

Sea Rite II

Designed for extra side visibility. Optional purge valve.

D 1034. Black.

Tenue

Nose pocket, purge valve (may be kept sealed).

D 1035. Black with white trim. Sizes: regular or Mini-Mondial (20% smaller).

Triton

Separate nose pads for equalizing pressure. Purge valve.

D 1036. Black.

Dolfino

"Nervi"

Hexagon-shaped lens of tempered glass. 92% natural rubber skirt with double feathered edge, finger wells. Adjustable split head strap.

D 1037. Black and yellow.

"Splendido"

High impact nylon frame, 5mm tempered lens. 92% natural rubber skirt with nose pocket and double feathered edge. Compact size.

D 1038. Black and yellow.

"Venice"

Wide view design, 5mm tempered glass lens, high impact frame. 92% natural rubber skirt with finger wells, optional purge valve, double feathered edge. Split strap.

D 1039. Black and orange.

"Professional"

Stainless steel or nylon frame, 5mm tempered glass, nose pocket, optional purge valve, double feathered edge, split strap.

D 1040. Black and yellow.

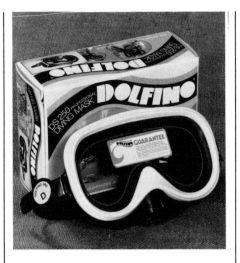

"Milano"

Modified oval shaped tempered glass lens, skirt with feathered edge, finger wells.

D 1041. Black and yellow.

"Genoa"

Oval shape, finger wells, stainless steel frame.

D 1042. Black and yellow.

"Roma"

For small faces. Safety lens, finger wells.

D 1043. Black and yellow.

"Elba"

Double feathered edge, stainless steel frame, tempered glass lens.

D 1044. Black and yellow.

"Capri"

Wide vision, double feathered edge, finger wells.

D 1045. Black and yellow.

"Scuba Dive"

Molded nose pocket, double feathered edge.

D 1046. Black, red and yellow.

"Lido Deep Diver"

Low volume. Narrow skirt with double feathered edge and double seal.

D 1047. Black and orange.

"Super Cyrano"

Two 5mm tempered lenses in molded frame. Nose pocket.

D 1048. Black and orange.

"Panorea"

Three 5 mil. tempered lenses for 180° positive vision, finger wells.

D 1049. Black and yellow.

Healthways

Scubarama®

Three pane lens with flex corner post joints. Stainless steel bands, soft rubber skirt with double seal, finger wells. Adjustable rubber head strap with locking tab on skirt. Purge valve optional.

D 1050. Black.

Scubamaster®

Goggle-shaped 5mm tempered glass lens for side and downward vision. Five-inch wide skirt opening. Rubber skirt with feathered edge, double seal, molded nose pocket. Aluminum band. Purge valve optional.

D 1051. Black.

Scubacat®

Low internal volume. Short skirt with feathered edge, double seal. Tempered lenses, molded rubber nose pocket, positive lock strap. Purge valve optional.

D 1052. Black (including band and head strap).

Scubaview™

Slopes back to top and sweeps down and to sides for upward, downward, and side vision. Five-inch wide skirt opening fits most faces. Rubber skirt with feathered edge, double seal, molded in finger wells, large purge valve. Molded rubber head strap with positive lock, 5mm tempered glass lens, stainless steel band.

D 1053. Black.

Scubalizer®

Oval shape. Rubber skirt with tapered edge and double seal. Convoluted finger wells. Head strap with positive lock, 5mm tempered glass lens, stainless steel band. Purge valve optional.

D 1054. Black. Sizes: 5″ wide skirt or junior size (narrower skirt).

Prismatic™

Low volume wrap-around design with glass and frame molded as single unit in three planes. Light weight, low profile. Mask-lok fastener allows one-handed underwater adjustment.

D 1055. Orange and blue.

Oceanic Farallon

Piuma

Tempered glass molded into ABS frame. Gum rubber skirt. Positive locking, easy adjusting strap. Light weight, low volume. Nose pocket.

D 1056. Blue.

Poseidon

Full Face Mask

Connects to Cyklon 300 regulator. Wide vision, low resistance. Equalizing nose pocket. Seals with Unisuit hood.

D 1057. Black. Poseidon Division of Parkway Fabricators, Inc.

Supervision

Three lenses. Flexible equalizer finger wells. Double sealing skirt. Split strap. Optional extra-large purge valve.

D 1058. Black.

Compact Supervision

Three lens design for smaller faces. Double water seal, nose pocket equalizer, split headband.

D 1059. Black.

Pro-Vision

Rectangular lens, flexible finger wells, double sealing edges, split head strap. Extra-large purge valve optional.

D 1060. Black.

Pressurizer II

Oval lens with flexible finger wells. Double water seal, split head strap.

D 1061. Black. Sizes: regular and compact.

Pressurizer II H/T Mask

Constructed of hypo-allergenic, translucent compound. Split head strap, flexible finger wells. Oval lens.

D 1062.

Pro-Vision H/T Mask

Translucent hypo-allergenic material, rectangular lens, flexible finger wells, split head strap. Extra large purge valve optional.

D 1063.

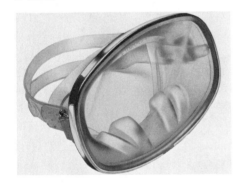

Scubapro

Optical Mask

Corrective lenses ground into optical quality crystal mask lens. Double sealing skirt, nose pocket equalizer. Also available with plain lens.

D 1064. Black.

Scubapro Mask

Basic oval lens, smooth water seal, split head strap.

D 1065. Black. Sizes: regular and compact.

Free Vision

Two lenses set close to face for wide vision, low volume.

D 1066. Black with red lens retainer.

Close-Up

Two lenses, minimum displacement, nose pocket.

D 1067. Black with blue lens retainer.

Seatec

Triport Mask

Three tempered lenses, nose pocket, double seal.

D 1068. Black.

Sea-Vision

Wide oval tempered lens, double seal, finger wells.

D 1069. Black.

Aqua-Vu

Oval tempered lens, finger wells, double seal.

D 1070. Black.

Sea Lad

Designed for small faces. Oval tempered lens.

D 1071. Black.

Sportsways

Equalizer

Slanted lens, short topskirt, finger wells. Purge valve optional.

D 1072. Black.

Vista Vue

Slanted oval lens, short topskirt.

D 1073. Black.

Catalina

Dual lens, low volume, double seal, nose pocket.

D 1074. Black.

Avalon

Rectangular lens, pure gum rubber sealing edge, optional purge valve.

D 1075. Black.

Hydronaut

Dual lens, low volume, wide visibility, double seal, nose pocket.

D 1076. Black and white.

Parabolic

Extremely low volume, light weight. Dual lenses with swept back design, nose pocket, double seal.

D 1077. Black and orange.

Dolphin Jr.

For smaller faces. Oval tempered lens, split head strap.

D 1078. Blue.

Tekna

Tekna Mask I

Light weight, low volume wrap-around. Strap-Loks are instantly adjustable. Four lenses, nose pocket, split strap.

D 1079.

Tekna Mask II

Twin lens design. Small radius double seal edge. Low volume, light weight. Split strap with instantly adjustable Strap-Loks. Nose pocket.

D 1080.

U.S. Cavalero

Equinaut

Low volume, wide angle, double lens, nose pocket, double edged seal.

D 1594.

Corsica

Contoured design, dual lens, double edged skirt, nose pocket.

D 1595.

St. Tropez

Low volume, minimum displacement dual lens design with nose pocket inner seal.

D 1596.

Gymnot

Rectangular lens, double sealing skirt with finger wells, choice of stainless steel or black or yellow plastic rim. Optional purge valve.

D 1597. Sizes: regular and mini.

Competition

Feathered edged skirt, oval tempered lens, large finger wells.

D 1598.

Tahiti

Wide oval tempered lens, soft edged seal, stainless steel rim.

D 1599.

U.S. Divers

Bella

Low volume double feather-edge seal. Nose pocket equalizer. Tempered glass lenses, stainless steel rim and buckles, split head strap.

D 1081. Black with yellow trim ring.

Wrap-Around

Three lenses, nose pocket, purge valve.

D 1082. Black.

Nova

Wide angle lens, nose pocket.

D 1083. Black with yellow trim ring.

Aqua-Naut® II

Rectangular skirt, purge valve, equalizer pockets.

D 1084. Black with yellow trim ring.

Pacifica® II

Large purge valve, equalizer pockets.

D 1085. Black with yellow trim ring. Sizes: regular and mini.

Atlantis® II

Rectangular skirt, equalizer pockets.

D 1086. Black with yellow trim ring. Sizes: regular and mini.

Fisheye

Lowest volume. Two wide-angled lenses. Equalizer pockets.

D 1087. Black with yellow trim ring.

Tahiti Deluxe

Rectangular lens. Trim ring covers nose.

D 1088. Black.

Equi-Purge

Oval lens, purge valve, equalizer pockets.

D 1089. Black, yellow, or hypo-allergenic silicone.

Equi-Rama

Oval lens, equalizer pockets.

D 1090. Black or hypo-allergenic silicone.

Sea Champ®

Oval lens, feather-edge flared skirt.

D 1091. Black or blue with yellow trim ring.

Sea Champ® Jr.

Rectangular lens for smaller faces.

D 1092. Black or blue.

U.S. Nemrod

Barcelona

Gum rubber skirt with purge valve. Three tempered lenses with flex corner posts. Cam-lock strap with stainless steel fittings.

D 1093. Black.

Denia

Three tempered lenses with flex corner-posts. Nose pocket with purge valve. Extra wide non-slip strap. Stainless steel lens

D 1094. Black.

Super Lux

Compact design. Double-edged seal, nose pad for equalization. Tempered safety lens with stainless steel band.

D 1095. Black with orange trim.

Toledo

Wide angle lens. Double-edge seal, feathered skirt. Tempered safety lens with stainless steel rim.

D 1096. Black.

Alicante

Double-sealed skirt. Tempered lens with stainless steel band. Purge valve and equalizer. Adjustable split strap.

D 1097. Black with yellow clamp ring.

Adra

Wide angle tempered safety lens. Double-edged seal. Equalizer nose pad.

D 1098. Black with yellow trim.

Coronado

Double-sealed skirt with purge valve and equalizer wells. Oval tempered lens with stainless rim. Adjustable split strap.

D 1099. Black.

Bali

Feathered skirt with bellows-type pockets. Tempered oval lens with stainless steel rim. Adjustable split strap.

D 1100. Black.

Atlanta

Designed for smaller faces. Equalizer nose pads. Tempered safety lens with stainless steel rim.

D 1101. Black with yellow trim.

Bermuda

Fits close to eyes for wide field of vision. Feathered skirt. Tempered safety lens, split strap.

D 1102. Black.

Colombo

Designed for young divers. Soft skirt. Oval tempered safety lens, stainless steel rim. Split strap.

D 1103. Black.

Cadiz

Lightweight, low displacement design. Rectangular wide-angle tempered safety lens. Split strap, feathered skirt.

D 1104. Blue.

Tarraco

Specially compounded rubber skirt. Plastic lens with pressure rim.

D 1105. Blue with white rim.

Marino

Designed for young divers. Skirt made of special rubber compound. Plastic lens.

D 1106. Black with amber lens.

Oporto

Oval lens, purge valve, stainless lens band.

D 1107. Black.

White Stag

Super View

Low volume dual lens with neoprene or hypo-allergenic translucent skirt, nose pocket. Optional corrective lenses (-2.0 through -7.5 diopters).

D 1108. Black or translucent.

Pinovision

Low volume single-lens design with nose pocket, double seal, rubber skirt. Optional prescription-ground lenses (-2.0 through -7.5 diopters).

D 1109. Black.

Perivision

Three lenses, double seal, nose pocket, purge valve.

D 1110. Black.

Super Stag

Rectangular lens, nose pocket, double seal.

D 1112. Black.

Aquavision

Oval lens, finger wells, double seal. Large or small purge valve optional.

D 1026. Black.

Stabilizator

Oval lens, small purge valve optional, feathered skirt, finger wells.

D 1113. Black.

Panavue

Wide view lens, finger wells, small purge valve optional, double seal.

D 1114. Black.

Panorama

Wide oval lens, finger wells, double seal, small purge valve optional.

D 1115. Black.

Mini Sea-Pro

Single lens nose pocket design for smaller faces. Double seal.

D 1116. Black.

Junior

Single oval lens for smaller face.

D 1117. Black.

Snorkel Buying Guide

The snorkel is a surface breathing aid which allows the diver to inhale without lifting his head out of the water. This advantage helps snorkelers to conserve energy while keeping their eyes on the scene below them.

Sport divers use snorkels in three different ways: pure snorkelers stay on the surface in shallow or particularly clear water. Skin divers use snorkeling gear but plunge beneath the surface. Scuba divers use snorkels to supplement their air supply, usually getting to and from a scuba-diving site. The kind of diving you intend to do should influence your choice of snorkel.

The key feature in a snorkel is its breathing ease, which is a combination of how smoothly the air is inhaled and exhaled, how easily any water is cleared out, and how comfortably the snorkel fits the mouth and face.

Most snorkels are reasonably simple affairs, shaped roughly like the letter "J". The barrel of the snorkel is the pipe which protrudes above the surface of the water. Next is the mouthpiece tube, the curved or otherwise contoured section which connects the barrel to the third snorkel component, the mouthpiece.

Snorkel barrels are generally made of rubber or plastic, 12"-14" in length. A barrel over 15"-16" is generally too long, since the water pressure 15 inches below the surface will prevent the diver's chest from expanding enough to inhale surface-pressure air. Slightly soft barrels cause less drag in the water than rigid ones.

Up to a point, the larger the bore (internal diameter) of the barrel, the easier the snorkel will breathe. Most barrels have bores between ⅝"-⅞". One good rule of thumb is: the larger the diver, the larger the bore. Belled or flared barrel tips can add up to 18% in breathing efficiency by decreasing turbulence in the barrel, which aids in exhaling as well as inhaling. Many snorkel barrels are also topped off with brightly-colored trim which can help a diver pick his buddy out of a crowd or murky water.

Contoured barrels are shaped to fit snugly around the side of the head. If properly designed, they can reduce drag, which should help the mouthpiece fit more comfortably.

Some snorkels are available in an "S" shape with a floatation valve (usually a ping pong ball in a holder) to keep water out of the snorkel when submerged. They frequently leak, close unexpectedly, and cause drag in the water. Even more dangerous are masks with built-in floation-closing snorkels, since the unwary diver could possibly inhale the leaked water. Anyone using a snorkel should learn the elementary techniques of clearing one when swamped, rather than relying on these undependable gadgets.

Most snorkels come with a "keeper" or mask strap adapter on the barrel, to secure the snorkel when the mouthpiece is out of your mouth. Be sure the keeper is compatible with the head strap of the mask you want.

The tube which holds the mouthpiece may be an extension of the barrel or a separate unit. Some tubes are gently curved, while others are more sharply bent in an "L" design. For the smoothest flow of air, the mouthpiece tube should have the exact same bore as the barrel.

Other mouthpiece tubes are made of flexible corrugated tubing which falls out of the way when not in use, to avoid fouling in other gear (especially helpful if you're alternating between scuba and snorkel). Flexible tubes also contour to any face and reduce drag on the mouthpiece.

However, the internal corrugations of flexible tubes tend to retain water even after clearing, causing what divers call "misting" on inhalation. Some models are corrugated outside but smooth on the inside to overcome this problem. Be sure any corrugated tubing is non-kinking and non-collapsible.

A compromise arrangement consists of a "bellows" connection — with two or three corrugations between the tube and the mouthpiece. This connection offers flexibility in positioning and less risk of "misting". Swivel connections between the barrel and tube or tube and mouthpiece can also aid in achieving a comfortable fit.

Tubes which curve too deeply or sharply can add turbulence in both the intake and exhalation of air, and can make it more difficult to purge water. Some tubes are fitted with purge valves designed to eject water below mouth level, rather than forcing it all the way out the top of the barrel. Most of these arrangements work better in theory than in practice.

Diver comfort is affected more by the mouthpiece than any other snorkel component. Mouthpieces come in different sizes, materials, and degrees of rigidity. There are many different features to consider, but the primary consideration is personal comfort.

A mouthpiece consists of a rubber flange which fits in front of the teeth and behind the lips, plus a biting surface (usually two "lugs") and an air hole allowing the diver to inhale and exhale.

When trying on snorkels, have the dive shop clerk wash the mouthpiece of those models that interest you, and show you how to put the mouthpiece in place. Notice the taste and smell of the mouthpiece and the air you get through it. Be sure the flange fits easily under your lips without irritating your gums. Bite down on the lugs to be sure they fit your own dental pattern. While using the snorkel, your teeth will be slightly clenched, so hold the mouthpiece firmly for a while to test for comfort.

Some snorkels come with special bite plates or hollow or moldable lugs which you may find more comfortable than the standard lugs.

Divers generally wear their snorkels on the left side of the head, to avoid fouling the tube in a single-hose regulator, which traditionally comes over the right shoulder. Even if you use double-hose regulator, or no scuba gear at all, this is a good habit to learn just for the sake of uniformity. Try the snorkel on in combination with the mask you desire. With snorkel keeper and mouthpiece in place, move the barrel backward and forward on the mask strap to see how much discomfort its drag may cause you.

Snorkels

AMF Voit

Swimaster Avalon

Rotating mouthpiece for adjustable positioning. Large bore, flared top. Built-in lug for permanent snorkel keeper, plus conventional keeper. Neoprene rubber.

D 1118. Black with red trim.

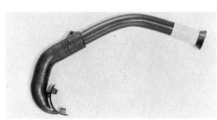

F8

Large bore, wrap-around design. Neoprene rubber.

D 1119. Black with red trim.

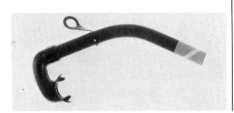

F5B

Corrugated mouthpiece tube (noncollapsing) with smooth inner wall. Soft mouthpiece.

D 1120. Blue and white.

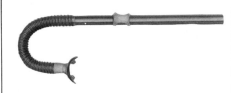

F6

All rubber one-piece J design with oval bite-plate. Venturi action at "U" aids in purging.

D 1121. Black.

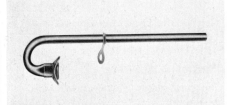

F1Y

Beginners model. Simple J design, soft mouthpiece.

D 1122. Orange with white mouthpiece.

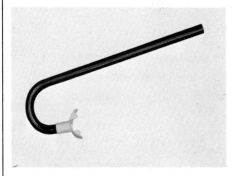

Swimaster Bello-Flex

Corrugated mouthpiece tube. Straight-top barrel design.

D 1123. Black with red, white and blue trim.

Swimaster Spearfisherman

Large bore barrel and mouthpiece opening.

D 1124. Black with red, white and blue trim.

Skin Diver

Two-piece J design, all-rubber mouthpiece.

D 1125. Orange and black.

Cressi-Sub

REX
Flexible L shaped tube. Soft mouthpiece.
D 1126. Black with luminous trim.

Areusa "Bellows"
Flexible rubber barrel, corrugated rubber tube to soft mouthpiece.
D 1127. Black with luminous trim.

Delfino Jr.
Flexible barrel, soft rubber mouthpiece.
D 1128. Luminous tube, black mouthpiece.

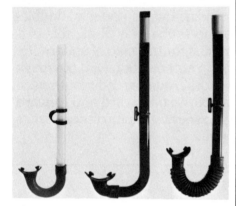

Gringo
Flexible angled barrel, soft rubber elbow and mouthpiece.
D 1129. Black with luminous trim.

Delfino
Rigid barrel. J design with soft rubber mouthpiece.
D 1130. Black.

Professional
Contoured barrel, soft mouthpiece.
D 1131. Black with clear, black, or yellow barrel.

Dacor

Turboflex®
Low convolution hose interior for more efficient clearing and inhalation. 360° swivel at flex tube connection. Offset mouthpiece with short flex section for easy access. Straight or contour tube.
D 1132. Black with red "Glo-Top"® trim.

Universal
Standard J design, lug type mouthpiece.
D 1133. Black with red "Glo-Top"® trim.

"L" Shape
Sharp bend around face to minimize drag. Lug type mouthpiece.
D 1134. Black with red "Glo-Top"® trim.

Spiral-Flex
Flexible non-crimping hose. Full oval bite-plate.
D 1135. Black with red "Glo-Top"® trim.

Flexible
Flexible non-crimping hose molded to lug type mouthpiece.
D 1136. Black with red "Glo-Top"® trim.

Standard
J design, plastic barrel, lug type mouthpiece.
D 1137. Black with red "Glo-Top"® trim.

Lightweight
J design with smaller-bore tube.
D 1138. Black with red "Glo-Top"® trim.

Big Barrel Wraparound
Extra large diameter barrel, 360° swivel at tube connection.
D 1139. Clear plastic tube with red "Glo-Top"® trim. Black mouthpiece.

Turbo
Large diameter flexible barrel, contoured mouthpiece, straight or contour tube.
D 1140. Black with red "Glo-Top"® trim.

Dolfino

"Rapallo"
Slightly contoured large bore barrel of crushproof flexible rubber.
D 1141. Black with red trim.

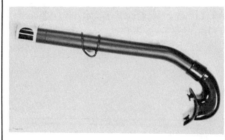

"Rimini"
Straight J design. Rubber mouthpiece.
D 1142. Black with red trim.

"Porto" Pro Flex
Mouthpiece tube of 92% natural accordian rubber, reinforced barrel.
D 1143. Black with red trim.

Healthways

Scubamaster® High Flow
Extruded and formed rubber tube with conical belled tip. Curved molded rubber mouthpiece angled at 30° to curve tube closely around head.
D 1144. Black with "Safety-Glo" red trim.

Scubamaster®
Big-bore barrel and mouthpiece tube smoothly curved for easy clearing. Molded rubber mouthpiece angled at 30°. Rigid high impact ABS barrel.
D 1145. Orange barrel, black mouthpiece.

Scubajet® Adjustable
Mouthpiece can be rotated 30° forward or backward to adjust to head position, with built-in stops to prevent over-rotation.
D 1146. Black with "Safety-Glo" red trim.

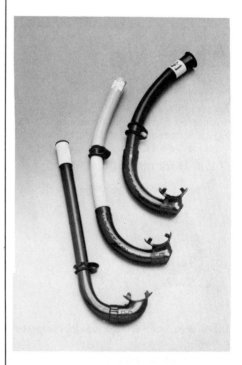

Scubadiver®
Lightweight clear plastic tube, molded rubber mouthpiece.
D 1147. Black mouthpiece, "Safety-Glo" red trim.

Scuba "J"™

Soft, flex-mounted mouthpiece with one piece rubber elbow and barrel.

D 1148. Black with "Safety-Glo" red trim.

Scubaflex®

"Accordion-flex" tubing. Wide mouthpiece opening with oval bite plate. Purge valve optional.

D 1149. Black with "Safety-Glo" red trim.

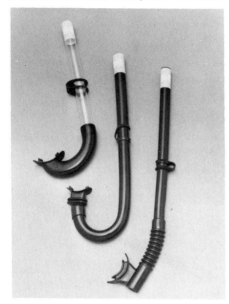

Oceanic Farallon

Moldable Mouthpiece Snorkel

Patented mouthpiece lugs can be heat-molded to diver's individual bite for extra comfort, improved grip, and positive seal. Large bore contoured barrel. Swiveled mouthpiece.

D 1150. Black with fluorescent trim.

Scubapro

Wrap Around Jet Snorkel

13/16" bore with patented "Jet" design. Contoured to hug head and minimize vibrations or snagging.

D 1151. Black with red trim.

Off-Set Jet Snorkel

Wrap-around 13/16" bore with mouthpiece specially tilted for use on left side of mask. Patented "Jet" design.

D 1152. Black with red trim.

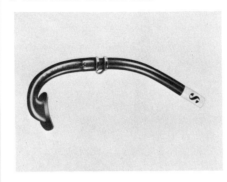

Swivel Tip Jet Snorkel

Mouthpiece tube swivels to position barrel angle to individual needs. Specially designed for use with back mounted buoyancy devices to facilitate surface swimming on on the back.

D 1153. Black with red trim.

Super Jet Snorkel

Purge valve below gum-rubber mouthpiece. 11/16" bore.

D 1154. Black with red trim.

Jet Snorkel

Patented "Jet" design bore in straight J shape. Large mouthpiece.

D 1155. Black with red trim. Sizes: regular (11/16" bore) and mini (9/16" bore).

Scubapro Snorkel

Mouthpiece bellows for comfortable fit in smaller mouths. 11/16" bore.

D 1156. Black with red trim.

Hydroflex Snorkel

Corrugated mouthpiece hose. 9/16" bore.

D 1157. Black with red trim.

Seatec

Sea Tube

7/8" bore with flared top, contoured barrel.

D 1158. Black.

Sea Diver

Straight J design, large bore barrel.

D 1159. Black.

Sea Flex

Corrugated mouthpiece tube, large bore barrel.

D 1160. Black.

Sportsways

Catalina

Straight J design, bellows-style mouthpiece.

D 1161. Black with red trim.

Malibu "Big Barrel"

Slightly contoured, extra-long, large bore barrel.

D 1162. Black with red trim.

Avalon Contour "Flex-O-Wrap"

7/8" diameter contoured barrel with close tolerance between inside of barrel and mouthpiece.

D 1163. Black with red trim.

Dolphin Jr.

Straight J design.

D 1164. Blue with red trim.

Tekna

Tube-Tab Snorkel

Big bore, contoured barrel, swiveling mouthpiece. All rubber construction. Patented tube tabs (hollow bite lugs) for comfort. Available with regular size or small mouthpiece.

D 1165.

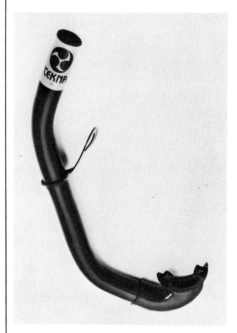

U.S. Divers

Aqua-Lung® Professional

Contoured crushproof 7/8" bore barrel.

D 1166. Yellow or black with yellow trim.

Power Tuned

Patented flared top.

D 1167. Black with yellow trim.

Snork-L

Flexible tube with flared top, 360° rotating mouthpiece.

D 1168. Black with yellow trim.

Super-Flex

convoluted non-kinking hose from barrel to mouthpiece. Optional purge valve.

D 1169. Black with yellow trim.

Aqua-Flex

Smooth bore convoluted hose from barrel to mouthpiece.

D 1170. Black with yellow trim.

Aqua-Master® II

One piece rubber barrel and tube with crushproof oval biteplate.

D 1171. Yellow or black with yellow trim.

Aquatic

Lightweight, soft mouthpiece.

D 1172. Yellow or blue.

U.S. Nemrod

Irun

1″ bore barrel, contoured for minimum drag. Soft mouthpiece.

D 1173. Black with red trim.

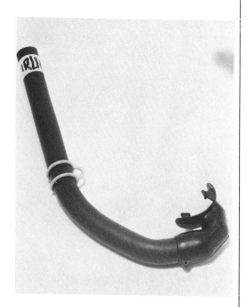

Menorca

Soft, all-rubber J design. Soft mouthpiece.

D 1174. Black with red trim.

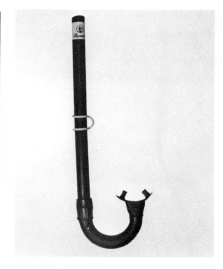

Menorca Flex

Flexible barrel, corrugated rubber tube. Soft mouthpiece.

D 1175. Black with red trim.

Tossa

Large barrel, soft mouthpiece.

D 1176. Black and blue.

Almeria

Angled plastic barrel with soft rubber mouthpiece.

D 1177. Black and orange.

Canaris

Soft, flexible plastic mouthpiece and plastic barrel.

D 1178. Yellow and orange.

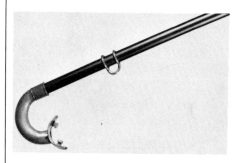

White Stag

Hydro-Stream

Contoured mouthpiece tube with large bore and optional adjustable curved barrel.

D 1179. Black with red and white trim.

Deep Dive Big Tube

Curved mouthpiece tube, ⅞″ bore. Optional swivel connector at mouthpiece and barrel.

D 1180. Black with red and white trim.

Bellows

Straight barrel, corrugated rubber tube, soft flexible mouthpiece.

D 1181. Black with red and white trim.

Dolphin

Designed for junior divers. Standard J design, rubber barrel.

D 1182. Black with red and white trim.

Junior

Designed for junior divers. Standard J design, plastic barrel.

D 1183. Black with red and white trim.

Fin Buying Guide

A good pair of swimming fins (or flippers) can almost triple your barefoot swimming speed, but divers are more concerned with power and efficiency than velocity. Fins give the diver added range and endurance, while leaving his hands free for other activities.

Swim fin efficiency is a function of the power supplied by the fin blade as it moves through the water. However, there is a broad range of blade designs, and you will find that some are more comfortable or efficient for you than others. Flippers with large and/or stiff blades provide the most power and thrust, but, because of the amount of resistance they encounter, can also cause cramping.

Fins that are too small or pliable to work efficiently can cause fatigue. If a fin blade doesn't snap back when bent, it's probably too flexible for serious diving. The right degree of blade rigidity depends on the diver's size and conditioning plus anticipated diving conditions.

There are many blade designs, each with its own characteristics. A straight blade works as a direct extension of the foot. The down-stroke of a straight blade is 1/3 as efficient as its upstroke. An offset blade is set at a 20°-30° angle to the foot, more in line with the plane of the leg. An offset blade provides the same power output as a straight blade, but the power is more equally distributed between the up and down strokes. Reportedly, this balanced thrust causes less cramping than the straight blade.

Most blades feature stabilizer rails, ribs, or vanes along the outer edges and, frequently, down both faces of the blade itself. Another popular feature is the power vent which minimizes propulsive resistance and helps hold the blade stable during the power phases of the kick. Sometimes these vents are fitted with overlapping blades that redirect water through and along the blade toward its tip. These vents equalize the force between the downstroke and the upstroke, producing the most thrust with the least energy output.

You'll find blades with both symmetrical and assymetrical designs. The chief advantage of symmetrically-shaped blades is that they can be worn on either foot — as long as the foot pockets themselves are symmetrical.

The foot pocket is the next most important fin component. Here the two basic styles are the open heel and full foot pocket (which covers the heel).

Open heel designs generally feature adjustable straps, so the foot pocket can be custom-fit to your own foot, or changed if the fins are shared by different divers. Flippers are generally worn over heavy athletic socks or wet or dry suit boots to prevent chafing, so be sure to try them on this way. Many divers wear open-heel adjustable fins over hard-soled boots for the combination of snug fit and heel protection.

In most cases, you should plan to wear your boots under your fins whether or not you wear any other part of your exposure suit, since the foot pocket is cut overlarge to accommodate the boot, and will be too large to accommodate your bare foot no matter how much you tighten the adjustable strap. Check the strap lock carefully, and see if there is a system for retaining loose strap ends.

Open heel fins are a bit easier to get on, although some full foot models come with rear pull-tabs to aid in this operation. Full foot flippers may also come off more easily in rough water, although some brands have instep straps or other accessories to help hold them on.

Whatever the stiffness of the blade you choose, look for a soft rubber foot pocket. Be sure the pocket isn't too tight across the instep, or chafing or numbness could result. Too loose a fit could cause blisters or loss of fins.

Other comfortable features, found most frequently in full foot fins, are open toes and/or drain holes. Both reduce drag by preventing

water from accumulating in the foot pocket, and the open toe feature helps prevent cramping, as well.

Flippers may be constructed for positive, neutral, or negative buoyancy. If you're planning on diving in murky water where you could lose sight of lost equipment easily, or shallow water where you can reach the surface with just one fin, floating flippers might be best for you. If you plan to be on the bottom for any extended periods, fins with negative buoyancy might be easiest to retrieve. For general diving, neutral buoyancy is recommended, since the lost fin stays at the same depth as the diver.

Fin sizes are generally given in U.S. adult shoe sizes. You'll find that prices usually go up with the size of a particular model.

Fins

AMF Voit

Duck Foot

New soft open heel foot pocket fits either foot. Stiff ribbed blade. Buoyant.

D 1184. Black with blue or orange. Sizes: 5-7, 7-8, 8-9, 9-11, 11-13.

Swimaster Mark X

Vented design for extra propulsion. Large oval vents reduce pressure drag. Open heel foot pocket with adjustable band, stainless steel buckle. Blend of natural and neoprene rubber.

D 1185. Black.

Voit Viking

Symmetrically curved blade with large stiff ribs. Soft stretch heel, stiff blade.

D 1186. Two-tone blue. Sizes: 4-9, 9-13, 11-13.

Swimaster Mark IX

Open heel with adjustable strap, stainless steel buckle. Blend of natural and neoprene rubber. Blade design based on original UDT Duck Foot.

D 1187. Black. Sizes: regular and mini (for smaller feet or without boots).

Sail Fins

Rubber blade with five stabilizer ribs. Replaceable adjustable neoprene strap.

D 1188. Blue. Sizes: up to 4, 4-8, 8 and up.

A8 Skin Diver

Rubber blade with six stabilizer ribs, open toed full foot pocket. Buoyant.

D 1189. Black. Sizes: 1-3, 4-5, 5-8.

54

Mini Duck Foot

Duck foot styling scaled down for children. Non-slip heel straps, soft and pliable construction.

D 1190. Blue. Sizes: up to 4, 4-8.

Swim Fins

Heel pad plus adjustable strap, vented blade with reinforced ribs.

D 1191. Black.

A10 Skin Diver Fins

Open toe full foot. Two-plane blade design. Buoyant.

D 1192. Black. Sizes: 5-7, 7-9, 9-11, 11-13.

Riviera

Lightweight Tecralene® blade, soft open toe foot pocket with heel tab.

D 1193. Black and blue. Sizes: 1-3, 3-5, 6-8.

A7 Skin Diver

Open toe full foot, 6 stabilizer ribs on blade.

D 1194. Black. Sizes: 1-3, 4-5, 5-8.

Cressi-Sub

Rondine Extra

Full foot, open toed design with extra long blade.

D 1195. Black. Sizes to 13.

Rondine Blue

Open toed full foot. Soft flexible rubber compound is slightly buoyant.

D 1196. Blue. Sizes: 4-5, 5-6, 7-8, 8-9, 10-11.

Rondine "S"

Vented blade. Open toed full foot.

D 1197. Black. Sizes: 5-6, 7-8, 8-9, 10-11.

Rondine "L"

Open toed full foot, long angled blade.

D 1198. Black. Sizes: 6,7,8,9,10,11,12.

Rondine "V"

Assymetrical blade, built-in arch in open toed full foot pocket.

D 1199. Black. Sizes: 8-9, 9-10, 10-11.

Comando USA

Open foot, adjustable strap, vented blade.

D 1200. Black. Size: fits 8-14.

Dacor

Turbo

Open heel style with adjustable straps. Three stabilizer ribs.

D 1201. Black.

Turbo II

Flow-through vent, four stabilizer ribs. Open heel, adjustable straps.

D 1202. Black.

Corda

Full-foot, open toe, extra-long blade, heavy side rails.

D 1203. Blue (floating), or black (non-floating).

Dolfino

"Marina" Swim Fins

Open toed full foot pocket, flexible blade. 92% rubber, buoyant.

D 1204. Black. Sizes: 1-3, 6-8, 9-10, 11-13.

"Stella" Junior Fins

Fully adjustable heel strap. Made of buoyant 92% natural rubber.

D 1205. Orange. Size: 1-7.

Jumbo "Hydra" Fins

Open toed full foot pocket, vented blade with four stabilizer ribs.

D 1206. Black. Sizes: 7-8, 9-10, 11-12.

Healthways

Scubamaster®

Six balanced vents for lateral stability. Adjustable cross-ribbed straps, with slotted retainers for loose strap ends. Rear of foot pocket compounded of softer rubber for comfort.

D 1207. Black.

Whaler™

Ribbed rubber blade, open-toe foot pocket with soft rear section. Adjustable straps with slotted retainers.

D 1208. Black.

Scubafin

Full foot pocket with open toe. Stiff rubber blade with side rails. Heel tab for easy entry. Buoyant.

D 1209. Black. Sizes from 5-14 (shoe size).

Imperial

Turtle Fins

Open heel, adjustable strap, vented blade with four stabilizer ribs.

D 1210. Black. Sizes: medium or large blade.

Oceanic Farallon

Fara-Fin™ I

Stainless steel flex-frame locks diver's leg to optimum angle. Instant heel strap adjustment.

D 1211. Black.

Fara-Fin™ II

Spring-loaded compression compensated heel strap for instant adjustment.

D 1213.

Scubapro

Jet Fins

Patented design based on "jet" principle which redirects kick-resisting water from top of foot to second blade area behind vents for extra thrust. Adjustable strap. Slightly negatively buoyant.

D 1214. Black. Sizes: 4-9, 7-11, 10-14.

Scubapro Full Foot Fins

Open toe full foot pocket with high heel for security. Ribbed blade.

D 1215. Black. Sizes: 5-7, 7-8½, 8½-10, 10-12, 12-14.

Skin Diving Fins

Inexpensive open toe full foot design.

D 1216. Blue. Sizes: 2-3, 3-4, 4-5, 5-7, 7-9, 9-11, 11-13.

Sportsways

"707" Floating Fins

Open heel, adjustable strap, vented blade with four stabilizer ribs.

D 1217. Black. Sizes: medium, large.

Regal Floating Fins

Open toe full foot pocket, tapered for snug fit at heel. Light, flexible blade.

D 1218. Black. Sizes: 5-7, 7-9, 9-11, 11-13.

Waterlung Floating Fins

Open toed, tapered full foot pocket. Tapered, extra-high external blade ribs.

D 1219. Black. Sizes: 4-5, 5½-6½, 7-8, 8½-9½, 10-11, 11½-13, 13½-16.

Dolphin Jr. Fins

Open toed full foot, three stabilizer ribs.

D 1220. Blue. Sizes: 2-3, 3-4, 4-5.

U.S. Cavalero

Hydrojet

Open heel with adjustable strap. Three vents, four stabilizing ribs on symmetrical blade.

D 1600.

Cavalero Navy Fins

Full foot or open heel with adjustable strap. Offset symmetrical blade, drain holes in foot pocket.

D 1601. Sizes: Adjustable 6-9, 9-13; Full foot 7-8, 9-11, 11-13.

U.S. Divers

Super Rocket®

Extra powerful open heel, adjustable strap with pull-on tab. Blade with four stabilizer ribs, three vents.

D 1221. Black. Sizes 10 and up.

Rocket®

Open heel, adjustable strap. Patented triple vent design and snap action ribs.

D 1222. Black. Sizes: adult and mini.

The Spoiler®

Open heel, adjustable strap. Internal high-pressure ducts cause venturi action for added thrust. High side ribs.

D 1223. Black. Sizes: all adult sizes.

Otarie®

Soft, open toe full foot pocket, symmetrical blade design. Choice of floating or non-floating.

D 1224. Blue or black. Sizes: 1-3, 3-4½, 4½-6, 6½-8, 8-9½, 9½-11, 11-13.

Aqua-Lung® Professional

Soft full foot pocket with open heel. Balanced, long, slender blade with three stabilizer ribs.

D 1225. Black. Sizes: 8-10, 10-11, 11-12, 12-13.

U.S. Nemrod

Venturi Power

Water is directed into toe pocket "Power Intake" and thrust out blade tip "Power Exhaust." Stabilizer vanes on both blade faces. Contoured open heel foot pocket, adjustable strap.

D 1226. Black. Sizes: 6-10, 8-15.

Venturi Delfin

"Power Intake" and "Power Exhaust" vents on blade. Large blade with lateral stabilizer vanes. Contoured full foot pocket.

D 1227. Black. Sizes: 8-10, 11-13, 14-15.

Cortez

Long blade with balanced rib-frame. Full foot pocket with open toe. Made of gum rubber.

D 1228. Black. Sizes: 2-4, 4-6, 6-8, 8-10, 10-12, 12-15.

Sevilla

Full sole with adjustable heel strap, stabilizer vanes on blade.

D 1229. Black. Sizes: 3-6, 7-10.

Suprema

Lightweight, non-marking rubber construction. Open toe full foot pocket, extra-wide blade.

D 1230. Blue. Sizes: 2-4, 4-6, 6-8, 8-10.

Buoyancy Devices Buying Guide

Factors such as depth, amount of air left in the scuba tank, and type of equipment being worn or carried can all change the diver's buoyancy during the course of a dive. In recent years a number of devices have been introduced to moderate these changes, so the diver can select whatever degree of buoyancy he chooses — positive, neutral, or negative — during any portion of the dive.

The very first buoyancy control devices were weights which offset the diver's natural positive buoyancy. At first weights were hand carried but soon divers began wearing them on their belts.

Weight Belts

Most modern weight belts consist of 2″ nylon webbing or some other non-deteriorating material fitted with a quick-release buckle. The buckle must be durable and non-corrosive, slip-proof, and easily operated — unseen — with one gloved hand. It's helpful if the quick-release buckle on your weight belt is a different design than the buckle on your scuba harness or any other gear, so you can single it out instantly.

Since the weight belt is the first piece of equipment you're liable to ditch in an emergency, be sure the one you buy is compatible with your other equipment. It should buckle on unencumbered by all other straps, hoses, and other protrusions, and fall away freely when released.

The weight belt is also one of the last pieces of equipment you put on. So be sure you can cinch it down snugly and fasten the buckle with all your other gear in place. If the belt is especially long, watch out for a flapping loose end that could hang up on other equipment.

A tight-fitting belt will keep weights from shifting and upsetting your diving trim. Some belts are designed to contract as the wet suit compresses, to retain a snug fit at any depth. One type is made entirely of rubber, which is less durable than nylon webbing. Other models use rubber "compensators" that take up any slack in the nylon belt. You'll find this depth compensating feature very helpful anywhere below 50 feet.

Other types of belts feature shot-filled vinyl pouches which are somewhat bulky, but conform to body contours. Various models of backpacks and buoyancy compensators also incorporate their own weight systems.

Weights

Most scuba divers (and even many skin divers) need some extra weight to offset their natural positive buoyancy. If you wear even the briefest wet suit protection, you will definitely require additional weights. Here are some techniques for determining how much extra poundage you should pack:

Hand carry a belt with five 2 lb. weights to the bottom of a pool or other calm, shallow water. Drop one weight at a time until you feel yourself becoming slightly buoyant. The amount remaining should be the right weight for you. If ten pounds is not enough, reverse the process by adding weights while floating, until you begin to sink after exhaling.

If you conduct this test in fresh water, figure on adding 2-5 lbs. for salt water. You can also plan to add 18-20 more pounds to overcome the buoyancy of a full neoprene wet suit.

Remember, these are only general guidelines. As soon as you enter open water, you should begin testing for your ability to achieve neutral buoyancy (ideally with the assistance of an experienced diver) and go *no farther* until you achieve it. Always pack a few extra weights in your gear bag, and don't hesitate to go back to the boat or shore to make adjustments. Diving while improperly weighted (too heavy *or* too light) can lead to frustration, exhaustion, panic, and tragedy. Get your buoyancy right at the start and you'll never regret it.

Most slip-on lead weights come in 1,2,3,4, and 5 lb. sizes. Some are specially slotted so they will stay stationary on the belt, or can be removed one at a time without disturbing the other weights. Some large size weights (5-10 lbs.) are contoured to fit compactly on the hips.

Vests

After weights, the next buoyancy device to be

introduced was the inflatable safety vest, an upgraded version of the WWII "Mae West." Most models include an oral inflation tube and a detonating mechanism for a CO_2 cartridge. As the name implies, the safety vest is primarily an emergency device to get the troubled diver up from the bottom or to support an exhausted or unconscious diver at the surface.

Most vests feature a "horse collar" design which distributes the buoyancy around the diver's chest and behind his head, to float him upright with his face out of the water. Many factors can affect the diver's positioning, however, and there are no guarantees these units will bring him to the surface face up

The inflator tube on a safety vest also doubles as a bleeder valve, so the diver can let excess pressure escape while he ascends and the ambient water pressure drops. Bleeding the vest in this way prevents rupturing the bladder or rising at a dangerously rapid rate.

Buoyancy Compensators

Most dive clubs, boat operators, and tour outfitters require the use of at least a safety vest for snorkeling as well as scuba diving. And many are turning to the far more sophisticated buoyancy compensator.

To illustrate the many advantages of a b.c., here is an example of a typical boat dive utilizing one: The diver enters the water with his b.c. slightly inflated so he can wait for his buddy on the surface. When he's ready to descend he "dumps" air until he is negatively buoyant, so he will sink to his desired depth without having to kick down. When his ears begin to ache, he inflates the b.c. until he reaches neutral buoyancy and clears his ears, then dumps the extra air and continues down again. On the bottom he adjusts for neutral buoyancy so he can swim without bumping into rocks and plants. If he picks up a heavy specimen or drops deep enough to compress his wet suit, a quick inflation restores his neutral buoyancy. When he wants to surface, he inflates the b.c. enough to lift him off the bottom then regulates his rate of ascent by valving off excess air until he arrives, relaxed, at the surface. If he has a surface swim back to the boat, he inflates the b.c. again, and it supports him like a diver's float.

Most buoyancy compensators are vest-like in appearance, but with a number of unique features. First, the oral inflator/deflator hose is usually a large-diameter, flexible corrugated tube with a special mouthpiece to help the diver switch easily between his scuba regulator and b.c. Second, buoyancy compensators usually contain an overpressure relief valve (also called an automatic purge valve) to discharge excess air before the bag bursts. The deflation feature of the inflator/deflator hose allows the diver to dump air manually before the overpressure valve activates.

Buoyancy compensators generally contain at least one CO_2 cartridge detonator for emergency floatation, and most include, or are adaptable to, power inflators which fill the b.c. from the scuba tank. A few models incorporate their own small compressed-air bottles, so they can be power-inflated independently. In some cases, it is even possible to use this extra compressed air as an auxiliary breathing supply.

With many styles and models available, the key factors in selecting a b.c. are comfort, convenience, lifting power, and, of course, reliability.

Your b.c. can affect your comfort in many ways. Since it adds a number of straps to your already-encumbered body, you should make sure that they can be fastened snugly without hampering your movement or any other equipment. Be sure to fully inflate the b.c. while you're trying it on, and check the fit of the straps and neck opening. If at all possible, try it in the water, to be sure the straps hold the inflation chambers in place and that there's not too much drag.

Look out for any difficulties putting the b.c. on or taking it off. Straps of nylon or other long-lasting synthetics with non-slip adjusting buckles are best. The outer bag fabric, while durable, should not be too abrasive.

Check the placement of the inflator hose. Is it long enough to reach your mouth in any position? Is the mouthpiece end secured to the vest where you can locate it easily, or will it float free underwater? Is the mouthpiece comfortable and does it make a tight seal with your lips? Is it readily distinguishable from your regulator mouthpiece?

Once you're satisfied with the comfort of a particular model, you can begin looking for conveniences.

Make sure you can reach all your other equipment with your b.c. in place (again, both inflated and deflated). Some b.c.'s are cut shorter than others, or designed with lower profiles, so be sure you get the best fit possible.

A manual purge button on the inflator hose will help assure that no water enters the vest during oral inflation. One or more pockets (especially with Velcro closures) can be helpful for carrying car keys or collecting small specimens.

You'll find a wide choice of b.c. sizes and lift capacities (usually expressed in terms of pounds of buoyancy at the surface). The minimum amount of lift should at least equal the amount of weight on your belt. A minimum of 25 lbs. of positive buoyancy is usually needed to support a fully-outfitted diver at the surface.

The maximum lift capacity (generally around 50 lbs.) should be determined by your own natural buoyancy, the depths you plan to dive to, the kinds of accessories or specimens you plan to carry, and whether you want to be prepared to support a helpless buddy in an emergency.

CO_2 cartridges are generally detonated only on the surface, since they won't provide the needed buoyancy at average scuba depths. As a rule, a 16 gram CO_2 cartridge is needed to hold a diver's head safely out of the water, and 19-25 gram cartridges are recommended. Some b.c.'s carry more than one cartridge. These are generally fired by a pull-string mechanism which should be made of rot-resistant material, and smoothly operated even with gloves on.

Many structural innovations have greatly increased b.c. reliability. One is double-bag construction with an outer bag of abrasion-resistant material and one or more inner bladders of puncture-proof material such as polyurethane. Removable inner bags are easiest to clean and rinse. Separate inflation chambers with individual overpressure relief valves provide an extra margin of safety. External seams should be double bonded, heat or ultrasonically sealed, or otherwise laminated inside and out for greatest strength. Mesh drains aid in flushing out the b.c.

The larger diameter inflator/deflator hose the better. For best results it should fit high on the left side of the vest body. The power inflator should operate easily with one hand. Separate power and oral inflation controls help reduce confusion. All working parts should be of corrosion-resistant material. Be sure the power inflator hose is long enough to connect up with the low pressure port on your regulator's first stage and still give you all the "stretch" you need. Learn to use your power

inflator as an underwater *emergency* device only, so you'll be prepared to inflate your b.c. orally in case your tank pressure is low.

If there is just one automatic overpressure relief valve, it should be located low on the vest body so that if it is activated, the remaining air will stay trapped above it. Some larger volume b.c.'s may also have an emergency dump valve activated by a pull cord to prevent an uncontrolled ascent if the vest is fully inflated too soon.

Recently, back-mounted and wrap-around style b.c.'s have been introduced. These models have advantages of concentrating the bulky air bags outside the diver's field of vision and reducing the number of straps needed to hold everything in place. A few come with integrated quick-release weight systems and/or protective "shells" so they serve as fully-contained buoyancy systems. Some are permanently attached to their own back-packs. Others can be fastened to your own pack.

Many of these back-mounted models increase swimming drag, and others are less efficient at holding the diver's face out of the water than the vest styles. Another disadvantage is that they cannot be used *without* the back pack for free diving.

Divers frequently debate the pros and cons of various systems. As long as any type of b.c. passes your key tests of comfort, convenience, lift capacity and reliable construction, such matters as style and color are strictly personal choices.

Buoyancy Devices

AMF Voit

8BC2 Swimaster Buoyancy Compensator Vest

Double bag construction with zippered neck for removing inner bag. Large bore oral inflator hose with pushbutton control. Over-pressure relief valve limits internal pressure to approximately 1½ psi over ambient pressure. Compact profile. CO_2 cartridge.

D 1246. Orange.

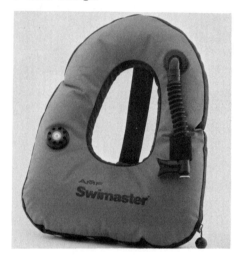

Swimaster Weights

Notched to slide easily on and off belt.

D 1247. Sizes: 2,3,5 lb.

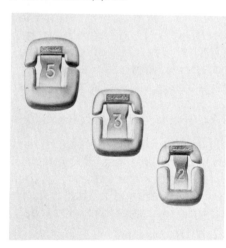

8BC1 Swimaster Buoyancy Compensator Vest

Triangular double bag construction. Oral inflator, CO_2 cartridge, pocket.

D 1248. Orange.

8BC3 Swimaster Mini Buoyancy Compensator Vest

Shorty style, single bag construction. Corrugated oral inflator, CO_2 cartridge.

D 1249. Orange.

Diver's Weight Belt

2" nylon, adjusts quickly underwater. Airplane-style quick release buckle.

D 1250. Black or orange.

6 Lb. Lead Weight

Contoured to fit on hip.

D 1251.

Cressi-Sub

Cressi Buoyancy Compensator

Nylon double bag construction. Oral inflator hose, dual CO_2 detonators. 40 lbs. buoyancy.

D 1252. Yellow and black.

Cressi Compensator 715

Single bag construction. Large oral inflator, automatic overpressure valve. 15 lbs. buoyancy.

D 1253. Yellow and black.

Cressi Compensator 723

Single bag construction. Large oral inflator, automatic overpressure valve. 23 lbs. buoyancy.

D 1254. Yellow and black.

Cressi Weight Belt

2" nylon webbing, airplane-type quick release buckle.

D 1255. Choice of three colors.

Cressi Weights

3 lb. and 5 lb. (contoured) lead weights fit 2" belts.

D 1256.

Dacor

Nautilus

Constant volume system integrating weights, buoyancy compensator, power inflator, and backpack in a hard shell unit. Features include water inlet valve for determining buoyancy, auto/manual buoyancy control regulator, overpressure relief valve and integrated weight rack. Provides up to 60 lbs. of surface buoyancy, fits 6.9" to 7.25" diameter tanks.

D 1257. Black and yellow.

"Seachute" Vest

Inflates orally, by CO_2 cartridge, or (as an option) from air tank.

D 1258. Red and Black.

50-Lb. Multiple Capacity Compensator Vest

Large volume, 50 lbs. of buoyancy at surface) inflated orally or by CO_2.

D 1259. Orange or charcoal.

Compensator Vest

Medium volume (20 lbs. of buoyancy at surface). Sewn-in key ring and ID holder.

D 1260. Orange.

25-Lb. Multiple Capacity Compensator Vest

Medium volume (25 lbs. of buoyancy at surface). Single pocket and CO_2 cartridge.

D 1261. Orange or charcoal.

Inflatable Vest

Oral inflator, 16 gram CO_2 cartridge. Nylon outer shell with inner bladder. Slash pocket.

D 1262. Yellow.

Mini Inflatable Vest

Oral inflator, 8 gram CO_2 cartridge. Nylon outer shell with inner bladder.

D 1263. Yellow.

Fold-Away Vest

Folds into a 10" x 20" pouch which opens automatically when inflation is required. Oral inflator plus 16 gram CO_2 cartridge.

D 1264. Yellow.

Compensator Weight Belt

Special expansion section adjusts belt as wet suit compresses. Supports up to 35 lbs. of weight, allows 3¼″ expansion.

D 1265. Black.

"Quick-Ditch" Weight Belt

Positive locking cam action buckle, 2″ nylon webbing.

D 1266. Yellow, blue, black, orange.

Weights

Contoured lead weights containing nickel for smooth finish, in 2 or 3 pound increments.

D 1267.

Healthways

Scubamaster® Buoyancy Compensator

Ultrasonically sealed polyurethane inner bladder, outer layer of nylon fabric. Lever actuated first stage scuba inflator valve with easy-disconnect hose. Large diameter flex hose oral inflator held in place with Velcro strip. CO_2 cartridge (25 gram) activated by lanyard at lower left corner. Large volume relief valve prevents over-pressurization. Wide neck opening to prevent squeeze. Utility pocket with snap closure.

D 1268. Yellow with black trim.

Buoyancy Compensator W/CO_2

Assymetrical bag design of nylon fabric with polyurethane inner bladder. One-inch flex hose on large bore oral inflator/deflator valve with soft extended mouthpiece. Snap-closure utility pocket. CO_2 inflator mechanism with 16 gram cartridge. Over-pressure relief valve screws out for bag flushing.

D 1269. Yellow with black trim.

Scuba Flotation Vest

Bib style with polyurethane-backed nylon fabric. 16 gram CO_2 cartridge for full surface inflation. Oral inflation tube and valve. Overpressure relief valve. Adjustable nylon thorax strap.

D 1270. Yellow with black trim.

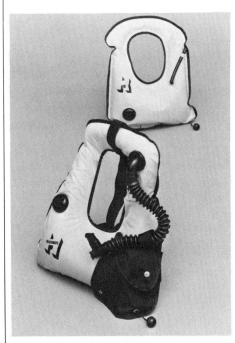

Scubamaster Weight System

Nylon webbing belt carries 5 lb. hip weights and nesting 2 and 3 lb. weights. Quick release adjustable stainless steel buckle.

D 1271. Black belt, metallic colored weights.

Oceanic Farallon

Elevator I B.C.

Pushbutton console for inflation/deflation. Remote-piloted dump valve/overpressure relief valve. Non-floating oral inflator, CO_2 cartridge.

D 1272. Orange or blue.

Elevator II B.C.

Low pressure inflation system (attaches to oral inflator). CO_2 cartridge.

D 1273. Orange or blue.

Elevator III B.C.

Double bag with oral inflator.

D 1274. Orange or blue.

Scubapro

Scubapro Buoyancy Control Pack

Attached to Scubapro contour ScubaPak. Power, oral, and two CO_2 inflators. Flotation bags stay out of sight, on back. Quick-release shoulder and waist strap buckles and tank band. Approximately 35 lbs. buoyancy.

D 1275. Orange.

Scubapro Buoyancy Compensator

Approximately 35 lbs. of variable positive buoyancy. Attaches with buckled waist and crotch strap. Power and oral inflators, two CO_2 cartridges. Fittings for attaching optional utility pocket.

D 1276. Orange. Sizes: regular and compact (25 lbs. buoyancy).

Mark I Diving Vest

Lined neck opening, no zippers. 1" dia. flexible hose inflator/deflator plus 12 gram CO_2 cartridge. Waist strap. Approximately 15 lbs. of surface buoyancy.

D 1277. Orange.

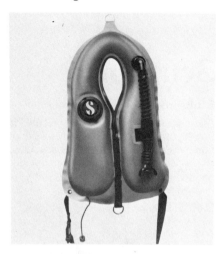

Scubapro Stabilizing Jacket

Heads-up flotation wraps entire torso in buoyancy. Easy entry or exit.

D 1278. Orange. Sizes: s,m,l,xl.

Scubapro Snorkeling Vest

Compact design. Oral inflation hose also serves as overpressure relief valve. 12 gram CO_2 cartridge, signal whistle.

D 1279. Orange.

Scubapro Independent Weight System

Weight chambers with quick-release pins attached to backpack harness to eliminate weight belt. Adjustable vertically and horizontally to desired diving trim. Large release pins easily operable with gloves.

D 1280. Black.

Scubapro E-Z On Weights

Slotted for adding or removing from weight belt without removing buckle. Contoured for comfort and molded to resist sliding.

D 1281. Sizes: 2,3,5 lbs.

Scubapro Hip Weights

Contoured to rest comfortably on hips and eliminate multiple small weights. Molded to resist slipping.

D 1282. Sizes: 6,7,8,9,10 lbs.

Jet Belt, Expanding

2" nylon belt with expander section that compresses up to 5". Airplane style quick release buckle.

D 1283. Black.

Scubapro Quick-Release Belt

54" long, 2" wide nylon belt. Airplane style quick release buckle.

D 1284.

IWS Weights

2½ lb. weights shaped for use in Scubapro Independent Weight System and also slotted to fit 2" wide belts.

D 1285.

Bullet Weight

Shaped like a bullet, slotted to fit on 2" belt. Approx. 2 lbs.

D 1286. Scubapro.

Seaquest

Seaquest B/C Pack

Back-mounted. Oral inflator, optional push-button low-pressure tank inflator. Overpressure valve. Double bag construction. 21" wide when fully inflated, provides 41 lbs. of buoyancy. Backpack not included.

D 1287. Yellow or black.

Rough Water B/C

Outer bag of ballistic nylon coated with polyurethane. Inner bag of polyurethane-coated nylon. Oral inflator secured by Velcro fastener, optional mechanical inflator and 25 gram CO_2 cartridge. high capacity overpressure valve, front pocket. Provides up to 40 lbs. of buoyancy in salt water.

D 1288. Orange.

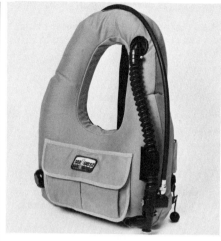

White Water B/C

Outer bag of 420 denier nylon backed with urethane, nylon inner bag. Oral inflator plus optional mechanical inflator and 25 gram CO_2 cartridge.

D 1289. Black, blue or yellow.

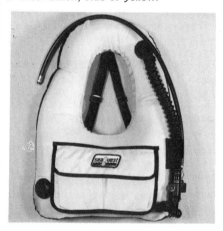

Deep Water B/C

Double bag. Polyurethane-coated nylon inner bag. Oral inflator, optional 25 gram CO_2 cartridge or two 16 gram cartridges. Overpressure relief valve. Mesh drain panels top and bottom. Purge mechanism on oral inflator. 35 lbs. of buoyancy in salt water.

D 1290. Yellow or black.

M-90

Extra-heavy gauge polyurethane-coated nylon outer bag. Short, compact design. Urethane inner bag. Oral inflator, optional 25 gram CO_2 cartridge. Nylon mesh drain panels. Provides 33 lbs. of buoyancy.

D 1291. Yellow.

M-92

Urethane-backed ballistic nylon outer bag, heavy gauge urethane inner bag. Front pocket. Short design. Oral inflator, optional 25 gram CO_2 cartridge. Provides 33 lbs. of buoyancy.

D 1292. Orange.

M-94

Double bag, outer bag of 420 denier nylon. Oral inflator, optional 25 gram CO_2 cartridge. Designed for smaller physiques. Front pocket with key ring holder sewn inside. Mesh drain panels.

D 1293. Yellow.

Open Water B/C

Single bag of 420 denier nylon. Spiral oral inflator/deflator hose. Overpressure valve, expansion pocket with Velcro flap. Optional 16 gram CO_2 cartridge.

D 1294. Orange.

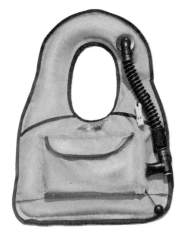

Blue Water B/C

Double bag, oral inflator, 25 gram CO_2 cartridge. 31 lbs. of buoyancy.

D 1295. Orange.

Shortie B/C

Single bag, 10" oral inflator hose, 16 gram CO_2 cartridge.

D 1296. Orange.

Seatec

Back Inflation Unit

Outer bag of "Tuff Tiger Threads" or urethane coated nylon, inner bladder of urethane. One hand power inflator, oral inflator, optional cam back pack, over-pressure valve and quick dump override.

D 1297. Blue, orange, yellow, or black. Sizes: regular and deluxe.

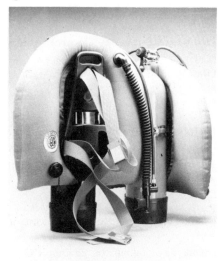

The Puffer

Choice of "Tuff Tiger Threads" or urethane coated nylon outer bag. Oral inflation hose, CO_2 detonator, automatic overpressure relief valve and quick dump override, spine and waist straps. Front pocket.

D 1298. Blue, orange, yellow, or black.

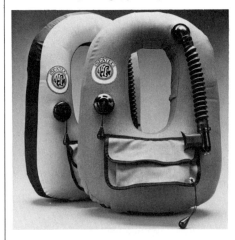

DV201

Urethane coated nylon. Oral inflator hose, overpressure relief valve, offset front pocket, CO_2 detonator.

D 1299. Yellow, black, or orange.

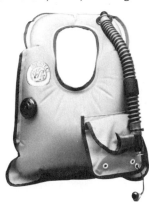

BCV

Urethane coated nylon outer bag, urethane inner bladder. Oral inflation hose, automatic overpressure relief valve and quick dump override, CO_2 detonator. Large pocket. Power inflator optional.

D 1300. Yellow, orange, or black.

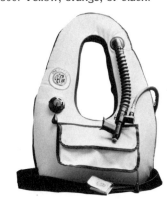

TD1002-3D

Expanding three dimensional design for added lift. Urethane coated nylon outer bag, urethane inner bladder. Oral inflation hose, CO_2 detonator, automatic overpressure relief valve. Large pocket.

D 1301. Yellow, black, or orange.

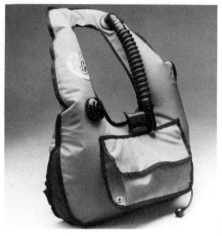

DV101

Small snorkeling vest. Oral inflator, CO_2 detonator, overpressure relief valve.

D 1302. Yellow.

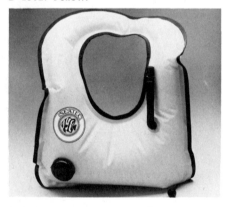

BC401

Flotation pillow with no neck collar. Urethane coated nylon outer bag, urethane inner bladder. Oral inflation hose, CO_2 detonator, overpressure relief valve. Front pocket.

D 1303. Orange and black.

BC3

Midsize vest. Oral inflation hose, CO_2 detonator, overpressure relief valve.

D 1304. Yellow, black, or orange.

Bluefin Stabilizing Vest

Over-the-shoulder design. Push button inflator, oral inflator, CO_2 detonator. Double bag construction.

D 1305. Orange and blue.

B.C. VI

Double bag construction, oral inflation, one CO_2 detonator and space for another one. Nylon mesh drains top and bottom.

D 1306. Blue or orange.

Seatec Weight Belt

2″ nylon with airplane-style stainless steel buckle.

D 1307. Black, yellow, red, or blue.

Selpac

SBC 50

Backpack unit, with or without power inflator. 42 lbs. of surface buoyancy.

D 1308. Blue with black trim.

SBC 42

Double bag construction, pull-cord dump valve on neck, with or without CO_2 or power inflator. 42 lbs. of surface buoyancy.

D 1309. Orange, yellow, or blue.

SBC 30

Double bag construction, smooth exterior material. With or without CO_2 or power inflator. 30 lbs. of surface buoyancy.

D 1310. Orange, yellow, or blue with black trim.

Sportways

Hydronaut Buoyancy Control System

Back-mounted, double bag construction. Oral inflator. Power inflator, cam pack optional. 60 lbs. surface buoyancy.

D 1311. Red.

High Seas Buoyancy Control Vest

Double bag construction. Oral inflator, 26 gram CO_2 cartridge, 40 lbs. surface buoyancy, pocket with Velcro closure.

D 1312. Red.

Deluxe Waterlung Buoyancy Control Vest

Double bag, oral inflator, 26 gram CO_2 cartridge, pocket with Velcro closure. 33 lb. surface buoyancy.

D 1313. Red.

U.S. Cavalero

Cavalero/Fenzy M-6 Buoyancy Compensator

Single bag with breathing mouthpiece, 4.2 cu. ft. air cylinder (3000 psi), dump valve integrated into oral inflator/deflator hose.

D 1602.

Cavalero/Fenzy M-5 Buoyancy Compensator

2.8 cu. ft. air cylinder, breathing mouthpiece, dump valve integrated into inflator/deflator hose.

D 1603. Orange.

Cavalero/Fenzy M-4 Buoyancy Compensator

Standard inflator/deflator hose. Optional 2.8 cu. ft. air cylinder can be used for emergency breathing.

D 1604. Orange.

Cavalero/Fenzy M-70

Aluminum 3000 psi air cylinder and low magnetic fittings per military specifications. Breathing mouthpiece, dump valve integrated into inflator/deflator.

D 1605. Black or orange.

U.S. Divers

Calypso® Compensator

Over-the-shoulder unit attaches to backpack. Urethane backed nylon fabric outer bag, removable polyurethane inner bladder. 50 lbs. of lift. One-way dump valve for trim buoyancy. Non-floating oral inflator, push button low pressure inflator, 38 gram CO_2 cartridge (43 lbs. of lift at surface).

D 1314. Yellow or black.

Aqua-Master B.C. Vest

Impregnated nylon fabric, over-the-head design. Oral inflator, 38 gram CO_2 cartridge. Overpressure relief valve. 30 lbs. of lift. Integral crotch strap, stainless steel harness fittings.

D 1315. Yellow or black.

BC I

Urethane backed nylon fabric outer bag with removable polyurethane bladder. Non-floating oral inflator with mouthpiece that fits into regulator mouthpiece. 38 gram CO_2 cartridge. Fitting for attaching low pressure inflator. One-way dump valve acts as automatic overpressure relief valve at 2½ psi overpressure. Front pocket with Velcro closure.

D 1316. Black or yellow.

B.C. II

Identical to B.C. I but with low pressure inflator and hose included.

D 1317. Yellow or black.

Ocean Explorer Vest

Over-the-head design. Single bag construction, 16 gram CO_2 cartridge.

D 1318. Yellow or black.

Sea Venturer Vest

Front zipper design. Single bag construction, 16 gram CO_2 cartridge.

D 1319. Yellow or black.

Slip-Quick Weight Belt W/Buckle

Weights can be added without removing kam action quick release buckle.

D 1320. Black.

Neoprene Weight Belt

2″ wide by ⅛″ thick belt with wire quick release buckle.

D 1321. Black.

Velcro Weight Belt

Velcro fastener for quick adjustment.

D 1322.

Weights

Available in 1, 2, and 3 lb. plus 6 lb. and 8 lb. contoured sizes.

D 1323.

U.S. Nemrod

Nemrod Scuba Vest With Bottle

Single bag construction. Self-contained high-pressure air bottle inflates vest to 36 lbs. buoyancy; can be used as emergency breathing device, refilled from scuba tank. Large diameter oral inflator hose with contoured mouthpiece and built-in buoyancy control valve. Automatic overpressure purge valve activates at 2 psi over ambient water pressure.

D 1324. Yellow and black.

Nemrod BC24

Single nylon fabric bag. Front zipper. 10″ corrugated oral inflator hose with push-button mouthpiece. 16 gram CO_2 cartridge. Front pockets, waist and spine

straps. Provides 18 lbs. of buoyancy.

D 1325. Yellow and black.

BC26

Double-bag design. Push-button oral inflator, 25 gram CO_2 cartridge. 40 lbs. buoyancy.

D 1326. Yellow and black.

Nemrod Buoyancy Compensator Vest

Single-bag. Oral inflator with automatic purge. 33 lbs. buoyancy.

D 1327. Yellow and black.

BC22

Single-bag. Push-button oral inflator, 25 gram CO_2 cartridge. 23 lbs. buoyancy.

D 1328. Yellow and black.

BC20

Single-bag. Oral inflator, 16 gram CO_2 cartridge. 15 lbs. buoyancy.

D 1329. Yellow and black.

Nemrod Nylon Weight Belt

Nylon webbing, adjustable chromed quick release buckle.

D 1330. Black.

BC26

Double-bag. Oral inflator, 25 gram CO_2 cartridge. 40 lbs. buoyancy.

D 1331. Yellow and black.

Adjustable Rubber Weight Belt

Rubber compounded for strength, stretch, and recovery. Quick release buckle.

D 1332. Black.

Nemrod Weights

Hardened lead weights for all 2″ belts. Available in 2 lb., 3 lb., 4 lb., and 5 lb. sizes.

D 1333.

Watergill

At-Pac

Back-mounted integrated weight and flotation system. Includes tank pack.

D 1334. Orange, blue, black, or red. Watergill

White Stag

Buoyansator IV

Nylon outer bag, polyurethane inner bladder, expandable oral inflator/deflator hose, overpressure valve, mesh drains top and bottom. Power and CO_2 inflators optional.

D 1335. Orange.

Buoyansator X

Nylon outer bag, polyurethane inner bladder, increased lift capacity. Mesh drains top and bottom, expandable oral inflator/deflator hose. Power and CO_2 inflators optional.

D 1336. Orange.

Buoyansator V

Single bag construction with bellows design to reduce length. Expandable oral inflator/deflator hose, overpressure valve. CO_2 optional.

D 1337. Orange.

Buoyansator III

Single bag, ultrasonically sealed. Expandable inflator/deflator hose, overpressure valve, CO_2 cartridge.

D 1338. Orange.

Buoyansator VI

Nylon outer bag, polyurethane inner bladder. Expandable inflator/deflator hose, overpressure valve, CO_2 cartridge.

D 1339. Orange.

Compensator Weight Belt

Stretch neoprene with airplane-style quick release buckle.

D 1340. Metallic and black.

Nylon Weight Belt

Nylon webbing belt with airplane-style quick release buckle.

D 1341. Metallic and black.

Knife Buying Guide

A knife is an indispensable diver's tool and safety aid — not a weapon as portrayed in so much underwater fiction. Over the years divers' knives have been upgraded to perform a number of useful functions

The best underwater knife blades are made of steel. Stainless steel resists rust and corrosion. High-tempered steel holds the best cutting edge and can be chrome-plated for rust and corrosion resistance. Both are strong enough to handle most prying, gouging, and digging chores as well.

Special designs can help the knife blade perform specific jobs. A serrated edge is useful for sawing. A line-cutter notch can be used to free the diver from fouled lines. A blunt pry tip can help dislodge specimens and shellfish such as scallops. Some knives even include scaling and filleting edges. Many carry inch markings which are helpful in measuring game or other specimens.

Blades come in a broad range of sizes and shapes. Generally they run 5-7" in length, and about 1¼" wide at the widest spot. There are many larger and smaller models available too.

The knife handle, first and foremost, must offer a secure grip, so it must be securely attached to the tang or extension of the blade. Look for a handle contour that fits your hand comfortably. In some knives the finger-guard is molded into the handle. This one-piece design offers the best security against slipping.

Many knife handles include a hammer-type butt cap or utility head which can be very useful for pounding. In some cases these butt caps are screwed to the hank, while in others they are welded on. If you plan to do any heavy-duty hammering, you'll want the more secure welded-on type.

Knife handles are generally made of plastic or rubber, and occasionally of wood. The key features here are non-slip comfort and durability. So be sure any rubber or wood handle you select is treated to withstand salt water, sun, and other corrosive influences.

You may still find a few underwater knives with floating handles, although these appear to be increasingly rare and are generally recommended only for skin diving. Most of today's knives are negatively buoyant.

Some models come with fittings for attaching wrist lanyards. If you use a lanyard, be sure it is large or elastic enough so you can free your hand if your knife should become trapped.

Knives can be worn at the waist, on the forearm, or — most commonly — on the leg. (Many divers place the sheath on the inside of one calf, where it is less subject to fouling and is accessible to either hand.)

Be sure the knife you select has a sheath that fits comfortably and conveniently where you want to wear it — that no other equipment interferes with taking the knife out or replacing it. If you're not sure where you'll eventually want to wear your knife, you can find sheaths adaptable to all positions.

The chief function of the sheath is to hold the knife securely yet release it quickly when you want it. Try the securing/releasing mechanism several times to be sure you can operate it blindly even with gloves on. Be sure it's sturdy enough to hold up under repeated use. The sheath you select should cover all sharp portions of the blade yet allow for drainage, so water will not accumulate in the sheath and add to drag.

If you plan any deep wet suit diving, you should consider a sheath with depth-compensating straps that tighten as the neoprene of the wet suit compresses. If your sheath has conventional straps, check the locking mechanisms to be sure they're fool-proof. Strap retainers can help prevent loose strap ends from fouling.

Knives

AMF Voit

8K8 Swimaster Diver's Leg Knife

Serrated 7″ stainless steel blade with line cutter, 6″ game scale, ABS handle with stainless steel hammer-face butt cap. Sheath included.

D 1342. Orange handle.

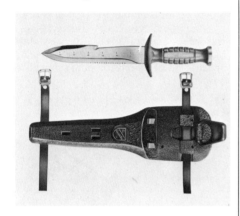

Swimaster Deluxe Diver's Knife

200 series stainless blade (serrated on back), finger grip handle.

D 1343. Black handle.

DK7 Diver's And Sport Knife

7″ stainless blade. Sheath fits leg or waist.

D 1344. Black handle.

8K4 Diver's Knife

Stainless blade, contoured plastic handle. Sheath fits waist or leg.

D 1345. Black handle.

Cressi-Sub

Panga

Contoured blade and handle. Fitting for wrist lanyard. Snap-out flow-through leg sheath.

D 1346.

Rocket

Heavy-duty serrated blade, double finger guard.

D 1347.

Killer

Small blade, butt end on handle.

D 1348.

Dacor

Combination Knife-Tool

Blunt working tip, two serrated segments, line cutter, rubber handle and sheath with expandable straps. Stainless steel blade carries inch measurements.

D 1349. Black handle, sheath.

400 Series Knife

Blade of 400 series stainless steel, 6″ or 7″ in length. Stainless steel finger guard. Serrated edge, inch measurements on blade.

D 1350. Black handle, sheath.

300 Series Knife

Blade of 300 series stainless steel 6″ or 7″ in length. Serrated edge, inch measurements on blade. Finger guard molded into handle.

D 1351. Black handle, sheath.

Commercial Diver's Knife

Pocketknife style. 4½″ stainless steel blade locks open. Rosewood grips on stainless steel body. Swivel hook for fastening to belt snap hook.

D 1352. Stainless steel with wood grain trim.

Small Knife

Specially designed 4½″ 400 series stainless steel blade with double serrated edge. Rubber belt sheath.

D 1353. Black handle, sheath.

Compact Knife

5″ blade of 420 series stainless steel with rough and fine serrated edges, line cutter, inch measurements.

D 1354. Black handle, sheath.

Folding Knife

Six separate multi-purpose tools (large and small blades and screwdrivers, cork screw, can opener, bottle opener, stripper, and reamer).

D 1355. Red Cycolac® grip.

Healthways

Scubamaster® Knife

Heavy duty stainless steel construction. Serrated cutting edge includes line cutter notch. Rubber handle with metal guard and utility head. 6″ scale game. Wedge grip sheath with snap open quick release. Blade is 6¾″ long.

D 1356. Black handle and sheath.

Scubadiver® Knife

6¾″ stainless steel blade with serrated cutting edge. Metal utility head. One piece molded rubber handle and guard. Wedge grip sheath, 6″ measuring scale.

D 1357. Black handle, sheath.

Seadiver® Knife

Molded soft plastic grip. 6¾″ stainless steel blade with serrated cutting edge and 6″ scale. Stainless steel guard and butt plate. Slimline sheath.

D 1358. Black handle, sheath.

Scubapro

The Knife

Choice of magnetic or non-magnetic stainless steel blade with forefinger notch opposite paring edge, serrated edge. Simulated bone handle with contoured grip. Includes sheath with compensating leg straps.

D 1359.

Diver's Knife

Cutting edge, serrated sawing edge, scalloped scraping edge on stainless steel blade. Hammerhead on handle. 6″ scale on blade. Sheath has compensating leg straps.

D 1360. Black handle.

Stiletto

Especially designed for spearfishermen, to cut lines or kelp, or clean game. One serrated edge on blade. Sheath with rubber compensating straps fits on arm or leg, as well as belt.

D 1361. Black handle.

Filet Knife

Flexible 8-inch stainless steel blade. Simulated bone handle. Includes sharpening stone and protective sheath.

D 1362.

Sportsways

"Navy" Knife and Sheath

Tapered 7″ hardened stainless steel blade with serrated area, 6″ measuring scale.

D 1363. Black, orange or yellow handle.

"Diver" Knife and Sheath

Contoured 7″ hardened stainless steel blade with concave serrated edge for sawing or scaling.

D 1364. Black, yellow, or orange handle.

U.S. Divers

Sea Hawk

Heavy 7¾″ polished stainless steel blade with 6″ scale, serrated back. Hammer-type

butt cap, gripping ridges on rubber handle. Contoured sheath with adjustable straps.

D 1365. Black, orange, or Americana (red/white/blue) handle.

Sea Master

7″ polished stainless steel blade with 6″ scale, serrated back. Forged butt cap. Contoured molded rubber handle. Double-sided blade guard. Low-profile contoured sheath with adjustable straps.

D 1366. Brown, yellow, black or orange handle.

Master Knife

7″ polished stainless steel blade with 6″ scale, serrated back. Hammer-type butt cap, molded non-slip handle with double-sided blade guard. Contoured sheath with adjustable straps.

D 1367. Black handle.

Nordic Knife

6″ blade with 5″ scale, serrated back, contoured sheath.

D 1368. Black handle, sheath.

Skinning Knife

Thin fileting blade 6⅛″ long. Protective case.

D 1369. Black handle, case.

U.S. Nemrod

Nemrod Knife & Sheath

Stainless steel blade with one serrated edge. Rubber grip with nylon wrist lanyard. Belt sheath.

D 1370. Black handle, sheath.

Professional Knife & Sheath

Serrated stainless steel blade, butt end, sheath fits leg or belt.

D 1371. Black handle, sheath.

Combat Knife & Sheath

Stainless steel serrated blade, rubber handle, leg sheath.

D 1372. Black handle, sheath.

Wenoka

Diver's Edge™ I

Safety guard is an integral part of shock resistant handle. Stainless steel butt cap welded to tang of blade. 7″ stainless steel blade with saw edge, line cutter. Includes sheath with 24″ depth compensating rubber straps.

D 1373. Black, yellow, or orange handle. Overall length: 12⅛″.

Diver's Edge™ II

Stainless steel finger guard. 7″ stainless steel blade with line cutter, saw edge, pry tip. Stainless steel butt cap screwed to tang of blade. Includes sheath with 24″ depth compensating rubber straps.

D 1374. Black, yellow, or orange handle. Overall length: 11¾″.

Diver's Edge™ III

Safety guard is integral part of shock-resistant molded handle. 6″ stainless steel blade with two saw edges, line cutter, pry tip. Sheath with 24″ vinyl straps included.

D 1375. Black, yellow or orange handle. Overall length: 11″.

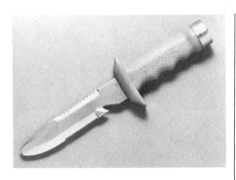

Diver's Edge™ IV

Stainless steel finger guard, screw-on butt cap. 6″ stainless steel blade with saw edge, line cutter, sharp point. Includes sheath with 24″ depth compensating rubber straps.

D 1376. Black, yellow, or orange handle. Overall length: 10⅝″.

Diver's Edge™ V

Balanced construction, pointed tip, line cutter, solid molded handle, solid stainless steel butt, saw blade. 7″ 400 series stainless steel blade.

D 1377. Black, yellow or orange handle. Overall length: 12⅞″.

Diver's Edge™ VI

Pry tip, saw blade, line cutter, 4½″ 400 series stainless steel blade. Solid molded handle with finger grips.

D 1378. Black, yellow, or orange handle. Overall length: 9¼″.

Diver's Edge™ VII

Pointed blade, saw edge and honed edge, line cutter, solid molded handle with stainless steel butt. 4½″ 400 series stainless steel blade.

D 1379. Black, yellow, or orange handle. Overall length: 9¼″.

Champion

6¾″ blade with sharp cutting edge, sawing area, line cutter. Molded handle with heavy stamped guard, butt cap. Sheath included.

D 1380. Black, yellow, or orange handle. Overall length: 11½″.

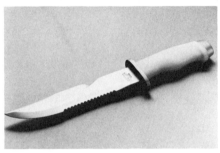

Moby Dick

Easy grip, one piece shock-resistant molded handle and guard. 6⅞″ blade with two saw edges, inch markings, sharp point. Sheath included.

D 1381. Black, yellow, or orange handle. Overall length: 12″.

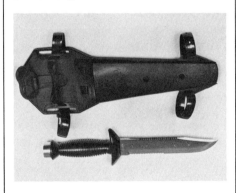

Sea Horse

One-piece guard and textured handle molded on blade. Extra large butt welded on blade tang. 6″ blade with double serrations, sharp point. Sheath included.

D 1382. Black, yellow, or orange handle. Overall length: 11″.

Mermaid

Sleek balanced design with molded one piece shock-resistant handle and guard. 5¾″ blade with double serrated edge, sharp point. Sheath included.

D 1383. Black, yellow, or orange handle. Overall length: 11″.

The Explorer II

Stiletto styling. 4⅞″ stainless steel blade with line cutter, serrated edge, sharp point. Stainless steel finger guard. Includes special sheath which fits on arm, leg, or belt.

D 1384. Black handle. Overall length: 8¾″.

Super Stag Knife

7½″ stainless steel blade with serrated edges, 6″ measuring scale. Neoprene handle textured for secure grip.

D 1385. Black handle. Overall length: 12¾″.

Exposure Suit Buying Guide

Unless you're strictly a "fair-water" diver, you'll need some sort of protection from the chill of the depths. An exposure suit can also protect you against cuts and scratches, as a quick examination of any used suit will confirm. Your choices of protective diving dress are profuse.

The most common choice for divers is the wet suit, made of multicellular foam neoprene which traps water so the body heat can warm it to form an insulating layer. Next come the dry suit and the inflatable variable-volume suit, both of which are designed to keep the water from contacting the diver's body at all.

A few other systems have been designed for commercial divers, but are not yet readily available to the general public. The constant volume suit is inflated on the surface. The diver's exhalations go directly into the suit, and automatic exhaust valves maintain a constant internal air volume during all phases of the dive. These suits are reported durable, but uncomfortable for underwater swimming.

There's also an open circuit hot water system, which consists of a wet suit with a pump and tubing that distributes hot water uniformly. Since the hot water is supplied from the surface via an insulated hose, this design is not suitable for scuba.

Another design, the closed circuit hot water suit, includes a heat source carried by the diver. Special underwear distributes hot water through built-in loops, and is covered by a dry suit. Current designs are reportedly quite restrictive.

Dry Suits

Dry suits were the first practical cold-water protection for sport divers. They are made of leakproof sheet rubber or rubbercoated fabric and designed to fit over warm undergarments (or, in extreme conditions, over a wet suit). To be effective, a dry suit must form fail-safe seals at all openings, which generally include the face, ankles, wrists, and point of entry.

Most dry suits are of one-piece design, either molded seamless or with seams cemented and stripped. Entry is made through chest or back openings which are then zippered or gathered and fastened. In two-piece suits, the jacket and pants are rolled together at the waist or sealed by a waist ring.

Dry suits that fit properly so all seals work well do the best job of staving off cold for extended periods. However, they have several disadvantages over wet suits.

Because they are more expensive to produce, dry suits cost more and are less readily available than wet suits. They can be less comfortable, particularly because of the necessarily tight seals. They're difficult to doff and don, often requiring the assistance of a buddy. They don't insulate well without wool or thermal underwear. In temperate water, the diver cannot wear only the top half of a two piece dry suit. If the sheet rubber rips, the suit will leak and is harder to repair than a neoprene wet suit. And dry suits are subject to suit squeeze with trapped air compressed by hydrostatic pressure wrinkling the suit and pinching the skin.

Variable Volume Suits

Variable volume suits are inflable to hold cold water away from the body. Because they are made from closed-cell neoprene, they are also known as wet-dry suits. These one-piece suits feature water- and pressure-proof zipper entries and sewn seams. They can be inflated orally or from the scuba tank, and the diver can adjust his buoyancy trim manually through the inflation/deflation hose. The use of a buoyancy compensator, however, is still recommended.

The bulk of the variable volume suit can make it fatiguing on long horizontal swims. The internal air can rush to the feet if they are elevated above head. Any leaks mean not only an inflow of cold water, but loss of buoyancy control, as well.

Wet Suits

By far the most popular form of thermal protection is the wet suit. The foam neoprene of the wet suit contains millions of nitrogen-filled bubbles which trap cold water to prevent it from flowing against the skin and drawing off body heat.

Neoprene for wet suits comes in various thicknesses. The most common are ⅛″, 3/16″, and ¼″. A few specialty suits are available in ⅜″ or even ½″. Depending on the suit's tailoring, the thickness of the neoprene determines the insulating effectiveness.

Consult Appendix A to determine the amount of protection you need for your own projected diving. When in doubt choose a ¼″ suit. A ¼″ suit is only slightly more binding than the thinner models, and if you need a suit at all, it won't overheat you. Remember, however, that neoprene thickness also affects suit buoyancy, so if you're trading up, plan to adjust your weights accordingly.

Neoprene comes in a variety of finishes. The cellular structure can be exposed (a rarity today) or treated to develop a skin. The skin can be smooth or textured for additional strength.

Most better grade suits feature a lining of nylon or other non-corroding stretch material on the inside, outside, or both sides of the suit. The lining strengthens the suit and, on the inside, makes it easier to doff and don and more comfortable to wear. Outside, it increases tear and abrasion resistance. While tears in the foam material can be mended easily with liquid neoprene, the lining requires sewing for a secure repair. Lining makes no difference in the suit's insulating capability, and may further restrict movement.

Fit is the paramount consideration in selecting a wet suit. It should be as close fitting as possible to restrict the general flow-through of water, especially down the spine and from the underarms down the sides where cold water can spread around the torso. However, the suit should not bind at the joints, restrict circulation, or be too difficult to put on or take off.

Zippers at the chest, wrists, and ankles can help in doffing and donning the suit, but may leak unless they are backed by neoprene flaps or gussets. Some women's models feature an additional zipper at the waist or hip. Be sure all zippers are made of nylon, stainless steel, coated nickel, or other corrosion-resistant material.

Most wet suits consist of separate jacket, pants, hood, boots, and gloves. Since hoods, boots, and gloves are usually sold separately, they will be described in our chapter on "Accessories." Many special features are available for the diver's comfort and convenience. Some may be ordered as options.

Farmer-style bib overall pants add a layer of protection around the torso, and help to neutralize any leakage from the jacket zipper. An extra-high jacket collar or attached hood can prevent cold water from seeping down the neck.

Optional pads and pockets are helpful. A spine pad can cushion the scuba tank and trap cold water from the back of the neck. Other pads can reinforce elbows, knees, and other abrasion-prone areas, although they may tend to restrict the joints. Pockets can be helpful for storing tools or small specimens.

Velcro closures at the throat, crotch strap, pockets, and other openings are secure, adjustable, and easily operated. Swivel locks (also called twistlocks) hold the crotch strap more securely than snaps.

Many wet suits come in a variety of colors. These colors can be helpful in distinguishing the diver in the water. But since the dyes used tend to weaken neoprene and nylon, colored suits can be less durable than plain black models.

Wet suits can be purchased "off the rack" or with various degrees of custom tailoring (from mixing and matching pre-cut parts to mail-ordering entire suits cut to the diver's individual measurements). If you are dissatisfied after trying a few different standard wet suit models, perhaps a custom suit is best for you.

Exposure Suits

Bayleysuit

Deluxe Eurekan Wet Suit

¼" or 3/16" neoprene with two-sided nylon, custom tailored jacket with attached hood, high collar, farmer-style pants.

D 1386.

Eurekan 100 Custom Wet Suit

¼" or 3/16" neoprene with two-sided nylon, custom tailored jacket, farmer-style pants.

D 1387.

Eurekan Pretailored Wet Suit

¼" or 3/16" neoprene with two-sided nylon. Farmer-style or waist high pants. Men's or women's models.

D 1388.

Aquastatic II Wet Suit

⅜" neoprene with two-sided nylon. Attached hood, Water Lockout Seal back entry. Custom tailored for men or women.

D 1389. Black.

Budget Pre-Tailored Wet Suit

¼" or 3/16" neoprene with two-sided nylon. Choice of farmer-style or waist high pants. Standard sizes or custom tailored for men or women.

D 1390.

Bayley One-Piece Wet Suit

¼", 3/16", or ⅛" neoprene with two-sided nylon. Stock sizes or custom tailored for men or women.

D 1391.

Cressi-Sub

Women's Wet Suit

Textured 3/16" neoprene. 6 zippers.

D 1392. Black with yellow trim.

Men's Wet Suit

Textured 3/16" or ¼" neoprene with 5 zippers.

D 1393. Black with yellow trim.

Nylon Two Wet Suits

3/16" or ¼" neoprene with nylon on both sides. 5 zippers.

D 1394. Black with yellow trim.

Super-Cold "Alaska" Wet Suit

¼" hooded jacket. 5 zippers, nylon inside and out.

D 1395. Black with yellow trim.

Dacor

Thermoskin® Men's Wet Suit

Jacket and pants of 3/16" or ¼" neoprene with Tuff-Textured exterior, nylon lining. Chest, sleeve, leg zippers.

D 1396.

Thermoskin® Women's Wet Suit

Features additional waist entry zipper, form fit bust cut, and contoured legs.

D 1397.

Del Mar

Deluxe Wet Suit

¼" or 3/16" neoprene with nylon inside, textured jacket, vest top pants, thigh and shoulder pockets.

D 1398. Black and blue.

Captain Kidd Wet Suit

⅛" neoprene with textured jacket and waist high pants. Designed for children.

D 1399. Black.

Super Reef Wet Suit

¼" or 3/16" neoprene with nylon inside. Textured jacket, vest top or waist high pants.

D 1400. Black.

Del Mar USA Wet Suits

⅛" textured neoprene with choice of smooth skin or nylon outside. Men's and women's styles.

D 1401. Black with red, white or blue trim. Sizes: xs, s, m, ml, l, xl.

Santa Cruz Wet Suit

¼" or 3/16" neoprene with two-sided nylon. Knee pads, rolled cuffs and ankles, contrasting arms. Custom tailoring.

D 1402. Black and blue.

Monterey Wet Suit

¼" or 3/16" neoprene with two-sided nylon jacket, vest top pants.

D 1403. Black.

Ventura Wet Suit

¼" or 3/16" neoprene with two sided nylon jacket, waist high pants.

D 1404. Black.

Eliminator Wet Suit

¼" or 3/16" neoprene. Jacket zipper opens into attached hood for easy entry. Velcro wrist and ankle straps.

D 1405. Blue and black.

Del Mar Custom Wet Suit

Two sided nylon with vest top pants, diagonal zippers on pants and jacket. Knee and spine pads, thigh, knife, and key pockets. Custom tailored.

D 1406. Black and blue.

Henderson Aquatics

Aqua-Tux M100-4 Wet Suit

⅛", 3/16", or ¼" neoprene with two-sided nylon, 5 nickle silver zippers, standard sizes or custom-tailored.

D 1407. Black.

Tex Skin Wet Suit

3/16" or ¼" neoprene textured outside, lined with doubleknit nylon inside. Choice of one or five zippers, men's and women's models. Twist lock crotch strap fasteners, all seams sewn.

D 1408. Black. Sizes: xs, s, m, l, xl.

Nylastic & Aquatic Exposure Suit

3/16" or ¼" neoprene with choice of textured or smooth exterior, nylon lining inside. Five stainless steel zippers, fully sewn and triple cemented seams, full flap under all zippers, twist lock crotch strap fasteners. Custom tailoring available.

D 1409. Black.

Zip-On Exposure Suit

3/16" or ¼" neoprene with choice of nylon outside or both sides. Fits loose until zipped up at torso, legs, and arms for diving. Fully sewn and triple cemented seams, Velcro fasteners at ankles and wrists. Anti corrosive zippers and twist locks.

D 1410. Black, orange, or blue.

One Piece Jump Suits

⅛", 3/16", or ¼" neoprene with nylon inside, choice of smooth, textured, or nylon exterior. Choice of one or five zippers. Velcro collar. Custom tailored or standard sizes.

D 1411. Black. Stock sizes: s, m, l, xl.

Aqua-Tux M100-2 Wet Suit

⅛", 3/16", or ¼" neoprene. Wrap-around Velcro collar, insulating gussets behind arm and leg zippers.

D 1412. Black (standard sizes), blue or orange (custom models).

Aqua-Tux M100-6 Wet Suit

¼" neoprene with two-sided nylon, single zipper.

D 1413. Black.

Cold Water Farmer John 435

3/16" or ¼" neoprene with two-sided nylon, farmer-style pants, choice of attached hood, turtleneck, or standard collar.

D 1414. Orange or blue and black.

Cold Water Farmer John 440

3/16", ¼", or ⅜" neoprene with nylon inside, choice of smooth or textured exterior.

D 1415. Black.

Henderson Dry Suit

¼" neoprene with two-sided nylon. Oral and automatic inflators. Custom tailored.

D 1416. Choice of color combinations.

Imperial

King Turtle

¼" or 3/16" neoprene with two-sided nylon. Available in five-zipper jacket and standard pants or six-zipper jacket and farmer john pants. Choice of King Turtle or Glowflex rubber. Leg sheaths, pockets optional.

D 1417. Blue or black.

Bubble Suit

Variable volume. Chest inflator (oral or automatic). Waterproof zipper across shoulders. Sealed at neck, ankles, and wrists. Choice of King Turtle or Glowflex rubber. Stock sizes or custom made.

D 1418. Blue, black, orange. Stock sizes: s, m, l, xl, xxl.

"Sitka"

¼″ or 3/16″ neoprene with two-sided nylon. Standard or farmer-style pants, men's and women's models. Single zipper. Customs available.

D 1419.

Penguin Wet Suit

¼″ or 3/16″ King Turtle or Glowflex rubber, standard or farmer-style pants. Custom made for men or women.

D 1420. Black, blue, or orange.

Baby Turtle

¼″ or 3/16″ Turtleskin rubber with nylon lining inside. Zippers on chest, wrists, ankles.

D 1421. Black.

Lord Byron

Partially Inflatable Wet Suit

¼″ nylon two sided inflatable top, ¼″ nylon farmer-style pants with nylon inside, smooth outside. Self-purging oral inflator can be converted to automatic. Knife and general purpose pockets on thighs, Velcro-fastened crotch strap. Self-locating waist seal vents air when diver is upended.

D 1422. Black, blue or orange.

O'Neill

O'Neill Supersuit

¼″ neoprene with nylon inside, full or partial nylon outside. Reversed turtleneck top. ¼″ nylon one cuffs bonded to sleeves and legs. Attached SunSock boots optional. Oral inflator with bypass purge valve to keep water out, adaptable to power inflation.

D 1423.

O'Neill Sealsuit

3/16″ or ¼″ neoprene with choice of one-sided or two-sided nylon. Farmer-style pants with Velcro shoulder entry. Rolled edges on neck and arms, ankle seals. All seams bonded with special tape. Partial zipper on jacket. Men's and women's models.

D 1424.

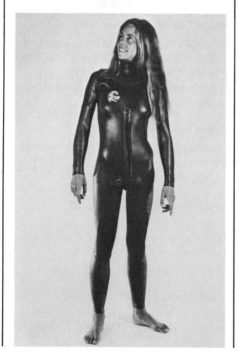

Parkways

Custom Choice Wet Suit

Custom fitted in ⅛″, 3/16″ or ¼″ nylon two-sided closed cell neoprene. Options include attached hood; arm and leg zippers; thigh pocket; spine, knee, and elbow pads; hidden pocket; tool pocket; knife pocket; overstitching.

D 1425. Blue, black or orange.

Sharkskin Vest/Pant Wet Suits

¼″ neoprene textured on both sides. One-piece coveralls with Velcro-fastened shoulder closure, ankle zippers. Jacket has front and wrist zippers and swivel crotch strap locks. Men's and women's styles.

D 1426. Black.

Sharkskin Two Full Wet Suits

⅛″, 3/16″ or ¼″ neoprene textured both sides. High waist and neck. 5 zippers for men, extra hip zipper for women.

D 1427. Black.

Youth's Wet Suit

¼″ neoprene textured outside, nylon lined inside. Jacket, pants, one zipper.

D 1429. Black.

Brute Suit

¼″ neoprene, nylon two sides. One-piece coveralls, jacket with angled front zipper.

D 1430. Black, orange, or blue outside.

Nylon-2-Sides Wet Suits

3/16″ or ¼″ neoprene lined inside and out with nylon. 5 zippers for men, 6 for women. High waisted pants, jacket with set-in sleeves.

D 1431. Black or orange.

One-Piece Jumpsuits

⅛″ neoprene lined inside and out with nylon. Velcro fastened collar. One zipper.

D 1432. Black or blue.

Nylon-2-Sides Vest/Pants Wet Suit

¼″ neoprene, nylon inside and out. One-piece coveralls, jacket, 5 zippers.

D 1433. Black or orange.

Combo Color Wet Suits

3/16″ or ¼″ neoprene, nylon inside and out. Available with pants or coveralls.

D 1434. Black and combination colors.

Hang Ten

Winter Suit

One piece full wet suit with nylon inside. Adjustable roll collar.

D 1435. Black with color panels.

Poseidon

Unisuit

Inflatable wet/dry system. Cycolac buoyancy control valves, optional 3000 psi "bailout" bottle, attached vulcanized rubber boots. Nylon lining inside and out.

D 1436. Black, blue or orange.

Scubapro

Scubaproflex™ Wet Suit

3/16″ or ¼″ neoprene bonded to Proflex fabric. Fully contoured. Men's and women's models.

D 1437. Blue. Sizes: xs to xl.

Farmer John Wet Suit

3/32″ neoprene with seams taped and sewn. Men's and women's models.

D 1438. Black and blue.

Undersea Systems

Viking Dry Suit

One piece rubber coated polyester fabric with watertight back opening zipper. Variable volume or constant volume models. Feet and hood attached.

D 1439.

U.S. Divers

Taskmaster II Wet Suit

Two-sided nylon, sewn inside and out, surged around edges. Farmer-style pants. Knee, elbow, spine pads. Single chest zipper, twistlock crotch snaps. ¼″ neoprene.

D 1440. Black with blue trim: Sizes: xs, s, sm, m, ml, l, xl.

Sea Diver Wet Suit

Two-sided nylon, farmer-style pants with adjustable Velcro shoulder tabs. One chest zipper, twistlock crotch fasteners. ¼″ neoprene.

D 1441. Black body and pants, blue sleeves. Sizes: xs, s, m, l, xl.

Super Sport Wet Suit

Textured pattern for flexibility, extra strength at joints. High waist. Available in one-zipper or five-zipper, 3/16″ or ¼″ neoprene.

D 1442. Black. Sizes: xs, s, m, l, xl.

Divemaster Wet Suit

Textured pattern for flexibility, seam strength. Farmer John pants with Velcro shoulder straps. ¼″ neoprene. One chest zipper, twistlock crotch fasteners.

D 1443. Black. Sizes: xs, s, m, l, xl.

Capri Wet Suit

Specially designed for women. Textured pattern ¼″ neoprene. High waist. Twistlock crotch snaps, six zippers (including extra hip zipper).

D 1444. Black. Sizes: xs, s, m, l, xl.

Capri II Wet Suit

Designed for women. Two-sided nylon over ¼″ neoprene. High waist, 6 zippers. Twistlock crotch snaps.

D 1445. Blue. Sizes: xs, s, m, l, xl.

Oceanaut Wet Suit

Two-sided nylon, blue in-black out. High waist. 3/16″ neoprene.

D 1446. Black. Sizes: xs, s, m, l, xl.

U.S. Nemrod

Canada Wet Suit

5mm (approx. ¼″) microcell neoprene, textured outside, nylon lined inside.

D 1447. Black with yellow tape on seams. Sizes: youth, small, medium, large, x-large.

Senora Wet Suit

5mm microcell neoprene, textured outside, nylon lined inside. Designed for women.

D 1448. Black with yellow tape. Sizes: s, m, l, xl.

Baltic Wet Suit

3/16″ closed-cell foam neoprene textured outside, nylon lined inside. Single zipper.

D 1449. Black.

White Stag

Thermal-Air II Inflatable Suit

Offset chest zipper entry. Nylon two ¼″ neoprene, knee pads. Attached boots optional.

D 1450. Black, blue, or orange. Sizes: s, m, ml, l, xl, custom available.

Thermal-Air III Inflatable Suit

Back zipper entry for optional placement of oral inflator. Nylon two ¼″ neoprene, knee pads. Attached boots optional.

D 1451. Black, blue, or orange. Sizes: s, m, ml, l, xl, custom available.

Super Stag Deluxe Custom Pro-Diver Wet Suit

3/16″ or ¼″ nylon two with contrasting color panels, custom tailoring available for men and women. Choice of regular or farmer-style pants.

D 1452. Black and blue or orange.

Super Stag Pro-Diver Wet Suit

3/16″ or ¼″ nylon two, legs patterned for bent leg swimming position. Custom tailoring available for men and women.

D 1453. Black, blue, or orange.

Super Stag Farmer John Wet Suit

3/16″ or ¼″ nylon two, farmer-style pants. Attached hood optional. Custom tailoring available for men and women.

D 1454. Black, blue, or orange.

Stag Custom Wet Suit

3/16″ or ¼″ nylon two, farmer-style pants optional.

D 1455. Black or blue.

Caribbean Jump Suit

One piece ⅛″ nylon two with front zipper. Reversible.

D 1456. Blue/orange. Sizes: men xs, s, m, ml, l, xl; women xs, s, m, l. Custom tailoring available.

Stag Pro-Diver Wet Suit

3/16″ or ¼″ nylon two, five zippers.

D 1457. Black or blue. Sizes: men xs, s, m, ml, xl; women xs, s, m, l.

Stag Farmer John Wet Suit

¼″ nylon two with farmer-style pants. Men's sizes only.

D 1458. Black or blue. Sizes: xs, s, m, ml, l, xl.

Commercial Diver Pro-Diver Wet Suit

3/16″ or ¼″ nylon inside, textured exterior, five zippers.

D 1459. Black. Sizes: men xs, s, m, ml, l, xl; women xs, s, m, l, customs available.

Commercial Diver Farmer John Wet Suit

¼″ nylon inside, textured exterior, farmer-style pants.

D 1460. Black. Sizes: (men only) xs, s, m, ml, l, xl, customs available.

Ocean Diver Pro-Diver Wet Suit

3/16″ or ¼″ nylon in, texture out, five zippers.

D 1461. Black. Sizes: men xs, s, m, ml, l, xl.

Ocean Diver Farmer John Wet Suit

¼″ nylon in, texture out, farmer-style pants. Men's sizes only.

D 1462. Black. Sizes: xs, s, m, ml, l, xl.

Scuba Equipment

The term "scuba" stands for "self-contained underwater breathing apparatus," and actually encompasses a number of different breathing systems — most of which are unavailable to the sport diver.

Closed-circuit scuba recirculates the exhaled air, drawing off the CO_2 and enriching the remainder with fresh oxygen. These rebreathers are popular for military use because they give off no tell-tale bubbles. But they are limited to use above one atmosphere (33 feet) because of the toxic effects of breathing oxygen below that depth.

Scientific and commercial divers sometimes use computerized closed-circuit mixed-gas scuba which contains oxygen and an inert gas such as helium in separate cylinders.

These units help to avoid nitrogen narcosis and decompression problems in dives as deep as 1000 feet.

A semi-closed circuit scuba rig recirculates a portion of the exhaled air, letting some of the nitrogen and other inert gases escape. These highly sophisticated units require extensive technological know-how and training for deep diving.

The typical sport diving scuba rig consists of a tank of compressed air fed to the diver by a demand-type mouthpiece. It is called an open-circuit unit because the diver's exhalations are expelled into the water, and not recirculated in any way. This is the only type of scuba marketed for the general public, so it will be the only kind discussed further in this chapter.

Scuba Tank Buying Guide

Compressed air scuba tanks are made of either chrome molybdenum steel or aluminum alloy 6351. All equipment companies marketing tanks use one of these two formulations, and also adhere to other strict specifications set down by the U.S. Department of Transportation (see Appendix C). Never use any tanks other than those specifically approved by the D.O.T. for scuba diving.

Steel tanks came first and are still the most widely used. The steel is treated with an anti-rust enamel inside, and is galvanized (coated with zinc) outside. Colorful teflon or epoxy coatings applied over the zinc may help protect against chipping and scuffing, but their effect is largely cosmetic. The galvanizing process is the steel tank's best protection against external corrosion.

Aluminum tanks require no internal treatment, because when the aluminum is exposed to air a thin aluminum oxide film (known as "alumina") forms to protect against further oxidation.

Tank sizes are usually given in terms of the number of cubic feet of surface pressure air they can hold. The standard steel tank contains 71.2 cu. ft. This cylinder can be filled to working pressure of 2250 pounds per square inch. When full it weighs about 39 lbs., and should allow about 50 minutes of normal breathing at 33 feet. A standard size aluminum tank holds 80 cu. feet of air, and can be filled to 3,000 psi. It weighs about the same as the smaller steel tank. Tank diameters are usually 6.9" or 7.25".

Other common tank sizes are 38, 42, and 50 cu. ft., and these are often manifolded together for extra breathing time. Twin tanks are less subject to sway and twisting on the diver's back, but they are heavier to carry and add drag in the water.

A scuba tank is fitted with an on-off valve that forms a watertight seal with the high pressure stage of a demand regulator through the use of an O-ring seal. The basic design is called the K valve because its inner air chambers approximate the shape of the letter "K". This valve also contains a burst-disc safety release plug. The plug is designed to blow out harmlessly if the air pressure exceeds 125-166% of the tank's working pressure (around 3400 psi for a tank with a 2250 psi rating). Therefore, the overpressure will be relieved well before it could build to an explosive situation. The actual burst pressure rating is stamped on the plug.

K valves provide a crude warning system when the air supply is low. Each breath becomes increasingly more difficult until the diver ascends and the ambient water pressure decreases. Then he will be able to breathe more easily, but will not be able to drop deeper again. This is *not* a trustworthy reserve system, and the sensation is only noticeable when the tank is dangerously low on air. A diver using a K valve cylinder should always carry a submersible pressure gauge to monitor tank pressure before it reaches such a crisis level.

The second common valve design is the J valve, which features a constant reserve mechanism. In the J valve, a spring-loaded shutoff device begins to restrict the airflow at a predetermined pressure (usually about 300 psi). When the diver notices his breathing becoming constricted he can override the shutoff device by pulling a "J"

shaped lever which mechanically compresses the spring, fully re-opening the valve. The remaining 300 lbs. of air can provide from 5-15 minutes additional breathing time, depending on the diver's depth and any factors affecting his rate of respiration. Some J valves can be adjusted to activate at higher pressures, providing an even greater reserve.

One advantage of the J valve is that, after it is activated, the diver can stay at the same depth or even descend to finish a task. Of course, this is not recommended. The greatest disadvantage of the J valve is that it is not infallible. The diver must remember to set the lever in the correct position before submerging. The lever can be inadvertently tripped with no warning to the diver. A submersible pressure gauge is now considered a necessity even with a J valve.

Tanks

Cressi-Sub

Cressi Tanks

Nickel-chromium and molybdenum steel alloy. 3000 psi working pressure. Oven painted exterior over galvanized finish.

D 1463. White. Sizes: 71.2 or 106 cu. ft.

Dacor

Dacor Aluminum Tanks

Casing of aluminum alloy (6351T6), coated with multiple polyurethane, capacity to 3000 psi. Available with K valves or J valves, and in double tank blocks.

D 1464. Grey, bronze, or blue. Sizes: 80 cu. ft. or 50 cu. ft.

Dacor Steel Tanks

Chrome molybdenum casing with ¾" O-ring seal. Available with K or J valves, and in double tank blocks.

D 1465. Galvanized. Size 71.2 cu. ft.

Healthways

Healthways Steel Tanks

Cold drawn from chrome molybdenum steel, with galvanized zinc exteriors (hot dipped vinyl overcoatings optional). Rated 2250 psig + 10%. Available with J or K valves with high impact molded control knobs.

D 1466. Yellow or blue vinyl or galvanized finish. Size: 71.2 cu. ft.

Scubapro

Scubapro Tanks

Galvanized steel. K valve or depth compensated adjustable J valve. Available in single or twin configurations.

D 1467. Galvanized, black or white epoxy finish. Sizes: 45 cu.ft. (2216 psi), 71.2 cu.ft. (2475 psi).

Selpac

Sherwood 7200G

Galvanized steel. Maximum fill pressure 2475 psig.

D 1468. Galvanized, blue or black vinyl finish. Size: 71.2 cu. ft.

Sherwood 9600G

Galvanized steel. 3300 psig maximum fill pressure.

D 1469. Galvanized. Size: 94.6 cu.ft.

SCS 104G

Galvanized steel. Maximum fill pressure 2640 psig. 7⅞″ diameter.

D 1470. Galvanized. Size: 104 cu.ft.

SCS 55G

Galvanized steel. Maximum fill pressure 1980 psig.

D 1471. Galvanized. 50 cu.ft.

SCS 45G

Galvanized steel. Maximum fill pressure 2216 psig.

D 1472. Galvanized. Size: 45 cu. ft.

SCA 72

Aluminum. Maximum fill pressure 3000 psig.

D 1473. Blue, yellow, or black. Size: 72 cu. ft.

Sportsways

Sportsways Diving Cylinders

Galvanized steel. ¾″ neck opening. Available with or without J or K valves, in single or double configurations.

D 1474. Galvanized, yellow, orange, or black finish.

U.S. Divers

Big Professional

Aluminum, 3000 psi, 7.25″ diameter. Available with J and K valves and in double tank blocks.

D 1475. Yellow, grey, or black epoxy enamel. Size: 80 cu. ft.

Mark I

Aluminum, 3000 psi, 6.9″ diameter. Available with J and K valves and in double tank blocks.

D 1476. Yellow, grey, or black epoxy enamel. Size: 71.2 cu. ft.

Mark II

Aluminum, 3000 psi, 6.9″ diameter. Weighs 22 lbs. Available with J and K valves and in double tank blocks.

D 1477. Yellow, grey, or black epoxy enamel. Size: 50 cu. ft.

U.S. Divers Steel Tanks

2475 psi, 6.9″ diameter. Available with J and K valves, and in double tank blocks.

D 1478. Galvanized finish. Size: 71.2 cu. ft.

U.S. Nemrod

U.S. Nemrod Galvanized Unlined Tank

Chrome-molybdenum steel. 2250 psi working pressure. Meets all DOT specifications. Side-mounted on-off knob.

D 1479. Galvanized or black vinyl (over galvanized). Size: 71.2 cu. ft.

White Stag

White Stag Steel Cylinders

Galvanized molychrome steel, 6.9″ diameter. Choice of J or K valve. Vinyl coating optional.

D 1480. Metallic, orange, or black. Size: 71.2 cu. ft.

Harness Buying Guide

Scuba tanks are usually sold in combination with backpacks or harnesses — either as original equipment from the manufacturer or in a package deal put together by the retailer. However, you can always opt for a particular pack or harness to suit your individual needs.

Harnesses

Harnesses are systems of straps (usually made of nylon webbing) designed to hold the tank securely against the diver's back. These arrangements are considered somewhat old-fashioned today, and are rarely offered. If you try on a tank with harness, make sure the straps adjust to fit your particular physique. For instance, when you tighten the waist band, you may find that the quick-release buckle winds up inconveniently positioned under your arm. You should also test the harness' ability to hold the tank securely underwater.

Backpacks

The backpack is designed to support the tank comfortably on a metal or plastic plate that is contoured to the diver's back and hips. Backpacks usually require fewer straps than harnesses (no crotch strap, for instance), and are therefore easier to doff and don. The back plates distribute tank weight more evenly than harnesses and keep the tank from swaying from side to side or riding up and bumping the back of the diver's head.

Look for a minimum of bulk and weight in a backpack. The waist and at least one shoulder strap (usually the left) should be equipped with quick release buckles or other rapidly-operated fasteners. Straps should be nylon webbing or similar non-rotting and non-abrasive material.

Some backpacks feature one or more carrying handles, which can be useful on land. The strongest handles are molded in as an integral part of the back plate.

A quick-release cam type tank band can be handy if you plan to change cylinders. Otherwise, a permanent-clamping band will give you the utmost security. Check on whether the back plate can handle bands of different diameters, or setups for twin bands. That way if you get new tank or set of twins later, you won't have to get a new pack for them.

Harnesses

Cressi-Sub

106 C.F. Anatomic

Designed for large capacity (106 cu. ft.) tank.
D 1212.

European Harness

Incorporates tank boot, 40mm wide nylon straps. Single and twin assemblies available.
D 1481.

Twin Harness

Nylon harness with metal tank bands. Fits 6.9" or 7.25" diameter tanks.
D 1482.

Twin Anatomic

Pack with dual bands for 6.9" or 7.25" diameter tanks.
D 1483.

Single Anatomic

Tank band, quick release buckle and fittings of stainless steel.
D 1484. Sizes: A fits 6.9" diameter tanks; B fits either 6.9" or 7.25".

Dacor

Dacor Plastic Pak

For steel and aluminum tanks, convertible for double tanks. Quick release tank-changing cam available.
D 1485. Black.

Dacor Aluminum Pak

Plate of heavy gauge marine aluminum. Adjusting screw, quick release cam for tank band. Carrying handle available.
D 1486.

Healthways

Scubamaster® Quick-Cam Scubapak®

Adjusts to fit tanks from 6.80" to 7.58" in diameter. Stainless steel cam mechanism

and band with non-slip rubber pad. Molded, high-density polyethylene frame with spine clearance groove. Three molded in hand grips for choice of carrying angles. Pliable roll-resistant polypropylene webbing for comfort on bare shoulders. Quick-release waist and shoulder buckles allow straps to be adjusted after donning unit.

D 1487. Black with blue trim.

Scubamaster® Scubapak

Band assembly tightens with screwdriver to fit tanks from 6.80″ to 7.58″ diameter. Quick-adjust/quick release buckle on left shoulder strap. Polyethylene frame with spine clearance groove, three molded in handles. Polypropylene webbing.

D 1488. Black with blue trim.

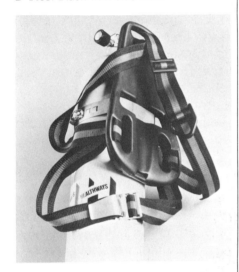

Scubapro

Deluxe Contour Scubapak Harness

Symmetrical back plate, three carrying handles. Wide cam-operated tank band.

D 1489. Black and metallic.

Twin Tank Contour Scubapak Harness

Contoured back plate, permanent tank bands with reserve pull rod guides.

D 1490. Black and metallic.

Standard Contour Scubapak Harness

Contoured back plate with three handles. Adjustable tank band.

D 1491. Black and metallic.

Seatec

Cam Pak

Quick release cam stainless band with neoprene sleeve.

D 1492. Black or blue.

Screw Down Pack

Contoured pack, screw down stainless band fits 6.9″ or 7.25″ dia. tanks.

D 1493. Black or blue.

Mariner Pac

High impact blow-molded polyethylene frame, stainless steel tank band, nylon webbing.

D 1496. Black. Sizes: fits 6.9″ and 7.25″ diameter tanks.

Mariner Kam Pac

Quick-release Kam, spring lock on handle.

D 1497. Black. Sizes: fits 6.9″ and 7.25″ diameter tanks.

Mariner II Pac

Velcro quick-release on left shoulder.

D 1498. Black. Sizes: fits 6.9″ and 7.25″ diameter tanks.

Sportsways

Deluxe Waterlung Pac

Quick-drain ports, molded-in top and side handles, stainless steel cam-action tank band. Fits steel and aluminum single or double tanks.

D 1494. Black with red straps.

U.S. Divers

Mariner III Kam Pac

Quick-release stainless steel mechanism with spring locking feature on handle. Fits 6.9″ and 7.25″ diameter tanks. Double D-ring quick release. Weightbelt-style quick release buckle on left shoulder.

D 1495. Black.

Mariner III Pac

Weightbelt-style quick release buckle on left shoulder.

D 1499. Black. Sizes: fits 6.9″ and 7.25″ diameter tanks.

Mariner Twin Pac

Additional carrying handle with stainless steel bolting.

D 1500. Black. Sizes: fits 6.9″ or 7.25″ diameter tanks.

Twin Tank Harness

Lightweight webbing with four-point mounting system.

D 1501. Black. Sizes: fits 6.9″ and 7.25″ diameter tanks.

U.S. Nemrod

U.S. Nemrod Back-Pack

Injection molded polyethylene. Nylon webbed straps with airplane-style quick release buckle. Quick release tank band.

D 1502. Black or orange.

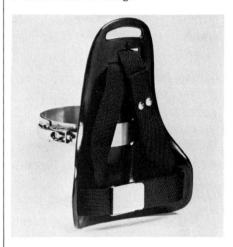

White Stag

Super Stag Delux

Contoured molded frame with handle at top. Stainless steel cam band adjusts to fit 6.9″ and 7.25″ tanks (double bands optional). Quick release buckles at waist and shoulder. Neoprene webbing optional.

D 1503. Black.

Super Stag

Contoured molded frame. Stainless steel cam band adjusts to 6.9″ and 7.25″ tanks (double bands optional). Quick release buckles at waist and shoulder. Neoprene webbing optional.

D 1504. Black.

Scuba Regulator Buying Guide

The purpose of a scuba regulator is to reduce the compressed air in the tank to ambient water pressure and deliver sufficient quantities to the diver on demand.

Two-Hose Regulators

Originally, all regulators were single-stage two-hose units. The reduction from cylinder pressure to ambient pressure took place entirely in one stage.

Today, two-hose models still exist, but now they employ two stages of pressure reduction. In the first stage, the air is reduced from tank pressure (as high as 3,000 psi) to approximately eight atmospheres above the ambient pressure — perhaps 100-130 psi. This air is fed to the second stage at a nearly constant pressure, to reduce breathing resistance. Then the second stage further reduces the pressure to ambient and feeds the diver exactly as much as he demands.

In two-hose regulators, both stages are contained in the housing mounted on the tank valve. A large-diameter, corrugated, low pressure hose carries the air around the right side of the diver's head to his mouthpiece. The mouthpiece is fitted with a one-way exhaust valve, so when the diver exhales, the used air is forced into the left-hand hose and carried back to the housing atop his tank, where it is expelled into the water.

Some divers still prefer two-hose regulators for a number of reasons. Bubbles escape behind the head and do not interfere with vision or hearing. The buoyant hoses help the mouthpiece sit comfortably. Because both stages are integrated into a single housing, they are easier to protect from freezing, making the better two-hose regulators most reliable for diving under ice and in subfreezing water.

The greatest disadvantage to the two-hose regulator is that the demand mechanism is located behind the diver's head, so that when the diver is swimming horizontally, there is a differential of six or more inches between his respiratory organs (where the demand is created) and the second stage (where ambient water pressure is sensed). When breathing in a face-up position, the difference in hydrostatic pressure between the diver's lungs and the demand mechanism can cause the regulator to free-flow — forcing out far more air than the diver can use. Two-hose regulators can also be difficult to purge since the diver must roll on his left side to force the water into the left-hand hose, then exhale sharply to clear the water out.

One-Hose Regulators

Far more popular is the light, compact one-hose design, with the first stage mounted on the cylinder valve and the second stage integrated into the mouthpiece. Both stages are connected by a medium-pressure hose. Exhaled air is expelled out of the mouthpiece through a one-way mushroom valve with bubbles directed away from the diver's face by exhaust ports.

Ideally, the regulator should provide precisely as much air as needed regardless of any changes in tank pressure, ambient pressure, or the diver's rate of respiration, so that breathing underwater is as effortless as breathing on land. To achieve this ideal, equipment manufacturers have devised a number of alternative designs.

The first and second stages operate basically the same way. A vacuum is created when the diver inhales, setting off a chain of mechanical events which allows air from the tank to rush in to fill the vacuum. Since the vacuum is created initially in the second stage, let's examine it first.

Second stage: All second stages contain a diaphragm with one side exposed to the water. When the diver inhales, a vacuum forms behind the diaphragm, and the water presses against it in an attempt to fill the vacuum. the diaphragm bends, activating one or more valves which allow air to enter the mouthpiece from the first stage, thus satisfying the diver's demand. The pressure of the water dictates how much the diaphragm bends and — therefore — how wide the valve opens. That is how the air is delivered at ambient water pressure.

The valves in a second stage may be either "upstream" or "downstream" in design. An upstream valve opens against the flow of air, and a downstream valve opens with it. Downstream valves require a counterforce such as a calibrated spring to close against the hose pressure air. These valves prevent pressure buildup in the second stage and will "free-flow" harmlessly if they malfunction. In some models, the spring tension can be adjusted to increase breathing ease.

Upstream valves are less comon in second stages. One example is the tilt valve, which tilts away from its seat when opened. A small spring clip holds the valve closed when the second stage is unpressurized. With a tilt valve, the higher the hose pressure, the greater the inhalation effort.

Pilot operated second stages have two valves. A pilot valve opens and closes the main valve, which controls the airflow to the mouthpiece. Instead of relying on simple leverage to operate the valve, this arrangement introduces the added power of pneumatic amplification.

A great advantage of the one-hose regulator is that the second stage diaphragm can be depressed manually to purge water from the mouthpiece when the diver doesn't have enough air left in his lungs to do the job. A "purge button" or clearly marked surface on the diaphragm is provided for this purpose.

First stage: The first stage has the dual job of holding back the cylinder pressure while supplying air to fill the vacuum in the second stage. Most first stages utilize upstream valves which require one spring to force the valve open against the tank pressure air and another to close it as the high pressure is reduced. First stages are activated by diaphragms or pistons, and may be "balanced" or "unbalanced."

In a standard or "unbalanced" diaphragm first stage, a push rod operated by the high pressure diaphragm opens an upstream valve. In a "balanced" diaphragm design, the cylinder pressure air is trapped in a mid-pressure chamber, which balances (or neutralizes) the effect of the high pressure on the valve. Therefore, only the mechanical force of the spring effects the valve operation, allowing for smoother operation. With this design, a larger valve orifice can be used, thereby allowing greater airflow capacity with no increase in respiration effort. Also, the spring can be adjusted to alter the airflow.

Some first stages utilize pistons instead of diaphragms. With an "unbalanced" piston, once the

vacuum is formed, water pressure and a bias spring push the piston down, opening the air valve. During exhalation the piston closes off the high pressure seat. A "balanced" (or "flow-through" or "flow-into") piston allows the high pressure air to distribute evenly around the valve, again neutralizing its effect on the valve operation. A precision ground spring ensures a constant flow of air over ambient pressure. With just one moving part, the piston design is relatively trouble free and easy to maintain.

Not all product literature spells out what types of valves and other mechanical devices are used in either regulator stage. Ask the salesperson for a full description if you have any questions.

First stages generally contain a high pressure port for attaching a submersible pressure gauge, and at least one low pressure port for a b.c. power inflator, "octopus" second stage, or other air-powered accessory. Others may feature a constant J type reserve or a sonic reserve which emits an audible warning when tank pressure reaches a predetermined level.

All regulator mouthpieces are similar in design to snorkel mouthpieces, and should be made of non-corrosive, flexible rubber, neoprene, or plastic.

There are many other special features available on individual regulator models. The key ones are mentioned in the following product reviews. All regulators listed are one-hose designs unless otherwise described.

Regulators

AMF Voit

MR12-II Swimaster

Vortex assist: special by-pass tube creates a vortex to assist breathing, particularly at high flow rates. Fully balanced first stage with two low-pressure and one high-pressure accessory ports.

D 1505. Metallic case.

MR12 Swimaster

Fully balanced adjustable first stage with one high-pressure and two low-pressure ports. Recessed purge button.

D 1506. Metallic and black.

R14 Swimaster Polaris II

Piston first stage with MR12 second stage. Chin rest built into exhaust tee.

D 1507. Metallic and black.

Cressi-Sub

Polaris 5 "S"

Balanced piston first stage.

D 1508. Metallic and black.

Polaris 5

One-hose. Recessed purge button, side exhaust.

D 1509. Metallic and black.

Dacor

Olympic Model 400

Balanced first stage, dual exhaust valve system, anti-free flow device, two high pressure outlets, one low pressure port. Optional modular constant reserve system (300 psi).

D 1510.

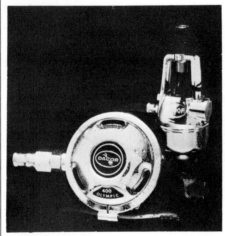

Olympic Model 800

Balanced first stage, dual exhaust valve system, anti-free flow device, two high pressure outlets, one low pressure port. Modular constant reserve system.

D 1511. Black and chrome-plated brass.

Olympic Model 200

Machined first stage, one high pressure and one low pressure port. Dual exhaust system, anti-free flow device.

D 1512. Black and chrome nickel plated body.

Olympic Model 100

Piston first stage, high pressure port, dual exhaust system, anti-free flow device.

D 1513.

Balanced Two Hose

Two stage balanced regulator. Bacteria resistant neoprene spiral hoses.

D 1514. Black and triple-plated chrome body.

Polar Olympic

Teflon-treated second stage and silicone fluid-operated first stage for ice-resistance.

D 1515. Black and chrome-plated body.

Healthways

Scubair Sonic

Low frequency sonic vibrations warn when tank pressure drops below 300 psig. Large piston first stage. Extra intermediate pressure port for connection of additional second stage or b.c. Submersible tank pressure gauge port with restricting orifice. 2475 psig service pressure.

D 1516. Chromed brass, black rubber.

Scubair II "J"

Balanced flow-through piston first stage with J reserve mechanism set at 250 psig. Extra ports for submersible pressure gauge, additional second stage, b.c. Yoke screw knob shaped to resist snagging.

D 1517. Chromed brass, black rubber.

Scubair II

Balanced piston first stage with extra intermediate pressure ports, designed for 3000 psig service pressure. Second stage (standard on all Healthways regulators) has air jet balanced silicone rubber diaphragm, downstream venturi action, large exhaust port with manifold which directs bubbles away from diver's face.

D 1518. Chromed brass, black rubber.

Scubair

Piston-operated first stage with intermediate pressure port, tank pressure gauge port. For use at 2475 psig service pressure.

D 1519. Chromed brass, black rubber.

Scuba Star

Piston-operated first stage with extra intermediate and high pressure ports. For use at 2475 psig service pressure. Scubair second stage.

D 1520. Chromed brass, black rubber.

Poseidon

Unisuit Cyklon 300

Two-stage construction with ports for gauge, air tools, octopus rig, hookah, and inflatable wet/dry suit. Anti-freeze cap protects first stage. Adapts to full face masks.

D 1521. Metallic and black.

Scubapro

Mark V

Balanced piston first stage with two high pressure ports. Multiple port swivel connection to second stage, which features adjustable breathing.

D 1522. Metallic and black.

Mark III

Piston-operated first stage, downstream second stage. Recessed purge button.

D 1523. Metallic and black.

Pilot Second Stage

Pneumatically amplified servo operated second stage can be used with any first stage. "Pre-Dive" switch prevents unwanted free-flow. Dual inlet ports allow choice of connections.

D 1524. Metallic and black.

Sherwood-Selpac

Sherwood SRB-3000

Designed for 3000 psig service pressure. Exhaust tee easily removed for inspection or cleaning. First stage has oversized piston, three low pressure ports, one high pressure port.

D 1525. Black.

Sherwood SRB 2000

Designed to handle 3000 psi service pressure. First stage has swivel yoke, large piston, three low pressure ports, one high pressure port with safety orifice to prevent hose whip.

D 1526. Black.

Sherwood SRB 4100J Or K

Designed to handle 4000 psig service pressure. Balanced piston first stage with four low pressure ports (can supply up to three octopus second stages at once). Optional J valve reserve on first stage. Second stage features large recessed purge button, airfoil assist for diaphragm, adjustable seat for individual breathing requirements, built-in chin support.

D 1527. Black.

Sportsways

Sportsways-Waterlung #W-200

Balanced flow-through piston first stage, three low pressure ports. 10 oz. second stage.

D 1528. Black.

Sportsways-Waterlung #ATM-500C

Pre-set piston first stage. Fully protected diaphragm in second stage.

D 1529. Black.

Sportsways-Waterlung Sport Diver V

Fully balanced, adjustable diaphragm first stage. Second stage constructed of Space Age resin for strength, lightness.

D 1530. Black.

Sportsways-Waterlung #W-600 Hydronaut

Balanced flow-through piston first stage has three low pressure ports plus special 1p port for b.c. power inflator. "Floating Piston" Orifice connector helps keep second stage tuned.

D 1531. Red and black.

Tekna

Tekna Regulator

Pilot-operated second stage with only five moving parts. Design allows for right or left-handed use.

D 1532.

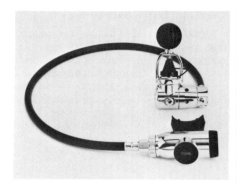

Undersea Systems

Aquastar Airmatic

Balanced first stage with low pressure setting designed for working pressures up to 5000 psi. Second stage of ABS plastic is neutrally buoyant. Mechanical reserve optional.

D 1533.

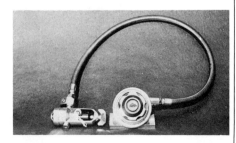

U.S. Divers

Calypso® XXX "J"

Forged yoke and body construction. Built-in constant reserve (300 psi tank pressure). Balanced first stage with reversible high-pressure seat and stainless steel piston. Two low-pressure ports, 45° angle high-pressure port.

D 1534. Black and chrome.

Calypso® VI

Depth compensating balanced piston first stage. Two low-pressure ports, one high-pressure port. Oversized exhaust tube and port. Patented venturi assist in second stage.

D 1535. Black and chrome.

Cornshelf® XIV

Balanced diaphragm. 360° swivel yoke for first stage. One high pressure port, two low pressure ports on first stage.

D 1536. Black and chrome.

Cornshelf® Supreme

Balanced diaphragm. First stage has 360° swivel yoke, one high pressure port, two low pressure ports. Ports isolated in silicone oil-filled chamber to prevent freezing and keep out contaminated water and dirt.

D 1537. Black and chrome.

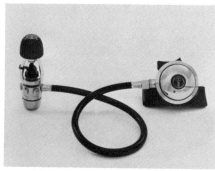

Aquarius®

Single piece forged body and yoke in first stage. Two low pressure ports. Venturi assist in second stage. Adjustable intermediate pressure.

D 1538. Black and chrome.

U.S. Nemrod

Meteor J

Balanced downstream design. Anti-freeze cap prevents leakage in warm water. Automatic Reserve Variator system in first stage includes balanced reduction valve, high-pressure port. Second stage houses downstream valve and large diaphragm with recessed purge button, side exhaust.

D 1539. Metallic and black.

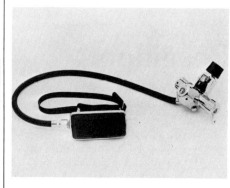

Delta II Downstream

First stage features diaphragm system, one high-pressure and one low-pressure port. Second stage houses downstream valve system, recessed purge button. Rotates 360° on non-kinking hose.

D 1540. Metallic and black.

Sirius Downstream

Diaphragm system first stage with one high-pressure and one low-pressure port. Second stage molded from Luran resin for light weight. Triangular housing features recessed purge button and downstream valve system.

D 1541. Metallic, black, orange.

Ibiza Downstream

Diaphragm system, high-pressure port in first stage. Downstream valve, recessed purge button in second stage. Flexible exhaust tee, adjustable retainer trap.

D 1542. Metallic, black, orange.

Snark III Silver

Two-hose. Venturi valve system.

D 1543. Black and chromed brass.

Watergill

Watergill FSDS-100

First stage has twin pistons, integral reserve mechanism, automatic b.c. inflation device. Downstream second stage.

D 1544.

Pressure Guage Buying Guide

Modern dive planning is based on constant knowledge of one's remaining air supply, making the submersible pressure gauge indispensable. Gauges are required in so many certification courses, on so many charter boats, at so many resorts, and by so many clubs, that it hardly makes sense to purchase a new regulator without one.

Even if your tank or regulator is equipped with a reserve device, a submersible gauge is still an important safety aid. And, if you establish your air consumption rate for a given activity, the gauge can be used as a "timer." For instance, if you consumed 400 pounds of air following a particular compass heading, you know you can return to your starting point by following the reciprocal heading until another 400 pounds is used up.

Some submersible gauges can be attached to the high-pressure outlet on the tank valve. Others hook up to the high-pressure port on the regulator's first stage. This is the more desirable combination, since the diver is far less likely to change regulators than tanks.

Be sure the high-pressure hose is long enough for you to easily grasp and read the dial of the gauge, but not so long that it becomes a nuisance. Some hoses come with snaps or other retaining devices that allow you to attach the gauge to other equipment. Try the gauge on with your other gear, to be sure you can reach and read it easily.

All gauges work similarly, so the things to look for are a large dial with luminous face or numbers you'll be able to read even in murky waters. Some gauges have swivel heads which can be an added convenience.

One word of advice: Pressure gauges can lose accuracy, particularly at the lower pressures where the readings are most critical. Check your submersible gauge against a reliable store gauge (at both high and low pressure) frequently, and have it serviced if any discrepancies come up.

Submersible Pressure Gauges

AMF Voit

Swimaster Underwater Pressure Gauge

Bourdon tube movement, dial face swivels 360°. Protective rubber cover with built-in shock absorbers, accessory slot. Calibrated to 4,000 psi, working pressure 3,000 psi.

D 1547. Black, luminescent face.

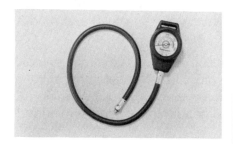

Dacor

Dacor Underwater Pressure Gauge

Phosphorescent dial scale to 3500 psi/240 kilograms, reserve scale indicator. 360° swivel head, overpressure relief valve.

D 1548. Black cover, luminous dial.

Dacor Combo

Air pressure gauge to 3500 psi/240 Kg plus capillary depth gauge on reverse side. Depth gauge reads to 250 feet or 80 meters.

D 1549. Black cover, luminous dial.

Healthways

Submersible Pressure & Depth Gauge

Side reading, swivel mounted gauge with stainless steel-braided, Teflon-lined high-pressure hose. Pressure gauge reads to 3500 psig. Capillary depth gauge on reverse side measures to 250 feet on luminous dial. Also available in metric units. Rubber retaining strap included.

D 1550. Black rubber housing. Healthways.

Submersible Pressure Gauge

Side reading, swivel mounted gauge with stainless steel-braided, Teflon-lined high pressure hose. Reads to 3500 psig (or in kilograms). Spiral bourdon tube mechanism, over-pressure relief device. Rubber retaining strap included.

D 1551. Black rubber housing.

Oceanic Farallon

Farallon Pressure Gauge

Reads to 4000 psi. Protective housing, luminous face. Modules to house other instruments can be added later.

D 1554. Black.

Scubapro

Scubapro Submersible Tank Pressure Gauge

Monitors tank air pressure to 3600 psi. Attaches to high-pressure port.

D 1555. Black case, luminous face.

Sportsways

Super Sea-Vue Gauge

3500 psi service pressure. Brass chrome plated housing, polycarbonate lens.

D 1556. Metallic, luminous dial.

Super Sea-Vue Gauge With Depth Meter

3500 psi service pressure gauge, capillary depth meter bezel reads to 250 feet.

D 1557. Metallic, luminous dial.

Econo Sea-Vue Gauge

Non-metallic housing with soft rubber cover. 3000 psi service pressure.

D 1558. Black, luminous dial.

U.S. Cavalero

Cavalero C.S.S.

Chrome-plated brass case, right-angle mounted with 360° swivel, reads to 3500 psi or metric equivalents.

D 1606. Metallic.

U.S. Divers

Dive Master

Console combining 250' oil-filled depth gauge and 4000 psi tank pressure gauge on same side.

D 1559.

Pro Dive I

Low profile gauge to 4000 psi tank pressure. Coiled bourdon tube mechansim. Housing of ABS material with protective rubber cover. Safety overpressure vent. 360° right-angle swivel mount. Snap-strap harness attachment. Metric dial optional.

D 1560. Black case, luminous dial face.

200' Pro Dive II

Bourdon tube 4000 psi tank pressure gauge with 200' capillary depth gauge around rim of dial. Safety overpressure vent on case. Lexan® lens, O-ring sealed.

D 1561. Black body, luminous face.

U.S. Nemrod

Nemrod Submersible Pressure Gauge

Large dial protected by rubber casing. Full swivel base. Fits all high-pressure ports. Galvanized steel mesh reinforced hose.

D 1562. Black.

White Stag

Deep-Air III

Side-mounted with swivel. 2" dial with luminous face reads to 4000 psi.

D 1563. Orange or black housing.

Deep-Air V

Includes capillary depth gauge on protective sleeve. 2" dial with luminous face reads to 4000 psi.

D 1564.

Depth Gauge Buying Guide

A depth gauge is a necessity for all scuba diving below 33 feet, and can be a helpful aid for skin divers who want to know how deep they're diving.

Basically, a depth gauge is a hydrostatic pressure gauge calibrated in depths (usually feet or meters). There are three major kinds of depth gauges, the capillary, bourdon tube, or diaphragm design.

Capillary Gauges

Simplest and least expensive of all is the capillary or air column gauge. Water enters a small diameter plastic tube and progresses along a calibrated dial the deeper the diver goes. Unfortunately, the scale of the dial is non-linear, so the calibrations become closer together and therefore less accurate at greater depths. This type of gauge is very reliable at shallow depths but becomes undependable below 60 feet.

Besides this disadvantage, the capillary tube can also clog with dirt. Air can get into the water column. And decreases in temperature will decrease the volume of air in the tube, so the gauge will read unrealistically deep.

Bourdon Tube

The most popular type of gauge mechanism is the bourdon tube, with a crescent-shaped hollow C spring, usually made of copper or beryllum brass. As pressure on the spring increases, the tube changes its curvature, activating the gauge needle. You'll find three types of bourdon tube gauges on the market today.

In the open bourdon tube, water enters the C spring through a small opening. As the spring straightens it moves a needle along the gauge dial.

With an oil-filled bourdon tube, the water presses up against a sealed neoprene cup which transmits ambient pressure to the oil, in turn straightening the C spring.

A sealed bourdon tube has a C spring in a partial vacuum filled with silicone or mineral oil. A neoprene diaphragm or flexible plastic surface transmits the ambient pressure to the oil, which in this case causes the C spring to coil tighter rather than straighten.

Oil-filled gauges retain their sensitivity longer and are less subject to internal corrosion than the open bourdon tube. They're also less fragile, because the oil cushions shocks.

If you take a bourdon tube gauge below its depth range, however, you could damage the mechanism.

Diaphragm Gauges

The third type of gauge features a sealed chamber with a flexible metal or silicone diaphragm stretched across an opening in the housing. Through a series of arms and gears, the diaphragm activates a needle which indicates depth on a calibrated dial.

Some gauges combine capillary and bourdon tubes to provide accurate shallow and deep readings. Depth gauges are also integrated with watches, thermometers, and submersible pressure gauges, and may be coupled with other instruments in special instrument consoles (see "Accessories").

A maximum depth indicator is a popular gauge feature for decompression or repetitive dive planning. A special pointer indicates the greatest depth reached, until reset by hand. Some gauges may be adjusted for accurate readings when diving at high altitudes.

No depth gauge is completely accurate. As a rule of thumb, the deeper the range on the dial face, the less accuracy at shallow depths. So you should choose a gauge that doesn't exceed your own dive limits.

Most depth gauges are designed to fit on the diver's wrist. Some are relatively low-profile, others are quite bulky. Be sure you can read the dial face easily in dim light and that you can fasten the strap easily over your wet suit. A stretch strap will help hold the gauge steady at any depth.

Dacor

Dacor LFG150 Gauge

Color coded dial identifies "non-decompression" and safe sport diving zones. Oil filled. Chrome bezel, Lexan® lens, phosphorescent dial face. Black stretch neoprene straps with pivot pins, stainless steel buckle. Reads to 150 feet/45 meters or 300 feet/90 meters.

D 1565. Chrome.

Dacor SFG150 Gauge

Color coded dial identifies "non-decompression" zone and zone below sport diving limit. Oil filled. Cycolac® body and rim, silver dial, black stretch neoprene straps with pivot pins, stainless steel buckle. Reads to 150 feet/45 meters or 300 feet/90 meters.

D 1566. Black.

Dacor Capillary Tube Depth Meter

Phosphorescent dial face, large numerals. Black Cycolac® case. Reads to 250 feet or 80 meters.

D 1567. Black.

Maximum Depth Indicator

Oil filled. Records maximum depth reached (can be reset by hand). Reads to 150 feet/45 meters or 300 feet/90 meters.

D 1568. Black band, metallic case.

Watch Band Capillary Gauge

Fits on most watch bands or depth gauge straps (as backup). Reads to 150 feet or 45 meters.

D 1569. White dial.

Healthways

Scuba Depth Gauge

Capillary tube depth indicator. Large white letters on contrasting dial. One-piece rubber case and strap. Chromed brass rim and buckle.

D 1570. Black. Healthways.

Oil Filled 250′ Depth Gauge

Low profile, pressure-proof silicon oil filled housing. Large numerals on reflective background. Brass and rubber case.

D 1552. Black case and strap, white dial face.

Bourdon 200′ Depth Gauge

Large black markings to 120/feet, red markings from 120-200 feet. One-piece rubber case and strap with chromed brass rim and buckle.

D 1553. Black and chrome case, white dial face.

Oceanic Farallon

Diaphram Depth Gauge

Rack and pinion movement. Reads to 150′.

D 1571.

Oil-Filled Depth Gauge

Ultrasonically sealed, with protective rubber boot. Reads to 150′ or 250′.

D 1572.

Scubapro

Capsule Depth Gauge — 325 Feet

Oil-filled ultrasonically sealed case with diaphragm. Temperature-compensated. "Depth Memory" feature stores maximum depth. Heavy duty rubber strap.

D 1573. Black with luminous face.

Capsule Depth Gauge — 250 Feet

Oil-filled, ultrasonically sealed case with diaphragm. Temperature-compensated 32° — 80° F. Reads to 250 feet.

D 1574. Black with luminous face.

Capsule Depth Gauge — 150 Feet

Oil-filled, ultrasonically sealed case with diaphragm. Temperature-compensated. Reads to 150 feet. Rubber strap.

D 1575. Black with luminous face.

Capillary Depth Gauge

No moving parts. Replaceable tube. Face scaled for easy-to-read shallow diving. Rubber strap.

D 1576. Black with luminous face.

Altitude Adjustment Depth Gauge

Provides accurate depth information at any altitude. Expanded shallow scale. Sealed case. Heavy-duty strap. Available in 500 or 250-foot scales.

D 1577. Black with luminous face.

Seatec

Seatec Capillary Depth Gauge

Reads to 150 feet. Comes with rubber strap.

D 1578. Black with luminous face.

Sportsways

Sportsways Oil-Filled Depth Gauge

Reads to 170 feet. One piece rubber housing and strap.

D 1579. Black with luminous dial.

U.S. Cavalero

Oil-Filled Depth Gauge

Sealed and shockproof low profile case marked in five foot increments to 210 feet. Decompression stops in red.

D 1607.

Piston Depth Gauge

Water pressure compresses a piston along a straight calibrated scale to 250 feet.

D 1608.

U.S. Divers

Depth Master I

Case of high impact ABS material. Screw on replaceable bezel. C-shaped bourdon tube mechanism. Neoprene boot around case. Neoprene strap, Lexan® lens. Reads to 150', 250' or 60 meters.

D 1428. Black with luminous face.

Depth Master II

Two-inch dial face. One-piece adonized and epoxy coated die-cast aluminum case with screw on replaceable bezel. Bourdon tube mechanism. Reads to 150' or 250'.

D 1580. Black with luminous face.

Depth Master III

Magnified capillary depth gauge mounted on bezel of bourdon tube dial. Both gauges read to 150' or 250'. Silicone oil filled mechanism.

D 1581. Black with luminous face.

Pro Depth Gauge

One-piece stainless steel case, floating lens. Reads to 250'.

D 1582. Luminous face.

Baltic Compass and Depth Gauge

Low profile, contoured case with intensified capillary depth gauge and fluid-filled luminescent compass.

D 1583. Black.

U.S. Nemrod

320' Depth Gauge

Flexible, oil-filled sealed case with bourdon tube mechanism.

D 1584. Black.

250' Gauge and Compass

Reads to 250 feet. Plastic strap.

D 1585. Black.

Nemrod Depth Gauge

Shock resistant, tested to 200 feet. Rubber base.

D 1586. Black.

White Stag

Deep IV & Deep V

Oil-filled. 2" luminous face, Velcro strap. Calibrated to 150' or 250'.

D 1587. Orange housing.

Deep IV & Deep V Depth Gauges/ Memory Pointers

Oil-filled. 2" luminous face with pointer to show deepest point of dive. Velcro strap. Calibrated to 150' or 250'.

D 1588. Orange housing.

Straight Capillary Gauge

Open tube gauge designed to fit on submersible pressure gauge hose. Reads to 100'.

D 1589.

Deep III

Oil-filled. 1½" luminous face calibrated to 150'. Velcro strap.

D 1591. Black housing.

Deluxe Capillary Magnified

Wrist-type open tube gauge with magnifying concave lens. Luminous face reads to 100'.

D 1592. Black housing.

Deep Capillary

Wrist-type open tube gauge with 2" luminous face that reads to 150'.

D 1593. Black housing.

Accessories

The word "accessory" can mean different things to different people. A piece of equipment that may be considered an "extra" by one diver could be a necessity to another, depending on his or her needs (underwater lights and thermometers are good examples).

In the previous chapter we discussed basic equipment for skin and scuba divers. In this chapter we present a sampler of optional gear which can greatly enhance your fun and safety, but which is not essential for general diving.

We have limited our selection to accessories which the sport diver can actually take into the water, and have omitted such topside items as compressors, clothing, jewelry, and chemicals (first aid kits, mask defoggers, etc.). We have also excluded spare parts and replacement hardware.

This sampler is meant to give you an idea of the type of merchandise available, and is not an exhaustive survey of every product in every category. We are grateful to the manufacturers who provided the following information, and invite any firms whose products were omitted to forward product literature and black and white glossy photos for our next edition.

For your convenience, we have grouped these accessories into the following categories: Communications Devices, Dive Boats and Vehicles, Flags and Floats, Game Collecting Aids, Instruments, Lights, Miscellaneous, Photo Equipment, Protective Outerwear, Salvage Aids, Scuba Attachments, and Spears and Guns.

A few of these products are available only by mail order (some just in kit form). Unless otherwise noted, however, most can be purchased or ordered through diving retailers. The addresses of all the manufacturers represented here can be found in Appendix H.

Most of the general buying tips at the beginning of the "Equipment" chapter also relate to these accessory products. However, since many accessories have highly specialized functions, we suggest that you make a thorough study before buying. If you're unsure of what accessories you might need, ask your instructor or salesperson for a rundown of the diving conditions you're likely to encounter, and for recommendations of accessories that will be useful in those conditions.

Accessories

Communication Devices

C-SLATE

Underwater writing slate fits on fore arm with Velcro fastener. Marking pen attached.

D2001. C-Slate Company.

CONSOLE SLATE

Designed exclusively for Pennform consoles. Pencil fits in out-of-way position.

D 2002. White. Pennform Plastic Products

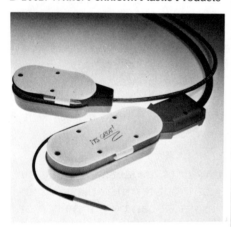

NEMROD SLATE AND PENCIL

Underwater writing instrument attached to its own slate.

D 2003. U.S. Nemrod, Inc.

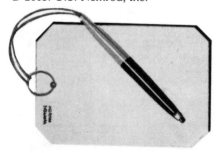

HELLEPHONE

Diver-to-diver or diver-to-surface communicator provides voice intelligibility over distances of up to ½ mile and depths to 300 feet. Diver unit Model 3117 (shown) and surface unit Model 3118 have acoustic outputs of ½ watt. The 3117 is encased in double O-ring sealed anodized aluminum cylinder which straps to tank. Earphone fits under mask strap or hood. Microphone is inserted into special mouth mask.

D 2004. Black. Helle Engineering, Inc.

HELLE PINGER RECEIVER

Especially designed to pick up electronic pinging signals from long distances. Linear array increases signal strength, and forms highly directional listening beam. Operates on single frequency (27 kHz) and includes sealed earphone for guiding diver to pinger location. Neutrally buoyant, operable to 700 feet.

D 2005. Black. Helle Engineering, Inc.

SEA-VOICE™

Projector diaphragm transmits conversation between divers up to 80 feet apart. Uses kinetic energy, no batteries or wires. Audible with no special equipment. Bladder of impedance matched sound transmitting neoprene stores in cone/base for compactness and protection. Diver removes scuba mouthpiece, speaks into Sea-Voice mouthpiece.

D 2006. Sea Sonics, Inc.

SPORTPHONE™

Ultrasonic scuba diver CB. Solid-state, no moving parts. Microphone attaches to regulator and mouthpiece. Transmits 100 yards laterally, down to 100 feet. Each set includes one transmitter/receiver, communication mask with microphone, and special bone conduction earphone. Powered by eight AA penlight batteries, operating time 6 hours. Weighs 1 lb in water.

D 2007. Sound Wave Systems, Inc.

WETPHONE™

Wireless portable underwater voice system. Voice-operated and manual switch-operated units for diver-to-diver or diver-to-surface communication. Voice operated unit can transmit and receive hands free. Normal operating range up to ¼ mile. Operates 8-10 hours on eight 1.5V Alkaline D size batteries. Surface unit (shown) has built-in tape recorder jack.

D 2008. Sound Wave Systems, Inc.

WETTAPE™

Diver-carried mini-cassette tape recorder with hands free voice recording down to 200 feet. One model has manual on/off switch, one has voice-operated system. Powered by standard 9V transistor battery, good for 10 hours.

D 2009. Sound Wave Systems, Inc.

WETWORD™

Diver-carried wireless underwater receiver. Receives signals from any diver-carried or surface Sound Wave unit. Ten hours of use from eight 1.5V alkaline AA penlight batteries. Rechargeable nicad battery pack available. Negative buoyancy.

D 2010. Sound Wave Systems, Inc.

WETBEACON™ AND WETFINDER™

Hand-held relocation system. WETFINDER receives acoustical impulses emitted by WETBEACON within range of 1000'. Light Emitting Diode shows when impulses are received; automatic gain control allows diver to home in on beacon with hands free operation. Beacon will pulse for up to 45 days, at depths of 300'. WETFINDER will run for up to 48 hours actual use on optional alkaline cell.

D 2011. Sound Wave Systems, Inc.

Dive Boats & Vehicles

AVON REDCREST

Four-person inflatable with oarlocks, rubbing strake fender, lifelines, fittings for engine mounting bracket, painter, inflatable thwart, stern seat. Bowdodger, marine plywood floorboards, CO_2 emergency inflator optional. Maximum h.p. 4.

D 2012. Grey and yellow. Length: 9'3". Avon/Seagull Marine.

AVON REDSHANK

Seven person inflatable with oarlocks, two inflatable thwarts, combined hand/foot bellows, dufflebag, fitting for outboard engine mount. Bowdodger, outboard mounting bracket, marine plywood floorboards, CO_2 emergency inflator optional. Maximum h.p. 5.

D 2013. Grey and yellow. Length: 12'3". Avon/Seagull Marine.

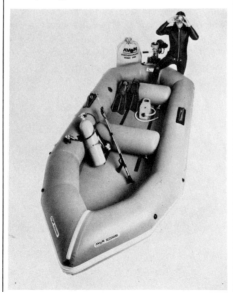

AVON SPORTBOATS

Inflatables with tapered buoyancy tubes, inflatable V-keel, maximum stern buoyancy to support motor, maximum floor area. Integral wooden transom, marine ply floorboards, optional adjustable seating. Maximum h.p. 6-65.

D 2014. Grey and red. Lengths: 9', 10'6", 12'6", 14'6", 16'6". Avon/Seagull Marine.

AVON SEARIDER SR4M

Four person inflatable with fiberglass V hull bonded to buoyancy tubes. Standard version has clear floor area, upholstered seats (2 or 4) optional. Includes bowdodger, fuel tank fittings, lifting handles, foot bellows, ski bolts, drain plug. Maximum h.p. 50.

D 2015. Grey and red. Length: 13'4". Avon/Seagull Marine.

AVON SEARIDER SR5M

Eight person inflatable seats four in comfort. Bowdodger, fuel tank fittings, rubbing strake fender, ski bolts, drain plug, lifting handles, davit lifting points, foot bellows. Deluxe version includes upholstered seats, remote steering, steering console, windscreen. Maximum h.p. 120.

D 2016. Grey and orange. Length: 17'11". Avon/Seagull Marine.

'CUDA INFLATABLES

Marine plywood floorboards, bow canopies of heavy vinyl coated nylon, inflatable keels. Include inflation pump and hose, maintenance kit, two carrying cases. Assemble in 15 minutes. Three sizes can carry from 20-35 hp. outboard engines.

D 2017. Lengths: 14'3", 12'6", 11'3". Avon/Seagull Marine.

BONAIR II

Four-section woodgrain-vinyl marine plywood floorboards, built-in transom with motor mounting pad. Nylon-vinyl bow canopy, optional windshield. Handrails and bow handle of elastic polyurethane, stainless steel towing rings on bow. Inflatable keel. Comes with pump and hose, maintenance kit, carrying cases. Assembles in 12 minutes. Handles 35 h.p. outboard.

D 2018. White and red. Length: 13". Bonair Boats, Inc.

BONAIR D-300 DINGHY

Constructed of 'Cudahide® fabric with two air chambers and separate inflation points. Optional motor mount, floorboards. Includes foot pump and hose, rigid bench seat, two-piece oars and detachable oarlocks, towing rings, maintenance kit, carrying case. Can accommodate 5 persons. Maximum h.p. 5.

D 2019. Length: 9'10". Bonair Boats, Inc.

330 — ARGONAUT

Six-person inflatable. Includes windshield, inflatable keel, rubbing strake, fitted weather bowdodger with zipper closure, heavy-duty oarlocks, inflatable pillow seat. Three airtight compartments. Engine capacity to 25 h.p. Weights 160 lbs.

D 2020. Grey and red. Length: 12'4". Camp-Ways Inflatable Boats.

331 — ARGONAUT

Five airtight compartments plus inflatable keel, 6 high-volume valves, zippered bowdodger, windshield, oarlocks, inflatable seat, painter, lifelines, bellows pump, treated wood floorboards. Maximum engine capacity 35 h.p. Weighs 200 lbs. (plus floorboards).

D 2021. Grey and red. Length: 13'6". Camp-Ways Inflatable Boats,

332 — ARGONAUT

Five airtight compartments plus inflatable keel fitted with high-volume valves. Includes windshield, rubbing strake, bowdodger with zipper closure, oarlocks, inflatable pillow seat, painter, lifelines, repair kit, bellows pump, carry bags and handles, treated wood floorboards. Weights 230 lbs. Maximum engine capacity 50 h.p.

D 2022. Grey and red. Length: 15'. Camp-Ways Inflatable Boats.

4-MAN DELUXE BOAT

Upturned bow for easier handling, high-volume valves for quick inflation/deflation. Includes wood motor mount, rubbing strake, oarlocks. Maximum capacity 4 h.p.

D 2023. Grey and red. Length: 10'. Camp-Ways Inflatable Boats.

6-MAN BOAT

Upturned bow for easier handling, high-volume inflation/deflation valves. Includes wood motor mount, mounted D-rings, rubbing strake, oarlocks. Made of 35 oz./sq. yd. coated nylon fabric (37 oz. on floor). Maximum engine capacity: 5 h.p.

D 2024. Grey and red. Length: 11'8". Camp-Ways Inflatable Boats.

ACHILLES INFLATABLE CRAFT D6-1328

Six-person inflatable with air keel, detachable spray dodger, oarlocks, carrying handles, wooden floor. Four chambers, one seat, outboard motor transom. Recommended engine capacity: 20 h.p.

D 2025. Grey and red. Length: 13'2". Diving and Fishing Boats, Inc.

SCUBA TOW

Do-it-yourself hand-held vehicle with two Byrd Model 1212 12VDC motors powered by a heavy duty 12VDC lead-acid motorcycle battery. Total thrust is 40 pounds, top speed of 3 m.p.h., running time of 50 minutes continuous or 80 minutes intermittent. Adjustable ballast tanks, operable to 100 feet plus.

D 2026. Plans and motors available from Kent Corporation.

ONE MAN SUB

Do-it-yourself single seat Delta-wing design. Semi-dry (portion of diver's body is in air pocket while underwater — no face mask required). Two model 2424 24VDC motors powered by 2 to 4 12VDC batteries. Two speeds (2-4 m.p.h.), range to 8 miles. Constant buoyancy valve, plywood and fiberglass hull, acrylic plastic bubble canopy. Maximum dive angle 15°, operable to 100 feet plus.

D 2027. Plans and motors available from Kent Corporation.

TWO MAN SUB

Do-it-yourself semi-dry or full wet two-seater sub. Two 2424VDC motors powered by 4 12VDC batteries. Two speeds (2-4 m.p.h.), range of 8 miles. Variable buoyancy valve. Hull fashioned from surplus aircraft drop tank with fiberglass sections, canopy of ¼" clear acrylic plastic. Aircraft type controls. Operable to 100 feet plus.

D 2028. Plans and motors available from Kent Corporation.

ONE-MAN SUBMARINE

Dry type single-seat submersible with twin external motors powered by 12-volt marine batteries. Pressure hull of ¼" gauge steel, conning tower hemisphere hatch blown from 1" thick acrylic sheet. Variable ballast tank system, bottom viewing port, snorkel system, emergency drop-lead weight, internal depth gauge. Speed 2½ knots, maximum operating depth 250 feet.

D 2029. Length overall: 11'8". Kittredge Industries, Inc.

NOVURANIA INFLATABLE BOATS

Two-piece wooden keel, wide diameter tubes for dryer ride. Skin of 840 density nylon, coated with hypalon. Marine multi-layered floor boards, marine plywood transom. Air pump, oars, carrying bags, bow-dodger, water repellent document pocket, lifelines, lifting and towing handles included. Twelve models (Poseidon IV shown).

D 2030. Grey, red, or yellow. Proko International.

ROYAK DIVERS FLOATS

Single person diver vehicle propelled by double blade kayak type paddle. Formed from Cycolac, with 2.3 cu. ft. of polystyrene floatation installed within hull. Cockpit designed so diver sits below water level for stability. Wet or dry aft storage compartment. Three models, from 51-59 lbs.

D 2031. Yellow. Royak, Inc.

OCEAN KAYAK

Fiberglass ocean vehicle with three separate air chambers, powered by double-bladed paddle with collapsible aluminum shaft. 5'10" watertight storage compartment. 14' waterline, cockpit in choice of s,m, l size.

D 2032. Yellow or optional colors. Seaboard Products.

SCUBA SCOOTER

Cruises at three times normal swimming speed for an hour of continuous running from fully charged 12 volt 35 AH lead-acid aircraft type battery. Slight positive buoyancy, anodized aluminum hull. Three-bladed propeller powered by .5 h.p. permanent magnet motor. Grasp switch motor controls, guided by wrist action on handles. Available directly from manufacturer.

D 2033. Yellow and black. Length: 37". Seatech Corporation.

SEVYLOR RUNABOUTS

Three-chamber hull construction. Inner chambers connected to wooden floorboards and transom support braces. Made of Neopryl with heat sealed seams. Two models: K68 handles two people, maximum 6 h.p. motor; K88 handles three people, maximum 10 h.p. motor.

D 2034. Yellow and black. Length: K68 9'2", K88 11'. Sevylor USA, Inc.

SHAKESPEARE SUBMOBILE®

Operates at 2 mph for approximately one hour. Powered by 12 volt D.C. 18 amp. 1750 rpm motor, two 6 volt D.C. 20 amp. batteries. Maximum operating depth 150'. Hand switch provides speed control, turns controlled by wrist action on grips. Positive buoyancy. Batteries interchangeable through rear port, recharger included.

D 2035. Yellow and black. Length: 24½". Shakespeare Products.

HYDROCOPTER

Variable buoyancy underwater vehicle which diver rides in sitting position. Buoyancy chamber filled by diver's exhaust bubbles, with valve controlling amount of air for neutral buoyancy. Allows diver to lift heavy items. Wishbone control swings propulsion motor through 90° arc to move up, down, or horizontally. Maximum depth 40'. Plans and parts available from manufacturer.

D 2036. U.S. Laboratory.

MARK I JUNIOR

Four-person inflatable with front spray hood, three section floorboard with inflatable keel. Two airtight compartments besides keel. Maximum engine capacity 10 h.p.

D 2037. Gray and yellow. Length: 10'6". Zodiac of North America, Inc.

MARK I DELUXE

Four-person inflatable with convertible spray hood, single inflation point, deep inflatable keel, two additional airtight compartments, two carrying handles. Maximum engine capacity 25 h.p.

D 2038. Gray and yellow. Length: 10'6". Zodiac of North America, Inc.

MARK II GR

Six-person inflatable with aluminum floorboards, marine mahogany plywood transom, lateral rubbing strakes. Three airtight compartments plus inflatable keel. Single-point inflating valve includes overpressure relief feature. Maximum engine capacity 55 h.p.

D 2039. Gray, black, and yellow. Length: 13'10". Zodiac of North America, Inc.

MARK III GR

Ten-person inflatable with aluminum floorboards, five airtight compartments plus inflatable keel, four interconnecting automatic overpressure relief valves, 2 anti-splash flaps on transom, fitting auxiliary for twin engines. Maximum engine capacity 65 h.p.

D 2040. Gray, black, and yellow. Length: 15'5". Zodiac of North America, Inc.

MARK IV GR

Twelve-person inflatable with aluminum floorboards, five airtight compartments plus inflatable keel, four interconnecting automatic overpressure relief valves, four carrying handles, two D rings for towing. Maximum engine capacity 85 h.p.

D 2041. Gray, black and yellow. Length: 17'6". Zodiac of North America, Inc.

CADET

Four-person inflatable with marine plywood floorboards in hinged sections, two airtight compartments plus inflatable keel, rubbing strake, bow carrying handle. Maximum engine capacity 10 h.p.

D 2043. Gray. Length: 9'10". Zodiac of North America, Inc.

SCUBA LADDER

Single-shaft ladder with open steps for small boat. Fits at angle to boat, providing room for fins and allowing diver to lean forward while boarding. Detachable or permanently mounted brackets. Constructed of aluminum, weight 8.5 lbs.

D 2044. Length: 63". Aquatic Specialties.

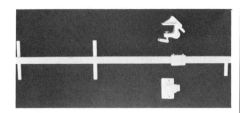

Floats

SIGNAL FLOAT

Inflatable plastic float with removable flag and 60 feet of ⅛" floating nylon line.

D 2045. Red, white, black. Cressi-Sub.

DACOR SMALL DIVER'S FLOAT

Self-righting inflatable buoy with rigid diver's flag. "DIVER BELOW" in large block letter.

D 2046. Red and white. Dacor Corporation.

PELICAN FLOAT

Neutrally buoyant portable with buoy helpful in marking items lost overboard, pinpointing diving spots, light salvage work, search and recovery work, even diver-to-surface communication. Solid plastic body body with 100 feet of 250 lb. test tether line and non-drag anchor.

D 2047. Orange and yellow body, yellow line. Pelican Products.

PRO BUOY 1

Oral-inflating 20" diameter float with weighted center pole that retains upright position at all times. 14" x 16" diver's flag comes with insertable stiffener. Assembles in one minute.

D 2048. Dayglo red and white. Pennform Plastic Products, Inc.

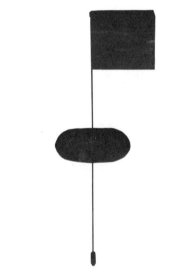

U.S. NEMROD DIVER'S BUOY

Vinyl. Inflates to 36" high, 20" diameter. Inflatable flag 11" x 12". Large drain plug. Mooring line cleat.

D 2049. Red-orange and white. U.S. Nemrod, Inc.

Game Collecting Aids

CATCH-ALL BAG

Smallest size fits on belt. Largest size is of heaviest 100% nylon mesh available. Snap closures.

D 2050. Sizes: XS, S, M, L. Cressi-Sub.

SCUBAMASTER® AB & DIVERS TOOL

16" long x 1½" wide x ¼"thick aluminum alloy tool with round edges and inch marked scale. Bonded on soft vinyl handle, adjustable neoprene lanyard. Useful for taking abalone and scallops, or as a pry bar or digging tool.

D 2051. Black handle. Healthways.

HENDERSON "BUG BAG"

Ligthweight heavy duty nylon mesh with non-corrosive metallic tubing, neoprene hinges. Stainless steel closing latch. Nylon handle on larger model.

D 2052. Standard size: 18" x 24"; large size: 26" x 28". Henderson Aquatics.

BUG BAG

Nylon mesh, 14" x 24". Heavy wire locking device on handles, attaching strap.

D 2053. White, U.S. Nemrod, Inc.

ABALONE TOOL

Meets California fish and game requirements. Stainless steel blade has seven-inch scale marked to show legal limits for various species of abalone. Molded shock-resistant rubber handle. Fitting for attaching lanyard. Sheath included.

D 2054. Black handle. Overall length: 12¾". Wenoka Cutlery.

WENOKA DIVERS TOOL

Molded shock-resistant rubber handle with lanyard fitting. 7¾" stainless steel blade with sawing and chopping edges, angled pry tip. Sheath included.

D 2055. Black handle. Overall length: 13". Wenoka Cutlery.

Instruments

SWIMASTER DELUXE LIQUID COMPASS

Rotating bezel and lubber line. Luminous markings. Single-handed operable strap with escapement buckle.

D 2056. Black with yellow strap. AMF Voit.

SEA QUARTZ 20 WATCH

Swiss quartz movement guaranteed accurate to one minute a year. Day-date calendar, stainless steel case with screw-down crown, elasped time bezel. Pressure-proof to 20 atms. (660'). Minimum battery life one year. Optional steel bracelet.

D 2057. Metallic with burgundy dial. Chronosport, Inc.

SEA QUARTZ 30 WATCH

Swiss quartz movement guaranteed accurate to within one minute a year. Scratch-resistant mineral crystal, one-way ratcheted bezel with luminous markers, screw-down crown. Pressure-proof to 30 atms. (1000').

D 2058. Metallic and black. Chronosport, Inc.

STAR DIVER WATCH

Andonized stainless steel case guaranteed pressure proof to 30 atms. (1000'). Scratch-resistant mineral crystal, screw-down winding crown, one-way ratcheted bezel. Self-winding, day-date calendar.

D 2059. Black. Chronosport, Inc.

LADIES' DIVETTE WATCH

Solid stainless steel case with internal rotating bezel. Self-winding movement with calendar. Optional stainless steel bracelet.

D 2060. Metallic. Chronosport, Inc.

MINI-DIVE

Automatic 17-jewel ladies' dive watch. Self-winding, calendar, rotating one-way bezel. Pressure-proof to 30 atms. (1000').

D 2061. Stainless case, black bezel, luminous markings. Chronosport, Inc.

SCUBA THERMOMETER

Large numbers (20°-120°) broken into color coded segments. Liquid filled capsule tested for 200 feet. Fits on watch or gauge strap.

D 2062. Nickel plated brass case, black dial. Healthways.

SCUBA COMPASS

Liquid filled capsule. Rotating bezel with needle alignment lines which glow in dark. Heavy gauge adjustable strap.

D 2063. Black with white markings. Healthways.

PRO COMPASS

Patented case eliminates corrosion and sticking bezel. Low profile bezel for better view of north needle, easily gripped even with gloves. Precision jewel bearing eliminates need for strong, magnetized needle, reducing influence of surrounding metal objects.

D 2064. Black. Ikelite Underwater Systems.

DOUBLE FACE COMBO

Houses pressure gauge plus depth gauge or compass.

D 2065. Black. Oceanic/Farallon.

HIRSCH "CONTAINER" DIVERS WATCH

Handwound 17 jewel, shockproof movement with date, rotating bezel. "Container" can be removed from bezel for easy exchange, eliminating repair waiting time. Guaranteed watertight to 120 feet.

D 2066. Black with orange hands and number indicators. Orange Coast International.

200 SERIES INSTRUMENT CONSOLE

Two-piece model polypropylene case with space for any combination of pressure gauge plus depth gauge or compass. Screw-on covers hold gauges in place. Accepts most major gauges.

D 2067. Blue, black, red, yellow or green. Pennform Plastic Products, Inc.

300 SERIES INSTRUMENT CONSOLE

Space for combination of pressure gauge, depth gauge, and compass (most major brands). Two-piece molded polypropylene cse. Screw-on covers hold gauges in place.

D 2068. Blue, black, red, yellow, or green. Pennform Plastic Products, Inc.

320 SERIES INSTRUMENT CONSOLE

Includes mounting section for watch, bottom timer, decompression meter, etc. Space to hold most major brands of pressure gauge, depth gauge, and compass. Molded polypropylene body, screw-on gauge covers.

D 2069. Blue, black, red, yellow, or green. Pennform Plastic Products, Inc.

BOTTOM TIMER

Automatically begins recording time of dive below 5-9 feet. If diver surfaces during dive, timer records total time spent below 5-9 feet. Pressure sensitive diaphragm activates and deactivates watch. Housed in ultra-violet resistant Lexan, outer cover of Kraton® thermoplastic rubber with Velcro strap. Optional Gage Mount for fastening to pressure gauge hose.

D 2070. Black. Princeton Tectonics.

RECTA COMPASS

Lightweight. Adjustable luminous sighting-arrow. Plastic construction. Optional depth gauge.

D 2071. Recta S.A.

SEA-DWELLER ROLEX CHRONOMETER

Patented valve allows helium and other gases to escape for decompression. Guaranteed pressure proof to 2000 feet. Self-winding, date indicator, rotating bezel. Extension strips in bracelet for wearing watch over wet suit.

D 2072. Stainless steel case and bracelet, black face. Rolex.

SUBMARINER

Guaranteed pressureproof to 660 feet. Triple locking winding crown protected by special shoulder. Rotating bezel, date indicator.

D 2073. Stainless steel or 18 kt gold. Rolex.

SCUBAPRO AUTOMATIC DECOMPRESSION COMPUTER

Indicates amount and location of decompression needed, if any, prior to surfacing. Pre-dive calibration indicator for determining instrument's readiness for diving. Rubber strap.

D 2074. Metallic case. Luminous decom stop marks and needle. Scubapro.

SCUBAPRO LS-I COMPASS

Can be read from top or side. Rotatable bezel remembers desired course or indicates bearings. Liquid-filled case, heavy-duty strap.

D 2075. Black with luminous dial. Scubapro.

SCUBAPRO DIVE TIMER

Shows "minutes" of breathing time based on tank air supply remaining at depth. Second depth-compensated gauge shows tank psi. Attaches to regulator high-pressure port. Comes with protective cover.

D 2076. Black case. Scubapro.

SCUBAPRO INSTRUMENT CONSOLE

All rubber case holds any Scubapro depth gauges (except capillary models), LS-1 compass, automatic decom computer. Fits onto Dive Timer or submersible tank pressure gauge.

D 2077. Black. Scubapro.

PROFESSIONAL WATCH

17 jewel self-winding movement, polished stainless steel case. Tested to 900 feet and 76° below zero. Maximum decompression limits marked on bezel.

D 2078. Orange face. U.S. Divers Company.

SHARK HUNTER WATCH

17 jewel self-winding movement, polished stainless steel case. Tested to 900 feet and 76° below zero. Maximum decompression limits marked on bezel.

D 2079. Black face. U.S. Divers Company.

SEA RAMBLER WATCH

17 jewel self-winding movement, polished stainless steel case. Tested to 900 feet and 76° below zero. Maximum decompression limits marked on bezel.

D 2080. Silver face. U.S. Divers Company.

NEMROD COMPASS

Luminous dial, jeweled pivot. Lubber lines on face. Gun type sight.

D 2081. Black. U.S. Nemrod, Inc.

THE DIPSTIK

Handheld digital sonar for underwater use. Displays depth or distance to target, analyzes echoes electronically to determine type of target. Pressureproof to 150′. Maximum range 600+ feet. Up to 500 individual 90 second operations between battery charges. Stainless steel case. Polyweb wrist strap, charging cord included.

D 2082. Metallic. Length: 11″. Vetronic Instruments.

Lights

RECHARGEABLE LIGHT

Provides two hours of usable light, recharges in 10-15 hours. Cycolac® body, electrogel battery.

D 2083. Red and black. Dacor Corporation.

DIVER'S FLASHER

Designed for night and limited visibility diving. Emits 50 flashes per minute (150,000 peak lumens per flash).

D 2084. International oranges. Dacor Corporation.

DIVEX 4500 HAND HELD LIGHT

Guaranteed to 1500 feet. Epoxy impregnated cast aluminum alloy. thumb-operated on-off switch. Powered by 6 volt battery. Strong enough to be used as hammer.

D 2085. Divex.

IKELITE II

Textured case and handle guaranteed unbreakable. Clear lens in front of #4546 sealed beam bulb. Contour handle position for ease in aiming. Fail-safe on/off mechanism with switch lock. Floats bulb up. Sealing foolproof to 400 feet.

D 2086. White and clear. Ikelite Underwater Systems

C-LITE

Push-on snap cap, compact size. Guaranteed unbreakable and safe to working depth of 800 feet. C-Lite I produces 10,000 initial beam candle power from six "C" size alkaline batteries. C-Lite II produces 6,000 initial beam candlepower from rechargeable ni-cad batteries.

D 2087. Black. Ikelite Underwater Systems.

MODULAR I

Utilizes six "D"size flashlight batteries (not included). May be converted to a higher intensity or to a movie light by adding a ni-cad battery pack and sealed beam lamp. Removable pistol grip handle, unbreakable GE Lexan case and cap.

D 2088. Black and clear. Ikelite Underwater Systems.

MODULAR X

O-ring seal push-on cap, rotating on/off/on switch with lock, interchangeable battery modules, removable pistol grip handle, Lexan case and cap. Powerful bulb requires alkaline type "D" cell batteries. Converts to Super Light or movie light.

D 2089. Black or clear. Ikelite Underwater Systems.

SEAPROBE FLASHLIGHT

Anodized aluminum construction with no-slip diamond grip knurling. Lanyard of 500 lb. strength braided rope with slip bead. Uses standard "D" batteries (two-cell to seven-cell models). Sealed and certified waterproof to 300 feet.

D 2091. Yellow and black. L.A. Screw Products, Inc.

SCUBAPRO UNDERWATER LIGHT

Pressure-proofed to 300 feet. "O"-ring seals on lens. Thumb-operated switch with lock. Non-corroding plastic body, lanyard connection. Uses standard flashlight batteries.

D 2092. Black. Sizes: 4 cell, 6 cell. Scubapro.

SERL DIVER LIGHT

Injection molded ABS housing resists corrosion from battery acid as well as salt water. Over-the-top handle for straight ahead aiming. Lamp (GE#965 or #500) set for narrow beam, powered by 10 standard "D" size batteries (not included). Tested for 300'. Beam-up floatation.

D 2093. Yellow. Serl Underwater Products.

TEKNA-LITE I

Light weight. Rechargeable modular ni-cad battery pack provides 1-hour running time. Rotating bezel switch. Includes 110 VAC charger and batteries.

D 2094. Tekna.

TEKNA-LITE II

Compact design. Can be used as flashlight, spotting light, or flasher. Two bulbs, one moving part. Velcro strap holder optional.

D 2095. Tekna.

THE BRIGHT LITE

Housing and bezel of high impact ABS material. Oversize handle protects on/off switch. Rated light output of 103,000 candlepower. Lens made with parabolic curve. Provides one hour and 45 minutes of light per battery charge. Recharges from 115 volt AC or 12 volt DC (DC recharging cord optional).

D 2096. Yellow with black bezel. U.S. Divers Company.

NEMROD DIVER'S LIGHT

Leak-proof magnetic switch. Floats beam up. Seals water tight to 150'. Takes 6 volt battery.

D 2097. Orange and black. U.S. Nemrod, Inc.

SUPER Q LITE

35,000 candlepower light powered by rechargeable ni-cad batteries for 1½ hour burn time. Batteries exchanged in seconds. Pressure tested to 2000'. Clear Lexan case allows visual inspection of O-ring seal. Halogen bulb. All parts glow in dark. 110 VAC charger, beam widener included.

D 2098. Clear. Underwater Kinetics.

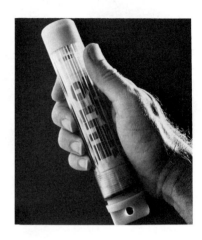

Miscellaneous

THE CREEPER

Underwater stabilizing device, for use in strong currents. Diver advances by moving handles forward in alternate fashion. Diver can attach himself to Creeper to work or rest with hands free. Can also serve as pivot for search rope. Constructed of steel rods with lead weights which can be removed or added to. Weighs about 45 lbs. as shipped.

D 2099. Aquatic Specialties.

BELT SNAP HOOK

1" polypropylene loop fits over belt and holds heavy duty brass snap hook. Three sizes for different jobs. Smallest size has a belt snap for quick removal.

D 2101. Black loop. Sizes: S, M, L. Dacor Corporation.

THE WATER GLASS

Practical tool for locating diving spots, treasure hunting, or underwater viewing. Weighs 9 lbs. Can be disassembled for storage.

D 2100. Size: 14" x 23". Catalina Marine.

CONSOLE RETAINER STRAP

Attaches to back pack waist or shoulder strap to hold pressure gauge/console hose and/or octopus regulator hose. Easily workable snap action.

D 2102. Blue, black, red, yellow, or green. Pennform Plastic Products, Inc.

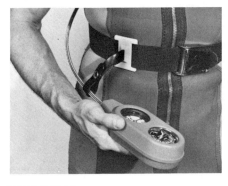

FIXE-PALM

Fits over instep and behind and under heel to hold full foot fins securely.

D 2103. Black. Sizes: 7-11, 9-16. Healthways.

BROWNIE'S THIRD LUNG

Three h.p. 4 cycle Briggs & Stratton engine turns diaphragm compressor to feed one diver as deep as 100' or two divers to 70 feet up to 2 hours on 2 quarts of gasoline. 26" diameter platform on 36" float. Includes two demand flow regulators, each on 40-foot lengths of hose.

D 2104. Various models for shallower depths. W.C. Brown Company.

RDC.1 REPETITIVE DIVE CHART

Waterproof, solid, laminated plastic. Tables 1-11, 1-12, and 1-13 on one side. Opposite side features Table 1-10, dive log, and checklist. Dive ladder for computing repetitive dives. Write and wipe surface, special marker and pen clip.

D 2105. Size: 8" x 10". Aquatic Research Engineering, Inc.

GUIDES TO MARINE FISHES

Laminated cards printed on both sides with illustrations of common fish in Florida and the Caribbean, Hawaii and the Central Pacific, North American West Coast, shoreline and reef, and U.S. East Coast (shown). Can be carried underwater.

D 2106. Black and white. Size: 3½" x 8½". Sea Sports.

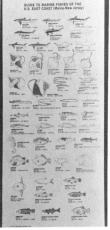

AQUA OPTICS

Individual spectacle correction bonded to diver's face plate. Near-sightedness, far-sightedness, astigmatism, bifocals, and prism correction can be incorporated. Lenses average twice as large (6 sq. in.) as spectacle lenses. Any style face-plate may be used. Mask can be ordered along with lenses.

D 2107. A.S. Newton, O.D.

ALL-AMERICAN SCUBA Rx LENSES

Bonded to face plates of virtually all types of diving masks. Single vision or bifocal, tempered to meet FDA regulations. Lens shape usually round or oval, cut to fit nose piece, depending on size and shape of mask.

D 2108. Benson Optical Company, Inc.

PRESCRIPTION FACE PLATES

Wide angle saftey lenses precision ground and bonded to mask face plate with 100% transparent epoxy optical cement. Any prescription, any style of mask. Compensated for focus adjustment if mask places lenses further from eyes than eyeglasses. Masks supplied at 10% discount.

D 2109. Leonard Maggiore, Optician.

Photo Equipment

SUNPACK MARINE 28 FLASH

Fits all Ikelite camera housings plus Nikonos cameras. Designed for use down to 325 feet. Rotating ball-and-socket head for flash positioning, quick-release bracket for instant off-camera lighting, leakage alarm, neutral buoyancy. Delivers guide number 90 with ASA 100 film, 45 with ASA 25 film. Comes with battery cartridge that holds six standard "AA" batteries.

D 2110. Size: 1.5″ x 3.5″ x 15.5″. Berkey Marketing Companies.

TOSHIBA TM-1

Manual strobe powered by 4 alkaline pen-light batteries. Provides approximately 250 flashes and recycle time of 5-7 seconds. Water-proof sync cord, off-camera flash bracket. Weighs 2.4 lbs. Surface guide number of 41 with ASA 25 film. Designed for use to 396 feet.

D 2111. Black. Elmo Manufacturing Corp.

LENS FOCUSER FOR NIKONOS CAMERAS

Aid to above water and underwater focus measurements with all Nikonos I, II, and III and Calypso lenses. Temporarily replaces camera body for ground glass focusing of lens at any focus control setting, any f/number, and with any diopter or extension tube combination.

D 2112. Black. fm Roberts Enterpises.

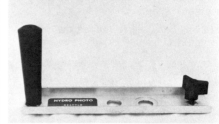

FUJICA MARINE-8 AX100

"Available light" AX100 8 mm movie camera in watertight case approved for depths to 133 feet. Stabilizer fins for underwater stability and maneuverability, wrist lanyard.

D 2113. Fuji Photo USA, Inc.

HYDRO PHOTO CLOSE-UP LENSES

Designed to fit the Nikonos 28mm and the Konica C35 Marine (shown) or the Nikonos 35mm (three models). Screw directly into camera, can be installed or removed underwater. Precision ground from optical glass. Distance wand fits flash shoe.

D 2114. Hydro Photo.

COBRA FLASH ARM

Five ball socket joints, each capable of bending 35 degrees in any direction or rotating. Tension control at base. Anodized aluminum tubes, stainless steel tension cable. Compatible with all present day underwater photography systems. Head fits Sub Sea 50, 150 and 225 strobes and custom arms can be special ordered for other lighting systems (no extra charge).

D 2115. Red. Length: 27″. Hydro Photo.

CAMERA BASE PLATE

Secure, versatile attachment. Holds camera in line without interfering with controls or frame counter. Also holds E.O. connector or Nikonos flash unit or Hydro Photo Cobra flash arm.

D 2116. Hydro Photo.

PHOTO FRAMER

Slips over Nikonos lens barrel, showing exact angle of lens coverage underwater. Works with distance wands to frame subject, then determine close-up lens focus. Available for Nikonos 35mm and 28mm lenses.

D 2117. Hydro Photo.

IKELITE MODULAR MOVIE LIGHT

Provides 3400°K cinema lighting coverage for a standard lens for about 12 minutes of filming before recharging or changing the ni-cad battery modules. Two or more lights can be used together.

D 2118. Black. Ikelite Underwater Systems.

TRIMCASE

Designed specifically for Kodak Pocket 10, 20, 30, 40, 50, 60; Trimlite 18, 28, 38, 48; Tele-Instamatic 608 and 708; plus Minolta 50, 60, 70, 200, 250, 270; and Canon 11OED. Foolproof sealing to 300 feet. Single control operates shutter release and film advance. Includes handle and underwater flash unit.

D 2119. Clear. Ikelite Underwater Systems.

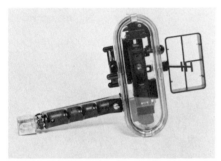

KODAK INSTAMATIC HOUSINGS

¾" plexiglass covers with stainless steel lid snaps, tested to 350 feet. Complete with handle assembly and power packs or connectors for addition of optional flash ur. Designed for Kodak models 104-124-134-304, 154-174-404-, X-45, 704-714, 804-814, X-90.

D 2120. Clear. Ikelite Underwater Systems.

35MM RANGEFINDER HOUSINGS

Automatic exposure control, removable handle assembly, battery pack and bulkhead for Ikelite SST flash system. Shutter release, film advance, focus, aperture, and/or shutter speed controls are included on housings for specific 35mm cameras.

D 2121. Clear. Ikelite Underwater Systems.

SLR CASES

Speed handle places shutter release and film advance controls at fingertips, facilitates horizontal and vertical photographs. Gear drive focus control for all lenses. Interchangeable port system. Controls for film advance, shutter release, shutter speed, and meter switch where applicable. Wired to work with Ikelite SST flash system. Models to fit most standard SLR cameras.

D 2122. Clear. Ikelite Underwater Systems.

2¼ SQUARE HOUSINGS

Specially built for individual camera models. Removable handle assembly, all controls, SST flash system. Removable magnifying viewer where applicable. Optional interchangeable fronts to fit various size lenses. Safe to 300 feet. Shown: housing for Hasselblad 500C, 500CM.

D 2123. Clear. Ikelite Underwater Systems.

POLAROID SX-70 CASE

Fits all folding SX-70 model cameras. Allows entire roll of film to be used as prints drop into special compartment. Shutter release, lighten/darken, and focus controls.

D 2124. Clear. Ikelite Underwater Systems.

IKELITE REFLECTOR FLASH

Satin anodized finish for evenly balanced lighting. Socket accepts all standard bulbs. Flash arm mounts on all Ikelite handle assemblies. Coil cord allows for hand held use underwater. Non-corrosive all metal construction.

D 2125. Metallic. Ikelite Underwater Systems.

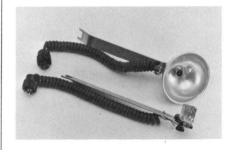

IKELITE HAND FLASH

Accepts flash cubes. Mounts on Ikelite handle assemblies, easily removed for hand holding. Coiled cord allows flexibility in positioning. Works with all Ikelite housings incorporating the SST system plus the Nikonos Power Pack.

D 2126. Black. Ikelite Underwater Systems.

SST STROBE SYSTEM

Solid state triggering device, for assured firing, incorporated in p.c. cord or in hot shoe design. Powered by 22½ volt battery/capacitor. Designed to withstand depths to 300 feet. Quick-release lid snap, room for filters or wide-angle diffuser, off/on control, waterproof cord which may be plugged or unplugged below surface.

D 2127. Clear. Ikelite Underwater Systems.

IKELITE NIKONOS POWER PACK

Incorporates selector switch for X and M sync plus 22½ volt battery. In X sync it fires strobes in Ikelite electronic flash housings; in M sync it fires bulb, cube, or hand flashes.

D 2128. Black. Ikelite Underwater Systems.

SPORTSFINDER

Allows accurate aiming and fast framing. Clips onto lid snap of all Ikelite housings and adapts to Nikonos camera. Front sight and framer fold down when not in use. Dimensionally correct for 35mm format, with square format markings.

D 2129. Black. Ikelite Underwater Systems.

OPTICAL VIEWFINDER

Sees more than eye can see comfortably. Functions like 15mm camera lens, with series of lenses. Includes assortment of framer masks to indicate picture area taken by camera with 28, 35, 50 and square 126/movie lenses. Complete with mounting provisions for all Ikelite housings and Nikonos cameras.

D 2130. Ikelite Underwater Systems.

MOVIE HOUSINGS

Plexiglass cases for Super 8 cameras by Kodak (shown: Kodak XL), Canon, Bolex, Eumig, Minolta, and 16mm cameras by Bolex, Canon, and Beaulieu. Custom installations also available.

D 2131. Clear. Ikelite Underwater Systems.

NIKONOS HANDLE UNITS

Large contour handle for easy grasping, long tray for attaching strobes and meters. Shutter release/film advance activated with thumb while holding handle. Molded of unbreakable plastic. Models to fit Nikonos 1, 2, and 3.

D 2132. Metallic and black. Ikelite Underwater Systems.

IDI ACL-4 UNDERWATER HOUSING

Cast aluminum housing for 16 mm 400 ft. film capacity Eclair ACL movie camera. Reflex viewing through standard camera reflex system, accessory viewfinder. Pressure tested to 200 feet. Viewable footage counter. Accessory mounting plate for meters, lights, etc. Total weight 39 lbs. including loaded camera and battery.

D 2133. Image Devices, Inc.

OCEANIC 2000 STROBE

Corrected front port. Recycling time of 6 seconds. Powered by two "C" alkaline batteries, produces up to 300 flashes between battery changes. Topside guide number of 35 with ASA 25 film. Available with choice of connectors.

D 2134. Size: 5" long by 2⅞" diameter. Oceanic/Farallon.

OCEANIC 2001 STROBE

Topside guide number of 55 with ASA 25 film, 6-second recycling time. Nicad batteries provide 360 flashes after four hour charge. Ready light, coiled connector cord.

D 2135. Oceanic/Farallon.

OCEANIC 2003 STROBE

Dual-powered. Low power setting provides surface guide number of 40, 4-second recycle time, up to 430 flashes. High power setting gives guide number of 65, 6.5-second recycle time, approximately 280 flashes per charge. Off-low-high switch, ready light, coiled connecting cord.

D 2136. Oceanic/Farallon.

PRO MOVIE LIGHT 100

Suited for 8mm and 16mm cameras. Cycolac shell. Interchangeable battery packs can be charged in or out of the housing. Nicad "F" batteries provide constant voltage over complete discharge time. Charges in 16 hours, provides 24 minutes of burning time.

D 2137. Oceanic/Farallon.

PRO MOVIE LIGHT 200

Cycolac shell. Battery pack of "D" size GE "goldtop" cells which reach full charge in 5 hours and burn for 12-14 minutes. Batteries may be charged in or out of housing.

D 2138. Oceanic/Farallon.

MINIFLASH

Compact strobe for close-up underwater photography. Includes coiled sync cord, camera mounting bracket, batteries. Guide number approx. 25 with ASA 64 film. Approximately 200 flashes with alkaline batteries, 6-10 seconds recycle time. Depth limit: 130 feet. Three models available.

D 2139. Clear. Nash Industries.

NIKONOS III

35mm underwater and all-weather sealed dual-body camera with interchangeable lenses. Single lever advances film and cocks, then releases shutter. Two knurled knobs control focus and aperture settings. All joints and lens socket O-ring sealed, operable to 160 feet.

D 2140. Black. Nikonos.

NIKKOR 15MM LENS

Exclusively for underwater use. Requires accessory optical viewfinder. Aperture range f2.8 - f22, angle of view 94°, minimum focus from film plane 12", filter size 84mm.

D 2141. Nikonos.

NIKKOR 35MM IC LENS

For use in and out of water. Underwater requires accessory frame finder. Aperture range f2.5 - f22; angle of view 46°30' underwater, 62° out of water; minimum focus from film plane 31.5"; filter size 52mm.

2142. Nikonos.

NIKKOR 80MM IC LENS

For use in or out of water. Underwater requires accessory frame finder. Aperture range f4.0 - f.22; angle of view 22° underwater, 30°20' out of water; minimum focus from film plane 39.4"; filter size 52mm.

D 2143. Nikonos.

UNDERWATER FLASH UNIT P

accepts No. 6 or 26 focal-plane flashbulbs or AG-1 bulbs with accessory adapter. Vinyl-covered sync cord with molded top for Nikonos III flash outlet. Requires regular 22.5V battery. Separate model available for Nikonos II.

D 2144. Metallic and black. Nikonos.

SCREW-IN LENS HOOD/FILTER HOLDER

Shields 28mm, 35mm, or 80mm lenses from extraneous light, required for attaching Nikon 52mm filters to lenses.

D 2145. Black. Nikonos.

PLASTIC LENS PROTECTOR

Screws into Nikkor 28mm f3.5, 35mm f2.5, or 80mm f4 lens for added safety and protection.

D 2146. Black. Nikonos.

CLOSE-UP OUTFIT

Coated auxiliary close-up lens, field frames for 28mm, 35mm, and 80mm lenses, and 3 field frame holders plus flash unit holder. May be used with any Nikonos model. Includes leather case.

D 2147. Metallic and black. Nikonos.

OPTICAL VIEWFINDERS

For Nikkor 15mm f2.8 lens (shown) and 80mm f4 lens. Includes mounting bracket.

D 2148. Black. Nikonos.

HIPPIE FOUR

Kodak Instamatic camera and Vivitar strobe in plastic housing with wrist lanyard. Camera and flash may be removed from housing for use on land. Camera has automatic frame counter and drop-in loading. Strobe gives hundreds of shots on two AA cells (not supplied).

D 2149. Sea Research/Bosco.

S'EASY GRIP

Cast aluminum tray and grip for Nikonos I and II. Grips camera with no special connector. Hand contoured grip, threaded tripod bushing. Drilled for most accessory flash or strobe arms.

D 2150. Black. Sea Research/Bosco.

SLIP ON

Close up adapter for Nikonos lenses with spring mounted probe. Achromat lens for full color saturation.

D 2151. Sea Research/Bosco.

CUSTOM 35MM SLR HOUSINGS

Housings for ½" optical grade plexiglass tested to 175 feet with full controls for all camera functions. All hardware of stainless steel. Sea Link male connector installed with internal PC cord for strobe or flash hookup. Choice of flat or water corrected domed lens ports. Grip and accessory shoe for left or right handed operation.

D 2152. Sea Research/Bosco.

CUSTOM SUPER 8 HOUSINGS

Housings of ½" optical grade plexiglass with controls for all camera functions. All stainless steel hardware. Includes spare main closure O-ring, extra lubricant.

D 2153. Sea Research/Bosco.

SEASTROBE 91

Pressureproof to 350 feet. Gives 400+ shots with 4 second recycle time. 5,800° color temperature. Handle and accessory shoe fitting, 3 foot coil cord included. On/off switch.

D 2154. Sea Research/Bosco.

SEA BRUTE

Self-contained underwater light. Three 650 watt 3400° Kelvin quartz halogen lamps deliver approximately 2 kilowatts. Rechargeable nickel cadmium battery. Adjustable buoyancy. 120 VAC charger recharges in 12 hours. One lamp burns 60 minutes, two lamps 40, three lamps 20 min.

D 2155. Sea Research/Bosco.

SEA LINK

Modular underwater connector for flash, strobe, flood, or sound. AC, DC or pulse. Installation time 5 minutes. Uses standard ¼" OD cable. Tested to over 1,000 feet. Can be adapted to Nikonos camera.

D 2156. Sea Research/Bosco.

SR 2000 STROBE

Smallest submersible strobe available. Surface guide number of 40 with 70° u/w beam angle. Three-second recycle interval with fresh charge. Nicad batteries yield approximately 150 flashes. Batteries recharge in 5 hours.

D 2157. Sonic Research.

SR 2000 SYSTEM KITS

Complete lighting packages for beginning or professional Nikonos photographer. Beginner model includes SR 2000 Sync with connector and ball joint, 3-D photo arm, mounting bracket and thumb release, warm-up filter, photo case. Professional system adds SR 2000 Slave with ball joint Nikonos bracket, second 3-D photo arm, tandem plate, neutral density filter.

D 2158. Sonic Research.

THE HELPING HAND

Stainless steel attachment to mount hand light to top or side of strobe. Fastens by hand with wing nut. Varios sizes to match up with most common strobe or movie lights and hand lights.

D 2159. World Below.

KRAMER FRAMERS

Stainless steel framing aids adjust underwater. Model 100 for use with Micro Lens III adjustable for surface or underwater settings. Model 200 for use with Hydro Photo #1 or #2 lens can be turned upside down when not taking closeup shots.

D 2160. Metallic. World Below.

Protective Outerwear

ZIPPER KNEE BOOTS

¼" neoprene with two-sided nylon. Available in standard or kneelength sizes. Zippers.

D 2161. Sizes: 4-6, 6½-7½, 8-9, 9½-11, 11½-12½. Henderson Aquatics.

HARD SOLE ZIPPER BOOTS

¼" neoprene with two-sided nylon, zippers. Sewn seams, non-skid soles.

D 2163. Sizes: 4-6, 6½-7½, 8-9, 9½-11, 11½-12½. Henderson Aquatics.

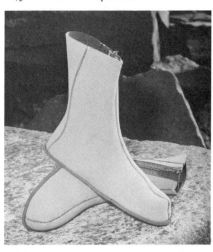

KNEE SOCKS

⅛", ", or ¼" neoprene with two-sided nylon. Extend to calf to protect lower leg and suit.

D 2162. Blue, black, or orange. Sizes: 4-6, 6½-7½, 8-9, 9½-11, 11½-12½. Henderson Aquatics.

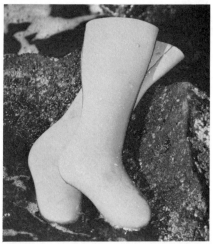

HARD-SOLE, NON—SKID DIVING BOOTS

⅛", 3/16", ¼", ⅜" neoprene with choice of two-sided nylon, or smooth or textured exterior. Non-skid foam insulating sole, dual seams on both sides of heel for strength.

D 2164. Black. Sizes: 4-6, 6½-7½, 8-9, 9½-11, 11½-12½. Henderson Aquatics.

111

ALL-PURPOSE 5-FINGER GLOVES

⅛", 3/16", ¼", or ⅜" neoprene with two-sided nylon, extra long sleeves, sewn seams.

D 2165. Black. Sizes: up to 7, 7-7½, 8-8½, 9-9½, over 9½. Henderson Aquatics.

DIVING MITTS

⅛", 3/16", ¼", or ⅜" neoprene with choice of smooth or textured exterior or two-sided nylon. Fully sewn seams.

D 2166. Sizes: up to 7, 7-7½, 8-8½, 9-9½, over 9½. Henderson Aquatics.

COLD WATER DIVING HOOD

3/16", ¼", or ⅜" neoprene with nylon lining, choice of smooth, textured or nylon-lined exterior. Extra wide bib, fully sewn seams.

D 2167. Sizes: under 6½, 6½-6¾, 6⅞-7⅛, 7¼-7½, over 7½. Henderson Aquatics.

STANDARD HOOD

⅛", 3/16", ¼", ⅜" neoprene with nylon inside, choice of smooth, textured, or nylon-lined exterior. Conforms to head contours.

D 2168. Sizes: under 6½, 6½-6¾, 6⅞-7⅛, 7¼-7½, over 7½. Henderson Aquatics.

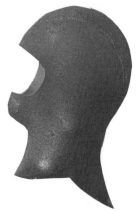

SEAL HOOD

¼" neoprene nylon lined. Special face seal designed specifically for use with O'Neill Seal Jacket or SuperSuit. Tapered neck, taped seams.

D 2169. O'Neill.

OTTER PAW

3/16" nylon lined neoprene mitten designed to seal on wrists of O'Neill suits. All seams bonded with tape.

D 2170. O'Neill.

COLOR WET SUIT SHORTIES

One-piece with short sleeves and pants. ⅛" neoprene lined with nylon outside or both sides (optional). One zipper. Men's and women's models.

D 2172. Black or blue. Parkway Fabricators.

PARKWAYS TUNICS

Zipper-front jacket with short sleeves, collar, swivel locks for crotch straps. ⅛" neoprene with nylon on outside or two sides (optional). Men's and women's models.

D 2173. Black or blue. Parkway Fabricators.

PARKWAYS HOODED WET SUIT SHIRT

⅛" neoprene with nylon lining inside (reversable). Generous arm and neck cut-outs to reduce chafing.

D 2174. Black. Parkway Fabricators.

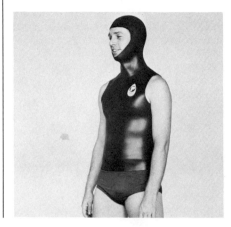

GAUNTLET GLOVE

Flexible five finger glove with gauntlet-style wrist. Nylon lined inside and out.

D 2175. Black. Sizes: XS to XL. Scubapro.

MOLDED SOLE BOOTS

Wrap-around sole with anti-slip tread. Double nylon backed 3/16" or 1/4" neoprene.

D 2176. Black and blue. Sizes: 6 through 13. Scubapro.

CONTOUR SOLE BOOTS

Molded rubber soles. Available in 3/16" or 1/4" neoprene with textured finish or nylon inside and out.

D 2177. Black. Sizes: XS, S, M, L, XL, XXL. U.S. Divers Company.

HARD SOLE BOOTS

Long wearing soles provide foot protection. Available in 3/16" textured neoprene or 1/4" with nylon lining inside and out.

D 2178. Black. Sizes: XS, S, M, L, XL, XXL. U.S. Divers Company.

SOFT SOLE BOOTIES

3/16" textured neoprene.

D 2179. Black. Sizes: XS, S, M, L, XL. U.S. Divers Company.

COLD WATER HOOD

Large skirt provides extra protection for neck, chest, and back. Available in textured 3/16" or 1/4" neoprene or 1/4" with nylon lining on both sides.

D 2180. Black. Sizes: S, M, L. U.S. Divers Company.

DIVERS HOOD

Available in 3/16" or 1/4" textured neoprene or 1/4" with nylon lining inside and out.

D 2181. Black with optional blue trim. Sizes: S, M, L. U.S. Divers Company.

GLUV MITTS

Separate thumb, index finger. 3/16" textured neoprene.

D 2182. Black. Sizes: XS, S, M, L. U.S. Divers Company.

FIVE FINGER GLOVES

Available in 3/16" neoprene, textured or with nylon lining inside and out.

D 2183. Black (textured) or blue (lined). Sizes: XS, SM, L, XL. U.S. Divers Company.

Salvage Aids

200 LB. TREASURE BAG

Push button bleed valve for buoyancy trim. Can be used for light salvage work, underwater construction. Brass snap bolt, nylon straps. Made of 10 oz. vinyl coated nylon fabric with stiff sewn collar.

D 2184. Yellow. Size: 40" x 28". Carter Bag Company.

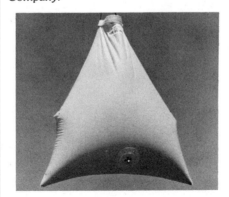

100 LB. TREASURE BAG

Compact when deflated. Can lift anchors, outboard motors, propellors, etc. Also doubles as marker-buoy, game bag, watertight surface container. Nylon straps, solid brass snap hook, easy to grab corners. Includes repair kit.

D 2185. Yellow. Size: 28" x 25". Carter Bag Company.

500 LB. TREASURE BAG

Constructed of 13 oz. vinyl coated polyester. Nylon lifting strap, galvanized steel snap hook. Screw type buoyancy trim valve. Small mouth prevents bag from turning over and dumping air on surface.

D 2186. Size: 56" x 26". Carter Bag Company.

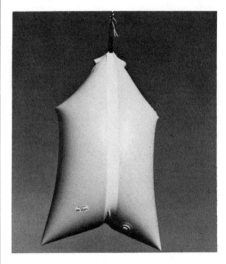

1500 LB. BOULDER BAG

Originally developed for moving boulders in shallow river gold dredging operations. Displaces less than 3 feet of water. Overpressure valve, attached inflation hose, screw-type purge valve. Constructed of vinyl coated nylon fabric. Purchase point at bottom of bag is stainless steel u-bolt.

D 2187. Size: 30" x 54" x 54". Carter Bag Company.

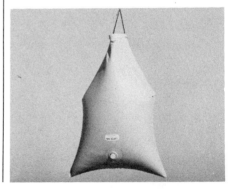

AQUA PRO TREASURE RAY

Underwater metal detector. In open air, will detect a large object from 6 feet, a penny from 11 inches. 200-foot service depth, slightly negative buoyancy. Visual and aural signaling modes. Acrylic barrel and headphone, filled polyester search head. Powered by ten size AA penlite cells, average battery life 50 hours. Operating temperature 0° - 120° F.

D 2188. White with red handle. J.K. Gilbert Co.

MARK I UNDERWATER METAL DETECTOR

Completely transistorized, with equal sensitivity in fresh or salt water. Will sense a penny at 4", larger objects at 3'. Detects all metals. 200-foot operating depth, slight negative buoyancy. Powered by standard 9 volt battery, weighs 4 pounds.

D 2189. Yellow and black. J.W. Fishers Mfg. Company.

MARK 3 UNDERWATER METAL DETECTOR

25% greater detection area than Mark 1. Senses a penny at 4", larger objects at 3'. 1MA meter indicates presence of metal. 5 lbs. Powered by heavy duty 9 volt battery.

D 2190. Yellow and black. J.W. Fishers Mg. Company.

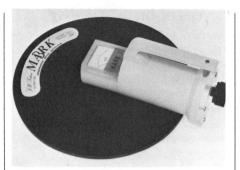

MARK 5 UNDERWATER METAL DETECTOR

Presense of metal is noted on 1MA meter and by audio frequency shift in special underwater earphone. 18" coil provides for maximimum penetration and large search area. Senses a penny at 4½", larger objects at 5½". Powered by large, surplus power 9 volt battery. Weighs 7 lbs.

D 2191. Yellow and black. J.W. Fishers Mfg. Company.

MARK 7 UNDERWATER METAL DETECTOR

Designed to be towed from boat, to locate large masses of metal. Search coil and control box interconnected by 150' cable. Sensitive up to 8½'. Powered by long lasting 9 volt battery, weighs 16 lbs.

D 2192. Black and yellow. J.W. Fishers Mfg. Company.

SPORTSMAN LIFT BAGS

High tensity neoprene impregnated nylon, .055" thick, with brass dump valve, two attachment eyes. Bottom of bag opens for easy filling and venting. Model 100 has lift capacity of 112 lbs., Model 200 has capacity of 210 lbs.

D 2193. Black. Sizes: 100 = 30" x 6" x 25"; 200 = 34" x 7" x 31". Subsalve Industries.

U.S. DIVER'S LIFT BAG

Vinyl impregnated nylon with buoyancy trim valve to control ascent. 2" criss-crossing nylon webbing.

D 2194. Yellow and black. Sizes: 100 lb., 200 lb., or 300 lb. lift capacity. U.S. Divers Company.

TREASUREMASTER AMPHIBIAN

Underwater metal detector powered by single 9-volt penlight battery. One control knob turns instrument on and adjusts it. Can detect a dime at 4", quarter at 5". Includes waterproof headphones.

D 2195. Length: 4". White's Electronics, Inc.

Scuba Attachments

SCUBA FRENCH CONNECTION

Adapter to fit U.S. regulators to foreign tanks.

D 2196. Andreassen Enterprises.

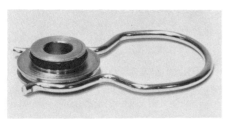

DACOR PONY TANK

Provides extra reserve (14 cut. ft. of air at 2015 p.s.i.). Aluminum casing 4⅜″ diameter by 19¼″ length (including valve).

D 2197. Grey. Dacor Corporation.

HOSE CLAMP RETAINER

Adjustable plastic strap holds rubber hose clamp for submersible gauge or regulator hose. Fits tanks up to 7.25″ diameter.

D 2198. Black. Dacor Corporation.

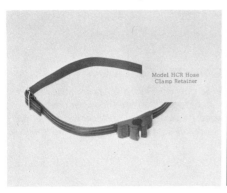

HYDRO CAP I

Guards against fouling or damaging regulator first stage and tank valve. Made of C.L. plastic to fit various size tanks.

D 2199. Blue, yellow, or orange. Hydro-Fairing.

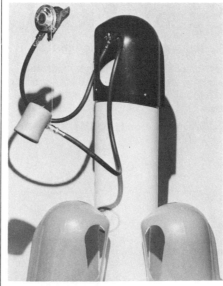

HYDRO FAIRING I

Consolidates loose equipment into one unit. Streamlines and protects rear b.c.s from puncture or fouling. Built-in tank boot, installs in seconds. Constructed of C.L. plastic.

D 2200. Blue, yellow, orange, or clear. Hydro-Fairing.

MANHANDLERS

Tank carrying handles — permanent type for bolt-fastened tank bands or detachable type for quick release bands. Handle is permanently molded over heavy steel insert. Especially helpful with back-mounted buoyancy devices.

D 2201. Blue or black. Pennform Plastic Products, Inc.

SCUBAPRO "OCTOPUS" VERSATILE

Variable breathing effort can help prevent unwanted free-flow. Large exhaust valve for easy clearing.

D 2202. Metallic and black with orange mouthpiece and exhaust tee. Scubapro.

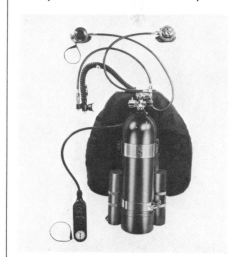

BUDDY CONNECTOR

Positive latch air flow fitting attaches between second stage regulator and air hose of one-hose regulator. Can be released to attach regulator to buddy's extra hose and fitting without removing regulator from mouth.

D 2203. Metallic. Sound Wave Systems, Inc.

TEKNA OCTOPUS

Pilot-operated second stage with only five moving parts. Designed for right or left-handed use. Weighs only 9 oz.

D 2204. Tekna.

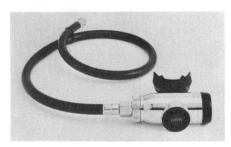

WABA

Hot water-powered heat conductor attaches between scuba tank and face mask or mouthpiece. Provides air temperatures above 80°F for two hours or more. prevents loss of body core temperature, allows longer, deeper dives in cold water and shorter waiting periods between dives. Operates to depths of 100 feet, breathing rate of 30 breaths/minute, 2 liters/breath.

D 2205. Yellow. Underseas Environmentals, Inc.

SIRIUS OCTOPUS HOOK-UP

Sirius second stage with 32" hose which threads into any regulator's low-pressure port.

D 2206. Metallic, orange, black. U.S. Nemrod, Inc.

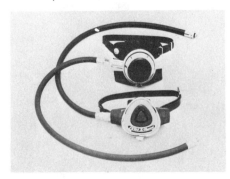

DELTA II OCTOPUS HOOK-UP

Delta II second stage with 32" hose which threads into any regulator's low-pressure port.

D 2207. Metallic and black. U.S. Nemrod, Inc.

Spears & Guns

SWIMASTER MAGNUM 450

Heavy-walled, tempered and anodized aluminum barrel resists barrel bow. Slings shaft, and spear set in straight line. Three slings.

D 2208. Metallic and black. Overall length: 75". AMF Voit.

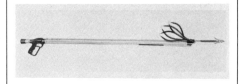

SWIMASTER MAGNUM SPEAR-FISHING GUN

Aluminum barrel, stainless steel shaft and fittings. Three slings. Double barbed spear-head.

D 2209. Metallic and black. Overall length: 62". AMF Voit.

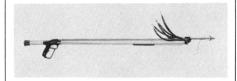

SWIMASTER SAWED-OFF MAGNUM

Compact. Two slings. Shaft has extra notch for conversion to three slings. Cocking butt. Double barbed spearhead.

D 2210. Metallic and black. Overall length: 53". AMF Voit.

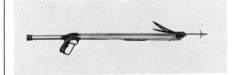

SWIMASTER CUSTOM GUN

Two slings. Short cocking butt. Single barbed spearhead.

D 2211. Metallic and black. Overall length: 30". AMF Voit.

SUPER CARBINE SPEAR GUN

Designed for fast-swimming fish, extra penetration. Fringe trigger, muzzle, slide ring and shaft all on one plane for accuracy. Two slings.

D 2212. Metallic and black. Size: 26" barrel. AMF Voit.

CARBINE SPEAR GUN

Single sling. Designed for working in dense vegetation and coral. Anodized aluminum barrel, single barb head.

D 2213. Metallic and black. Size: 17" barrel. AMF Voit.

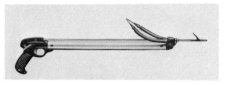

G48 POLE SPEAR

Anodized, tempered aluminum tubing with stainless steel and chromeplated brass fittings. Adjustable sling length, trident spear-head.

D 2214. Red. Overall length: 48". AMF Voit.

POLE SPEARS

Tapered aluminum tubing with anodized aluminum finish. Fittings of stainless steel or chrome-plated brass. Extensions available, spearheads available but not included.

D 2215. Black. Sizes: 48" or 66" overall. AMF Voit.

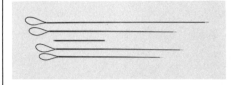

GARY BLACK WIDOW

Pole gun with internal shock-absorbing mechanism. Rubber sling, double-barbed spearhead. Constructed of aircraft grade anodized seamless aluminum and stainless steel.

D 2216. Sizes: 76" or 54". Belcher Industries, Inc.

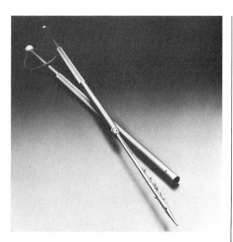

GARY SUPERSHAFT

Hawaiian sling-style gun. Hexagonal heat-treated stainless steel shaft produces less friction and drag in exit from housing. Single rubber sling, single-barbed spearhead.

D 2217. Length: 5′ or 4′. Belcher Industries, Inc.

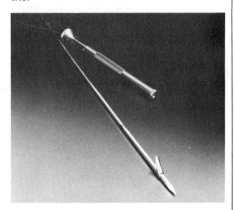

GARY SUPERSLING

Hawaiian sling-style gun constructed of aircraft-grade metals. Weighs only 4.5 oz. Barrel is 10″ for accuracy. Single rubber sling, single-barbed spearhead.

D 2218. Belcher Industries, Inc.

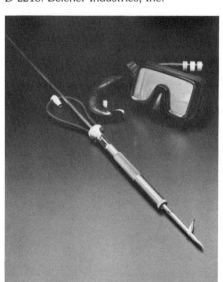

GARY BANGSTICK III

Air-filled barrel permits full ignition of powder for maximum gas production and bullet velocity. Permits rapid repetitive firing through interchangeable preloaded barrels. Sealed barrel prevents misfires due to wet powder.

D 2219. Belcher Industries, Inc.

GARY BANGSTICK II

.357 magnum or .38 caliber load in 6-inch air-filled barrel. Instantly interchangeable pre-load barrel allows rapid repeating. Weighs only 20 oz. O-ring sealed barrel prevents misfires due to wet powder. Comes with vinyl carrying case.

D 2220. Length: 4′. Belcher Industries, Inc.

GARY BANGSTICK I

.357 magnum or .38 caliber load, 6-inch air-filled barrel. Instantly interchangeable pre-loaded O-ring sealed barrels for rapid repeating. Weighs 17 oz. Comes with adjustable back-pack mounting bracket. inertial firing pin and safety pin prevent accidental discharge.

D 2221. Length: 26″. Belcher Industries, Inc.

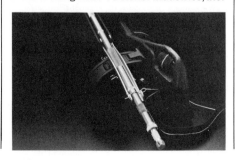

SINGRAY® SPEARGUNS

Arbalete style. Cadmium plated steel shafts from 24″ to 47″ overall length. Separated, wrap-around elastics (3 on 47″ model, 2 on others). Straight back trigger pull, thumb control safety, automatic line release.

D 2222. Dacor Corporation.

COMPETITION CUSTOM

36″ long, 5/16″ diameter stainless steel shaft with two notches. Two black latex rubber slings. 9½′ of floating polypropylene line. Double barb spearhead. Contoured, center balanced hand grip with pistol grip butt. Quick release rear seal mechanism. Die-cast aluminum handle, butt and muzzle with epoxy coating.

D 2223. Black. Healthways.

COMPETITION COMPACT

24″ long, 5/16″ diameter shaft with two notches. Two black latex rubber slings. 6 1/3′ of floating polypropylene line. Single barb spearhead.

D 2224. Black. Healthways.

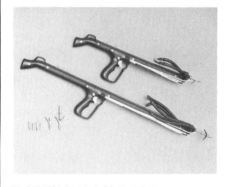

SPORTSMAN COMPACT

Double notch, 25½″ long, 5/16″ diameter shaft. Cadmium plated steel shaft, aluminum barrel, rear hand grip. One piece latex rubber sling. Push button, thumb operated safety, molded in line release. Braided nylon line.

D 2225. Black and metallic gray. Healthways.

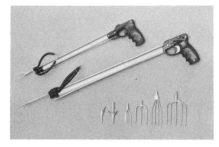

117

HEAVY DUTY SPEARGUN

⅜" shaft for long game, quick-reload open muzzle, extra strength grooved barrel to eliminate shaft whip. safety lever blocks sight line when engaged. Long cocking-butt aids elbow-locked aiming. Gun floats without shaft. Slings and spearhead no included.

D 2227. Metallic and black. Scubapro.

BANTAM SPEARGUN

For quick shooting of small game in restricted areas. Comes with single sling and Trident Spearhead. Floats without shaft. Thumb-operated safety.

D 2228. Metallic and black. Scubapro.

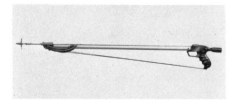

LIGHTWEIGHT SPEARGUN

Spearshaft groove in barrel adds strength and eliminates shaft whip. Thumb-operated safety. Floats without shaft. Equipped with two-barbed spearhead and power sling.

D 2229. Metallic and black. Scubapro.

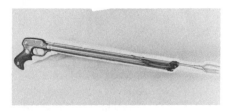

TIBURON III

Buoyancy chamber in barrel for stability and balance. Two sets of rubbers.

D 2230. Metallic and black. Size: 3'5". U.S. Nemrod, Inc.

TIBURON I

Grip set well back on barrel. Single-barb head. Comes with one set of rubbers.

D 2232. Metallic and black. Size: 2'1". U.S. Nemrod, Inc.

TIBURON II

Shoulder support for accuracy. Two sets of rubbers.

D 2231. Metallic and black. Size: 2'6". U.S. Nemrod, Inc.

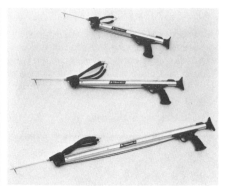

FALCON CORTO

Positive safety trigger lock. Single rubber.

D 2233. Blue and black. Size: 25½". U.S. Nemrod, Inc.

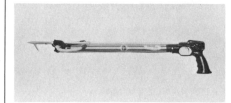

FALCON MINI

For use around rocks or jetties. Single rubber, positive safety.

D 2234. Blue and black. Size: 18½". U.S. Nemrod, Inc.

LINE REEL

For fast return. Comes with 50' of nylon line.

D 2235. Blue and black. U.S. Nemrod, Inc.

MARINER 2

Pneumatic (piston-driven). Three-position power selector. Lightweight. No bubbles or currents when fired. Range: 15 to 25'.

D 2236. Blue and black. Size: 36". U.S. Nemrod, Inc.

CLIPPER HUNTER SPECIAL

Piston-powered pneumatic. Gun, spear and knife combined in lightweight leg holster.

D 2237. Red grip, metallic barrel, black holster. U.S. Nemrod, Inc.

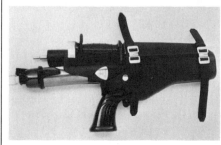

CLIPPER I

Piston-powered pneumatic with one-time charging feature. Reinforced muzzle. Weighs 3½ lbs.

D 2238. Metallic and red. Size: 27". U.S. Nemrod, Inc.

CLIPPER II

Piston-powered pneumatic. One-time charging feature. Stainless steel harpoon.

D 2239. Metallic and red. Size: 36". U.S. Nemrod, Inc.

CLIPPER III

Piston-powered pneumatic, with one-time charging feature.

D 2240. Red grip, metallic barrel. Size: 48". U.S. Nemrod, Inc.

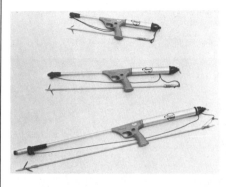

MINI CLIPPER

Piston-powered pneumatic with 15' range Weighs 3 lbs.

D 2241. Metallic and red. Size: 18½". U.S. Nemrod, Inc.

Publications

From the lyric memoirs of Guy Gilpatric, Hans Haas, Jacques Cousteau and other early divers, a rich literature has grown up around the sport of diving. This chapter lists the most popular sport diving books and periodicals in print.

Technological advances can make yesterday's books, like yesterday's equipment, obsolete. Some older books are fascinating for their historical perspective, but they may present as fact some outmoded theories. If you're planning to use any book as a how-to reference, check the date of the copyright and any subsequent revisions. Don't depend on the technical information in any book or magazine more than three years old without checking it against a more recent source.

If a book is meant to be a carry-along reference, its durability is of added importance. Some modern fish guides and other reference books are printed on waterproof stock, so they can be used on an open boat, or even underwater.

Dive shops and book stores rarely carry more than a few of the books described here, and a number of the periodicals we list are not available on newstands. In most cases the books or periodicals must be ordered directly from the publishers, special ordered by your local book store or they may be ordered through The Great Outdoors Trading Company, 24759 Shoreline Highway, Marshall, CA 94940. For price information, please see the notice opposite the inside front cover of this book.

Books

How-To

SAFE SCUBA

Student textbook for the National Association of Scuba Diving Schools. Chapters include an introduction to the underwater experience, skin and scuba diving techniques, environmental protection, bouyancy control, air management, open water buddy team techniques, physiological effects of pressure, safe diving tables, techniques of diving planning and a section on marine life. Color and black and white photos and illustrations. By Richard Hammes and Anthony G. Zimos.

D 3120. Softcover. 8½" x 11". 264 pages. ©1978. Published by NASDS.

BASIC SCUBA

Operation, maintenance and use of scuba and other dive gear. Chapters on diving dynamics, diving maladies, learning to use scuba, self-rescue and water safety, cold water survival, special diving problems, and spearfishing and photography. Hundreds of black and white photos and drawings. By Fred M. Roberts.

D 3018. Soft cover. 6" x 9". 488 pages. ©1963 (second edition). Published by Van Nostrand Reinhold Company.

FELL'S TEEN-AGE GUIDE TO SKIN AND SCUBA DIVING

Step-by-step instructions for teen-agers and their coaches. Traces the development of diving skills and equipment, surveys contemporary gear, explains safety measures and provides methods for coping with underwater emergencies. Black and white

photos and drawings. By George Sullivan.

D 3009. Hard cover. 5¾" x 8½". 99 pages. ©1965 (Revised 1975). Published by Frederick Fell, Inc.

SKIN & SCUBA DIVER'S DIGEST

Fundamentals, techniques and equipment for novice and expert divers. Covers diving physics, technology, water safety, underwater communication, photography, marine life, spearfishing, treasure hunting, search and salvage procedure, history, products, schools, and travel adventures. Hundreds of black and white photos and drawings. By Robert R. Springer.

D 3008. Softcover. 8½" x 11". 288 pages. ©1965. Published by DBI Books.

SCUBA DIVING & SNORKELING

Basic children's introduction to sport diving, with large type, color and black and white photos. Covers typical diving activities, equipment, undersea life, diving careers. By Peter B. Mohn.

D 3017. Hardcover. 7¾" x 9¼". 31 pages. ©1975. Published by Crestwood House, Inc.

SPORT DIVING THE INSTRUCTIONAL GUIDE TO SKIN & SCUBA

How to use and perfect your knowledge, equipment, and technique, to explore the underwater world. Covers wreck diving, treasure hunting, archeological search, photography, night and cave diving. Includes a step-by-step guide through the basics, with procedures from major diving instructor organizations. Hundreds of black and white photos and drawings. By Mort Walker.

D 3007. Softcover. 5¾" x 9". 315 pages. ©1977. Published by Henry Regnery Company.

THE COMPLETE UNDERWATER DIVING MANUAL

Designed especially for the scientist-diver. Covers physiology and first aid, equipment and breathing media, how to perform biological surveys, how to conduct search and recovery operations, underwater photography, saturation diving, decompression. Hundreds of black and white charts, photos and drawings. Compiled by National Oceanic and Atmospheric Administration and Office of Marine Resources.

D 3019. Softcover. 6¾" x 9¾". 370 pages. ©1977. Published by David McKay Company, Inc.

THE COMPLETE BEGINNER'S DIVE TO SKIN DIVING

Instruction in techniques and safety rules for breathhold diving. Covers equipment, underwater exploration, photography, spearfishing, underwater games, diving hobbies, and career opportunities. Written for youngsters. Black and white photos and sketches. By Shaney Frey.

D 3010 Hardcover. 6¼" x 9½". 116 pages. ©1965. Published by Doubleday & Company, Inc.

SPORT DIVER MANUAL

Part of a multi-media training program, the manual covers equipment, diving physiology, the underwater environment, and diving techniques. Sold in conjunction with kits which include workbook, record folder, and an optional audio-visual course. Color and black and white photos, other illustrations. Prepared by Jeppeson Sanderson, Inc.

D 3020. Softcover. 6" x 9". 280 pages. ©1976. Published by Jeppeson Sanderson, Inc.

DIVE! DIVE! DIVE!

Sport diver's guide, including chapters on buying equipment, underwater photography, wreck hunting, underwater archeology, marine biology, and diving around the world. Black and white photos and drawings. By David Hodgson.

D 3006. Hardcover. 5½" x 8⅞". 176 pages. ©1975. Distributed in U.S. by Transatlantic Arts, Inc.

THE NEW SCIENCE OF SKIN AND SCUBA DIVING

Comprehensive diving text. Chapters include basic requirements for skin and scuba diving, diving physics, diving medi-cine, fundamentals of compressed gases, basic equipment, skills, first aid for diving accidents, underwater environment, and planning a dive. Hundreds of line drawings and tables. Prepared by the Council for National Cooperation in Aquatics.

D 3021. Softcover. 6½" x 10". 288 pages. ©1974 (Revised edition 1975). Published by Association Press.

THE SKIN DIVER

A comprehensive guide to the underwater world by one of the pioneers of sport diving. Separate chapters on snorkeling, spear-fishing, where to dive, the aqualung, skin diving safety, marine life, exploring sunken ships, photography, and underwater vehicles. Hundreds of black and white photographs and drawings. By Elgin Ciampi.

D 3016. Hardcover. 6" x 9¼". 315 pages. ©1960. Published by the Ronald Press Company.

LET'S GO DIVING

Condensed diving instruction manual. Chapters on diving requirements, basic equipment, techniques, physics, physiology, marine life, and do's and don'ts. Illustrated with two-color drawings. By Bill Barada.

D 3011. Softcover. 5½" x 8½". 101 pages. ©1962 (Revised edition, 1977). Published by U.S. Divers Co.

SCUBA DIVING
HOW TO GET STARTED

Step-by-step pre-course training guide to basic skills, water entries, surface dives, choosing instruction, and selecting equipment. Written as a head start for anyone planning to take a certification course. Over 100 instructional black and white photos. By William Koelzer.

D 3022. Hardbound. 7¼" x 10¼". 120 pages. ©1976. Published by Chilton Book Company.

THIS IS DIVING

Aquatic instruction book for beginners and novices. Teaches skills for a safe scuba dive of over 60 feet. Subjects covered include marine flora and fauna, first aid, chemistry and physics of diving. Over 300 drawings and photographs, all in color. By Duilio Marcante.

D 3005. Hardcover. 7½" x 8". 144 pages. ©1976. Published by Sail Books, Inc.

SPORT DIVING A TO Z

Tips and techniques for advanced or experienced divers. Subjects covered include deep diving procedures, first aid, equipment improvements and maintenance, high alititude diving, night and limited visibility diving, mouth-to-mouth resuscitation, dive planning, search and recovery, and others. Black and white illustrations. By Dennis Graver.

D 3012. Softcover. 6" x 9". 167 pages. ©1976. Distributed by U.S. Divers Co.

PRACTICAL DIVING

Manual for compressed air divers, from basic safety guidelines for students to detailed technical computations for advanced divers and instructors. Over 50 black and white illustrations. By Tom Mount and Akira J. Ikehara.

D 3023. Softcover. 5½" x 8½". 191 pages. ©1975. Published by University of Miami Press.

THE COMPLETE GUIDE TO CAVE DIVING

Includes individual essays on equipment and procedures, the lure of caves, suggested safety rules, cave diving drowning statistics, proper equipment, and the proceedings of a 1968 seminar on the subject. Black and white photos and illustrations.

D 3013. Softcover. 8½" x 11". 47 pages. ©1973. Published by National Association of Underwater Instructors.

DIVING FOR FUN

Textbook for students, instructors, and advanced divers. Written to satisfy requirements of all national certification programs. Chapters on underwater world, physics, physiology, pressure and its effects, underwater safety, and diving skills. Black and white photos and illustrations. By Joe Strykowski.

D 3024. Softcover. 8⅛" x 10¼". 135 pages. ©1974. Published by Dacor Corporation.

UNDERWATER EDUCATION

A training text for institutions of higher learning. Sections include prerequisites for diving (physical and psychological fitness, watermanship, academic training), diving physics and techniques, equipment, oceanography and diving physiology, quizzes, reading assignments and suggested projects after each chapter. Over 100 instructive sketches. Written by Albert A. Tillman.

D 3004. Softcover. 8½" x 11". 149 pages. Fourteenth printing 1973. Published by Wm. C. Brown Company.

SCUBA SAFE AND SIMPLE

A simple text geared to NAUI teaching requirements, designed to give the reader the knowledge of a diver just completing a basic scuba course. The 14 chapters cover skills, lifesaving and first aid techniques, equipment, marine animals, specialty diving, and underwater photography. By John Reseck, Jr.

D 3025. Softcover. 5¾" x 9". 240 pages. ©1975. Published by Prentice-Hall, Inc.

ALTITUDE PROCEDURES FOR THE OCEAN DIVER

Manual for sport divers planning to dive in fresh water lakes, especially at high altitudes. Includes rules for adjusting buoyancy, modifying decompression schedules, correcting depth gauges, plus altitude dive tables. By C. L. Smith.

D 3014. Softcover. 8½" x 10¾". 46 pages. ©1976. Published by National Association of Underwater Instructors.

SCUBA DIVER'S GUIDE TO UNDERWATER VENTURES

Guide to underwater activities for divers with a minimum of 20 hours of underwater experience. Chapters on photography, treasure diving, ice diving, fresh water and ocean fish, live specimen collecting, cave diving, and diving careers. Over 100 black and white photos. By Judy Gail May.

D 3003. Softcover. 5" x 8⅜". 222 pages. ©1973. Published by Stackpole Books.

THE SKIN DIVER'S BIBLE

Basic guide to scuba and snorkel diving, with sections on equipment, physiology, learning techniques, hazards, underwater communications, diving accidents, underwater photography. Over 100 black and white photographs and drawings. By Owen Lee.

D 3026. Softcover. 7¾" x 10⅛". 160 pages. ©1968. Published by Doubleday & Company, Inc.

COLD WEATHER AND UNDER ICE SCUBA DIVING

Discussion of the unique aspects of cold-stress physiology, effects of cold on diving equipment, and under-ice orientation problems. Sections on proper equipment, special techniques, and training tips. Black and white photos. By Lee H. Somers, Ph.D.

D 3015. Softcover. 8½" x 11". 40 pages. ©1973. Published by National Association of Underwater Instructors.

LEGAL ASPECTS OF UNDERWATER INSTRUCTION

Discussion of diving legalities for underwater instructors, equipment suppliers, and others involved in teaching programs. Chapters cover basic legal concepts, professional liability, teaching defensively, instructor liability insurance, equipment and product liability, etc. Edited by Jeanne B. Sleeper and Thomas B. Anderson.

D 3002. Softcover. 8¼" x 10¾". 48 pages. ©1976. Published by National Association of Underwater Instructors.

PROFESSIONAL RESOURCE ORGANIZER MANUAL

Detailed teaching guideline to meet NAUI standards for skin diving, basic scuba, and sport diving courses. Loose leaf format for adapting and adjusting course level material. Black and white illustrations. By Ted Boehler.

D 3001. Hardcover. 11" x 11½". 419 pages plus appendices. ©1977. Published by National Association of Underwater Instructors.

DISCOVER THE UNDERWATER WORLD

Introductory guide to important aspects of skin and scuba diving. Designed as preparation for a certification course. Chapters on various underwater activities, practical oceanography, marine life, diving physics, body functions, and medical aspects of diving. Black and white and color photos and illustrations. By Ralph D. Erickson.

D 3028. Softcover. 7¾" x 10¼". 132 pages. ©1972. Published by U.S. Divers Co.

Dive Sites

A GUIDE TO SNORKELLING AND DIVING IN SEYCHELLES

Tri-lingual (English/French/German) listing of the more accessible snorkelling and diving spots on the Seychelles Bank of the Indian Ocean. Chapters include hints on snorkelling and fishwatching, and writeups of specific sites keyed to maps. Black and white and color photos and illustrations. By Rod Salm.

D 3118. Softcover. 8¼" x 8". 60 pages. ©1977. Published by Octavian Books.

DIVER'S GUIDE TO FLORIDA

Guidebook to scuba diving and snorkeling, treasure hunting, spearfishing, lobstering and other activities in the fresh and salt water of mainland Florida and the Keys. Includes locations of shipwrecks, air stations. Special information on diving laws and hazardous marine life. Color photos, black and white maps. By Jim Stachowicz.

D 3032. Softcover. 6" x 9". 64 pages. ©1976. Published by Windward Publishing, Inc.

DIVING GUIDE TO THE VIRGIN ISLANDS

Favorite diving locations of expert divers in the U.S. and British Virgin Islands. Each site is identified with a rough-drawn map, and corresponding writeups include divers' personal impressions. Color photographs,

including a portfolio of common fish specimens. By Gail Glanville and Armando Jenik.

D 3035. Hardcover. 6⅝" x 8¼". 64 pages. Published by Argos, Inc.

DIVER'S GUIDE TO THE IOWA GREAT LAKES

Historical and practical guide for skin and scuba divers. Includes maps of each lake, and descriptions of individual dive sites, with black and white surface photos for ease of location. Information on artifacts and other collectables. By Tom W. Tourville.

D 3031. Softcover. 5½" x 8½". 36 pages. ©1977. Published by the author.

DIVING GUIDE TO THE BAHAMAS

Guide to specific dive sites in the Bahamas, Turks, and Caicos Islands. Includes descriptive comments on anticipated depths and what might be expected in each area. Illustrated with 25 maps and 16 pages of color photographs. By Gordon Lomer.

D 3036. Hardcover. 6½" x 8⅛". 56 pages. Published by Argos, Inc.

BAHAMAS DIVER'S GUIDE

Guide for typical sport diver visiting the Bahamas. Each site listing includes an exact navigational fix by land, sea, and air. History of the islands, explanations of reef terrain and marine topography, and a fish index to 65 of the most common species. Underwater and surface color photos, with map overlays. By Shlomo Cohen.

D 3033. Hardcover. 6" x 10¾". 184 pages. ©1977. Published by Seapen Books.

UNDERWATER HOLIDAYS

Guide to 422 diving spots in the U.S., Canada, the Caribbean, the Bahamas, and Mexico. Where to stay, what to look for, local regulations, where to take lessons, how to buy equipment, how to take photos underwater. Black and white photos. By Janet Viertel.

D 3038. Softcover. 8" x 10¾". 256 pages. ©1978. Published by Grosset & Dunlap.

GREAT DIVING — I

Guide to dive sites in the Eastern U.S. and around the Gulf Coast. Includes an introduction to each distinct area, plus writeups of individual sites. Emphasis on diving features, hazards, regulations. Includes brief state-by-state listing of dive shops. Over 50 black and white photos and sketches. Written by Judy and Dean May.

D 3030. Softcover. 5¼" x 8¼". 256 pages. ©1974. Published by Stackpole Books.

RED SEA DIVER'S GUIDE

Compilation of favorite diving sites in the Gulf of Eilat, with introductory sections on the history, geography, weather, marine topography, and peoples of the area. Individual areas are plotted on maps, and illustrat-

ed with color surface and underwater photos. Includes photos of common fish species, a section on photography, and other helpful information. By Shlomo Cohen.

D 3034. Hardcover. 6" x 10¾". 182 pages. ©1975. Published by Taracoda.

141 DIVES in the protected waters of Washington and British Columbia

Personally-recorded descriptions of 141 dive sites between Olympia, Washington and Kelsey Bay, B.C. Each listing includes the recommended level of diving skill, descriptions of features, access, bottom conditions, hazards, and nearby facilities, plus a photo and nautical chart of the area. Written by Betty Pratt-Johnson.

D 3029. Softcover. 5½" x 8½". 394 pages. ©1976. Published by Gordon Soules Economic and Marketing Research/The Writing Works, Inc.

Marine Life

THE LIVING REEF

A picture book of corals and fishes of Florida, Bermuda, the Bahamas and the Caribbean. Chapters on hard and soft corals, sponges, invertebrates and crustacea, fish, squid and octopus, marine tropicals, and dangerous specimens. Includes data on the more than 100 full-color photographs. By Idaz and Jerry Greenberg.

D 3047. Softcover. 6" x 9". 110 pages. (Third printing 1974.) Published by Seahawk Press.

LIVING SHORES OF THE PACIFIC NORTHWEST

Guide to seashore plants and animals of Oregon, Washington and British Columbia. Species are grouped by type of beach where they're most frequently found. Each specimen identified by common names as well as scientific names. Over 140 photographs, many in full color. By Lynwood S. Smith.

D 3058. Softcover. 6" x 9". 160 pages. ©1976. Published by Pacific Search Books.

DANGEROUS MARINE ANIMALS

Handbook for identifying marine creatures that bite, sting, shock, or are non-edible, and for treating illnesses and injuries caused by them. Tooth structure of biting organisms and stinging apparatus of stinging species are shown. Hundreds of black and white photos and illustrations. By Bruce W. Halstead, M.D.

D 3048. Hardcover. 6¼" x 9½". 146 pages. ©1959. Published by Cornell Maritime Press.

THE MARINE COLLECTOR'S GUIDE

How to catch salt water specimens alive, including necessary equipment, likely places to look for popular specimens, how to hold and market them. Special chapters on collecting sea horses and bay specimens, invertebrates, and corals. Black and white and color photographs. By Robert P. L. Straughan.

D 3046. Hardcover. 9½" x 12½". 222 pages. ©1973. Published by A. S. Barnes and Company.

SEA TURTLES

Survey of the seven species of marine turtles in the subtropical and tropical waters of the world, and the turtle industry of the West Indies, Florida, and the Gulf of Mexico. Sixteen line drawings, 15 photographs, and 29 tables help describe each species. By Thomas P. Rebel.

D 3049. Hardcover. 5½″ x 8½″. 250 pages. ©1974. Published by University of Miami Press.

THE UNDERWATER WORLD

Introduction to underwater life. Describes different groups of aquatic animals and the relationships between them. Separate chapters on plankton, seashores, coral reefs, sea floor life, fishes of the open sea, unique species, and life in fresh waters. Black and white illustrations. By Gwynne Vevers.

D 3059. Hardcover. 5½″ x 8¾″. 168 pages. ©1971. Published by St. Martin's Press.

FISHERWATCHER'S GUIDE TO WEST ATLANTIC CORAL REEFS

Color illustrations and descriptions of over 180 species of fish in the waters from Florida to Venezuela. Printed on plastic, the volume is waterproof, greaseproof, and washable. Text by Charles C. G. Chaplin, illustrations by Peter Scott.

D 3045. Softcover. (Waterproof). 5½″ x 8½″. 64 pages. ©1972. Published by Harrowood Books.

SEA TURTLES

Nature-science book for children describing the major species of sea turtles—leatherback, breen, loggerhead, hawksbill, and ridley. Black and white sketches. By Francine Jacobs, illustrations by Jean Zallinger.

D 3050. Hardcover. 6½″ x 8½″. 63 pages. ©1972. Published by William Morrow and Company.

IN THE CORAL REEFS

Description of underwater life in the Caribbean, Bahamas, Florida and Bermuda. Includes sections on specific species, underwater geography, treasure hunting, and various institutions of oceanographic research. Color and black and white photographs. Edited by Hans W. Hannau.

D 3060. Hardcover. 9″ x 10″. 135 pages. ©1974. Published by Argo Books.

THE SEAWEED HANDBOOK

Guide to seaweeds of the East Coast from North Carolina to the Arctic. Chapters on identifying seaweed, seaweed reproduction, collection and uses of seaweeds and keys to 78 specific varieties. Over 100 black and white photos and sketches. By Thomas F. Lee, illustrated by Wendy Webster.

D 3051. Hardcover. 8″ x 9″. 217 pages. ©1977. Published by The Mariners Press.

GUIDE TO CORALS & FISHES of Florida, The Bahamas and the Caribbean

260 species of corals and fishes shown in full color with brief, simple text. Species include sharks and commensals, rays, game fish, tropical fish, sea turtles, 11 varieties of coral, plus crustacea. One chapter describes 11 species which are poisonous to touch. By Idaz and Jerry Greenberg.

D 3044. Softcover. (waterproof) 6″ x 9″. 64 pages. ©1977. Published by Seahawk Press.

FISHWATCHERS' GUIDE TO THE INSHORE FISHES OF THE PACIFIC COAST

Field guide to 93 of the most commonly observed species from Alaska to Baja California, in depths from 10 to 150 feet. Descriptions of each species, including tips on identifying and locating them. Underwater color photos of each species. By Daniel W. Gotshall.

D 3052. Softcover. 6″ x 9″. 108 pages. ©1977. Published by Sea Challengers.

THE SHARK: SPLENDID SAVAGE OF THE SEA

Accounts of shark studies during a two-year expedition in the Red Sea and Indian Ocean. Part of the Cousteau Undersea Discoveries series. 124 full color photographs plus black and white photos, sketches, and maps. By Jacques-Yves and Philippe Cousteau.

D 3061. Hardcover. 7¼″ x 10¼″. 277 pages. ©1970. Published by Doubleday & Company, Inc.

UNDERWATER CALIFORNIA

How to recognize and understand the natural features of California's underwater environment. Information on habitats, communities, and species identification plus diving locations. Black and white drawings and color photographs. By Wheeler J. North.

D 3043. Softcover. 4¾" x 8". 276 pages. ©1976. Published by University of California Press.

SHADOWS IN THE SEA — THE SHARKS, SKATES AND RAYS

Guide to the various members of the Selachian family. Covers dangerous species, and the conditions which make them dangerous, how man can protect against them, man's uses of sharks for commercial, medical and other purposes. Over 100 black and white photos and illustrations. By Harold W. McCormick, Tom Allen and Captain William Young.

D 3053. Hardcover. 6" x 9". 415 pages. ©1963. Published by Chilton Book Company.

LIFE AND DEATH IN A CORAL SEA

Studies of great coral areas in the Indian Ocean and Red Sea. Part of the Cousteau Undersea Discoveries series. 122 color and 20 black and white photographs, 20 line drawings. Appendices and illustrated glossary. By Jacques-Yves Cousteau and Philippe Diolé.

D 3062. Hardcover. 7¼" x 10¼". 302 pages. ©1971. Published by Doubleday & Company, Inc.

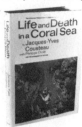

DIVING COMPANIONS — SEA LION — ELEPHANT SEAL — WALRUS

Studies of marine mammals off Capetown and Baja California, and in the Arctic. Part of the Cousteau Undersea Discoveries series. 126 full color photos, plus black and white photos, maps, illustrations. Appendices and illustrated glossary. By Jacques-Yves Cousteau and Philippe Diolé.

D 3042. Hardcover. 7¼" x 10¼". 304 pages. ©1974. Published by Doubleday & Company, Inc.

THE SHARK BOOK
LORD OF THE SEA

Facts and folklore about shark attacks, defenses against sharks, sport fishing for sharks. Includes a section of shark profiles. Full color and black and white photos and illustrations. By Sandra Romashko.

D 3054. Softcover. 9" x 6". 64 pages. ©1975. Published by Windward Publishing, Inc.

FISH MEN FEAR . . . SHARK!

Thumbnail guide to major species of dangerous sharks in the waters of Florida and the Caribbean. Chapters on sharks in captivity, shark research, sharks' sense of sound, sight, and smell. One chapter on rules to follow in shark-infested waters. Over 50 black and white underwater photographs. Written and illustrated by Idaz and Jerry Greenberg.

D 3027. Softcover. 5¼" x 8¼". 48 pages. Fifth printing 1977. Published by Seahawk Press.

OCTOPUS AND SQUID
THE SOFT INTELLIGENCE

Studies of cephalopods conducted in the Mediterranean, Pacific, and Puget Sound area. Part of the Cousteau Undersea Discoveries series. 124 full color photographs, 20 black and white photos, plus maps and drawings. Appendices, illustrated glossary. By Jacques-Yves Cousteau and Philippe Diolé.

D 3063. Hardcover. 7¼" x 10¼". 304 pages. ©1973. Published by Doubleday & Company, Inc.

LIVING CORAL AND OTHER INHABITANTS OF THE REEF

Explanation of reef civilization, tips for reef exploring, how to clean coral specimens, species of coral, sponges, reef fish and other reef dwellers. Over 100 full color photographs. By Sandra Romashko.

D 3099. Softcover. 6" x 9". 64 pages. ©1976. Published by Windward Publishing, Inc.

THE WHALE — MIGHTY MONARCH OF THE SEA

Accounts of encounters with sperm whales in the Pacific and Indian Oceans, gray whales along the coast of California, and killer whales in the Indian Ocean and in captivity. Part of the Cousteau Undersea Discoveries series. 124 full color photographs, plus black and white photos, drawings and maps. By Jacques-Yves Cousteau and Philippe Diolé.

D 3064. Hardcover. 7¼" x 10¼". 304 pages. ©1972. Published by Doubleday & Company, Inc.

ATLANTIC REEF CORALS

Handbook of common reef and shallow-water corals of Bermuda, the Bahamas, Florida, the West Indies and Brazil. Chapters on distribution of coral reefs around the world, formations of reefs, structure and habits of living corals, associates of corals, collection and preparation of corals, and coral taxonomy. Closeup black and white photos. By F. G. Walton Smith.

D 3041. Hardcover. 5½″ x 8¼″. 164 pages. ©1971. Published by University of Miami Press.

THE SHELL BOOK

Identifies more than 300 shells common to the Atlantic, Gulf of Mexico, and Caribbean. Species are grouped by bivalves, univalves, and others. Includes a natural history of shells, and tips on collecting and cleaning. Hundreds of full-color illustrations. By Sandra Romashko.

D 3056. Softcover. 6″ x 9″. 64 pages. ©1974. Published by Windward Publishing, Inc.

TROPICAL MARINE INVERTEBRATES OF SOUTHERN FLORIDA AND THE BAHAMA ISLANDS

Guide to the six most common invertebrate phyla in the region covered. Individual chapters devoted to the polyp animals, flatworms, mollusks, segmented worms, arthropods, and echinoderms. Nearly 250 full-color photos of living specimens. By Warren Zeiller.

D 3065. Hardcover. 7¾″ x 9½″. 132 pages. ©1974. Published by John Wiley & Sons.

SUBTIDAL MARINE BIOLOGY OF CALIFORNIA

Field guide and reference work on the plants and animals most frequently encountered near shore waters and offshore islands of California, especially the southern part of the state. Chapters on individual biological families. Black and white and color photographs. By Robert Galbraith and Ted Boehler.

D 3040. Softcover. 5⅜″ x 8⅜″. 128 pages. ©1974. Published by Naturegraph Publishers, Inc.

BENEATH THE SEAS OF THE WEST INDIES

Guide to undersea life in the Caribbean and off the Bahamas, Florida, and Bermuda. Includes chapters on reef ecology, marine archeology, underwater hunting, and introductions to the various families of marine fauna. 175 color photographs. By Dr. Hans W. Hannau and Bernd H. Mock.

D 3066. Hardcover. 6¾″ x 8½″. 104 pages. Published by Argos, Inc.

THE CORAL BOOK

A guide to collecting and identifying the corals of the world. Explanations of coral's underwater civilization and how to clean coral specimens. More than 50 species are identified and pictured as collector's specimens and as live animals, many in full color.

By Sandra Romashko.

D 3057. Softcover. 6″ x 9″. 64 pages. ©1975. Published by Windward Publishing, Inc.

THE SEA I LOVE

Personal evocation of the underwater world of the Red Sea, including observations of some of the 1,000 species of fish that inhabit the Gulf of Eilat. Full-color photographs and illustrations. By Shlomo Cohen.

D 3039. Hardcover. 9½″ x 8¾″. 85 pages. Published by Seapen Books.

DOLPHINS

Survey of research into dolphin intelligence and communication, plus personal accounts of observations, encounters, experiments in the Atlantic and Mediterranean. Part of the Cousteau Undersea Discoveries series. 105 full color photographs, plus black and white photos, drawings, and maps. By Jacques-Yves Cousteau and Philippe Diolé.

D 3068. Hardcover. 7¼″ x 10¼″. 304 pages. ©1975. Published by Doubleday & Company, Inc.

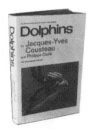

Photography

DIVERS & CAMERAS

Textbook for students, instructors, and advanced underwater photographers. Chapters on phenomena of light, cameras, housings, the photographic eye, exposures, film and filters, miniature photography, movies. Black and white photos and illustrations. By Joe Strykowski.

D 3074. Hardcover. 6″ x 9¼″. 212 pages. ©1974. Published by Dacor Corporation.

BASICS OF UNDERWATER PHOTOGRAPHY

Step-by-step guide through the complexities of underwater photography. Chapters include physics of light underwater, films and filters, equipment, shooting with natural and artificial light, close-up techniques, film developing, and printing. Color and black and white photos. By Doug Wallin.

D 3073. Softcover. 8″ x 10″. 128 pages. ©1975. Published by American Photographic Book Publishing Co., Inc.

UNDERWATER STROBE PHOTOGRAPHY

Guide to strobe equipment and techniques for those with working knowledge of underwater camera equipment. Information on basic and close-up exposures, plus single and multiple strobe techniques, and troubleshooting flash failures. Black and white and color photographs. By Jim and Cathy Church.

D 3071. Softcover. 5½″ x 8½″. 64 pages. ©1976. Published by the authors.

PHOTOGRAPHS UNDERWATER

Practical knowhow for both novice and advanced underwater photographers.

Discussions of light conditions, underwater housing design, the Rolleimarin system, lenses and portholes, and histories of early photographers. Includes 80 prize winning photos. By Bob Kendall.

D 3075. Hardcover. 8½″ x 11″. 104 pages. Published by ICER Press.

UNDERWATER PHOTOGRAPHY

Traces the evolution of the field from its early days off the French Riviera to the development of modern sophisticated systems. Includes chapters on underwater movies and television, archeology, and vehicles, as well as how-to advice on still photography. Black and white and color photographs. By Dimitri Rebikoff and Paul Cherney.

D 3070. Hardcover. 6¼″ x 9¼″. 143 pages. ©1975. Published by American Photographic Book Publishing Co., Inc.

UNDERWATER PHOTOGRAPHY SIMPLIFIED

Step-by-step account of what to expect and do when first taking a camera underwater. Chapters include potential of underwater photography, available equipment, lenses and filters, black and white or color with available light, flash techniques, and how to market photos. Over 50 black and white photos. By Jerry Greenberg.

D 3076. Softcover. 5¼″ x 8¼″. 48 pages. ©1972. (Fifth edition). Published by Seahawk Press.

UNDERWATER WITH THE NIKONOS & NIKON SYSTEMS

Practical guide to underwater photography with the amphibious Nikonos camera and other Nikon models in watertight housings. Separate chapters on lenses and accessories; shooting underwater with available light, flashbulbs, and electronic flash; close-up photography; housings; and practical tips on storage, maintainence and troubleshooting. Color and black and white photographs. By Herb Taylor.

D 3072. Hardcover. 6¼″ x 9¼″. 160 pages. ©1977. Published by American Photographic Book Publishing Co., Inc.

DEEP-SEA PHOTOGRAPHY

Compilation of technical papers on development of underwater photography and its use in oceanography. Includes innovations in hardware, techniques. Black and white and color photographs, some in stereo (stereo viewer included). Edited by John Brackett Hersey.

D 3069. Hardcover. 8½″ x 11¼″. 310 pages. ©1967. Published by The John Hopkins Press.

BEGINNING UNDERWATER PHOTOGRAPHY

An introduction to underwater photography beginning with basic concepts up through advanced techniques. Included are sections on choosing a camera and lenses, synchronization, using flashbulbs and strobes underwater. Black and white and

color photographs. By Jim and Cathy Church.

D 3077. Softcover 5½″ x 8½″. 56 pages. ©1975. Published by the authors.

Wreck Diving

ENCYCLOPEDIA OF AMERICAN SHIPWRECKS

Compilation of over 13,000 wrecks in U.S. territorial waters. Includes basic information on every known shipwreck in the American continental shelf of fifty gross tons or more. Information presented in regional listings. By Bruce D. Berman.

D 3088. Hardcover. 6⅜″ x 9½″. 308 pages. ©1972. Published by The Mariners Press.

ADVENTURES IN UNDERWATER TREASURE HUNTING

The personal story of a successful modern treasure hunter. Includes accounts of author's battles with barracuda, shark, and giant octopus while hunting Caribbean wrecks. Includes sketches, treasure maps, and photographs of relics and salvaged treasures. By Lieut. Harry E. Rieseberg.

D 3084. Hardcover. 5½″ x 8½″. 141 pages. ©1965. Published by Frederick Fell, Inc.

GREAT LAKES TREASURE WRECK ATLAS

Maps of each of the five Great Lakes with treasure sites and wrecks marked and described. Over 360 separate listings, all

also included in The Treasure Map Atlas. By Thomas P. Terry.

D 3083. Softcover. 8″ x 11″. 31 pages. ©1974. Published by Treasure Division of Specialty Publishing Company.

IN THE WAKE OF THE GOLDEN GALLEONS

Autobiographical account of treasure-diving ventures in the Caribbean. Includes histories and salvage attempts of a number of wrecked treasure ships, and stories of authors' associations with such famous treasure-hunters as Mel Fisher, Kip Wagner, Art McKee, Bob Marx and Art Hartman. Black and white photographs. By Roy Volker and Dick Richmond.

D 3089. Softcover. 6″ x 9″. 149 pages. ©1976. Published by OroQuest Press.

TREASURE MAP ATLAS

Fifty-state map guide to lost treasure in the U.S. More than 5,000 treasure locations are listed on individual state maps. Brief descriptions of each reported treasure are keyed to map locations. By Thomas P. Terry.

D 3082. Softcover. 8″ x 11″. 142 pages. ©1974. Published by Treasure Division of Specialty Publishing Company.

DIVING FOR SUNKEN TREASURE

Account of an expedition to the Silver Bank reef in the Caribbean to search for ancient shipwrecks. Includes historical tales of adventures along the Spanish Main. Part of the Cousteau Undersea Discoveries series. 112 full color photographs, plus black and white photos, drawings, and maps. By Jacques-Yves Cousteau and Philippe Diolé.

D 3090. Hardcover. 7¼″ x 10¼″. 302 pages. ©1971. Published by Doubleday & Company, Inc.

FELL'S GUIDE TO SUNKEN TREASURE SHIPS OF THE WORLD

Over 1,000 sites of treasure wrecks, listed continent by continent. Details on equipment and large-scale salvage methods. One chapter on sunken cities. Black and white photographs. By Lieut. Harry E. Rieseberg and A. A. Mikalow.

D 3085. Hardcover. 5½″ x 8½″. 221 pages. ©1965. Published by Frederick Fell, Inc.

MORE DOUBLOONS & OTHER BURIED TREASURE

A continuing collection of legends and locations, some on land, some in U.S. lakes. Over 500 lost, wrecked, or sunken steamboat locations are described. Maps and black and white photos. By Thomas P. Terry.

D 3081. Softcover. 5½″ x 9½″. 168 pages. ©1970. Published by the author.

DIVING FOR TREASURE

Personal account of nearly thirty years of searching for sunken ships. Includes stories of other marine archeologists. Chapters on specific wrecks, divers, treasures, underwater surveying and photography, reconstructing shipwrecks, and the politics of treasure diving. Black and white photographs and eight pages of color plates. By Peter Throckmorton.

D 3091. Hardcover. 8¾″ x 9¾″. 136 pages. ©1977. Published by The Viking Press.

SHIPWRECKS OF THE WESTERN HEMISPHERE

Guide to major shipwrecks in the Western Hemisphere, and an introduction to underwater archeology, treasure diving, and underwater exploration. Includes chapters on ancient sailing vessels and what they carried, tales of early salvors and treasure hunters, and how-to information. Black and white photos. By Robert F. Marx.

D 3080. Hardcover. 6¼" x 9¼". 482 pages. ©1975. Published by David McKay Company, Inc.

THE SEA OF TREASURE

Highlights of author's treasure diving career. Personal experiences through the waters of the Caribbean, Gulf of Mexico, and the West Coast of South America, from the Bahamas across the Spanish Main and down to Ecuador. Black and white photos. By Lieut. Harry E. Rieseberg.

D 3086. Hardcover. 5½" x 8½". 217 pages. ©1966. Published by Frederick Fell, Inc.

THE TREASURE OF THE GREAT REEF

Personal account of salvaging treasure from an ancient shipwreck on the reef off Ceylon. Includes nearly 100 black and white photographs and 16 pages of color photos. New edition contains an epilogue with updates on individuals in the original expedition. By Arthur C. Clarke.

D 3092. Softcover. 5¼" x 8". 278 pages. ©1974. Published by Ballantine Books, Inc.

THE UNDERWATER DIG

Introduction to marine archeology, from shipwrecks to submerged cities. Chapters include an historical background and techniques for research, search, excavation, dating and identification, preservation and publication, and speculations on the future of archeology underwater. Black and white photos and drawings.

D 3079. Hardcover. 6" x 9". 250 pages. ©1975. Published by Henry Z. Walck, Inc.

THE LURE OF SUNKEN TREASURE

Personal accounts of treasure hunting exploits by one of the best-known names in the field. Introduction provides a history of underwater salvage. Adventures include discovery of two of Columbus' caravels, the sunken pirate city of Port Royal, and the raising of the Swedish man-o'-war Vasa. Black and white and color photos and other illustrations. By Robert F. Marx.

D 3087. Hardcover. 7¼" x 10¼". 158 pages. ©1973. Published by David McKay Company, Inc.

WRECK! THE NORTH CAROLINA DIVER'S HANDBOOK

Guide to diving in the Graveyard of the Atlantic. Chapters include a history of shipping in the area, how to find wrecks, charter boats and skippers, selected wreck sites, and maps with wrecks pinpointed and described. Black and white photos. By Jess Barker and Bill Lovin.

D 3078. Softcover. 5½" x 8¼". 74 pages. ©1976. Published by Marine Grafics.

DIVING AND DIGGING FOR GOLD

Techniques for locating placer deposits and mining them. Chapters include What to Take, Where to Go, Tips from Old Timers, Tools, Amalgams and Retorts, Life and Death of a Mine, and Where to Sell Gold. Historical and current day photographs and drawings. By Mary Hill.

D 3093. Softcover. 5¼" x 8". 47 pages. ©1974. Published by Naturegraph Publishers, Inc.

Cookbooks

THE SAVORY SHELLFISH OF NORTH AMERICA

Natural history, habitat, harvesting techniques and recipes for the most commonly-found species of lobster, crawfish, crab, shrimp, abalone, conch, squid, mussel, clams, oysters, and scallops. Black and white and color photos. By Sandra Ramashko.

D 3096. Softcover. 6" x 9". 64 pages. ©1977. Published by Windward Publishing, Inc.

THE EDIBLE SEA

Over 250 recipes from around the world for crustaceans, mollusks, fish, marine reptiles and mammals, echinoderms, seaweeds, and seawater. Descriptions of what is and isn't edible, where to find it, how to catch and gather it. Over 140 line drawings and photos of edible and toxic specimens plus catching equipment. Written by Paul and Mavis Hill.

D 3095. Hardcover. 6¾" x 10¼". 276 pages. ©1975. Published by A. S. Barnes and Company.

BOTTOMS UP COOKERY

Complete guide to identifying, catching, and preparing fish and shellfish most commonly encountered by sport divers. Includes tips on diving, outdoor cooking, cleaning and filleting fish. Black and white photos and sketches. By Robert B. Leamer, Wilfred H. Shaw and Charles F. Ulrich.

D 3094. Softcover. 6" x 9". 263 pages. ©1975. Published by Fathom Enterprises.

THE FREE FOOD SEAFOOD BOOK

How to find, gather, and cook more than 140 delicacies from the ocean borders of North America. Separate sections on bivalves, crustaceans, coastal fish, and exotics such as abalone, octopus, squid, and conch. Recipes follow general descriptions of each species. Over 100 black and white sketches. Written by Peggy Ann Hardigree.

D 3097. Softcover. 6" x 9". 228 pages. ©1977. Published by Stackpole Books.

Medicine

ADVANCED FIRST AID FOR ALL OUTDOORS

A guide for those who venture beyond the range of immediate professional medical assistance. Covers instant aid; simple fractures, dislocations and sprains; wounds, compound fractures and amputation; near-drowning and diving accidents, and many other specifics. Dozens of photos and sketches. Written by Peter F. Eastman, M.D.

D 3100. Softcover. 6" x 9". 160 pages. ©1976. Published by Cornell Maritime Press.

HOW TO COPE WITH DANGEROUS SEA LIFE

A guide to animals from the Western Atlantic, Caribbean, and Gulf of Mexico that sting, bite, or are poisonous to eat. Includes sections on how to avoid endangering oneself, and rules to follow if bitten, stung or poisoned. Underwater color photos or illustrations of species. By Edwin S. Iverson and Renate Skinner.

D 3102. Softcover. 5¾" x 9". 64 pages. ©1977. Published by Winward Publishing, Inc.

MEDICAL ASPECTS OF SPORT DIVING

Layman's discussion of causes of diving injuries and accidents, how they can be avoided, and how to administer to them once they occur. Common respiratory problems and dangerous marine animals are described. Several black and white drawings. By Christopher W. Dueker.

D 3104. Softcover. 7¾" x 8½". 232 pages. ©1970. (Fifth printing). Published by A. S. Barnes and Co., Inc.

HUMAN PERFORMANCE AND SCUBA DIVING

Proceedings of symposium on underwater physiology held at Scripps Institution of Oceanography, April 10-11, 1970. Includes effect of diving equipment on diving performance, physiologic processes of diving, diving behavior and work methods. Black and white photos and illustrations.

D 3103. Softcover. 6" x 9". 170 pages. ©1970. Published by The Athletic Institute.

INTERNATIONAL LISTING OF CHAMBERS

Listing of all shore-based decompression chambers in Canada, Bahamas, Japan, Mexico, Germany, plus the U.S. and its territories and possessions. Also includes information on diving hazards requiring chamber use and their prevention and treatment.

D 3101. Softcover. 8½" x 11". 42 pages. Revised edition 1974. Published by National Association of Underwater Instructors.

FIRST AID FOR SKIN & SCUBA DIVERS

How-to information on general first aid, injuries caused by marine life, pressure-related illness and injury, and ingredients for a well-stocked first aid kit. Forms for recording personal health data and emergency information. Dozens of black and white sketches. Edited by Bernard E. Empleton.

D 3098. Pocketbook (waterproof). 4" x 5¾". 65 pages. ©1977. Published by Association Press.

Miscellaneous

AIR DECOMPRESSION AND CHAMBER OPERATION

Dive supervisor's aid, extracted from U.S. Navy Diving Manual. First section contains color-coded decompression tables for various situations. Second section contains standard rules for diagnosing diving-related medical emergencies. The book is waterproof and heat resistant to 200°F.

D 3099. Pocketbook. (waterpoof). 3¾" x 6". 140 pages. First printing 1976. Published by Hydroquip Corporation, Inc.

MAN BENEATH THE SEA

Review of underwater ocean engineering, covering hardware, bioscience, life support, and future trends in ocean technology. Chapters on technical history of diving, diving systems, life support systems, pressure vessels, umbilicals, tools, diving physiology, and ocean environment. Black and white photos and drawings. By Walter Penzias and M. W. Goodman.

D 3116. Hardcover. 6¼" x 9¼". 831 pages. ©1973. Published by John Wiley & Sons, Inc.

Photo not available.

STRANGE MYSTERIES OF THE SEA

Fifteen different tales of strange occurences on and under the sea, including the case of the "missing frogman," British Commander Lionel Crabb. Other stories deal with ship disappearances, "ghost" ships and sea-serpents. By Len Ortzen.

D 3117. Hardcover. 5⅝" x 8¾". 192 pages. ©1976. Published by St. Martin's Press.

SCUBA TANKS

Basic introduction to the technology of compressed air cylinders. Chapters on valves, steel vs. aluminum tanks, buying tips, tank care, hydrostatic testing, visual inspections. Black and white illustrations. By Bob Gonsett.

D 3113. Softcover. 8½" x 11". 48 pages. ©1973. Published by National Association of Underwater Instructors.

EQUIPMENT SAFETY PROGRAM

Procedures for visual inspection of scuba cylinders. Sections on tank corrosion, inspection procedures and standards. Appendices include sample inspection record sheet, inspector application, and inspection standards of the Compressed Gas Association. Black and white photos and illustrations. By Ron Miscavich.

D 3114. Softcover. 8¼" x 11". 32 pages. ©1977. Published by National Association of Underwater Instructors.

DIVE LOG

Set up to provide the diver a record of personal diving experiences. Includes sections on personal identification, lists of buddies, training record, individual dives, repetitive dive work sheet, boat diving plan, check lists and equipment records, photo log, standard signals, etc. By R. J. Shourot.

D 3108. Softcover. 5" x 8". 96 pages ©1961.

(Revised 1976). Published by Sea Press Company.

WAVES AND BEACHES

The dynamics of the ocean surface. Includes chapters on ideal waves, wind waves, waves in shallow water, tides and seiches, impulsively generated waves, measuring and making waves, the surf, beaches, the Littoral Conveyor Belts, and shoreline defenses against waves. Black and white photos and sketches. By Willard Bascom.

D 3109. Pocketbook. 4" x 7". 267 pages. ©1964. Published by Doubleday & Company, Inc.

THE EARTH BENEATH THE SEA

Account of geological forces that shape the topography of the ocean floor, based largely on research work at Scripps Institution. Includes personal experiences from author's 40-year career in marine studies. Black and white photos and illustrations. By Francis P. Shepard.

D 3106. Hardcover. 6" x 9". 242 pages. ©1967. Published by The John Hopkins Press.

WOMEN IN SPORTS - SCUBA DIVING

Adventures and careers of five well-known women divers: Valerie Taylor, Eugenie Clark, Kati Garner, Zale Parry, Sylvia Earle. Written primarily for children. Numerous black and white photographs. By Hillary Hauser.

D 3105. Hardcover. 6" x 8¾". 80 pages. ©1976. Published by Harvey House.

EXPLORERS OF THE DEEP

Accounts of 18 individuals who furthered the exploration of the ocean, from Benjamin Franklin to Scott Carpenter. Includes pioneers in submersibles, marine biology, marine geology, undersea habitats, and other aspects of oceanography. Full color photos and illustrations. By Donald W. Cox.

D 3107. Hardcover. 7¼" x 10¼". 93 pages. ©1968. Published by Hammond, Incorporated.

THREE ADVENTURES - GALAPAGOS - TITICACA - THE BLUE HOLES

Accounts of underwater expeditions to the historic Galapagos archipelgo, Lake Titicaca in the Andes, and the Blue Holes of the Caribbean and Bahamas. Part of the Cousteau Undersea Discoveries series. 125 full color photos, plus black and white photos, drawings and maps. By Jacques-Yves Cousteau and Philippe Diolé.

D 3110. Hardcover. 7¼" x 10¼". 304 pages. ©1973. Published by Doubleday & Company, Inc.

DIVING AND LOG BOOK AND TRAINING RECORD

Actually two separate diaries in one plastic cover, which comes in a watertight Zip-Loc plastic pouch. Training record can be used to detail achievements and experiences to date. Log book allows diver to keep records of each dive.

D 3111. Pocketbooks. Each 3¾" x 5¼". Each 32 pages. ©1973. Published by National Association of Underwater Instructors.

SUBMERGE!

The story of divers and their crafts, from the beginning to predictions about tomorrow beneath the seas. Chapters on undersea explorers, vehicles, and dwellings. Black and white illustrations. By Anabel Dean.

D 3112. Softcover. 6½" x 9". 111 pages. ©1976. Published by The Westminster Press.

SCUBA REGULATORS

Basic introduction to the workings of regulators including explanations of the different types, components, and accessories. Tips on choosing and caring for regulators. Black and white illustrations including many cutaway diagrams. By Bob Gonsett.

D 3115. Softcover. 8½" x 11". 60 pages. ©1975. Published by National Association of Underwater Instructors.

UNDERWATER WILDERNESS

Illustrated guide to life around the world's great reefs. Part I offers an explanation of the makeup of coral colonies. Part II is a site-by-site description of the greatest underwater wilderness areas. 306 color photographs plus 60 maps and drawings. By Carl Roessler.

D 3021. Hardbound. 9" x 12". 316 pages. ©1977. Published by Chanticleer Press, Inc.

SEASHELLS OF NORTH AMERICA

Field guide for identifying 850 species of marine mollusks on the Atlantic and Pacific coasts of North America. General information on mollusk physiology and behavior, and specific chapters on each class within the *phylum Mollusca*. Full-color illustrations. By George F. Sandstrom. Written by R. Tucker Abbott.

D 3119. Pocketbook. 4½" x 7½". 280 pages. ©1968. Published by Western Publishing Company, Inc.

SKIN DIVER'S GUIDE TO HAWAII

Underwater guidebook to the 50th state. Includes profiles of common reef fish, spearfishing equipment and techniques, tips on specific diving areas off Oahu, photography, shells and corals, research and salvage, fish and game regulations, and lists of retailers and diving services. Carries advertising, and includes black and white photos. By Gordon Freund.

D 3037. Softcover. 5½" x 8¼". 72 pages. Published by author.

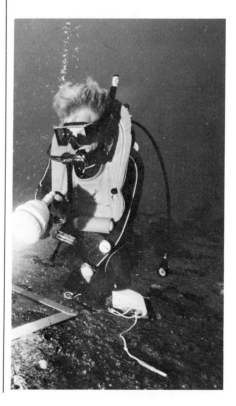

Periodicals

SKIN DIVER

Special interest magazine covering the sport and industry of skin and scuba diving. Regular features on diving medicine and technology, news of diving clubs and organizations, calendars of upcoming events, listings of dive shops. Feature articles on diving locales, vacation packeges, marine life, dive techniques, equipment, and photography. Glossy paper, color and black and white illustrations.

D4001. Monthly. 8″ x 11″. Approximately 98 pages. Published by Petersen Publishing Company.

SPORT DIVER

Jounal covering all aspects of skin and scuba diving. Regular features on diving locations, conservation, equipment. Departments include Edible Sea, Instructor Notes, closeup studies of marine life, Underwater Photography, Navy Diver, and Dive Shop Directory. Glossy paper, color and black and white illustrations.

D4002. Quarterly. 8″ x 11″. Approximately 128 pages. Published by Hass/Littlefield Publishing Company.

NAUI NEWS

Instructive articles on diving skills, teaching techniques, new programs and materials from NAUI, book reviews, diving medicine, and business and employment opportunities. Non-glossy paper, black and white illustrations.

D4008. Monthly. 8½″ x 11. Approximately 30 pages. Published by National Association of Underwater Instructors.

ADVENTURE TRAVEL

Magazine of The American Adventurers Association, a membership organization promoting "the participation of men and women in adventurous activities throughout the world." Feature articles on specific adventures, regular departments on travel news, low-cost adventures, conservation, gear, reading matter, and photo esays. Glossy paper, color illustrations.

D4004. Bi-monthly. 8½″ x 11″. Approximately 64 pages. Published by Adventure Travel Publications.

MARINE TECHNOLOGY SOCIETY JOURNAL

Compilation of technical papers on ocean topics, plus book reviews, and calendars of marine meetings and events. Edited for professionals and the interested public. Non-glossy paper, black and white illustrations.

D4009. 8½″ x 11″. Bi-monthly Approximately 64 pages. Published by the Marine Technology Society.

SEA FRONTIERS

A publication of The International Oceanographic Foundation, with articles on sea life, underwater technology, aquaculture, travel, vessels, and ocean-oriented arts and crafts. Glossy paper, color and black and white illustrations.

D4006. Bi-monthly. (Alternates with Sea Secrets.) 6″ x 9″. Approximately 128 pages. Published by The International Oceanographic Foundation.

SEARCH

Journal of undersea archeology, emphasizing maritime history and related fields. Individual technical papers cover marine archeological techniques, accounts of recent discoveries, historical accounts of marine culture and adventures plus present day marine technology. Non-glossy paper, black and white illustrations.

D4010. Quarterly. 8½″ x 11″. Approximately 40 pages. Published by Fathom Eight.

SEA SECRETS

Educational newsletter of The International Oceanographic Foundation. Features include answers to members' questions, news updates on marine technology, information on IOF travel and instructional programs, plus a calendar of upcoming oceanographic meetings. Non-glossy paper, black and white illustrations.

D4005. Bi-monthly. (Alternates with SEA FRONTIERS.) 6″ x 9″. Approximately 16 pages. Published by The International Oceanographic Institution.

UNDERCURRENT

Diving newsletter with information on trip planning, buying and maintaining equipment, diving insurance, and the dive industry. Includes reviews of dive resorts, diver surveys on equipment, and tips on evaluating dive shops and other services. Non-glossy paper, occasional black and white illustrations.

D4012. Monthly. 8½″ x 11″. Approximately 16 pages. Published by Undercurrent, Inc.

OCEANS

Official publication of the Oceanic Society, covering diving, ocean travel, maritime history, oceanographic research, fishing, the literature of the sea, ocean ecology and protection, maritime arts and sciences, marine research, sailing, boating, and other marine activities. Glossy paper, color and black and white illustrations.

D4011. Bi-monthly. 8½″ x 11″. Approximately 72 pages. Published by The Oceanic Society.

MARIAH

Coverage of expeditions on land and in the water. Tips on joining expeditions or planning your own. Advice on equipment and survival techniques. Glossy paper, color and black and white illustrations.

D4003. Quarterly. 8½″ x 11″. Approximately 84 pages. Published by Mariah Publications Corporation.

THE UNDERSEA JOURNAL

Publication of the Professional Association of Diving Instructors. Features include articles on instruction methods, special equipment, marine animals, diving medicine, new magazine and book reviews, and descriptions of PADI services. Glossy paper, color and black and white illustrations.

D4007. Bi-monthly. 8½″ x 11″. Approximately 30 pages. Published by Professional Association of Diving Instructors.

DIVER AND UNDERWATER ADVENTURE

Formerly Pacific Diver, now published in regional editions. Articles on diving sites, equipment, diving technology and medicine, marine life. Features on industry, club and association news, upcoming events, new books and products, and listings of air stations. Glossy paper, color and black and white illustrations.

D 4015. Bi-monthly. 8½″ x 11″. Approximately 46 pages. Published by Seagraphic Publications Ltd.

DIVE CANADA

Magazine of the Ontario Underwater Council. Articles on diving technology and techniques, dive sites (including histories of old wrecks), reports of conference proceedings, diving careers, and features on marine life, photography, and diving medicine. Non-glossy paper, black and white illustrations.

D 4016. Bi-monthly. 8½″ x 11″. Approximately 28 pages. Published by Ontario Underwater Council, 559 Jarvis St., Toronto, Ontario, M4Y 2J1.

OUTSIDE

Guide to enjoyment, understanding, and preservation of the outdoors. Accounts of land and water-based adventures, photo-essays of natural scenic attractions, plans and instructions for outdoor projects, features on current know-how and traditional lore, evaluations of ecological legal action, equipment reviews, and a calendar of outdoor events. Glossy paper, color and black and white photographs.

D 4014. Monthly. 8½″ x 11″. Approximately 84 pages. Published by Rolling Stone.

DIVERS WORLD

Newspaper reporting items of interest to manufacturers, tour operators, dive shops, and sport divers. News items on new products, club activities, industry personnel changes, upcoming conferences and other events, profiles of diving personalities, and educational programs. Newsprint, black and white photos.

D 4013. Monthly. 1½″ x 18″. Approximately 24 pages. Published by Toss, Inc.

Schools

You can learn skin and scuba diving from a variety of sources: governmental bodies like the military or the National Oceanic and Atmospheric Administration, universities, some municipal recreation departments, public service agencies like the YMCA, diving clubs, resorts, dive shops, or — last and by all means least — from a friend.

No matter how much confidence you have in a diving friend, if he doesn't urge you to seek professional instruction, you should automatically question his judgment. With diving technology and equipment evolving constantly, it would be foolish to accept anything less than the most up-to-date, professional training you can get.

A friend may introduce you to the basics of the sport in the comfort and safety of a backyard pool, but before you venture into open water, get professional training. Then, once you've mastered the basics, your friend will be able to pass along practical tips which you'll be better prepared to understand, evaluate, and utilize.

There are many advantages to learning from a certified instructor. For one thing, professionals are trained in teaching techniques, while friends usually are not. Learning from a pro will be easier, as well as more thorough. And, you'll be plugging into the mainstream of current diving theory, learning the same techniques as thousands of other divers all over the world. Compatibility of techniques can be very important when diving with new buddies or groups.

There's also an imminently practical aspect to this advice: without a recognized diving certification, most shops will refuse to sell you air or rent you gear, and most diving charter boats will refuse to let you in the water.

So your best bet is to find a school which offers one of the nationally or internationally recognized diving certifications. These certifying bodies will be discussed in detail at the end of this chapter. They include:

- Association of Canadian Underwater Councils
- Confederation Mondiale des Activities Subaquatiques
- National Association of Scuba Diving Schools
- National Association of Underwater Instructors
- Professional Association of Diving Instructors
- Scuba Schools International
- YMCA National Scuba Headquarters

Even within the overall guidelines of a national program, individual courses can vary from school to school, even from instructor to instructor. You may even find different certifications offered through the same school or shop, depending on the training of the instructors. Some instructors are also cross-trained, and can offer a choice of certifications.

Choosing a Course

Before shopping for a scuba course, first determine what level of training you desire. Some organizations offer as many as 20 different certifications. These range from introductory "quickies" which give you a taste for diving, up through advanced sport diver levels. Specialty courses may be offered in such activities as cave diving, ice diving, search and recovery, photography, or wreck diving. Some programs are designed as continuing education systems, to encourage that diver to refresh old skills and keep current on new developments in the sport. Professional level courses are available to prepare experienced sport divers as dive masters, or instructors.

Once you've determined the level of training you want, check to be sure you're qualified. Most courses have minimum age and health requirements, and some may require proof of previous experience. Usually a recent medical statement will be called for, but, in addition, you should look into the physical demands that will be made on you in the water sessions. If they seem arduous, you should do some preparatory conditioning before enrolling.

Next, get to know the instructor who'll be leading your particular class. Since the end goal of the course is to give you realistic confidence in the water, choose an instructor you respect. Does he or she seem to care about you personally and how much you learn? This attitude is very important, but beware of the instructor who's *too* helpful; learn to perform every task by yourself, so you'll be fully independent of the instructor when the course is over.

While you're visiting the school, inspect the equipment used in the classes (preferably with an experienced friend). Are the models reasonably current? Are there obvious signs of wear or poor maintenance? Is there a variety of brands and models, and will there be enough to go around? Since using different brands and models in your training will help you make buying decisions later, does the course equipment look like the kind of gear you might want to own?

Look at the pool. Is it deep enough to be challenging when practicing a breathhold dive? Is it large enough to accommodate a typical-size class? Check the temperature — it should be neither too warm nor too cold. Are the changing facilities clean and adequate? Is the pool open for practice sessions outside of class time?

Ask where the open water diving will be done. If you can, go visit the sites (ideally there will be more than one, with varying conditions). What kind of access is there: beach, rocks, pier, etc.? Is there any surface support at the dive site, like a raft or float? Will a boat be used for any open water dives?

Now ask about the course itself. Check the student/teacher ratio. The maximum for open water work should be 10 to 1, with one assistant for each additional four students. Ask to see a course outline, or some sample teaching materials. At the very least, the curriculum should cover:

- Diving Physics
- Underwater Physiology
- Diving Medicine
- Equipment Use and Maintenance
- Safety/Emergency Procedures
- Underwater Environment
- Underwater Activities
- Diving Skills and Practices

Look into the duration of the course. A basic scuba certification should take at least 27 hours, 16 of them in the water (at least two in open water). More advanced certifications usually last 24-40 hours, with individual segments broken down this way: lectures, 10-16 hours; pool sessions, 12-16 hours; open water, 2-8 hours. Does the class meet at a convenient time for you? (Some convene on weeknights, others over successive weekends.) Are makeup classes available? Be sure you can realistically make the entire class schedule.

Find out for sure how the open water dives will be conducted. In a scuba course, at least a third of the open water time should be spent on scuba techniques. Be sure the open water dives are true learning sessions—not just "check-outs."

The laws of diving under pressure cause divers to adopt some techniques which are contrary to our normal instincts (exhaling while ascending, for instance). These techniques must be *overlearned* so they, in fact, become instinctive underwater. This kind of training takes time and repetition under a variety of conditions. The best place to practice these techniques is in open water, after thorough lecture and pool sessions. Be sure plenty of time is set aside for this.

Finally, pin down the full cost of the course, including any "extras" which may not be immediately apparent. What gear must the diver buy? What is provided by the shop, and what must be rented? Are there charges for air fills, boat transportation or other services? What about books, classroom materials and other items, such as the certification card itself. Also, what's the school's policy if you should fail your final check-out? Must the entire course be repeated, or can you take some remedial work in your weak areas? Any extra charges for this service? When in doubt, get it in writing, either in a brochure or in a signed course description including costs.

For a subjective "feel," you may want to see if you can sit in on a classroom or pool session. You can also talk to past students of your instructor. Get references if you wish. You might ask these graduates whether they got everything that was promised to them, whether there were any surprises, and whether they felt truly confident in the water as a result of the course.

Once you're enrolled, try to vary your learning experiences as much as possible. Work with different equipment and different buddies if you can. Try to take your open water dives in as many different locations, under as many different condi-

tions, as possible. A varied training experience helps in overlearning the new techniques you'll have to master, and gives you confidence that you can handle any situation that comes up.

Certifying Agencies

The key national and international agencies offering diving certifications are:

Association of Canadian Underwater Councils
333 River Road
Vanier, Ontario, Canada K1L 8B9
(613) 746-5797

Formed by a union of regional councils in 1964, ACUC developed its own training standards in 1969. Today, each provincial or territorial council conducts its own training programs through participating shops, clubs or independent instructors. You can contact the regional council for a list of local Diving Training Institutes.

Training standards are spelled out in the ACUC Standards and Procedures Manual and Total Training System Standards Book. Training bulletins and other publications are also issued to instructors, to keep them updated. Instructors are required to requalify every two years.

ACUC offers one snorkel and four scuba diving certifications. The basic scuba certification is designated Diver Level I, and is open to students as young as 15. In addition to classroom and pool time, the course requires three open water scuba dives to a maximum depth of 10 meters.

Diver Level II is for those divers 16 and older who have held a Diver Level I certificate for at least a year, logging at least 15 dives in that period, with a minimum of 10 hours underwater. Level III divers must be at least 17 and have held a Level II certificate for a year or more, with at least 30 dives logged for the year. This is ACUC's highest sport diver proficiency rating.

Those holding Diver Level III certificates can also take specialty courses, including underwater archeology, photography, military diving, and search and recovery.

ACUC instructor candidates can apply for the following teacher certificates:

Snorkel Diver Instructor. Open to individuals 16 and older who are aquatic instructors, lifeguards or certified scuba divers, and who have taken a recognized first aid course. Candidates must pass an ACUC snorkel instructional techniques program. These people can train and supervise classes, issue Snorkel Diver certifications, and assist in evaluating Snorkel Diving Instructor candidates.

Instructor Level I (Assistant). Open to those holding Level III certifications for at least one year, with a recommendation from an ACUC Instructor. These assistants can work, under supervision, in classroom, pool, and open water training for Divers Level I and II, and may issue certifications for Snorkel Divers.

Instructor Level II. Those who have been Assistant Instructors (Level I) for one year, have served as divemasters, and hold a recognized first aid certificate can enroll in a Level II certification program. Upon completion they can supervise Instructors Level I, conduct preparatory courses for Diver Level II, assist in Instructor Level I and II programs, and certify Snorkel Divers, Snorkel Instructors, and Divers I and II.

Instructor Level III. The highest level of ACUC teaching competence. Open to those with at least a year's experience at Instructor Level II working in three or more Level I or II certification programs. These individuals can conduct diving courses and certify divers at all levels, and participate in Instructor Level I, II, and III certification programs.

Instructor Level IV. These individuals constitute the ACUC national college, developing diving on a national level and implementing national policies regionally.

ACUC offers cross-certification with the international agency CMAS (see below) and has recently begun cross-certifying instructors with NAUI.

Confederation Mondiale
des Activites Subaquatiques
34 Rue de Colisee 75008
Paris, France
(tel: 225 60 42)

CMAS, or the World Underwater Federation as it is known in English, is the recognized certifying body in Europe and other non-English speaking lands, some 52 nations in all. It was founded in 1959 and in a few remote areas is still the only recognized certification.

North American divers planning far-off vacations can have ACUC, PADI or NAUI credentials cross-certified to an equivalent CMAS ranking. CMAS has three levels each of sport diver and instructor certification.

National Association of
Scuba Diving Schools, Inc.
P.O. Box 17067
Long Beach, CA 90807
(213) 595-5361

NASDS was formed in 1962 as the National Association of Skin Diving Stores. Today over 250 retailers in the U.S. (including Alaska, Hawaii and Puerto Rico) as well as the Caribbean and Africa offer NASDS instruction and certification. The organization estimates it has certified over 600,000 divers and 2,000 instructors.

The backbones of the NASDS teaching system are a manual called the Gold Book used to set course standards, and the NASDS textbook *Safe Scuba* (reviewed under "Publications"). To control its standards, NASDS prohibits instructors from giving lessons independently of member schools.

NASDS offers two sport diving certifications. The "Basic Diver" rating is considered a license to learn and the course consists of a minimum of 10 three-hour lectures, 10 three-hour pool sessions plus a structured open water class under the supervision of an Open Water Instructor. Most schools also offer an additional fun dive. Divers may continue their education with an "Open Water" course stressing underwater navigation, boat diving, surf entry, dive planning procedures, night diving and other advanced techniques. This course is available in three or more additional open water sessions.

Those interested in teaching diving can earn four levels of instructor certification through NASDS:

Instructor Provisional: Applies to individuals enrolled in an NASDS in-store training program. These people must teach under the direct supervision of an NASDS Open Water Instructor for three to six months and pass an NASDS Instructional-Sales Clinic before moving up to the next grade of instructor certification.

Instructor: Earned by attending an Instructional-Sales Clinic (held four times a year, combining advanced instruction and marketing programs). Instructors may teach in the classroom and pool. They may lead one open water class under the supervision of an Open Water Instructor. They may also sign certification cards.

Open Water Instructor Provisional: For people who have completed the NASDS Open Water Instructor College (see below) or a Clinic program, but who have a small deficiency that can be upgraded by teaching 50 students and providing a letter from the member school requesting the upgrading.

Open Water Instructor: Awarded to those performing perfectly at an Instructional-Sales Clinic. These people can teach all phases of the NASDS program.

Open Water Instructor College: For those planning to pursue diving instruction as a full time career. The six year old College in San Diego, California offers a 10-week course in retailing practices and diving instruction technology. Graduates receive Senior Life Saving Certificates and are trained in basic underwater photography, equipment maintenance, and repair. They are also taught how to organize, sell and conduct overseas diving trips.

NASDS member store/schools are urged to refrain from the practice of "cross-certifying" students or instructors holding certification cards from other instructional agencies. However, NASDS offers a type of C-card that divers from all associations may purchase, which identifies the certifying agency in addition to providing a microfilm record of the owner's diving and medical history and equipment serial numbers.

*National Association of
Underwater Instructors
P.O. Box 630
Colton, CA 92324
(714) 783-1862*

Incorporated as a non-profit organization in 1960, NAUI has trained over 6,000 instructors and 770,000 divers internationally.

NAUI offers its instructors voluminous teaching aids and manuals, with standardized curricula and teaching procedures. NAUI instructors may operate independently of dive shops.

NAUI offers its instructors voluminous teaching aids and manuals, with standardized curricula and teaching procedures. NAUI instructors may operate independently of dive shops.

There are 20 different NAUI sport diving certi-

fications, starting with a 2-8 hour introductory or resort course. Next comes Skin Diver (minimum age: 8 years) and Senior Skin Diver (minimum age: 12). Then there is a Junior Scuba Diver course for those aged 12-14.

NAUI's Basic Scuba Diver course, for those aged 15 and up, entails a minimum of 27 hours, 16 or more in the water (at least 2 in open water, with at least 45 minutes on scuba).

A Sport Scuba course is offered for divers who have completed a Basic Course and desire additional training or have been inactive for some time. An Experienced Scuba Diver certification is available for divers with experience but no recognized certification.

Ten Specialty Diver courses are also offered by NAUI. The specialties covered include cave diving, deep diving, ice diving, wreck diving, diving leadership, underwater photography, search and recovery, underwater environment, hunting and collecting, and professional diving.

Divers seeking true expertise in the sport can take Advanced Diver and Divemaster courses. NAUI Divemasters are trained to organize and conduct group dives, and may assist certified instructors in the open water training of students.

There are three NAUI teaching certifications:

Assistant Instructor: Certified through attendance at an Instructor Qualification Course or by an individual NAUI Instructor. These individuals may assist in teaching sanctioned diving courses under the supervision of a NAUI instructor and may serve as safety divers in open water training. They may not issue certifications.

Skin Diving Leader: Trained and certified by individual NAUI instructors, these individuals may independently teach sanctioned skin diving (but not scuba) courses. They may also perform as Assistant Instructors in NAUI diving courses (including scuba if they are certified in scuba).

Instructor: Granted only to graduates of a NAUI Instructor Training Course or "other agency to NAUI crossover." The courses last a minimum of 80 hours (8 or 9 straight days, 5-6 successive weekends, or a full college semester or quarter). They are open to NAUI Assistant Instructors or instructors of other associations. Over 20 ITCs are held each year across the U.S. and in Canada, Japan, and Europe.

NAUI offers a weekend crossover certification

for qualified instructors from other agencies, with both written and open water evaluations. The association also has an Instructor Referral Service which allows local divers to find the names of NAUI instructors or the schedules of Sport, Advanced, or Specialty Diver courses in their areas.

*Professional Association
of Diving Instructors*
2064 N. Bush Street
Santa Ana, CA 92706
(714) 547-6996

Formed in 1966, originally to service the Midwest, PADI has grown into an international organization with more than 9,000 certified instructors in 50 countries.

Like NAUI, PADI offers a broad range of certifications, including Introductory Scuba, Skin Diver, Junior Scuba, and Basic Scuba. Minimum recommended duration for the Basic Scuba course is 27 hours, including one skin dive and two scuba dives in open water.

There is also a Forgotten Diver course for uncertified old salts, and such advanced certifications as Open Water, Advanced Open Water, and Divemaster. Specialty courses include underwater photography, hunting and collecting, search and recovery, rescue, equipment specialization, research diving, plus wreck, deep water, cave and ice diving. Those acquiring five of the specialty certifications enter PADI's highest sport diving classification: Master Scuba Diver.

PADI offers six levels of instructor certification:

Assistant Instructor: Open to certified PADI Divemasters. These people may teach and certify skin divers independently and assist in classroom and open water sessions for students up through the Advanced Open Water Diver course. To become an Assistant Instructor, a trainee must observe one complete Open Water Diver course and assist an active PADI instructor in a second course.

Underwater Instructor: Affiliate membership rating for qualified instructors from other recognized agencies accepted on individual application. These individuals may not certify PADI Assistant Instructors or staff PADI Instructor Training Courses.

Open Water Scuba Instructor: Issued to graduates of PADI sponsored Instructor Training Courses or to those achieving equivalent orientation to PADI programs, standards, procedures, philosophies, and teaching methods. The Instructor Training Courses last a minimum of 80 hours, over at least eight days, although they may be taken over weekends or college semesters or quarters. Courses are offered periodically in local areas.

Specialty Instructor: Open to PADI Underwater Instructors, Open Water Scuba Instructors, and Master Instructors. These ratings are granted upon acceptance of an application calling for a resume of qualifications and an outline of the proposed course.

Master Instructor: Available to those certified as PADI Open Water Instructors, as well as Water Safety, First Aid, and Cardio-Pulmonary Resuscitation Instructors, with additional involvement in PADI activities over at least two years. This rating is also granted on application and authorizes the holder to conduct sanctioned courses on all levels through the Assistant Instructor rating, except for specialties in which the holder had not received a Specialty Instructor Rating.

Course Director: Master Instructors may attend a Course Directors Workshop to qualify to conduct sanctioned training to Instructor levels.

PADI offers certified divers a Positive Identification C-card with the diver's photo and personal data encased in waterproof plastic. Divers certified by NAUI, YMCA, NASDS, SSI, or CMAS can cross-certify for one of these cards.

*Scuba Schools
International*
1449 Riverside Drive
Ft. Colins, CO 80521
(303) 482-0883

SSI began in 1970 as a non-profit educational organization and a professional retail dive store association. Today SSI courses are offered internationally through dive shops, schools and resorts.

In 1975, SSI and Jeppesen Sanderson introduced the Jeppesen Sport Diver Learning System, a combination of audio-visual, text, and workbook materials which is used to standardize SSI courses.

SSI offers three levels of sport diving instruction. The first is a snorkeling program for the traveling diver, designed to be offered through local travel agencies by cooperating dive shops. The next level is the Advanced Open Water certification, lasting a minimum of 41 hours and requiring six open water classes. SSI offers no basic certification.

The last sport level is actually a semi-professional certification, known as Dive Control Specialist. Graduates of the 45-hour DIVECON course receive advanced training in equipment, group control problems, diving physics and physiology, and rescue techniques. They can teach the SSI snorkeling program.

SSI has three instructor certifications:

Instructor Trainee: An introduction for the DIVECON graduate to teaching and retail dive store operation. Instructor trainees may teach snorkeling programs.

Advanced Open Water Instructor: Earned by graduates of an SSI Instructor School. This program consists of nine 8-10 hour days, and covers instruction, repair, and sales. Instructors certified by other agencies can earn this rating at an SSI Recertification Clinic.

DIVECON Instructor: Granted upon satisfactory completion of an application by a qualified instructor. These are the only individuals certified to teach SSI's DIVECON program.

In addition, SSI offers a Dive Rescue Specialist course to law enforcement officers, fire department personnel and underwater search and rescue teams. These courses are hosted by local participating SSI member stores, and taught by a staff of experienced former police officers.

*Young Men's
Christian Association
Center for
Underwater Activities*
P.O. Box 1547
Key West, FL 33040
(305) 294-0341

The YMCA Scuba Program began in the early 1950s in individual Ys and became standardized nationally in 1959. The program is now taught in 83 countries around the world. Today some 2,000 YMCA instructors are certifying approximately 30,000 divers a year.

The YMCA program offers four levels of sport certification. The *Basic Course* consists of a minimum of 14 hours of theory and 18 hours of pool work, plus one open water free dive and two open water tank dives.

Also offered is an Environmental Course with ten open water experiences designed to show the new diver the spectrum of diving available in the area, augmented with lectures on the special equipment and techniques being utilized and the nature of the environment and marine life being experienced.

An Advanced Course encompassing first aid, lifesaving, and sophisticated diving skills is also available, as are Specialty Programs including cave diving, ice diving, underwater photography, search and recovery, and diving medicine. Not all specialties (eg: ice diving) are available in all areas.

YMCA's Leadership Programs are broken down into three levels:

Teaching Assistant: Open to those 15 and over who have logged at least 15 dives. Duties include helping in pool instruction, while preparing as an assistant instructor.

Assistant Instructor: For trainees who pass a 20 hour program of testing and teaching in classroom, pool, and open water. Assistant Instructors may teach skin diving, lecture in scuba classes, and take charge of up to four scuba students in the pool and open water (under supervision).

Instructor: Issued to graduates of an Instructor Institute (similar in format but three times as long as the Assistant Instructor program). Instructors may teach basic, environmental or advanced courses, and specialty courses if they have completed the training for that specialty.

Not all local YMCAs offer scuba training, but YMCA certification is sometimes given by colleges and universities, recreation departments, apartment complexes, private swim clubs, dive shops, YMHA's, and other outlets. Check your local Y or contact the national center listed above to see if any of these programs are offered in your area.

Local Schools

Following is a list of dive schools throughout the United States, U.S. Possessions and Canada offering one or more of the recognized certifications discussed in this chapter. The list is arranged alphabetically by state and city, and the certifications offered are noted by initials.

Schools

U.S.

ALABAMA

Southern Skin Divers Supply
506 S. 45th St.
Birmingham, AL 35222
PADI

Diving Unlimited
205 Oak St.
Decatur, AL 35601
PADI

Sea Divers
121 Walnut Drive
Enterprise, AL 36330
NAUI

Aquarius Scuba School
8130 W. Main
Glencoe, AL 35905
NASDS

Ripp-Tide Dive Center
2805 S. 18th St.
Homewood, AL 35209
SSI

Aquaspace
7250 Governors Dr. W.
Huntsville, AL 35805
NASDS

Gulf Coast Divers Supply
512 Houston St.
Mobile, AL 36605
PADI

Southern Water Sports
1284 Hutson Dr.
Mobile, AL 36609
NASDS, SSI

Capitol Dive Center
42 Carol Villa Dr.
Montgomery, AL 36109
NASDS

Outdoor World
1317 Avalon
Muscle Shoals, AL 35660
PADI

Planet Ocean Scuba School
Rt. 3, Box 7294
Sylacauga, AL 35150
NASDS

Champion Scuba Divers
400 E. Sloan Ave.
Talladega, AL 35160
PADI

Professional Divers Service
3113 - 9th St.
Tuscaloosa, AL 35401
NAUI

ALASKA

Divers World
1534 Campbell
Anchorage, AK 99501
NAUI

Juneau Diving School
Box 362
Juneau, AK 99801
NASDS, NAUI

Alaska Aquatic Dive Center
503 Water St.
Ketchikan, AK 99901
NASDS, PADI

Commercial Diving Services
P.O. Box 1554
Kodiak, AK 99615
PADI

Alaska Black Dolphins
P.O. Box 601
Seward, AK 36609
NASDS

Southeastern Divers Supply
P.O. Box 1476
Sitka, AK 99835
NASDS

ARIZONA

Havasu Scuba & Sports, Inc.
1668 McCulloch Blvd.
Lake Havasu City, AZ 86403
NAUI

El Mar Diving Center
2245 W. Broadway
Mesa, AZ 99901
PADI

Aqua Sports
4230 S. Indian School Rd.
Phoenix, AZ 85012
NASDS, NAUI

Scuba Sciences
2620 W. Butler
Phoenix, AZ 85021
NASDS, NAUI

Scuba Sciences
4265 N. Brown Ave.
Scottsbluff, AZ 85251
NASDS

Scuba Sciences
616 S. Myrtle
Temple, AZ 85281
NASDS

Desert Diving School
7810 Apple Tree Drive
Tucson, AZ 85730
NAUI

Desert Reef Tech Sports
1123 E. 6th St.
Tucson, AZ 85719
NAUI

H. Cook Sporting Goods
El Con Center
Tucson, AZ 85716
NAUI

Tucson School of Scuba Diving
3575 E. Speedway
Tucson, AZ 85716
NASDS, NAUI

Aqua Dive Shop
356 W. 24th
Yuma, AZ 99901
PADI

Aqua World of Yuma
3014 - 4th Ave.
Yuma, AZ 85364
NAUI

ARKANSAS

Scuba Services Co.
1205 N. 6th Terrace
Barling, AR 72923
PADI

Starkey Marina
Rt. 2, Box 170
Eureka Springs, AR 72632
NAUI

Professional Ski N Scuba
P.O. Box 831
Heber Springs, AR 72543
PADI

J & T Dive Shop
Route 7 N. Culberhouse
Jonesboro, AR 72401
PADI

Cap'n Frogs of Arkansas
11401 Rodney Parham Rd.
Little Rock, AR 72205
NASDS

Lynn's Ski 'N Scuba
3408 S. University
Little Rock, AR 72204
PADI

Sports Co.
1115 S. Hwy. 71
Springdale, AR 72264
NASDS

CALIFORNIA

Divers Exchange
1104 Lincoln Ave.
Alameda, CA 94501
NAUI

California Skin Diving School
1083 N. Harbor Blvd.
Anaheim, CA 92801
NASDS

N. Orange County Regional
   Occupational Program
2360 W. La Palma
Anaheim, CA 92801
NAUI

Scuba Schools of Anaheim
1640 W. Lincoln Ave.
Anaheim, CA 92801
NAUI, PADI

Undersea Services
1631 Placentia Ave., Unit F
Anaheim, CA 92806
NAUI

Arcadia Pool & Dive
21 W. Durante Rd.
Arcadia, CA 91006
NASDS

Auburn Ski Hut
585 High St.
Auburn, CA 95603
NAUI

Catalina Island School
P.O. Box 796
Avalon, CA 90704
NAUI

Bamboo Reef
2110 Winchester Blvd.
Campbell, CA 95008
NAUI

The Comstock Shop
1040 Village Lane
Chico, CA 95926
NAUI

South Bay Diving Center
618 Broadway
Chula Vista, CA 92010
NAUI

Skip Sports, Inc.
Corte Madera Center
Corte Madera, CA 94925
NASDS

Laguna Sea Sports
1951 Newport Blvd.
Costa Mesa, CA 92627
NAUI

Menfish Underwater Inter.
P.O. Box 1265
Cupertino, CA 95014
NAUI

Amphibian Dive Shop
2123 Junipero Serra Blvd.
Daly City, CA 94015
NAUI

Black Barts Aquatics
34145 Coast Hwy.
Dana Point, CA 94145
NAUI

The Diving Bell
901 E. 3rd St.
Davis, CA 95616
NAUI, PADI

Lockheed MBL
P.O. Box 398
Avila Beach, CA 93424
NAUI

Innerspace
1303 N. Chester
Bakersfield, CA 93308
NASDS

Scuba Tech
9422 Alondra
Bellflower, CA 90706
NASDS

Bamboo Reef
1111 University Ave.
Berkeley, CA 94702
NAUI

Sunland Sports Lodge Dive Shop
8677 Wilshire Blvd.
Beverly Hills, CA 90211
NAUI, PADI

Aloha Diving Schools
2910 W. Magnolia
Burbank, CA 91505
NASDS

Aqua Ventures
2172 Pickwick Drive
Ponderosa North
Camarillo, CA 93010
NAUI, PADI

Divers Corner
11200 Old River School Rd.
Downey, CA 90241
NASDS

Diving Locker
348 E. Grand
Escondido, CA 92025
NASDS

Mosbarger, Inc.
425 3rd St.
Eureka, CA 95501
PADI

Pro Sport Center
508 Myrtle Ave.
Eureka, CA 95501
PADI

Coastal Sporting Goods
18601 N. Hwy. 1
Ft. Bragg, CA 95437
NASDS

O'Brien's Scuba
37313 Maple St.
Fremont, CA 94536
NAUI

Bob's Dive Shop of Fresno
1312 Blackstone
Fresno, CA 93703
NASDS

G. E. Monahan & Co.
3142 Belmont
Fresno, CA 93701
NASDS

Aqua Lung Center
3141 E. Yorba Linda Blvd.
Fullerton, CA 92631
PADI

Undersea Services
3043 Topaz Lane, N.B.
Fullerton, CA 92631
NAUI

Bob's Diving Locker
500 Botello Rd.
Goleta, CA 93017
NAUI

The Anchor Shack
571 Jackson St.
Hayward, CA 94544
NASDS, NAUI

Kelp Monsters Diving Center
11317 Posthill Rd.
Lakeside, CA 92040
NAUI

New England Divers
8363 Center Dr.
La Mesa, CA 92041
NAUI, PADI

Desert Scuba
512 W. Lancaster Blvd.
Lancaster, CA 93534
NAUI

San Diego Divers Supply
7522 La Jolla Blvd.
La Jolla, CA 92037
NASDS

Scuba Divers Supply
635 Pearl St.
La Jolla, CA 92037
NAUI

Lodi Skin Diving School
430 W. Lockeford St.
Lodi, CA 95240
NASDS

Paynes Demersal Divers
117 South H St.
Lompoc, CA 93436
NAUI

Scuba Schools of Long Beach
4740 E. Pacific Coast Hwy.
Long Beach, CA 90806
NAUI, PADI

Foothill College
12345 El Monte Rd.
Los Altos Hills, CA 94022
NAUI

Los Angeles Atheltic Club
431 W. 7th St.
Los Angeles, CA 90014
NAUI

New England Divers
11830 W. Pico Blvd.
Los Angeles, CA 90064
PADI

Malibu Divers
21231 Pacific Coast Hwy.
Malibu, CA 90265
PADI

California Wreck Divers
P.O. Box 9922
Marina Del Rey, CA 90291
NAUI

California Skin Diving School
4420 Holt Blvd.
Montclair, CA 91763
NASDS

Aquarius Dive Shop
2240 Del Monte Ave.
Monterey, CA 93940
NASDS

Ed Brawley Skindiving School
598 Foam St.
Monterey, CA 93940
PADI

Monterey Dive Center
763 Lighthouse Ave.
Monterey, CA 93940
PADI

El Camino Skin Diving School
1015 W. El Camino Real
Mountain View, CA 94040
PADI

Skip Sports, Inc.
3144 Jefferson St.
Napa, CA 94558
NASDS

South Bay Dive Center
105 W. 18th St.
National City, CA 92050
NAUI

Colo-Riv-Val Divers School
1920 Rio Vista
Needles, CA 92363
NASDS

Aquatic Center
4535 W. Coast Hwy.
Newport Beach, CA 92663
NASDS, NAUI, PADI

The Pinnaclis Dive Center
875 Grant Ave.
Novato, CA 94947
NAUI

Coastal Diving Co.
320 - 29th Ave.
Oakland, CA 94612
NASDS

S & S Scuba School
306½ Wisconsin
Oceanside, CA 92054
NASDS, NAUI

Westwind Divers, Inc.
1891 N. Tustin Ave.
Orange, CA 92665
NAUI, PADI

Pacheco Skin Diving Center
5775 Pacheco
Pacheco, CA 94520
NASDS, NAUI

Anderson's Skin & Scuba School
541 Oceana Blvd.
Pacifica, CA 94044
NAUI

Al's Sporting Goods
750 Price St.
Pismo Beach, CA 93449
NAUI

Oshman's
3303 N. Main St.
Pleasant Hill, CA 94523
NASDS

Nor-Cal U/W
7375 Spring Br. Rd.
Redding, CA 96001
NAUI

Dive N' Surf
504 N. Broadway
Redondo Beach, CA 90277
NASDS

Sea d Sea
1911 S. Catalina Ave.
Redondo Beach, CA 90277
NASDS, PADI

Aloha Diving Schools
7626 Tampa Ave.
Reseda, CA 91335
NASDS

Scuba Duba Dive
7126 Resenda Blvd.
Reseda, CA 91335
NAUI

California Skin Diving School
9762 Magnolia Ave.
Riverside, CA 92503
NASDS

California Skin Diving School
8099 Indiana Ave.
Riverside, CA 92503
NASDS

Cassotta Diving Instr.
4930 Pacific St.
Rocklin, CA 95677
PADI

Dolphin Swim School
1530 El Camino Ave.
Sacramento, CA 95815
NAUI

Ed Brawley Skindiving School
2147 Hurley Way
Sacramento, CA 95825
PADI

Mother Lode Dive Shop
2020 H St.
Sacramento, CA 91324
PADI

California Skin Diving School
1173 E. St.
San Bernardino, CA 92408
NASDS

Sea to Sea Scuba School
804 E. 16th St.
San Bernardino, CA 92404
NAUI

Diving Locker
1148 Delevan Dr.
San Diego, CA 92102
NASDS

Diving Locker
1020 Grand Ave.
San Diego, CA 92109
NASDS, NAUI

Naval Training Center
c/o Special Services
San Diego, CA 92133
PADI

New England Divers of San Diego
3860 Rosecrans
San Diego, CA 92110
NAUI, PADI

San Diego Divers Supply
4004 Sports Arena Blvd.
San Diego, CA 92110
NASDS

Aqua-Gear
1254 - 9th Ave.
San Francisco, CA 94122
NASDS

Bamboo Reef
584 Fourth St.
San Francisco, CA 94107
NAUI

Ocean Rovers
USMACTHAI JUSMAG Box 474
APO San Francisco, CA 96346
NAUI

Competition Ski & Sports
8958 Huntington Dr.
San Gabriel, CA 91775
NASDS

Bamboo Reef
1959 W. San Carlos
San Jose, CA 95128
NAUI

South Valley Skin Diving School
3852 Monterey Rd.
San Jose, CA 95111
NASDS

Stan's Skin Diving
554 S. Bascom Ave.
San Jose, CA 95128
NAUI

Water Pro
280 Higuera
San Luis Obispo, CA 93401
NASDS

Sports World
2477 Huntington Dr.
San Marino, CA 91108
NASDS

The Nautilus
3986 Huntington Dr.
San Marino, CA 91108
PADI

Ed Brawley Skindiving School
514 S. Bayshore Blvd.
San Mateo, CA 94402
PADI

Monterey Dive Center
13 W. 41st St.
San Mateo, CA 94403
PADI

Pacific Sporting Goods
1719 S. Pacific Ave.
San Pedro, CA 90731
PADI

Marin Skin Diving
3765 Redwood Hwy.
San Rafael, CA 94903
PADI

Oshman's
3rd & Grand
San Rafael, CA 94901
NASDS

Skip Sports
47 Paul Drive
San Rafael, CA 94903
NASDS

Aquatic Center
312 N. Harbor Blvd.
Santa Ana, CA 92703
NASDS, PADI

Diver's Den
22 Anacapa St.
Santa Barbara, CA 93101
NASDS

Underwater Sports
Marina Breakwater
Santa Barbara, CA 93109
NAUI

Nautilus Scuba School
2636 The Alameda
Santa Clara, CA 95050
NASDS

San Jose Divers School
2221 The Alameda
Santa Clara, CA 95050
NAUI

Steele's Sporting Goods
2350 El Camino Real
Santa Clara, CA 95051
NAUI

O'Neill's Dive Shop
2222 E. Cliff Drive
Santa Cruz, CA 95062
NAUI, PADI

Dive West
123 W. Main St.
Santa Maria, CA 93454
NAUI

Scuba Haus
2501 Wilshire Blvd.
Santa Monica, CA 90403
NAUI

Diving Center of Santa Cruz
2696 Santa Rosa
Santa Rosa, CA 95401
NAUI

Oshman's
1620 Mendicino Ave.
Santa Rosa, CA 94504
NASDS

Skip Sports, Inc.
733 - 4th St.
Santa Rosa, CA 94504
NASDS

Seaquest Scuba Schools
4380 Eileen St.
Semi Valley, CA 93063
NAUI

Diving Locker
155 S. Hwy. 101
Solano Beach, CA 92075
NASDS

Valley Skin Diving School
7831 Thornton Rd.
Stockton, CA 95027
NASDS

Scuba Duba Dive
12538 Ventura Blvd.
Studio City, CA 91604
NAUI

Diver's Dock
1020 W. El Camino
Sunnyvale, CA 94087
NAUI

Odyssey Dive
1586 Benton St.
Sunnyvale, CA 94087
NAUI

Seaquest Scuba Schools
1520 Thousand Oaks Blvd.
Thousand Oaks, CA 91360
NAUI

Ukiah Skin & Scuba
328 N. State St.
Ukiah, CA 95482
NAUI, PADI

Pelican Dive Shop
1645 Broadway
Vallejo, CA 94594
NASDS

Innerspace Diving Instruments
1420 Roleen Drive
Vallejo, CA 94590
NAUI

Laguna Sea Sports
7066 Van Nuys Blvd.
Van Nuys, CA 91405
NAUI

Ventura County Skin & Scuba
2805 Palma Dr.
Ventura, CA 93003
NASDS

Visalia Scuba Center
1933 B.W. Caldwell
Visalia, CA 93277
NASDS

Ed Brawley Skindiving School
2756 Camino Diablo
Walnut Creek, CA 94596
PADI

Olympic Dive & Travel
2595 N. Main St.
Walnut Creek, CA 94596
NASDS, NAUI

Scuba Tech
1613 Garvey Ave.
West Covina, CA 91790
NASDS

Commercial Diving Center
272 S. Fries
Wilmington, CA 90744
NAUI

Cal Aquatics
22725 Ventura Blvd.
Woodland Hills, CA 91364
NAUI

Scuba Hut
1181 Bridge St.
Yuba City, CA 95991
NAUI

COLORADO

Divers Reef, Inc.
3014 N. Nevada
Colorado Springs, CO 80907
PADI

Colorado Divers World
557 Milwaukee Ave.
Denver, CO 80206
NASDS

Diving Unlimited, Inc.
Happy Canyon Shopping Center
Denver, CO 80237
PADI

A-1 Diving Co.
4730 S. Lipan
Englewood, CO 80110
PADI

Rocky Mountian Diving Center Ltd.
1920 Wadsworth Blvd.
Lakewood, CO 80215
NAUI, PADI, SSI

Blue Mesa Scuba Center
123 Akard Ave.
Montrose, CO 81401
SSI

The Sports Arena
405 W. 8th St.
Pueblo, CO 81003
NASDS

Pueblo Divers Supply
4400 Thatcher
Pueblo, CO 81005
NAUI, PADI

CONNECTICUT

Orbit Marine
3273 Fairfield Ave.
Bridgeport, CT 06605
NAUI, PADI

The Diving Bell
RD 5, U.S. Route 7
Brookfield, CT 06804
PADI

Innerspace Diving Supply Co.
115 Center St.
Manchester, CT 06040
NAUI

Jack's Dive Center, Inc.
466 East St.
Plainville, CT 06062
NAUI, PADI

Bat-Liz Pro Divers Supply
20 Russell Rd.
Stratford, CT 06497
NAUI

The Scuba Shop
Foot of Broad
Stratford, CT 06497
NAUI, PADI, SSI

The Borowski Institute
370 Tudor St.
Waterbury, CT 06704
NAUI

Will Jacobs Dive Shop
1153 New Britian Ave.
West Hartford, CT 06110
PADI

DELAWARE

First State Sports, Inc.
2150 New Castle Ave.
New Castle, DE 19720
NAUI

Delaware Diving Academy.
P.O. Box 157
Ocean View, DE 19970
NASDS

First State Sports, Inc.
4109 Newport Gap Pike Rt. 41
Wilmington, DE 19808
NAUI

FLORIDA

Sundown Divers
208 Grace Blvd.
Altamonte Springs, FL 32701
NAUI

Seacamp Assn.
Big Pine Key, FL 33043
NAUI

Underseas, Inc.
P.O. Box 319, U.S. 1
Big Pine Key, FL 33043
PADI

Atlantic Coast Divers, Inc.
825 N. Federal Hwy.
Boynton Beach, FL 33435
PADI

Boca Dive Shop
251 N. Federal Hwy.
Boca Raton, FL 33432
NASDS, SSI

The Wreck Dive Shop
5905 N. Federal Hwy.
Boca Raton, FL 33432
PADI

Gulfview Divers Headquarters
101 Bridge St.
Bradenton Beach, FL 33510
PADI

Robby Sporting Goods
4517 Manatee Ave. W.
Bradenton, FL 33505
PADI

Charlotte Diver
861 SE Tamiami Trail
Charlotte Harbor, FL 33950
PADI

Pop's Scuba School
1754 Drew St.
Clearwater, FL 33515
NASDS

Mac's Scuba, Inc.
600 Mandalay Ave.
Clearwater, FL 33515
NASDS

Underwater Ltd.
216 Palermo Ave.
Coral Gables, FL 33134
NAUI, NASDS

Plantation Inn Marina
P.O. Box 1093
Crystal River, FL 32629
NASDS

Port Paradise Paquet Boat
P.O. Box 516
Crystal River, FL 32629
PADI

Kiefer's Sporting Goods
306 E. Pasco Ave.
Dade City, FL 33525
PADI

Atlantic Scuba Academy
20 N. Atlantic Ave.
Daytona Beach, FL 32018
NASDS, PADI

Herb's Dive Shop
2434 Atlantic Ave.
Daytona Beach, FL 32018
NASDS

Professional Diving Schools of Florida
210 N. Federal Hwy.
Deerfield Beach, FL 33441
PADI

Duck Key Divers
Indies Inn & Yacht Club
Duck Key, FL 33050
PADI

Aqua-Marine Water Safety School
485 SW 6th Court
Florida City, FL 33030
NAUI

Divers Haven
1530 Cordova Rd. SE
Ft. Lauderdale, FL 33316
NAUI

Dive Shop of Ft. Lauderdale
913 N. Atlantic Blvd.
Ft. Lauderdale, FL 33304
NAUI, PADI

Underseas Sports
609 S. Federal Hwy.
Ft. Lauderdale, FL 33301
NAUI

B & C Sports Diving
Rt. 3, Box 409 Miners Plaza
Ft. Myers, FL 33901
NAUI, PADI

Underseas Sports, Inc.
850 N. Federal Hwy.
Ft. Lauderdale, FL 33304
NAUI

Underwater Explorers
6068 McGregor Blvd.
Ft. Myers, FL 33901
NAUI

Under Sea World
521 N. 4th St.
Ft. Pierce, FL 33450
NASDS

Ocean Sports
129 E. Miracle Strip Pkwy.
Ft. Walton Beach, FL 32548
NAUI

Allen's Aquatic Center
3448 W. University Ave.
Gainsville, FL 32601
NASDS, NAUI

Divers Unlimited, Inc.
4231 Hollywood Blvd.
Hollywood, FL 33021
PADI

Seven Seas Dive Shop
2210 Hollywood Blvd.
Hollywood, FL 33020
PADI

Holiday Isle Dive Shop
P.O. Box 482
Islamorada, FL 33036
PADI

American Scuba Schools
5627 Arlington Rd.
Jacksonville, FL 32211
PADI

Florida P.A.D.I. Clinic
13638 Beach Blvd.
Jacksonville, FL 32224
PADI

Florida P.A.D.I. College
4593 St. Johns Ave.
Jacksonville, FL 32210
PADI

Florida State Skin Diving Schools
4172 Phillips Hwy.
Jacksonville, FL 32207
NASDS

Pro Dive Shop
4564 Atlantic Blvd.
Jacksonville, FL 32207
PADI

Bill Crawford's Tropic Isle Dive Shop
P.O. Box 755
Key Largo, FL 33037
PADI

Capt. Bob Klein
Holiday Inn Scuba Shop
Key Largo, FL 33612
PADI

C Gages Diving
Box 111, U.S. 1
Key Largo, FL 33037
NAUI

Coral Reef Park Co.
P.O. Box 13-M
Key Largo, FL 33037
NAUI, PADI

Key Largo Diving Hdq.
Rt. 1, Box 293
Key Largo, FL 33037
NAUI

Ocean Divers
P.O. Box 1113
Key Largo, FL 33037
SSI

Ocean Reef Dive Shop
Rt. 1, Box 274-B
Key Largo, FL 33037
NASDS

Sea-Dwellers Dive Center
P.O. Box 1796
Key Largo, FL 33037
PADI

Angler's Dive Shop
U.S. 1 Stock Island
Key West, FL 33040
PADI

Key West Pro Dive Shop
1605 N. Roosevelt
Key West, FL 33040
NASDS

Lakeland Diving Center
715 Alicia Dr.
Lakeland, FL 33801
PADI

Koller's Scuba School
810 Lake Shore Drive
Lake Park, FL 33403
NAUI

The Sport & Dive Shop, Inc.
740 Park Ave.
Lake Park, FL 33403
NAUI

Reef Dive Shop
304 E. Ocean Ave.
Lantana, FL 33462
NASDS

Atlantic Coast Divers, Inc.
409 Lake Ave.
Lakeworth, FL 33460
PADI

Hall's Dive Shop
1688 Overseas Hwy.
Marathon, FL 33050
PADI

Cliff's Fishing & Diving Center
2001 S. Melbourne Court
Melbourne, FL 32901
NAUI

Hatt's Diving Headquarters
2006 E. Front
Melbourne, FL 35901
NASDS, PADI

Missle Skin Diving
691 Courtenay N.
Merritt Island, FL 32952
NASDS

Culter Ridge Dive Center
20850 S. Dixie Hwy.
Miami, FL 33189
NAUI

Divemaster, Inc.
8350 SW 186 St.
Miami, FL 33157
NAUI

Divers Den South
12614 N. Kendall Dr.
Miami, FL 33186
PADI

The Diving Locker
295 Sunny Isles Blvd.
Miami Beach, FL 33160
NASDS

New England Divers
2945 NE 2nd Ave.
Miami, FL 33157
PADI

Underwater Unlimited
8429 SW 132nd St.
Miami, FL 33143
NASDS

U.S. Aquatics Diving School
971 SW First St.
Miami, FL 33130
PADI

Sous Marine Enterprises
449 McDonald St.
Mt. Dora, FL 32757
PADI

Scuba-Ski
118 - 9th St. S.
Naples, FL 33940
PADI

The Diving Bell
1700 E. Tamiami Trail
Naples, FL 33940
PADI

Ft. Lauderdale Scuba Academy
3410 NW 9th Ave.
Oakland Park, FL 33309
NASDS

Matheny's Aquatics Unlimited
556 Kingsley Ave.
Orange Park, FL 32703
NASDS, PADI

Bob's Scuba/Sport Center
55275 Orange Blossom Trail
Orlando, FL 32809

NAUI, PADI

Florida State Skin Diving Schools
1900 N. Mills Ave.
Orlando, FL 32803

NASDS, SSI

Jim Hollis Scuba World
5107 East Colonial Dr.
Orlando, FL 32807

PADI

Scots Swim & Scuba School
3465 Edgewater Drive
Orlando, FL 32804

NAUI

Diving Don's Dive Shop
333 S. Yonge St.
Ormond Beach, FL 32074

PADI

Ozona Dive Shop
300 Orange St.
Ozona, FL 33560

PADI

Norene Rouse Scuba
Buccaneer Yacht Club
143 Lake Drive
Palm Beach Shores, FL 33404

NAUI

C & G Sporting Goods
2144 Cove Blvd.
Panama City, FL 32401

NASDS

C & G Sporting Goods
137 Harrison
Panama City, FL 32401

NASDS

Divers Den
P.O. Box 10606
Panama City, FL 32401

NAUI

Hydrospace International
5323 N. Lagoon Drive
Panama City, FL 32401

NAUI

Kingry's Fishing Hole
2814 W. Hwy. 88
Panama City, FL 32401

NAUI

Pro Divers Shop
1218 Beck Ave.
Panama City, FL 32401

NAUI

Dive World
3090 N. Pace Blvd.
Pensacola, FL 32505

NAUI, PADI

Dot's Divers Professional Scuba
Instruction, Inc.
858 N. 72nd Ave.
Pensacola, FL 32506

NAUI

Gulf Coast Divers Supply
700 New Warrington Rd.
Pensacola, FL 32506

NAUI

Ray Manuel Diving
6134 N. 9th Ave.
Pensacola, FL 32504

PADI

Skipper's Diving, Inc.
408 E. Wright St.
Pensacola, FL 32501

NASDS, SSI

Tackle Shack
7801 - 66th St.
Pinellas Park, FL 33565

NASDS

Ft. Lauderdale Divers, Inc.
33 E. Acre Dr.
Plantation, FL 33317

NASDS, SSI

Aquatic Gateways
15 N. Federal Hwy.
Pompano Beach, FL 33062

NASDS

Chris Aquatics
222 N. Pompano Beach Blvd.
Pompano Beach, FL 33062

PADI

Treasure Cove Diving Center
20 NE 28th Ave.
Pompano, FL 33062

NAUI

Tropical Aquatics
2124 E. Atlantic Blvd.
Pompano Beach, FL 30062

NAUI

Colonnades Undersea Center
2525 Lake Drive
Riviera Beach, FL 33404

NAUI

Seapro, Inc.
U.S. Hwy. #1
Riviera Beach, FL 33404

PADI, SSI

Seaview Divers
6826 Gulf of Mexico Dr.
Long Boat Key
Sarasota, FL 33577

NASDS

The Tackle Box
1568 Main St.
Sarasota, FL 33577

PADI

American Divers Co.
415 Anastasia Blvd.
St. Augustine, FL 32084

PADI

Blue Water Marine Supplies
3511 SE Dixie Hwy.
Stuart, FL 33494

NASDS

Carter's Sporting Goods
3001 W. Tennessee St.
Tallahassee, FL 32304

NASDS

Dixie Divin Shoppe
2015 N. Monroe St.
Tallahassee, FL 32303

SSI

Central Florida Divers
10022 N. 30th St.
Tampa, FL 33612

PADI

Pelican Swim Center
1010 S. 76th St.
Tampa, FL 33691

NASDS

World of Water
3625 W. Kennedy Blvd.
Tampa, FL 33609

NASDS

Aquapro, Inc.
Mile Marker 91.5
Tavarnier, FL 33070

PADI

Barnacle Bills Dive
1556 Cypress Drive
Tequesta, FL 33458

NAUI

The Dive Shop
1325 S. Washington
Titusville, FL 32780

PADI

Aquatic Associates
5831 W. Hallandale Bch. Blvd.
West Hollywood, FL 33023

NASDS, PADI

Divers World
601 S. Olive Ave.
West Palm Beach, FL 33401

PADI

UNEXSO
Box 15933
West Palm Beach, FL 34406

NAUI

YMCA Recreation Center
2400 Ware Drive
West Palm Beach, FL 33409

NAUI

Deep Six Divers Service
505 Ave. "O" SE
Winter Haven, FL 33880

NAUI

Polk County Skin Diving School
P.O. Box 1678
Winter Haven, FL 33880

NASDS

Joe Hall the Scubaman
525 Kilshore Lane
Winter Park, FL 32789

SSI

Diveco Diving Systems
50 Royal Palm Blvd.
Vero Beach, FL 32960

NAUI, PADI, SSI

GEORGIA

Diving Locker
AITS Shopping Center
1490 Baxter St.
Athens, GA 30601

PADI

Airco The Diver
634 Lindbergh Way NE
Atlanta, GA 30324

PADI

Dive & Leisure Sports of Atlanta
3365 Main St.
College Park, GA 30337

PADI

W. Georgia Skin Diving School
2111 Wynnton Rd.
Columbus, GA 31906

NASDS

Dixie Divers
2546 Mellville Ave.
Decatur, GA 30032

SSI

Aqua Shop
131 E. Montgomery Crossroads
Savannah, GA 31406

NASDS

Garrard Pro Diver
2536 S. Cobb Dr.
Smyrna, GA 30080

PADI

Statesboro Scuba
28 S. Zetterower
Statesboro, GA 30458

NASDS

Sub Aqua Specialties
2232 Bemis Rd.
Valdosta, GA 31601

PADI

GUAM

Coral Reef Marine Center
P.O. Box 2792
Agana, Guam 96910

NAUI

International Divers Assn.
P.O. Box 6657
Tamuning, Guam 96911

PADI

Marianas Divers
P.O. Box 1116
Agana, Guam 96810

PADI

HAWAII

Aloha Dive Shop
Koko Marina Trade Center
Honolulu, HI 96825

NASDS

Dan's Dive Shop, Inc.
1382 Makaloa St.
Honolulu, HI 96814

NASDS, NAUI

Honsport, Ala Moana Pearl Ridge
2868 Kaihikapu
Honolulu, HI 96819

NAUI

Kukui Diving
3649 Kawelolani Place
Honolulu, HI 96816

NAUI

L. Reck's Skin & Scuba School
1042 D Llima Drive
Honolulu, HI 96817

NAUI

Fau Hana Dive
514-C Piikoi St.
Honolulu, HI 96814

NAUI

Skin Diving Hawaii
1667 Ala Moana Blvd.
Honolulu, HI 96815

NAUI

South Seas Aquatics
1125 Ala Moana Blvd.
Honolulu, HI 96814

NASDS, NAUI

Aaron's Dive Shop, Inc.
39 Maluniu Ave.
Kailua, HI 96734

NASDS, NAUI

Kirwan's School of Diving
450 Kaha St.
Kailua, HI 96734

NAUI, PADI

Dive Kona
Box 3005
Kailua Kona, HI 96740

NAUI

Hawaiian Divers
P.O. Box 572
Kailua-Kona, HI 96740

PADI

Professional Divers Hawaii
P.O. Box 1252
Kamuela, HI 96743

NAUI

Water Rats Dive Shop
46-020 Alaloa St.
Kaneohe, HI 96744

NAUI

Sea & Sage Diving Center
4544 Kukui St.
Kapaa Kauai, HI 96746

NAUI

Skin Diving Hawaii, Inc.
1993 S. Kihei Rd.
Kihei, Maui, HI 96753

NAUI

Havaiki Sail 'N Dive
RR 1, Box 554
Kona, HI 96740

NAUI

Beach Fun of Maui
Kaanapali Beach Hotel
Lahaina, HI 96761

NAUI

Central Pacific Divers
780 Front St.
Lahaina, HI 96761

NAUI, PADI

M. Foster Prof. Diving Tours
175 Baker St., H-21
Lahaina, Maui, HI 96761

NAUI

Scuba Wagon
Slip 70, Lahaina Yacht Harbor
Lahaina, Maui, HI 96761

NAUI

Sun Diver's
848 Front St.
Lahaina, Maui, HI 96761

NAUI

Garden Island Marine
RR 1, Box 180B
Lihue, Kauai, HI 96766

NAUI

Hawaiian Pacific Divers
10 Market St.
Wailuku, HI 96793

NAUI

Bojac Dive Shop
94-366 Pupupani St.
Waipahu, HI 96797

NAUI, PADI

IDAHO

Underwater Realm, Inc.
1812 W. State St.
Boise, ID 83702

PADI

Divers West
R 5 - 1675 W. Appleway
Coeur d'Alene, ID 83814

NAUI, PADI

ILLINOIS

Berry Distributors
12003 S. Cicero
Alsip, IL 60658

PADI

Aquaventure Diving School
Arlington Park Towers
Arlington, IL 61312

NASDS

Aqua Center, Inc.
717 Morton Ave.
Aurora, IL 60506
NASDS

Sea-Sun Sports Specialties
6932 W. Sixteenth St.
Berwyn, IL 60402
NAUI

Berry Diving Centers, Inc.
6059 W. Addison St.
Chicago, IL 60634
PADI

Erickson Underwater
Swimming School
6033 N. Sheridan Rd.
Chicago, IL 60660
PADI

Scuba Unlimited, Inc.
1440 W. Fullerton Ave.
Chicago, IL 60614
PADI

Aquaventure Diving School
1655 Oakton St.
Des Plains, IL 60018
NASDS

Scubaschools, Inc.
4915 Pershing Rd.
Downers Grove, IL 60615
NAUI

Elmer's Watersports
2609 Broadway
Evanston, IL 60201
NAUI

The Flipper Locker
1924 E. Illnois
Evansville, IL 47711
NASDS

Illinois Institute of Diving
P.O. Box 1096
Glendale Heights, IL 60137
NAUI

Illinois Institute of Diving
25 E. Parkside
Lombard, IL 60148
NAUI

Underseas Scuba Center
226 S. Main St.
Lombard, IL 60148
PADI

Black Magic Dive Shop
071 Oak St.
Mundelein, IL 60060
PADI

Blue Hole, Inc.
4817 W. Farmington Rd.
Peoria, IL 61604
NAUI, PADI, YMCA

Pope's Diving Supply
1828 - 222nd Place
Sauk Village, IL 60411
PADI

International Scuba Center
3919 Oakton St.
Skokie, IL 60076
PADI

Aquatic Sports Center
1703 W. Washington
Waukegan, IL 60085
NASDS

Anchor In Scuba Center
315 W. Ogden Ave.
Westmont, IL 60559
NAUI, SSI

INDIANA

Aqua Den
705 E. 8th St.
Anderson, IN 46012
NASDS

Southern Indiana Scuba
1025 S. Walnut St.
Bloomington, IN 47401
PADI

Lake County Sheriffs Marine Unit
P.O. Box 1206
Cedar Lake, IN 46303
PADI

Divers Supply Co., Inc.
3315 N. Illinois St.
Indianapolis, IN 46208
PADI

Fair Weather Dive Shop, Inc.
8805 E. 38th St.
Indianapolis, IN 46208
PADI

Indiana State Police Dept.
Room 304, State Office Bldg.
Indianapolis, IN 46204
NAUI

Midwest Scuba Center
9508 Ross Lane
Indianapolis, IN 46268
PADI

Marcos Dive
8 Widewater Drive
Lafayette, IN 47904
NAUI

Michigan City Scuba Center
2519 E. Michigan Blvd.
Michigan City, IN 46360
PADI

Scholl's Pro Dive Shop
(U.S. 12) 503 E. Second St.
Michigan City, IN 46360
NASDS, PADI

IOWA

The Scuba Shop
904 Kellog
Ames, IA 50010
NAUI

Iowa State Skin Diving Schools
Scuba & Ski
P.O. Box 428
Arnold Park, IA 51331
NASDS

Aquatic Corporation
2238 W. River Dr.
Davenport, IA 52802
NASDS

Iowa State Skin Diving School
216 Euclid
Des Moines, IA 50317
NASDS

Matt Leydens Dive Shop
1213 Locust
Des Moines, IA 50309
NAUI

Divers Pro Shop
1011 Arthur St.
Iowa City, IA 52240
NAUI, PADI

Professional Diving Schools, Inc.
1145 W. 8th Ave.
Marion, IA 52302
PADI

KANSAS

The Dive Shop, Inc.
3606 W. 95th St.
Leawood, KS 66206
PADI

Diver's Equipment & Repair
7804 Foster
Overland Park, KS 60204
NASDS

Topeka Dive Shop
1425 Lane
Topeka, KS 66604
NAUI

Frank's Dive Shop
1226 E. Harry
Wichita, KS 67211
NASDS

Midwest Diving Center, Inc.
1107 Parklane
Wichita, KS 67218
PADI

KENTUCKY

Lexington Dive Shop, Inc.
829 Euclid Ave.
Lexington, KY 40502
PADI, SSI

Divers, Inc.
4807 Dixie Hwy.
Louisville, KY 40216
PADI

Kentucky Diving Headquarters
3928 Shelbyville Rd.
Louisville, KY 40207
SSI

Aquarius Dive Shop
802 Elm St.
Ludlow, KY 41016
PADI

LOUISIANA

Innerspace Dive Shop
P.O. Box 1568
Covington, LA 70433
PADI

Vineyards Dive Shop
1400 W. Esplanade Ave.
Kenner, LA 70062
NAUI, PADI, SSI

Aquatic Dive Shop
1903 Johnston St.
Lafayette, LA 70501
NAUI, PADI

Louisiana State Schools of Diving
427 Rena
Lafayette, LA 70501
NASDS, SSI

Harry's Dive Shop, Inc.
4709 Airline Hwy.
Metairie, LA 70001
PADI

Aqua Sports
609 Park Ave.
Monroe, LA 71201
NAUI

Aquasports
2215 Liberty
Monroe, LA 71201
NAUI

Kerry's Aquatics, Inc.
4958 Gallier Dr.
New Orleans, LA 70126
PADI

New Orleans Skin Diving School
4417 Dryades St.
New Orleans, LA 70115
NASDS

Adventure Sports
1817 Texas
Shreveport, LA 71103
NAUI

Ark-La-Tex Diving School
9118 Bloom Blvd.
Shreveport, LA 71108
NAUI

Temento's School of Diving
435 Sala Ave.
Westwego, LA 70094
PADI

MAINE

Skin Divers Paradise
RFD #3, Turner Rd.
Auburn, ME 04210
NASDS, SSI

Valley Sports
10 Minat Ave.
Auburn, ME 04210
NAUI

Aqua Diving Academy
999 Congress St.
Portland, ME 04102
NASDS

MARYLAND

Cheasapeake Divers
P.O. Box 537-A, Bay Dr. Rt. 15
Baltimore, MD 21220
PADI

Divers Den Sport Center
8105 Hartford Road
Baltimore, MD 21234
NASDS, NAUI

Dynamo, Inc.
8906 Rhode Island Ave.
College Park, MD 20740
NAUI, PADI

The Scuba Hut
418 Crain Hwy. SW
Glen Burnie, MD 21061
NASDS, PADI, SSI

Catalina, Inc.
176 Great Mills Rd.
Lexington Park, MD 20653
NASDS

Divers World
923 Gist Ave.
Silver Spring, MD 20910
NASDS

MASSACHUSETTS

New England Divers, Inc.
Tozer Road
Beverly, MA 01915
NAUI, PADI

Underwater Safaris
P.O. Box 291, Back Bay Annex
Boston, MA 02117
NAUI

Aquatic Development
236 Wood Road
Braintree, MA 02184
NAUI

Brockton Scuba Center
Cape Cod School of Skin Diving
1 Perkins Ave.
Brockton, MA 02401
NASDS, SSI

East Coast Divers
213 Boylston St.
Brookline, MA 02146
NAUI

Marine Educators
P.O. Box 515
Cambridge, MA 02139
NAUI

Cape Cod School of Skin Diving
39 Main St.
Fairhaven, MA 02719
NASDS

Mass. School or Skin Diving
484 S. Main St.
Fall River, MA 02724
NASDS

Atlantic Diving Company
Parket St.
Gloucester, MA 01930
PADI

Lakeville Divers Supply, Inc.
Bedford St., Rt. 18
Lakeville, MA 02346
NASDS

Inland Divers
100 S. Main St.
Leicester, MA 01524
NAUI

Eastern Divers Supply
196 Middlesex St.
Lowell, MA 01852
NASDS, NAUI

The Scuba Shack
1293 Ocean St., Rt. 139
Marshfield, MA 02050
NAUI, PADI

The Dive Shop
945 Ashley Blvd.
New Bedford, MA 02740
NAUI

Innerspace Dive Center
120 Linden St.
Pittsfield, MA 01201
NAUI

South Shore Skin Divers
511 Washington St.
Quincy, MA 02169
NASDS

Boston School of Diving
United Divers, Inc.
57 Washington St.
Somerville, MA 02143
NASDS

Holyoke Underwater Supply
50 No. Main
So. Hadley Fall, MA 01075
NAUI, PADI

The Aquatic Center
244 W. Boylston St.
W. Boylston, MA 01583
NAUI

Robert E. Kaufman
P.O. Box 524
Williamstown, MA 01201
NAUI

MICHIGAN

Recreational Diving Systems, Inc.
3380 Washtenaw Ave.
Ann Arbor, MI 48104

PADI, SSI

Divers Supply
G-4142 Fenton Rd.
Flint, MI 48507

NASDS, PADI

Underwater Spc.
G 4084 Corunna Rd.
Flint, MI 48504

NAUI

Lubberts Dive Shop
4389 Chicago Dr.
Grandville, MI 49418

PADI

The Skamt Shop
5055 Plainfield Ave.
Grand Rapids, MI 49505

NASDS

Higgens Lake Sporting Center
9982 W. Higgens Lake Dr.
Higgens Lake, MI 48627

SSI

Fun, Inc.
254 River Ave.
Holland, MI 49423

NASDS

Holly Scuba Center
3525 Grange Hall Rd.
Holly, MI 48442

NASDS

Subaqueous, Inc.
1806 E. Michigan Ave.
Lansing, MI 48912

PADI

Michigan Underwater School of Diving
3280 Fort St.
Lincoln Park, 48146

NASDS

Advanced Aquatics
1545 Elliot
Madison Heights, MI 48071

NAUI

Scuba World
320 E. 12 Mile Rd.
Madison Hgts., MI 48071

SSI

N.M.U. Scuba School
N. Michigan University
Marquette, MI 49855

PADI

Seaaquatics, Inc.
28 Ashman Circle
Midland, MI 48640

NAUI, SSI

W. Michigan School of Diving
347 S. Hancock
Pentwater, MI 49449

NASDS

Underworld Systems
411½ Howard St.
Petoskey, MI 49770

NAUI, PADI, SSI

Pontiac Scuba Center
208 S. Telegraph
Pontiac, MI 48053

PADI

Blue Water Diving
1722 Lapeer
Port Huron, MI 48060

SSI

Recreational Diving Systems
4505 N. Woodward
Royal Oak, MI 48072

PADI, SSI

Bob's Coastal Marine Dive Shop
1109 Ashmun St.
Sault Ste Marie, MI 49783

PADI

Scuba North
13258 W. Bayshore Drive
Traverse City, MI 49684

NAUI, PADI

Underwater Outfitters
2579 Union Lake Rd.
Union Lake, MI 48085

NAUI

Scuba-Ventures Underwater
  School of Diving
46014 Van Dyke
Utica, MI 48087

NASDS

Macomb Diver Dive Shop
28869 Bynert
Warren, MI 48093

NAUI

MINNESOTA

Sports Craft, Inc.
Rt. 7
Brainerd, MN 56401

NASDS

Lake Superior Divers
Supply & School
3028 W. 3rd St.
Duluth, MN 55806

PADI

Club Scuba, East
2280 Maplewood Dr.
Maplewood, MN 55109

NASDS

Scuba Center
5015 Penn Ave. SW
Minneapolis, MN 55419

NAUI

Galleon, Inc.
Hwys. 10 & 75 No.
Moorhead, MN 56560

NAUI

Rochester Skin & Scuba, Inc.
528 S. Broadway
Rochester, MN 55901

NASDS

Scorpio Scuba Div. of Inland Aquatics
6429 Lyndale Ave.
S. Richfield, MN 55423

NAUI

The Argonautes
5500 S. Snelling Ave.
St. Paul, MN 55116

NAUI, PADI

Club Scuba, Inc.
1300 E. Wayzata Blvd.
Wayzata, MN 55391

NASDS

MISSISSIPPI

Diver's Hide-A-Way
1506 W. Howard Ave.
Biloxi, MS 39530

PADI

Earl's Dive Shop
401 Boulsog St.
Gulfport, MS 39501

NASDS

Skippers Diving, Inc.
4441 N. State St.
Jackson, MS 39206

NASDS, SSI

Gulf Coast Divers Supply
3313 Ingalls Ave.
Pascagoula, MS 39567

PADI

MISSOURI

Skin N Scuba Dive Shop, Inc.
407 N. 7 Hwy.
Blue Springs, MO 64015

PADI

John the Diver
S.R. 1, Box 459 Indian Point
Branson, MO 65616

NASDS

Inner World Diving Center
4714 Bridgeton Sta. Rd.
Bridgeton, MO 63044

PADI

Hughes Dive Co.
437 Broadway
Cape Girardeau, MO 63701

SSI

Divers Equipment & Repair
5800 Barrymore Dr.
Kansas City, MO 64134

NASDS, PADI

Divers Village
P.O. Box 329
Lake Ozark, MO 65049

SSI

Diver's Equipment & Repair
301 NE 58th St.
North Kansas City, MO 64118

NASDS

Scuba World
1231 E. Republic Rd.
Springfield, MO 65804

SSI

The Diving Chamber
4047 Gravois
St. Louis, MO 63116

PADI, SSI

NEBRASKA

Bonsall Pool & Scuba Center
540 N. 48th St.
Lincoln, NE 68504

NAUI, SSI

Midwest Diving School & Supply
Lake McConaughy
Ogallala, NE 69153

SSI

Sea Locker, Inc.
1267 S. 120th St.
Omaha, NE 68144

NASDS, PADI

Sports Corner
286 Italia Mall-Westroads
Omaha, NE 68114

NASDS

Fathom Diving School
1620 E. Overland
Scottsbluff, NE 69361

NASDS, PADI

NEVADA

Colorado River Divers
532 Eighth St.
Boulder City, NV 89005

NAUI

Desert Divers Supply
5720 E. Charleston
Las Vegas, NV 89122

NAUI, PADI

Scuba Center
553 E. Sahara
Las Vegas, NV 89107

NASDS

Sierra Diving Co.
Box 5568
Reno, NV 89502

NAUI

NEW HAMPSHIRE

Underwater Works
P.O. Box 601
Durham, NH 03824

NAUI

Keene Divers Supply
27 Water St.
Keene, NH 03431

PADI

Underwater Sports of N.H.
334 Park Ave.
Keene, NH 03431

NAUI

Divers Den Dive Shop
730 Mammoth Rd.
Manchester, NH 03104

PADI

Kimball Union Academy
Meriden, NH 03770

NAUI

La Porte's Skindiving Shop
Box 53, Route 103
Newbury, NH 03255

PADI

Undersea Enterprises, Inc.
46 State St.
Portsmouth, NH 03801

PADI

Atlantic Aqua Sport
522 Sagamore Rd.
Rye, NH 03870

NASDS

Northeast Air Supply
North Main St.
Wolfeboro, NH 03894

NAUI

NEW JERSEY

Cedar Grove Divers Supply
492 Pompton Ave., Rt. 23
Cedar Grove, NJ 07009

NASDS, SSI

The Skin Diving Center
1659 Hwy. 27
Edison, NJ 08817

NASDS, NAUI

Divers Den
232 Route 22
Greenbrook, NJ 08812

NAUI

The Quarry
Rt. 517
Hamburg, NJ 07419

NASDS

Dive Shop of New Jersey
228 Celsea Drive
Hurffvill, NJ 08080

NAUI

North Jersey Sports Divers
1587 Kennedy Blvd.
Jersey City, NJ 07305

PADI

Atlantic Wreck Diving
150 Longview Ave.
Lake Hiawatha, NJ 07034

NAUI

Divers Cove
State Hwy. 35
Laurence Harbor, NJ 08879

NAUI

Scuba Services, Inc.
246 Main St.
Lincoln Park, NJ 07035

NASDS, SSI

Professional Divers
Neptune City Shop. Ctr.
Hwy. 35
Neptune City, NJ 07753

NASDS, NAUI, PADI, YMCA

Underwater Schools of South Jersey
1340 Tilton Rd.
Northfield, NJ 08225

NASDS

So. Jersey School of Diving
P.O. Box 71
Pitman, NJ 08071

NAUI

Four Divers, Inc.
56 Broadway
Point Pleasant Beach, NJ 68472

PADI

Princeton Aqua Sports
306 Alesander St.
Princeton, NJ 08540

NAUI

Underwater Sports of New Jersey
Rt. 17
Rochelle Park, NJ 07662

NASDS

Sup/Sea Schools
P.O. Box 611
Willington, NJ 08046

NAUI

NEW MEXICO

New Mexico Marine Supply
5004 San Mateo NE
Albuquerque, NM 87109

PADI

Scuba School
625 Amerst NE
Albuquerque, NM 87106

NASDS

Watersports
5009 Menaul NE
Albuquerque, NM 87110

PADI, SSI

New Mexico School of Diving
4101 Cedar Dr.
Farmington, NM 87401

PADI

NEW YORK

Coastal Diving Academy
112 W. Main St.
Bay Shore, NY 11706

NAUI, PADI

Divers Way
596 Sunrise Hwy.
Bay Shore, NY 11706

NAUI

Central Skin Divers
2608 Merrick Rd.
Bellmore, NY 11710
PADI, YMCA

Brooklyn Divers
2917 Ave. 1
Brooklyn, NY 11210
PADI

Kings County Divers Corp.
3040 Ave. U
Brooklyn, NY 11229
NASDS, SSI

Professional Dive Trips, Inc.
3662 Shore Park Way
Brooklyn, NY 11235
PADI

Couger Sports, Inc.
3470 Webster Ave.
Bronx, NY 10467
NASDS

Dip 'N' Dive
500 Niagara Falls Blvd
Buffalo, NY 14223
NAUI

Divers-in-Depth
37 Franklin St.
Buffalo, NY 14202
NAUI

Niagara Scuba Sports
2048 Niagara St.
Buffalo, NY 14207
PADI, SSI

B F V Pro Dive Shop
City Pier
Canadaigua, NY 14424
NAUI

Scubar
P.O. Box 475
Canton, NY 13617
NASDS

Bill's Scuba Center
363 Lake Shore Drive E.
Dunkirk, NY 14048
YMCA

The Divers Den
127 Central Ave.
Dunkirk, NY 14048
PADI

North Shore Diving Center
58 Larkfield Rd.
E. Northpoint, NY 11731
NASDS, NAUI

Ed's Dive Shop
92 Oakland Ave.
Elmira Heights, NY 14903
PADI, YMCA

Dom's Scuba Emporium
297 Mosley Rd.
Fairport, NY 14450
NAUI

Hampton Bay Divers, Inc.
1140 Flanders Rd.
Flanders, NY 11901
PADI

Danzinger, Inc. Skin Diving
School of Long Island
70 S. Main St.
Freeport, NY 11520
NASDS

Innerspace Dive Shop, Inc.
57 Forest Ave.
Glen Cove, NY 11542
NASDS

Night Star Divers
P.O. Box 1
Highland Falls, NY 10928
PADI

Divemaster Center
57 Mill Lane
Huntington, NY 11743
PADI

Diving Center of Liverpool
504 Old Liverpool Rd.
Liverpool, NY 13088
NASDS

Seaquatic Systems
29 Heidt Ave.
Middletown, NY 10940
PADI

Underwater Services Unlimited
Nine Quiet Court
Miller Place, NY 11764
PADI

Underwater Advisors
8 East Second St.
Mineola, NY 11501
NAUI

Central N.Y. School od Skin Diving
1716 Burrstone Rd.
New Hartford, NY 13413
NASDS

Central N.Y. School of Skin Diving
Tennissland-Kellogg Rd. Mall
New Hartford, NY 13413
NASDS

Poseidon Underwater Systems
14 Deerpath Drive
New Paltz, NY 12561
NAUI

Atlantis Divers World & Tours
500 Ave. of the Americas
New York, NY 10011
PADI

European Divers Assn.
435th TAW
(Frankfurt, Germany)
APO NY 09057
NAUI

Guantanamo Bay Reef Raiders Assn.
Box 13, Cuba
FPO NY 09593
NAUI

World Wide Divers
155 E. 55th St.
New York, NY 10022
SSI

Central N.Y. School of Skin Diving
27 North Broad St.
Norwich, NY 13815
NASDS

Rockland Co. YMCA
35 S. Broadway
Nyack, NY 10960
NAUI

Central N.Y. School of Skin Diving
28 Oneida St.
Oneida, NY 13820
NASDS

Skin & Scuba
190 Callingham Rd.
Pittsford, NY 14534
PADI

Sub-Aqua Unlimited
69 Miller St.
Plattsburgh, NY 12901
PADI

Porthole Dive Shop
807 Route 25A
Pt. Jefferson, NY 11776
NAUI

Diving Center of Rochester
1889 E. Main St.
Rochester, NY 14609
SSI

Brice's Diving Equipment
420 William St.
Rome, NY 13440
PADI

Couger Sports, Inc.
590 Central Park Ave.
Scarsdale, NY 10583
NASDS

Schenectady School of Skindiving
33 Winslow Dr.
Schenectady, NY 12309
PADI

Divers Cove II
1724 Hylan Blvd.
Staten Island, NY 10305
NAUI

Aqua-Dome Dive Center
RD No. 1
Sterling, NY 13156
NAUI

The Stony Brook School
Route 25A
Stony Brook, NY 11790
NAUI

National Aquatic School
1425 Erie Blvd.
Syracuse, NY 13210
NASDS, PADI

Thrasher's Dive Shoppe
Box 72, R.D. No. 1
Troy, NY 12180
NAUI

Advanced Underwater Diving
215 Bert Ave.
Westbury, NY 11590
PADI

Pro Diver's Supply
27 Mohawk St.
Whitesboro, NY 13492
SSI

NORTH CAROLINA

Discovery Diving Co.
Atlantic Beach Causeway
Atlantic Beach, NC 28512
PADI

Diving Co., Ltd.
505 Stanley Ave.
Charlotte, NC 28205
NAUI

Underwater Unlimited
2438 Park Rd.
Charlotte, NC 28203
NASDS

Underwater World
5532 S. Boulevard
Charlotte, NC 29210
PADI

Sea Wolf Dive Shop
P.O. Box 707
Clinton, NC 28328
NAUI

Key West Diving Co.
P.O. Box 35062
Fayetteville, NC 28303
PADI

Undersea Center
4762 Yadkin Rd.
Fayetteville, NC 28393
NASDS, PADI

Aqua Sports, Inc.
2313 Randleman Road
Greensboro, NC 27406
PADI

Blue Dolphin Dive Shop
2510 English Rd.
High Point, NC 27260
PADI

Ed Huff's Underwater School
2007 Lejeune Blvd.
Jacksonville, NC 28543
NAUI

Innerspace Specialists Scuba Center
1909 Le Jeune Blvd.
Jacksonville, NC 28540
PADI

Underwater School of N.C.
2007 Lejeune Blvd.
Jacksonville, NC 28540
NASDS

Discovery Diving Company
11 Summerhill Terrace
Kinston, NC 28501
PADI

Aqua Haven
5212 Holly Ridge Dr.
Raleigh, NC 27612
NASDS

Sea Wolf Den
2110 Hillsborough Street
Raleigh, NC 27607
NAUI, PADI

Three Brothers Diving Center
222 S. River Drive
Southport, NC 28461
NAUI

Adventure World, Inc.
5328 Oleander Drive
Wilminton, NC 28402
NAUI

NORTH DAKOTA

Commercial & Sport Diving Center
531 Hamline St.
Grand Forks, ND 58201
NAUI

Underwater Scuba Instructor
Dept. of HPER
Univ. of North Dakota
Grand Forks, ND 58201
NAUI

Benthus, Inc.
102-1 Avion Way
Minot, ND 58704
NAUI

OHIO

Tri-County Dive Shop
469 East South St.
Akron, OH 44311
NAUI

Buckeye Diving School
46 Warrensville Center Rd.
Bedford, OH 44146
NASDS, PADI, SSI, YMCA

Aqua Hut International
521 S. Prospect St.
Bowling Green, OH 43402
PADI

Aqua World
313 Main St.
Bridgeport, OH 43912
NAUI

Ka Puka Wai Dive Shop
Meyers Lake Plaza
1506 Whipple Ave. NW
Canton, OH 44708
NASDS

Creelman Diver Supply
2117 Beechmont Ave.
Cincinnati, OH 45230
PADI

Underwater Specialties
338 Northland Blvd.
Cincinnati, OH 45246
NASDS, SSI

Aqua Specialists
1857 East 17th St.
Cleveland, OH 44115
NAUI

Scuba East Diving School
17021 Loraine Ave.
Cleveland, OH 44111
PADI

Ask Diving School
49 W. Long St.
Columbus, OH 43215
NAUI, PADI

Central Ohio School of Diving
3120 Indianola Ave.
Columbus, OH 43214
NASDS

Pier 161 Scuba Center
2355 W. Granville Rd.
Columbus, OH 43085
PADI, SSI

C & J Scuba School
5932 N. Dixie Dr.
Dayton, OH 45414
SSI

Scuba East Diving School
21950 Lake Shore Blvd.
Euclid, OH 44123
PADI

Treasure Cove Scuba
1840 N. State St.
Girard, OH 44420
PADI

Dive, Inc.
4615 Park Ave., West Rd. #12
Mansfield, OH 44903
NASDS, SSI, YMCA

Aquanetic Center
203 Brownell St.
Napoleon, OH 43545
YMCA

Sub-Aquatics, Inc.
10333 Northfield Rd.
Northfield, OH 44067
NAUI, PADI

Chafee's Marina
2707 NE Catawba Rd.
Port Clinton, OH 43452
NASDS

Sub-Aquatics, Inc.
8855 E. Broad St.
Reynoldsburg, OH 43068
NAUI, PADI

Salem School of Scuba
403 E. State St.
Salem, OH 40560
NASDS·

Bruce Reger's Pro Dive Shop
280 West Ave.
Tallmadge, OH 44278
PADI

Duke's Diving Service
844 Circleview Drive
Toledo, OH 43615
NAUI

Underwater Sports of Ohio
703 S. Main St.
Urbana, OH 43079
PADI

The Aqua Shack, Inc.
440 E. Dixie Dr.
W. Carrollton, OH 45449
NASDS

Midwest Underwater, Inc.
29006 Lakeland Blvd.
Wickliffe, OH 44092
NASDS

Aquatics Unlimited
302 North 7th St.
Zanesville, OH 43701
NAUI

OKLAHOMA

Ski N' Dive
604 E. 10th St.
Ada, OK 74820
NASDS

Oklahoma Divers Supply
103 S. Commerce
Ardmore, OK 73401
NASDS

Gene's Aqua Pro
Rt. I, Box 324
Ft. Gibson, OK 74434
NASDS, PADI

Gene's Aqua Pro
Tenkiller Aqua Park
Gore, OK 74435
NASDS

The Dive Shop
1411 Gore
Lawton, OK 73501
NAUI

Chalet Sports
2824 Country Club Dr.
Oklahoma City, OH 73116
SSI

Underwater Sports Shop
2533 NW 10th
Oklahoma City, OK 73107
NASDS

Divers Den
5122 S. Vandalia
Tulsa, OK 74135
PADI

The Blue Hole, Inc.
5733 E. Admiral Pl.
Tulsa, OK 74115
NASDS

The Dive Shack
8500 E. 11th St.
Tulsa, OK 74112
PADI

OREGON

Ron's Dive Shop
207 SE Willow Lane
Bend, OR 97701
PADI

Northwest Divers Supply
852 Broadway
Coos Bay, OR 97420
NASDS

Aqua Sports
964 Circle Blvd.
Corvallis, OR 97330
NAUI

Eugene Skin Divers Supply
1090 W. 6th Ave.
Eugene, OR 97402
PADI

Oregon Diving School
1677 Coburg Rd.
Eugene, OR 97401
NASDS

Divers World
255 Humberd Ln.
Grants Pass, OR 97526
PADI

Mapleton Skin Divers Supply
10932 Hwy. 36
Mapleton, OR 97453
PADI

Cap'n Frogs of Medford
312 N. Central
Medford, OR 79501
NASDS

Scuba Unlimited
16585 SE McLaughlin
Milwaukie, OR 97222
NAUI

Deep Sea Bill's
Box 213 South Jetty
Newport, OR 97365
PADI

Aquarius Underwater Center
7660 SW Barbur Blvd.
Portland, OR 97219
PADI

Trans Global Divers, Ltd.
5405 A N. Lagoon Ave.
Portland, OR 97217
NAUI

Tri-West School of Skin Diving
13604 SE Powell
Portland, OR 97236
NASDS

Valley Scuba Center
10803 SW Barbur Blvd.
Portland, OR 97219
NASDS

Pacific Scuba Center
760 NW Hill Pl.
Roseburg, OR 97470
NASDS

Anderson's Sporting Goods
141 Commercial NE
Salem, OR 97301
PADI

Dick's Diving Service
4947 River Road N.
Salem, OR 97303
NAUI

Oregon Diving School
1790 Center Ave.
Salem, OR 97301
NASDS

The Underwater Works
5330 NW Broadway St.
W. Linn, OR 97068
NAUI

PENNSYLVANIA

Aqua Marine Company
2411 South Law St.
Allentown, PA 18103
PADI

Scuba Swim
20 Hawley Ave.
Bellevue, PA 15202
NAUI

Ocean Devils Dive Shop
33 Swamp Rd.
Doylestown, PA 18901
PADI

Divers World
1539 W. 8th St.
Erie, PA 16505
NAUI

J & S Dive Shop
4203 Alvin St.
Erie, PA 16510
NAUI

B & B Marine Specialties
Box 277
Hillsville, PA 16132
NASDS

Underwater World
373 Easton Road
Horsham, PA 19044
NAUI

S & R Ski & Dive Shop
217 E. Main St.
Lansdale, PA 19446
NASDS

Divemasters
428 W. Bridge St.
Morrisville, PA 19067
NAUI

Teach Tour Diving Co.
Box 390
Nazareth, PA 18064
PADI

Thompson's Dive Shop
RD 3
New Bethelhem, PA 16242
NAUI

Atlantis Diving Center
4363 Main St.
Philadelphia, PA 19127
NAUI

Gilligan's Isle, Inc.
6545 Roosevelt Blvd.
Philadelphia, PA 19149
NASDS

The Diving Bell
681 N. Broad St.
Philadelphia, PA 19123
NAUI

Gainsford Scuba Swim
167 Carnation Ave.
Pittsburgh, PA 15229
NAUI

Sub-Aquatics, Inc.
1593 Banksville Rd.
Pittsburgh, PA 15229
NAUI, PADI

Aquanautics
111 Taft Ave.
Reading, PA 19605
NAUI

Professional Diving Service Co.
726 Pittsburgh St.
Springdale, PA 15144
PADI

PUERTO RICO

Underwater Services
No. 61 Ponce de Leon Ave., Stop 27
Hato Rey, Puerto Rico 00919
NAUI

Skin Diving School of Puerto Rico
P.O. Box 3925
Mayaguez, Puerto Rico 00708
PADI

The Water Emporium
Hyatt Rio Mar, P.O. Box P
Palmer, Puerto Rico 00721
NAUI

Caribbean School of Aquatics
Hyatt La Concha, Box 4195
San Juan, Puerto Rico 00905
NAUI

Caribe Water Sports
P.O. Box 1872
San Juan, Puerto Rico 00903
NAUI

Vieques Divers
c/o Duffy's Esperanza
Vieques, Puerto Rico 00765
PADI

RHODE ISLAND

Scuba Systems
1180-R Pontiac Ave.
Cranston, RI 02920
NAUI

5 Fathom Divers
307 Taunton Ave.
E. Providence, RI 02914
NAUI

Hammond's Hardware & Sporting
1 Narragansett Ave.
Jamestown, RI 02835
NAUI

University of Rhode Island
Kingston, RI 02882
NAUI

Rhode Island Academy of Skin Diving
111 Bellevue Ave.
Newport, RI 02840
NASDS, NAUI, YMCA

Demarco Divers
11 Vireo St.
N. Providence, RI 02904
NAUI

Rhode Island Academy of Skin Diving
209 Elmwood Ave.
Providence, RI 02907
NASDS

SOUTH CAROLINA

Scuba Divers Inc.
Hyw. 24 - Pier 24
Anderson, SC 29622
PADI

The Wet Shop
5121 Rivers Ave.
Charleston, SC 29405
PADI

Aqua-Venture Dive Center, Inc.
4357 Jackson Blvd.
Columbia, SC 29205
NASDS

Underwater Works Limited
1023 Bush River Rd. #7
Columbia, SC 29210
PADI

Aqua Nautica
Shops of the Seven Seas
U.S. Hwy. 17
Garden City, SC 29577
PADI

Carolina Divers Center, Inc.
423 Churchill Circle
Greenville, SC 29605
PADI

Divers World
3303½ Agusta Rd.
Greenville, SC 29605
NASDS

Neptune Dive & Ski
133 Georgia Ave.
N. Agusta, SC 29841
NASDS, NAUI

Scuba Divers, Inc.
495 E. St. John St.
Spartanburg, SC 29301
PADI

The Dive Shop
507 East St. John St.
Spartanburg, SC 29302
PADI

SOUTH DAKOTA

Scuba Supply
1607 St. Joe
Rapid City, SD 57701
PADI

Coral Reef
1113½ S. Minnesota Ave.
Sioux Falls, SD 57105
NASDS

TENNESSEE

Aquarius School of Scuba
6863 Lee Hwy.
Chattanooga, TN 37421
PADI, SSI

Currint Enterprises, Inc.
600 Magnolia Ave.
Knoxville, TN 37917
NAUI, PADI

Aqualanders Enterprises
3515 Ramill Rd.
Memphis, TN 38128
NAUI, PADI

Dive Shop
3149 Poplar
Memphis, TN 38108
NASDS

Tennessee Divers
4110 Gallatin Rd.
Nashville, TN 37206
NASDS

TEXAS

Key City Dive Shop
4249 Don Juan
Abilene, TX 79605
PADI

School of Scuba
1009 Walnut St.
Abilene, TX 79601
NASDS

Aqua Shop
319 Hudson
Amarillo, TX 79108
NAUI

Arlington Scuba Center
2414 West Park Row Drive
Arlington, TX 76013
PADI

J. Rich Sport's Ltd.
420 Northcross Mall
2525 Anderson Lane
Austin, TX 78757
NAUI, PADI

Scuba Institute
4320 N. Lamar
Austin, TX 78756
SSI

Scuba Point Travis
Rt. 7, Box 863
Austin, TX 78703
NAUI, PADI

Texas Skin Diving Schools
Intersection 2222 Hwy. 620
Austin, TX 78703
NASDS

Texas Skin Diving School
4320 N. Lamar
Austin, TX 78703
NASDS

La Mar Corbet Pro Dive Shop
1447½ Grand
Beaumont, TX 77701
SSI

Scuba Dive Shop
2373 Texas Ave.
Bridge City, TX 77611
SSI

Copeland's Marine Divers, Inc.
4041 S. Padre Island Dr.
Corpus Christi, TX 78411
NASDS

Padre Island Dive Shop
4455 S. Padre Island Dr.
Corpus Christi, TX 78418
NAUI

Aqua Sports
11116 Harry Hines
Dallas, TX 75229
NAUI

Thad Moore's Pro Scuba Hdqtrs.
13933 N. Central Expressway
Dallas, TX 75243
PADI

The Dive Shop
2719 Live Oak
Dallas, TX 75204
NASDS, NAUI

Scuba Shop
1407 Cedar Drive
Edinburg, TX 78539
NAUI

Southwest Scuba Divers
9993 Agena Lane
El Paso, TX 79924
PADI

Skin Diving School of Ft. Worth
3807 Southwest Blvd.
Ft. Worth, TX 76116
NASDS

Schaefer Diving Co.
02 First St.
P.O. Box 1096
Freeport, TX 77541
PADI

Aqua-Trek, Inc.
804 University Blvd.
Galveston, TX 77550
PADI

Aramco Marine & Dive
P.O. Box R
Galveston, TX 77552
NAUI

The Dive Shop
5718 Stewart Rd.
Galveston, TX 77550
NAUI, PADI, SSI

Scuba Point
Box 150 Star Rt.
Graford, TX 76045
NAUI, PADI

Tucker's Dive Shop
2025 E. Main
Grand Prairie, TX 75050
NAUI

Blue Water Diving School
910 Westheimer
Houston, TX 77006
SSI

Champions Dive Center
3203 West F.M. 1960
Houston, TX 77068
SSI

Divers World
810 Uvalde
Houston, TX 77015
NAUI

Houston Scuba Academy
13628 Alameda Rd.
Houston, TX 77045
NASDS, NAUI

Houston Scuba Academy, Inc.
14609 Kimberly
Houston, TX 77024
NASDS

Texas Scuba
8718 F.M. 1960 West
Houston, TX 77070
SSI

The Ocean Corp.
5709 Glenmont
Houston, TX 77081
NAUI

The Trinarc
5705 Glenmont
Houston, TX 77036
NAUI

Scuba Technology
3001 - 28th St.
Lubbock, TX 79401
NAUI

Scuba Sports
500 N. McCoil
McAllen, TX 78501
NAUI

Stovall's Dive Shop
1900 W. Front St.
Midland, TX 79701
PADI

Aquarius Dive Shop
P.O. Box 183
Nederland, TX 77627
NAUI

Texas Divers Co.
Fm FD 306 at Canyon Dam
New Braunfels, TX 78130
NASDS, NAUI

Houston Scuba Academy
3321 Red Bluff
Pasadena, TX 77503
NASDS

Neptune's Locker
2819 Red Bluff Rd.
Pasadena, TX 77503
PADI

Divers World
632 S. Central Expressway
Richardson, TX 75080
NAUI

Scuba Den de San Antonio
1106 Austin Hwy.
San Antonio, TX 78209
NAUI

Texas Divers Co.
2110 West Ave.
San Antonio, TX 78201
NASDS

The Divemasters
447 McCarty Rd.
San Antonio, TX 78216
SSI

The Dive Shop, Inc.
1426 Ranch Rd. 12
San Marcos, TX 78666
PADI

Ken Lees Aqua Sport
P.O. Box 806
S. Houston, TX 77587
NAUI

Temple Diving School
211 South 25th St.
Temple, TX 76501
PADI

Dungan Divers Supply
No. 12 Holly Ridge
Texarkana, TX 75501
NAUI

VIRGIN ISLANDS

Pressure Ltd., Dive Tours
P.O. Box 3612
Christiansted, St. Croix
U.S. Virgin Islands 00820
NAUI

V. I. Divers
Pan Am Pavilion
Christiansted, St. Croix
U.S. Virgin Islands 00820
NAUI, PADI

The Dive Shop
Box 161, Cruz Bay
St. John
U.S. Virgin Islands 00830
NAUI, PADI

Aqua Action
Wintberg Peak
St. Thomas
U.S. Virgin Islands 00801
NASDS

Joe Vogel Diving Co.
33 Raadets Gade
St. Thomas
U.S. Virgin Islands 00801
NAUI

Scuba Ventures
Caneel Bay Plantation
Box 9707, St. Thomas
U.S. Virgin Islands 00801
SSI
Virgin Islands Diving School
P.O. Box 1704
St. Thomas
U.S. Virgin Islands 00801
NASDS, NAUI, PADI, SSI

UTAH

Mountain Man Sports
927 N. Main St.
Logan, UT 84321
NAUI

USAFECO Diving School
2909 Washington Blvd.
Ogden, UT 84401
NASDS

Wolfe's
23rd & Washington Blvd.
Ogden, UT 84401
PADI

Wolfe's Scuba Center
1250 S. State
Orem, UT 84057
PADI

Adventurer Sports
5210 S. State St.
Salt Lake City, UT 84107
NAUI

Scuba Utah
2356 S. Redwood Rd.
Salt Lake City, UT 84119
PADI, SSI

Wolfe's Scuba Centers
6151 Highland Drive
Salt Lake City, UT 84121
NAUI, PADI

Wolfe's Scuba Center
250 South State
Salt Lake City, UT 84111
NAUI, PADI

USAFECO Diving School
3500 S. State St.
Salt Lake City, UT 84115
NASDS

VERMONT

Hydronautics
Rd. 1, Rt. 2
Milton, VT 05468
NAUI

Northern Divers, Inc.
54 Lake St.
St. Albano, VT 05478
NAUI

VIRGINIA

Ski & Dive, Inc.
1545 N. Quaker Lane
Alexandria, VA 22302
NASDS

Dad's Dive Den
RFD 2, Box 211, Old Ivy Road
Charlottesville, VA 22901
NAUI

American Water Sports of Virginia
821 W. Broad St.
Falls Church, VA 22046
PADI

National Diving Center
7502 Leesburg Park
Falls Church, VA 22043
NASDS, NAUI, PADI

"The" Dive Shop
2814 Graham
Falls Church, VA 22042
PADI

Bob Brown Co.
Kennewick Parkade
Kennewick, WA 99336
NAUI

The Diving Hole
8025 Lake Drive
Manassas, VA 22110
NAUI

Aqua Lung Diving Center
9601 Jefferson Ave.
Newport News, VA 23601
PADI

Aqua Lung Diving Center
805 W. Little Creek Rd.
Norfolk, VA 23505
PADI

Universal Divers Supply
14547 Jefferson Davis Hwy.
Woodbridge, VA 22191
NASDS

WASHINGTON

The Dive Shop
Box 607
Anacortex, WA 98221
PADI

Bellevue Community College
3000 - 145th Place SE
Bellevue, WA 98007
NAUI

Silent World Divers, Inc.
14444 Sunset Hwy.
Bellevue, WA 98007
NASDS, NAUI

Northwest Divers
2720 W. Maplewood
Bellingham, WA 98225
NASDS

Washington Divers
932 N. State St.
Bellingham, WA 98225
NAUI, PADI

Divers Hut
4831 Arsenal Way
Bremerton, WA 98310
NAUI

Sound Dive Center
2805 Wherton Way
Bremerton, WA 98310
PADI

Chelan Divers & Sporting Supply
South Lakeshore Rd.
Chelan, WA 98816
PADI

Prof's Rock Shop & Sporting Goods
56 N. College Ave.
College Place, WA 94324
NAUI

Edmonds Diving Center
138 Railroad Ave.
Edmonds, WA 98020
NAUI

Columbia River Divers Shop
115 Nob Hill Drive
Ephrata, WA 98823
NAUI

Everett Skin Diving School
3515 Broadway
Everett, WA 98201
NAUI

Victorian Divers Supply
3813 Rucker
Everett, WA 98201
NAUI

New England Divers, Inc.
2507 South 252nd St.
Kent, WA 98031
PADI

154

Gil's Divers Supply
1054 - 15th
Longview, WA 98632
NAUI

Aquarius Skin Diving School
20801 Hwy. 99
Lynnwood, WA 98036
NASDS

Whidbey Divers Scuba School
P.O. Box RR-80th NW & 900 W.
Oak Harbor, WA 98277
NASDS

Eason's Marine Service
9020 Martin Way
Olympia, WA 98506
PADI

Scuba Supplies
738 Marine Dr.
Port Angeles, WA 98362
NASDS

Aqua Masters
201 Meridian, North
Puyallup, WA 98371
NASDS

Lighthouse Dive 'N Ski
350 Sunset Blvd. N.
Renton, WA 98055
PADI

New England Divers
1009 - 1st Ave. S
Seattle, WA 98168
NAUI, PADI

Sea Star Diving Services
711 N. 80th
Seattle, WA 98103
NAUI

Underwater Sports
10455 Aurora Ave.
Seattle, WA 98133
NAUI

Mike's Diving Center
Rt. 5 Box 916
Shelton, WA 98584
PADI

Spokane Scuba School
N. 1908 Hamilton
Spokane, WA 99207
NASDS

Divers Reef
2515 - 6th Ave.
Tacoma, WA 98406
NAUI

Divers Reef, Inc.
6132 Motor Ave. SW
Tacoma, WA 98499
NAUI

Northwestern School of Skin Diving
2315 Ruston Way
Tacoma, WA 98402
NASDS

Pacific Frogman
7516 - 27th West
Tacoma, WA 98466
PADI

Underwater Instr., Inc.
8209 Hwy. 99
Vancouver, WA 98665
NAUI

Sea Anchor
3004 Airway St.
Wenatchee, WA 98801
NASDS

WASHINGTON,D.C.

National Diving Center
4932 Wisconsin Ave. NW
Washington, DC 20015

NASDS, NAUI, PADI

WEST VIRGINIA

YMCA of Bluefield
College Ave.
Bluefield, WV 24701
NAUI

Reef Raiders Dive Shop
929½ Dunbar Ave.
Dunbar, WV 25064
PADI

Huntington Sport & Comm. Diving
209 Bridge St.
Huntington, WV 25702
PADI

WISCONSIN

3 Little Devils Scuba Shop
Hwy. 123, Devils Lake
Baraboo, WI 53913
PADI

Sea 'N Ski
Brookfield, WI 53005
NASDS

Surfside Scuba, Inc.
604 George St.
DePere, WI 54115
PADI

On The Rocks
Rt. 1, Box 164
Ellison Bay, WI 54210
NASDS

Fontana Army-Navy Store, Inc.
P.O. Box 307 Hwy. 67
Fontana, WI 53125
PADI

Sea 'N Ski
Fox Point, WI 53217
NASDS

Schroeder's Liquor & Sport Shop
560 Mill St.
Green Lake, WI 54941
NAUI

Seaway Sports, Inc.
1255 Main St.;
Green Bay, WI 54302
NASDS

Eru's Diving Equipment
10751 W. Parnell Ave.
Hales Corner, WI 53130
NAUI

Geneva Area Dive Shop
611 Main St.
Lake Geneva, WI 53147
PADI

Fontana Army-Navy Store, Inc.
251 State St.
Madison, WI 53703
PADI

Pirates Cove, Inc.
1103 W. Oklahoma Ave.
Milwaukee, WI 53215
PADI

Sea 'N Ski
4248 N. 76th St.
Milwaukee, WI 53222
NASDS

Inland Seas Diving Academy
310 N. Commercial St.
Neenah, WI 54956
NASDS

Blue Water Divers Supply
Rt. 3
New Auburn, WI 54757
PADI

R.S. Diving Supply Co.
833 Lincoln S.
Rhinelander, WI 54501
PADI

Bennett Academy of Ski & Scuba
114 N. Main St.
Theinsville, WI 53092
PADI

Wisconsin State Divers Assn.
122 W. Broadway
Waukesha, WI 53186
PADI

Bennett Academy of Ski & Scuba
6509 W. North Ave.
Wauwatusa, WI 53092
PADI, SSI

West Bend Aqua Shop
1829 N. Main St.
West Bend, WI 53095
PADI

Rapid School of Scuba
1355 Badger Shopping Center
Wisc. Rapids, WI 54494
NASDS

WYOMING

Scuba World
P.O. Box 1194
Rock Springs, WY 82901
SSI

Canada
ALBERTA

Alberta Scuba Divers Council
P.O. Box 205
Edmonton, Alberta
Canada T5J 2J1
Write for ACUC member schools.

Ozzie's Sports Centre, Ltd.
8407 Elbow Dr.
Calgary, Alberta
Canada
PADI

Skin Scuba Schools of Alberta
533 - 11 Ave. SW
Calgary, Alberta
Canada
NASDS

The Dive Shop
2008 - 36 St. SE
Calgary, Alberta
Canada
PADI

Divers Den, Ltd.
10550 - 109 St.
Edmonton, Alberta
Canada
PADI

Mount Ocean Dive Center, Ltd.
10133 - 82 Ave.
Edmonton, Alberta
Canada T6E 1Z5
NAUI

B.C.

British Columbia Safety Council
96 E. Broadway, Suite 205
Vancouver, B.C.
Canada V5T 1V6
Write for ACUC member schools.

Innerspace Adventures
2450 Townline Rd. RR 1
Abbotsford, B.C.
Canada
NASDS

All-Canada Dive, Ltd.
4408-B Napien St.
Bby, B.C.
Canada
NAUI

Sea Fun Divers, Ltd.
1761 Island Hwy.
Campbell River, B.C.
Canada V9W 2A8
NAUI

Seafun Divers, Ltd.
540 Comox Rd.
Courtenay, B.C.
Canada V9N 3P6
NAUI

A & M Nielsen
Box 6925
Fort St. John, B.C.
Canada Y1J 4J3
SSI

Okanagan Scuba Academy
2970 Pandosy St.
Kelowna, B.C.
Canada
NASDS

Rimpac Divers, Ltd.
9818 - 5th St.
Sidney, B.C.
Canada
PADI

Diving Locker
1398 Main St.
Vancouver, B.C.
Canada
NAUI

Diving Locker
2745 W. 4th Ave.
Vancouver, B.C.
Canada
NAUI

MANITOBA

Manitoba Underwater Council
P.O. Box 711
Winnipeg, Manitoba
Canada R3C 2K3
Write for ACUC member schools.

Laurentian Trading Post
1952 Bank St.
Ottawa, Ontario
Canada
PADI

Sault S.C.U.B.A. Centre
398 Pin St.
Sault Ste Marie, Ontario
Canada
PADI

Tim's Place
11 Ivy Green Cres.
Scarborough, Ontario
Canada
PADI

Canada Scuba School
4164 Kingston Rd.
Searborough, Ontario
Canada
PADI

Scotia Scuba
169 Portland St.
Dartmouth, N.S.
Canada
NAUI, PADI

Gary's Scuba
234 Dominion St.
Glace Bay, N.S.
Canada
NAUI

Aquahaven Industries
Boutiliers Point - St. Margarets
Halifax, N.S.
Canada
NAUI

Atlantic Surf & Cycle Shop
6100 Lady Hammond Rd.
Halifax, N.S.
Canada
NAUI

Commercial Divers, Ltd.
3341 Robin St.
Halifax, N.S.
Canada
NAUI

Timberlea Dive Shop
Timberlea - Bay Road
Halifax, N.S.
Canada
NAUI

Acadian Underwater Service
Meteghan Centre, N.S.
Canada
NAUI

Island Divers
79 Queen St.
Charlottetown, P.E.I.
Canada
NASDS

NEW BRUNSWICK

New Brunswick Underwater Council
169 Glenwood Dr.
Moncton, New Brunswick
Canada E1A 2Z2
Write for ACUC member schools.

NORTH WEST TERRITORY

North West Territory Underwater Council
Dept. of Natural & Cultural Affairs
Govt. of the North West Territory
Yellowknife, N.W.T.
Canada X1A 2L9
Write for ACUC member schools.

NOVA SCOTIA

Chamber's Diving Services
Site 3, Box 36, RR 5
Armdale, N.S.
Canada
NAUI

Aqua Dive
Woodside Shopping Centre
211 Pleasant St.
Dartmouth, N.S.
Canada
NAUI

Central Scuba
101 Main St., Westphal
Dartmouth, N.S.
Canada
NAUI

Canadian Scuba Diving School
Box 2194, D.E.P.S.
Dartmouth, N.S.
Canada
PADI

Dominion Diving, Ltd.
26 Panavista Dr.
Dartmouth, N.S.
Canada

NAUI

ONTARIO

Ontario Underwater Council
559 Jarvis St.
Toronto, Ontario
Canada M4Y 2J1

Write for ACUC member schools.

Aquasport
223 King St. W.
Brockville, Ontario
Canada

NASDS

Northern Ontario Diving Supplies
Manitoulin Scuba Centre
West End Gov't Dock
Little Current, Ontario
Canada

PADI

Aquasport
1187 Hurontario St.
Mississauga, Ontario
Canada

NASDS

Aqua-Systems Dive Shop
1730 Dundas St. E.
Mississauga, Ontario
Canada L4X 1L8

NAUI

Thunder Country Diving
538 Bay
Ontario,
Canada P7B 2R9

NASDS

Aquasport
105 Mann Ave.
Ottawa, Ontario
Canada

NASDS

N. Ontario Diving Supplies
Sub-Aqua Centre
250 Lasaile Blvd.
Sudbury, Ontario
Canada

PADI

Aquasport
Main Square
2575 Danforth Ave.
Toronto, Ontario
Canada

NASDS

C-Way Diving Center
12 Front St. S.
Thorold, Ontario
Canada

PADI

Price Diving Services
45 Dunfield Ave., Suite 301
Toronto, Ontario
Canada M4S 2H4

NAUI

Subanautique, Ltd.
5791 Tecimseh Rd. E.
Windsor, Ontario
Canada

NASDS

Prince Edward Island Underwater
P.O. Box 2612
Charlottetown, P.E.I.
Canada C1A 8C3

Write for ACUC member schools.

QUEBEC

Centre de plongee Sous
   Marine de Cap, Inc.
190 Vachon
Cap de la Madeleine, Quebec
Canada G8T 3T9

PADI

Aquasport
1175 Provost St.
Lachine, Quebec
Canada

NASDS

Aquasport
Auberge de la Lanterna
Georgeville Rd.
Magog, Quebec
Canada

NASDS

Aquanaut Scuba Centre, Ltd.
5317 Sherbrooke St. W.
Montreal, Quebec
Canada

NASDS

Waddell Aquatics
6044 Cote St. Luc. Rd.
Montreal, Quebec
Canada

NASDS

Bo-Lan
85 Laviqueur St.
Quebec
Canada G1R 1A8

SSI

Nautilus Sports
1594 Chemin St. Louis
Quebec,
Canada

NASDS

Nautilus Sports
583 St. Jean
Quebec,
Canada

NASDS

Octo-Bulles, Ltd.
949 Decarie Bl. N.
Saint-Laurent, Quebec
Canada

NASDS

Centre De Plungee Nepteau
1035 Despachers
Sherbrooke, Quebec
Canada

NAUI

SASKATCHEWAN

Saskatchewan Underwater Council
P.O. Box 1883
Saskatoon, Saskatchewan
Canada S7K 3S2

Write for ACUC member schools.

YUKON TERRITORY

Federation Quebecoise Des
   Activities Subaquatriques
1415 est rue Jarry
Montreal, Quebec
Canada H2E 2Z7

Write for ACUC member schools.

Yukon Territory Underwater Council
Room 225, Federal Bldg.
Whitehorse, Yukon Territory
Canada

Write for ACUC member schools.

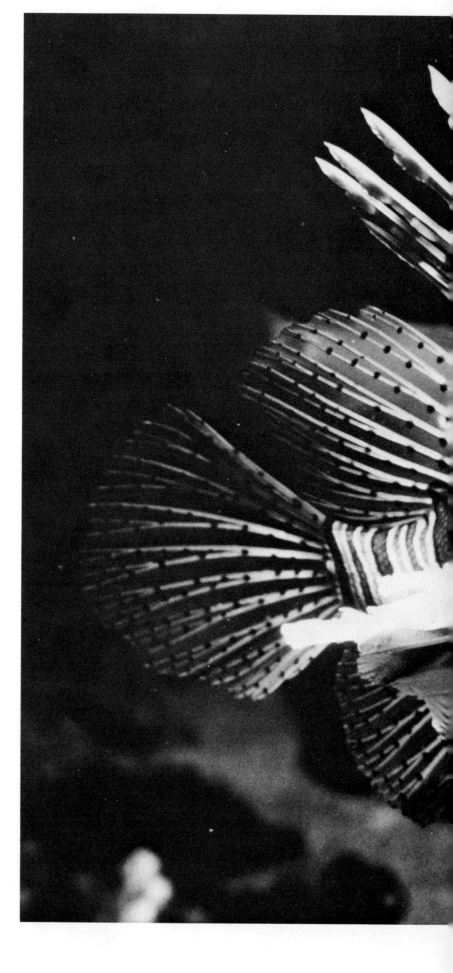

Clubs and Organizations

The growth of sport diving has been not only fast, but fragmented as well. Divers tend to be independent by nature, and so are the entrepreneurs—manufacturers, retailers, tour and resort operators—who supply and service them. As a result, no unifying, single-voiced force has emerged in diving, the way the National Rifle Association or Sports Car Club of America have in those sports.

Certifying Agencies

Probably the most powerful institutions in sport diving, besides the large manufacturers, are the major certifying agencies, which function as retail associations, lobbyists, consumer groups, and promoters of the sport at the same time. One of the greatest contributions of the certifying agencies has been the development of standards for the sport and the industry that serves it.

An obvious area of standardization has come in the field of diver education. As detailed in our chapter on "Instruction," each of the certifying agencies has a distinct training curriculum, but with the growth of cross-certification these programs generally teach similar techniques and rules of thumb. For the most part, it is the teaching methods and learning materials that differ from agency to agency.

As retail associations, the certifying agencies have spearheaded codes of ethics for divers as well as for instructors and salespeople. These codes have been important in promoting diving safety and in keeping governmental regulation of the sport to a manageable level.

The most tangible contributions of the certifying agencies are the safety equipment innovations they have pioneered. These advances include the near-universal use of submersible pressure gauges and personal buoyancy devices (vests or compensators), and safeguards like octopus second stages, dive floats and flags, plus repetitive tables and calculators. Research programs conducted by these agencies have also brought improvements in diving medicine and accident prevention techniques.

Most of the certifying agencies double as diver associations, providing benefits to divers they have certified. Here is a brief description of what each major agency offers besides diver training:

*Association of Canadian
Underwater Councils*
333 River Rd., Vanier
Ontario, Canada K1L 8B9

Represents divers belonging to member councils in the provinces and the Yukon and Northwest Territories. The organization disseminates recognized safety standards and provides a national information bureau.

ACUC conducts competitions in underwater navigation, hockey, football and photography. A Divers Pure Air Programme checks compressor installations and conducts air analyses. ACUC conducts seminars and issues certifications for visual tank inspectors. The association also conducts diving tours on request.

In addition, ACUC offers instructor liability insurance and diver accident insurance.

Members receive a newsletter, ACUC "I",

periodically (approximately six times a year), and communiques on topical subjects. ACUC also makes available a wide choice of informative pamphlets on specific underwater subjects.

National Association of
Scuba Diving Schools Inc.
P.O. Box 17067
Long Beach, CA 90807

Operates the Club Aquarius program with charter boats in Southern California and a full-scale diving resort, Cay Club Aquarius, near Belize. (See "Tours and Expeditions".) Club Aquarius also serves as a full service travel agency. NASDS member stores can put together groups for reduced rates at the resort, and frequently schedule local dives, river runs, fish fries, and other diving and social activities.

National Association
of Underwater Instructors
P.O. Box 630
Colton, CA 92324

The NAUI Diving Association encourages continuing education about the underwater environment. NAUI-certified divers receive the monthly *NAUI News* (reviewed under "Periodicals") and discounts on selected publications from NAUI as well as other publishers. Each member also gets a free diving log book. Non-divers, or those not certified by NAUI, can join the association and receive the newsletter by paying annual fees.

Two important NAUI projects are the annual International Conference on Underwater Education, open to divers, instructors, and the general public, and the Equipment Safety Program which trains and authorizes individuals to conduct visual tank inspections.

Professional Association
of Diving Instructors
2064 N. Bush Street
Santa Ana, CA 92706

Provides graduates with subscriptions to its professional technical magazine *The Undersea Journal* (see "Periodicals"), and a log book/training record. PADI also distributes diving texts to members at discounts, and issues periodic training bulletins.

For professionals, PADI operates an instructor placement service, and offers member stores an International Training Facility Program and Pure Air Program which combine technological

standards and merchandising aids.

Educational Organizations

A number of non-profit marine educational organizations have been established in recent years. Following is a sampling of some of the better known national and international organizations with particular appeal to divers:

International Oceanographic Foundation
3979 Rickenbacker Causeway
Virginia Key, Miami, FL 33149

Almost 70,000 members from 107 countries have joined the Foundation since its inception in 1953. Membership is open to anyone "interested in the oceans, in furthering research, education and public information." A major purpose of the Foundation is "encouraging and developing today's oceanographic exploration and scientific research."

The IOF operates a permanent marine science show, Planet Ocean, an educational facility and tourist attraction in the complex of ocean science institutions at Virginia Key, Miami.

Member services include a system for personally answering inquiries about marine subjects, as well as discounts on recommended books and film rentals. Members also receive the bi-monthly magazine *Sea Frontiers* and question-and-answer newsletter *Sea Secrets* (see "Periodicals").

Each year, the IOF bestows its prestigious Gold Medal Award for Outstanding Contributions to Oceanography on a deserving individual prominent in the field.

Oceanic Society
240 Fort Mason
San Francisco, CA 94123

Founded in 1973, the Society has 50,000 members in the U.S. and abroad. The only qualification for membership is concern for the ocean, since the Society is dedicated to "the conservation of the marine environment and ocean ecosystems."

Local chapters conduct educational courses and seminars, film and lecture series, and field trips. Members are encouraged to assist in local research activities, monitoring and testing programs and other volunteer activities. The Society also makes speakers and audio-visual programs available to interested groups.

Oceanic Expeditions offers a series of travel packages with an emphasis on marine sciences, and sponsors research expeditions. Many of these voyages offer unique sailing and diving experiences (see "Tours and Expeditions").

Members receive the slick bi-monthly magazine *Oceans* (see "Periodicals") and may also receive newsletters from their local chapters.

Fathom Eight
P.O. Box 8505
San Marino, CA 91108

Formed in 1974 as a means of grouping independent research in marine archeology, Fathom Eight is open to individuals who support that field of study. The organization accumulates data and recovered materials, distributes artifacts to museums and qualified institutions for public display, and presents findings to the public and to concerned institutions.

Through its membership seminars and other presentations, Fathom Eight encourages sophistication in marine archeological equipment, excavation and restoration. Membership publications include *Search,* the journal of undersea archeology (see "Periodicals"), an annual report recapping the preceding year's accomplishments, plus releases of important findings, events, or developments as they occur.

The Cousteau Society
777 Third Avenue
New York, NY 10017

Spearheaded by Jacques-Yves Cousteau and his son Philippe, the Society has acquired 150,000 members around the world since it was founded in 1973. It is dedicated to educating everyone in "the vital importance of a healthy ocean and of a clear water system."

Many of Cousteau's popular television series have been produced under the Society's banner, including "The Undersea World of Jacques Cousteau," "Oasis in Space," and the most recent "Cousteau Odyssey." The Society also produces filmstrips and books for high schools and colleges, paperback books on important marine issues, and articles and columns for magazines around the world.

In addition, the Society organizes lectures throughout the country and undertakes or sponsors research in fields not pursued by government or industry. A scholarship fund has been established for students to work on marine environmental problems at the university or laboratory level.

The Society fosters direct public involvement with environmental issues through local "Involvement Days," which focus attention on local and global problems. A program of communication with legislators on key issues had also been established.

Members receive a bi-monthly newsletter called the *Calypso Log* which includes information about current activities, international ocean issues, marine life, and environmental trends, plus a four-color poster with each issue. A special edition for young people, the *Dolphin Log,* is also available. Periodically, the Society also issues speeches, special reports, and answers to members' questions.

The Jean-Michel Cousteau Institute
P.O. Drawer CC
Harbor Town
Hilton Head, SC 29928

This organization is headed by Captain Cousteau's other diving son, Jean-Michel. The Institute has produced educational films and is working on a television series. A reference library is being set up to collect and disseminate audio-visual programs, educational material, and research data.

The primary member benefit of the Institute is its Project Ocean Search, a series of tour-study programs investigating the ecosystems of unique marine environment here and abroad. Each of the tours is personally hosted by young Cousteau and is open to divers and non-divers.

Council for Underwater
Resources and Oceans
P.O. Box 530173
Miami, FL 33153

A recent offshoot of the Council of Underwater Resort Operators, CURO has a worldwide membership who share a "common interest and concern in the ocean and its resources." The Council serves as a forum for the exchange of information between members and for the education of the public.

Besides underwater resort operators, CURO members include tourist boards, dive shops, equipment manufacturers, airlines, researchers, educators, diving and water-oriented publications, tour operators, certification agencies, divers, and interested laymen.

The young organization's plans call for the establishment of a correspondence service which will answer members' questions on underwater and diving technology, a speakers' bureau for interested groups, travel tips and specific information on new or improved diving areas, a rental library of underwater slides and films, career guidance in resort operation and marine science, a central training facility for diving resort operators, and government involvement.

CURO is planning a World Congress on Underwater Resources and Oceans, an interational communications forum scheduled for Europe in late 1980. Plans are also in the works for a CURO museum of diving history at the IOF's Planet Ocean exhibit.

Additional projects include a program to upgrade industry standards by providing rating forms for resorts and stylized log books for divers, plus the development of a comprehensive liability insurance program for resort operators.

CURO members receive a newsletter, *CURO Currents,* which covers activities of the organization and other information on the ocean and its resources. Various books and publications can also be ordered through CURO headquarters.

*American Association
of Certified Scuba Divers
P.O. Box 3820
Stamford, CT 06902*

Limited solely to divers certified by NASDS, NAUI, PADI or the YMCA, the Association has grown to 10,000 members since it began in 1976.

AACSD offers members group life term insurance covering most types of diving (often not covered under standard policies), group travel rates (see "Tours and Expeditions"), and discount tickets to underwater film festivals and seminars. The organization sponsors touring seminars with nationally certified instructors discussing scuba-related topics. An information center distributes copies of new scuba safety and training material issued by government and certifying agencies, as well as periodic briefs on current scuba accidents and fatalities.

Members receive the AACSD newsletter *Deep Thoughts* with news of member activities plus developments in diving technology and legisla-

tion. In addition, members can subscribe to *Skin Diver* Magazine at discount rates.

*Underwater Photographic Society
P.O. Box 7088
Van Nuys, CA 91409*

Founded in 1957 as a regional organization, UPS has begun to establish chapters in other cities as well. It is open to divers and photographers who wish to encourage amateur or professional underwater photography and cinematography, and to exchange knowledge and information on those subjects.

The Society sponsors the International Underwater Photographic Competition and Exhibition. Local chapters are encouraged to plan film showings, technical sessions, field trips, intrachapter photo contests, workshops, boat trips, tours, and similar activities.

A monthly newsletter details chapter activities and includes other articles of interest to underwater photographers.

*Underwater Society of America
732 50th Street
West Palm Beach, FL 33407*

The Society was formed in 1958 as an affiliation of regional dive councils, which are in turn made up of local dive clubs. Clubs not affiliated with a regional council, or independent divers, can join the Society as Associate Members. USA works for the interests of divers and the promotion of diving, and as a spokesman for the wants and needs of divers across the nation.

Since 1960, the Society has offered members a group accident insurance program. Other member benefits include a decompression sickness fund, a scholarship program, and continuous diver programs.

Members receive a quarterly newspaper, *Underwater Reporter,* and may also order a variety of how-to booklets published by the Society.

The listing of dive clubs which follows is by U.S. state and Canadian province, and alphabetically by city. This represents our best effort to locate all clubs in North America, but undoubtedly there are others we were unable to find.

Where we have been able to locate state or regional councils of divers and/or clubs, they appear at the beginning of each state or province.

Clubs and Organizations

United States

ALABAMA

Mobile Sea Wolves
61 S. Conception St.
Mobile, AL 36602

ARIZONA

Sand Dabs
4226 E. Indian School Rd.
Phoenix, AZ 85018

ARKANSAS

Arkansas Scuba Assn.
P.O Box 391
N Little Rock, AF

CALIFORNIA

Central California Council of Diving
Clubs
P.O. Box 779
Daly City, CA 94017

No Mama Dive Club
1640 W. Lincoln
Anaheim, CA 92801

East Bay Barnacles
2612 Truman Ct.
Antioch, CA 94509

Central Coast Sea Lions
5345 Magnolia Ave.
Atascadero, CA 93422

Penn Aqua Phantoms
508 San Bonito Ave.
Atherton, CA 94025

Bakersfield Frogmen
71 E. Pacheco Rd.
Bakersfield, CA 93307

Greater Los Angeles Council of
Divers
PO Box 1533
Beverly Hills, CA 90213

Gulls & Buoys
315 N. Ontario
Burbank, CA 91505

Sea Stars
2814 Empire
Burbank, CA 91504

Kelp Klippers
6154 Orsi Cir.
Carmichael, CA 95608

West Valley Divers Assn.
P.O. Box 481
Chatsworth, CA 91311

Sierra Aqua Fins
Box 976
Chester, CA 96020

Newport Harbor Sub Mariners
2164 Meyer
Costa Mesa, CA 92626

Hoffman Dive Club
967 Gramont
Covina, CA 91722

Peninsula Aqua Knights
10141 Denison
Cupertino, CA 95014

Black Barts Buccaneers
34145 Pacific Coast Hwy.
Dana Point, CA 92629

Five Fathom Dive Club
11200 Old River School Rd.
Downey, CA 90241

Laguna Skin Divers
7844 E. Vista Del Rosa
Downey, CA 90204

Sea Sabres
12145 S. Woodruff
Downey, CA 90241

Berkeley YMCA Senior Divers
7820 Eureka Ave.
El Cerrito, CA 94530

Sea Urchins
4933 Petit Ave.
Encino, CA 91316

Humbolt Skin Divers
624 Highland - Box 259
Eureka, CA 95502

Aqua Lancers
35370 Gustavo Ct.
Fremont, CA 94536

Fresno Serpent Divers
3008 N. Fisher
Fresno, CA 93703

Fresno Sport Divers
1224 W. Fedora
Fresno, CA 93705

IDS, Glendale Chapter
735 E. Lexington
Glendale, CA 91204

Chickens of the Sea
19619 Kirkwall Rd.
Glendora, CA 91740

Aqua Tatus
62 Whitney Ct.
Hayward, CA 94541

Neptune Raiders
3200 Rio Lindo Ave.
Healdsburg, CA 95448

Orcas Skin & Scuba Club of
Garden Grove
17672 El Nopal Ln.
Huntington Beach, CA 92646

Sea Stars
951 Foothill
La Canada, CA 91011

Reef Hunters
8811 Pacific Coast Hwy., No. 40
Laguna Beach, CA 92651

Lakeport Sea Bats
960 60th St.
Lakeport, CA 95453

Vaqueros Del Mar
P.O. Box 8782
Livermore, CA 94550

Delta Divers
314 W. Pine St.
Lodi, CA 95240

Hapa'ia Dive Club
2306 Wellesley Ave.
Los Angeles, CA 90064

Lung Dusters
4612 Strang
Los Angeles, CA 90022

Los Angeles Fathomiers
1855 Montiflora
Los Angeles, CA 90041

Nisel Kelp Tanglers
1638 Norton Ave.
Los Angeles, CA 90019

Surf Raiders
9851 S. Sepulveda Blvd.
Los Angeles, CA 90045

Merced Aquanauts, Inc.
918 Birch
Los Banos, CA 95635

San Jose Barbs
16290 Roseleaf Ln.
Los Gatos, CA 95030

California Wreck Divers
PO Box 9922
Marina Del Rey, CA 90291

Sierra Club Dive Section
4133 Via Marina No. 111
Marina Del Rey, CA 90291

Aqua Knights
PO Box 14
McClellan AFB, CA 95652

Los Santos Del Ondo
1686 Rocky Mountain Ave.
Milpitas, CA 95035

Stanislaw Co. Finmen
508 E. Rumble Rd.
Modesto, CA 95350

Monterey Sea Otters
851 Archer St.
Monterey, CA 93940

Pelican Divers
2500 MacGregor Ct.
Napa, CA 94558

Recreational Dive Assn.
1220 W. Pacific Coast Hwy.
Newport Beach, CA 92260

S.C.U.B.A.
4535 W. Pacific Coast Hwy.
Newport Beach, CA 92660

Kelp Kreepers
7553 Irvine Ave.
N. Hollywood, CA 91505

Cormorants
9361 Bining Ct.
Orangevale, CA 95662

Kelp Kats
205 E. Nectarine
Oxnard, CA 93031

Pasadena Torgutes
554 Chester Ave.
Pasadena, CA 91106

Petaluma Aqua Ducks
1177 Western Ave.
Petaluma, CA 94952

Orcas Underwater Group
34 Phyllis
Pleasant Hill, CA 94952

Marin Skindivers, Inc.
Box 67
Point Reyes, CA 94956

Pomona Valley Skin Divers
661 Parcelles St.
Pomona, CA 91766

Peninsula Aqua Phantoms, Inc.
56 Old Spanish Trail
Portola Valley, CA 94025

Aquaducks
Box 604 - RT 1
Quincy, CA 95971

Shasta Divers
3517 Alta Mesa Dr.
Redding, CA 96001

International Diving Club
7110 Reseda Blvd.
Reseda, CA 91335

Riverside Dive Club
17975 Choasset St.
Reseda, CA 91335

Richmond Y Divers
4017 Clinton Ave.
Richmond, CA 94805

San Pablo Dolphins
1600 26th St.
Richmond, CA 94806

Rio Makos
200 Gardiner Way
Rio Vista, CA 94571

Kelp Klippers
2073 51st Ave.
Sacramento, CA 95822

Reef Raiders
2871 Lorin Ave.
Sacramento, CA 95828

Seals
6100 Stockton Blvd.
Sacramento, CA 95824

Skin & Scuba Divers of
Greater Sacramento
104 Meister Way
Sacramento, CA 95819

Sea Dippers
400 Cresent Way
Salinas, CA 93902

Addicts
1742 39th St.
San Diego, CA 92105

Club Aquarius, San Diego Chapter
4004 Sports Arena Blvd.
San Diego, CA 92138

San Diego Underwater
Photographic Society
PO Box 82782
San Diego, CA 92138

Sea Dogs
3045 Sterne St.
San Diego, CA 92106

Sea Slobs
6645 Vigo Dr.
San Diego, CA 92115

Mid Valley YMCA Scuba Club
PO Box 5235
San Fernando, CA 91340

Cormorants
22 Lee Ave.
San Francisco, CA 94101

San Francisco Ocean Club
115 Foote Ave.
San Francisco, CA 94102

San Jose Flipper Dippers
554 S. Bascom Ave.
San Jose, CA 95128

San Jose Skin Divers
1098 Craig Dr.
San Jose, CA 95125

Sea Foxes
1454 Quartz Way
San Jose, CA 95118

Sea Sabres
33971 Calle De Borego
San Juan Capistrano, CA 92675

Deep Six
1725 141st Ave.
San Leandro, CA 94578

Underwater Photographic Society
2279 Belvedere Ave.
San Leandro, CA 94577

Aqua Tutus
Box 494
San Lorenzo, CA 94580

Sea Crawlers
2135 Via Rancho
San Lorenzo, CA 94580

Central Coast Sea Lions
2557 Greta
San Luis Obispo, CA 93401

Aquaholics
116 10th Ave.
San Mateo, CA 94401

Tiburon Scuba Club of San Mateo
PO Box 6023 Sta. A
San Mateo, CA 94403

Santa Cruz Aquatechs, Inc.
PO Box 3
Santa Cruz, CA 95063

Santa Barbara Divers
PO Box 30491
Santa Barbara, CA 93105

Santa Monica Blue Fins
PO Box 1763
Santa Monica, CA 90406

Scuba Haus Divers
2501 Wilshire Blvd.
Santa Monica, CA 90406

Sonoma City Reef Runners
2719 Mohawk
Santa Rosa, CA 95401

Garden Grove Orcas
24122 El Mirage
South Laguna, CA 92677

Hydro Knights
424 Wildwood Dr.
S. San Francisco, CA 94801

Skin Divers, Ltd.
8444 Kinross Way
Stockton, CA 95207

Scuba Duba Whalers
12538 Ventura Blvd.
Studio City, CA 91604

San Joaquin Sport Divers
303 Harrison St.
Taft, CA 93268

Seaweed Syndicate
South High School
Torrance, CA 90510

Pacific Grove Looney Gooney
151 Teddy Dr.
Union City, CA 94587

Van Nuys Teen Center
17100 Victory
Van Nuys, CA 91408

United Sport Divers
13415 Killion St.
Van Nuys, CA 91401

Kelp Kats
339 Lynbrook Ave.
Ventura, CA 92003

Kelp Rats
415 S. Howard St.
Ventura, CA 93003

Sea Bears
8635 Roswell St.
Ventura, CA 93003

East Bay Barnacles
144 Montanya Ct.
Walnut Creek, CA 94596

Coral Scratchers
2205 E. Walnut Creek Pkwy.
West Covina, CA 91790

Feather River Skin Divers
125 N. 10th St.
Williams, CA 95987

Descenders
227 S. Sonoma St.
Willows, CA 95988

Mariam Skin Diving Club
Oak Grove Ave.
Woodacre, CA 94973

COLORADO

Boulder Water Buffalos
15 S. 38th
Boulder, CO 80302

Colorado Gypsy Divers
229 N. Yucca
Pueblo, CO 81005

CONNECTICUT

Connecticut Council of
Diving Clubs
238 Blakeslee St.
Bristol, CT 06010

New Haven Barnacles
21 Third Ave.
Branford, CT 06405

Westport Diving Club
18 Short St.
Bridgeport, CT 06605

Eastford Sea Searchers
Eastford, CT 06264

Associated Skin Divers
88 Old County Hwy.
East Granby, CT 06026

Viking Skin & Scuba Divers
17 Williamson Rd.
Hamden, CT 06415

Blue Fin Diving Club
Box 432
Jewett City, CT 06351

Women Divers of Connecticut
141 Birch St.
Manchester, CT 06040

Sea Kings
225 Curtis St.
New Britain, CT 06053

Connecticut Dolphins
19 Meridian St.
New London, CT 06320

Milford Underwater Divers
11 Rangeley Dr.
Trumball, CT 06611

South Eastern Conn. Skin
Divers, Inc.
24 Baldwin Ct.
Uncasville, CT 06382

Sea Dragons of Connecticut
268 Crest St.
Wethersfield, CT 06109

DELAWARE

Diamond State Skin Divers
4 Carl Rd.
Augustine Hills
Wilmington, DE 19899

DISTRICT OF COLUMBIA

Pioneer Skin Diving Club
2116 Glendora St.
Washington, DC 20028

Sea Trolls Diving Club
2616 Riviera St.
Washington, DC 20031

FLORIDA

Daytona Beach Skin Divers
1309 Margina Ave.
Daytona Beach, FL 32019

De Bary Cudas
27 Columbia Tr.
De Bary, FL 32713

Flipper Flappers
4430 Hill Dr.
Fort Meyers, FL 33901

Sea Urchins
2602 S. 15th St.
Ft. Pierce, FL 33450

Florida Reef Raiders
382 Gardner Dr. NE
Ft. Walton Bch., FL 33548

Barnacle Busters
PO Box 12823 Univ. Sta.
Gainesville, FL 32601

Aqua Addicts
200 NW 12th Ave., Apt. 3D
Hallandale, FL 33009

Suncoast Sharks
148 Clark St.
Hudson, FL 33568

Bold City Divers
PO Box 52171
Jacksonville, FL 32201

Divers of the Golden Crown
4067 Starrett Rd.
Jacksonville, FL 32226

Jax Jetty Jumpers
5648 Floral Ave.
Jacksonville, FL 32211

Skipjacks
PO Box 1648
Jacksonville, FL 32201

KSC Barracudas
Box 21023
Kennedy Space Ctr., FL 32899

Bottoms Up Diving Club
PO Box 1297
Lake Alfred, FL 33850

Gold Coast Aquanauts
702 Wright Dr.
Lake Worth, FL 33460

Suncoast Seals
229 Andrea Dr.
Largo, FL 33540

Aqua Nuts
PO Box 1027
Melbourne, FL 32901

Sea Dragons
210 Catalina Isles Dr.
Merritt Island, FL 32952

Glug Clugs
9825 NW 13th Ave.
Miami, FL 33152

Miami Makos
249 Springs Ave.
Miami, FL 33166

South Florida Divers
12460 SW 33rd St.
Miami, FL 33165

Reef Raiders
755 Arabia Ave.
Opa Locka, FL 33054

Orlando Otters
PO Box 7084
Orlando, FL 32804

Ormond Anchor Chasers
PO Box 1934
Ormond Beach, FL 32074

Aqua Masters
4196 Arbor Way
Palm Beach Gardens, FL 33165

Diving Damsels
1245 Island Rd.
Riviera Beach, FL 33404

Venice Scuba Diving Club
Suite 1001 Sarasota Bank Bldg.
Sarasota, FL 33577

Castaways Diving Club
PO Box 2215
Satellite Beach, FL 32937

St. Pete Underwater Club
4026 31st Ave. N.
St. Petersburg, FL 33713

Sunshine Fins
8214 22nd Ave. N.
St. Petersburg, FL 33710

Independents
4014 Howard Ave.
Tampa, FL 33607

Tampa Tridents
PO Box 8334
Tampa, FL 33604

Underwater Picnic Society
813 W. 130th Ave.
Tampa, FL 33612

Bull Dolphins Skin & Scuba
2778 Pineridge Ave.
Titusville, FL 32780

Sea Dragons
PO Box 5501
Titusville, FL 32780

Sarasota Scuba Diving Club
950 Cooper St.
Venice, FL 33595

Underwater Team
6901 Carissa Cir.
W. Palm Beach, FL 33406

GEORGIA

Argonauts
PO Box Y
Albany GA 31702

Cruso Spearfishing Club
3047 Lenox Rd.
Atlanta, GA 30304

Sr. Divers of Georgia
1621 Cecilla Dr. SE
Atlanta, GA 30316

Augusta Scuba Nauts
YMCA Broad St.
Augusta, GA 30901

Gainsville Skin Divers
Box 23
Gainesville, GA 30501

Telfair Co. Catfish
1 Ave.
McRae, GA 31055

Waycross Skin Divers
2318 Eastover Dr.
Waycross, GA 31501

HAWAII

Hawaii Council of Diving Clubs
PO Box 298
Honolulu, HI 96809

Camp Smith Jellyfish
Camp Smith, HI 96861

Hui Lu'u Kai
66-009C Waialua Beach Rd.
Haleiwa, HI 96712

Alii Holo Kai
3446 Pakui St.
Honolulu, HI 96816

Hana Hana Lu'u
1236-B Palamea Ln.
Honolulu, HI 96817

Ka Imi Kai Scuba Divers
954 Kului Pl.
Honolulu, HI 96821

Pearl Divers
913 Murray Dr.
Honolulu, HI 96818

Salt Water Quarium Society
of Hawaii
1984 Hott-Smith Dr.
Honolulu, HI 96822

Tiki Divers
807 N. Vineyard Blvd. A15
Honolulu, HI 96817

Aku Marines Dive Club
PO Box 1050
Kailua, HI 96734

Bojac Dive Club
94-366 Pupupani St. #117
Waipahu, HI 96797

IDAHO

Boise Skin Divers
Box 961
Boise, ID 83701

Hell Divers
1218 Longmont
Boise, ID 83706

ILLINOIS

Illinois Council of Skin
& Scuba Divers
3147 Kentwood Pkwy.
Rockford, IL 61109

Sea Hawks Scuba Club
112 Lynhaven Dr.
Belleville, IL 62223

Aqua Divers Club
3039 E. 91st St.
Chicago, IL 60617

Chicago Aquanauts
2424 Touby Ave.
Chicago, IL 60645

Dirty Old Men's Sking Diving
Protective League, Ltd.
841 Glenwood Rd.
Glenview, IL 60025

Bubblemasters
PO Box 36, Mitchell Branch
Granite City, IL 62040

Rockford Divers Assn.
PO Box 1544
Rockford, IL 61110

INDIANA

Aqua Addicts Diving Club
711 Fulton Ave.
Elkhart, IN 46518

Indiana Aqua Divers
350 N. Meridian
Indianapolis, IN 46204

Aqua Lads
2145 Hollywood Place
South Bend, IN 46616

IOWA

Scuba Snoopers
Rt. 2
Ames, IA 50010

Quad City Divers
1841 E. 31st St.
Davenport, IA 52807

Subaquanauts Diving Club
648 32nd St.
Des Moines, IA 50312

Aqua Hawks Club
819 Loretta
Waterloo, IA 50702

KANSAS

Aqua Hunters, Inc.
Rt. 1 Box 217
Augusta, KS 67010

Jayhawks Divers of Pittsburg
Box 487
Pittsburgh, KS 66762

Martini's Scubaneers
450 S. Evergreen Ln.
Wichita, KS 67209

Wichita Desert Divers, Inc.
628 S. Chautauqua
Wichita, KS 67211

KENTUCKY

Mermen of Kentucky
1153 Liberty Rd.
Lexington, KY 40505

Kentucky Scuba Divers
3104 Hunsinger Blvd.
Louisville, KY 40202

Piranha Skin & Scuba
4215 Dolphin Rd.
Louisville, KY 40202

MAINE

Rocky Coast Divers
62 Turner St.
Auburn, ME 04210

Casco Bay Aqua Divers
100 Prospect St.
Biddeford, ME 04005

Brunswick Sea Lions
River Rd.
Brunswick, ME 04011

MARYLAND

Chesapeake Divning Club
109 Camrose
Baltimore, MD 21225

Maryland Hydronauts
1910 N. Forest Park Ave.
Baltimore, MD 21207

Maryland Waterbugs
921 Cromwell Bridge Rd.
Baltimore, MD 21204

Belair Divers
12514 Saber Ln.
Bowie, MD 20715

Groupers
205 Bucknell Rd.
Bryans Road, MD 20616

Sub Committee YMCA
7215 Baybrook Ln.
Chevy Chase, MD 20015

American Underwater Divers
5821 Mentona St.
New Carrolton, MD 20784

Atlantis Rangers
PO Box 96
Riverdale, MD 20840

Aquanauts
13200 N. Hampshire Ave.
Silver Springs, MD 20902

Bunker Hill Divers
10402 Leslie Ct.
Silver Springs, MD 20902

Talbot Co. Diving Club
c/o Guy Reeser
St. Michaels, MD 21683

MASSACHU-SETTES

Athol Frogmen
7 Pleasant St.
Athol, MA 01331

Water Wizards
198 Linden St.
Boylston, MA 01505

Cape Cod Tridents
Rd. 1
Centerville, MA 02632

Fairhaven Whaler Diving Club
Box 225
Fairhaven, MA 02719

Fall River Aquamen
85 Chace St.
Fall River, MA 02724

Gardner Skin Diving Club
Ligget Bldg.
Gardner, MA 01440

Atlantic Skin Divers
22 Parallel St.
Salem, MA 01970

Scuba Deep Sea Club
70 Dearborn St.
Salem, MA 01970

Bay Divers Club
322 County St.
Seekonk, MA 02771

Somerset Aquamasters
49 Adams St.
Somerset, MA 02725

Nemrods
50 N. Main St.
S. Hadley Falls, MA 01075

Massachusetts Sea Lions
518 Southhampton Rd.
Westfield, MA 01085

Lowell Underwater Explorers
Forest Rd.
Westford, MA 01861

Newton Nautileers
429 Cherry St.
W. Newton, MA 02165

Yankee Flippers
15 Bellevue St.
W. Rosbury, MA 02132

Dauntless Dolphins
74 Coolidge Ave.
Weymouth, MA 02188

Flubadubs
6 Jamesbury Dr.
Worcester, MA 01609

Worcester Aqua Divers
309 Hamilton St.
Worcester, MA 01604

Spear Fishermen
Holt Rd.
Holden, MA 01520

Central Mass. Aquanauts
c/o Inland Divers
100 S. Main St.
Leicester, MA 01524

Sea Diving Club
10 Roberts Pl.
Lowell, MA 01854

Lynn Lone Sharks
274 Eastern Ave.
Lynn, MA 01902

Marblehead Underwater Group
33 Haley Rd.
Marblehead, MA 01945

Neponsett Valley Bluefins
744 Neponsett St.
Norwood, MA 02062

North Shore Frogmen
PO Box 604
Peabody, MA 01960

Berkshire Skin Divers
YMCA
Pittsfield, MA 01201

Boston Sea Rovers
174 Beech St.
Rockland, MA 02370

MICHIGAN

Cheboygan Skin Divers
Box 284
Cheboygan, MI 49721

Champion Divers
12772 Wilfred
Detroit, MI 48213

Depth Chargers
32552 Clairview Dr.
Farmington, MI 48024

Aquaholic Divers
4224 Brousville
Lincoln Park, MI 48146

Viking Diving Club
51 E. Cicotte
River Rouge, MI 48218

Saginaw Underwater Explorers
3286 Northwood Pl.
Saginaw, MI 48603

Scubalancers
6715 Bailey
Taylor, MI 48180

Aqua Mates Skin Divers
6801 Roby Rt. 4
Union Lake, MI 48085

Wyoming Pirate Divers
930 40th St. SW
Wyoming, MI 49509

MINNESOTA

N. Star State Divers
4251 Nicollet Ave.
Minneapolis, MN 55409

MISSISSIPPI

Jackson Aqua Bees
YMCA
Jackson, MS 39205

MISSOURI

White River Lakes Divers
Indian Point Boat Dock
Branson, MO 65616

Hydronauts
904 Euclid
Carthage, MO 64836

Show Me Divers
617 N. Byers
Joplin, MO 64801

Inland Sea Devils
8012 Belleview
Kansas City, MO 64114

Kansas City Frogman Club
6806 E. 114 Terr.
Kansas City, MO 64134

Knights of the Deep
404 E. 10th St.
Kansas City, MO 64106

St. Louis Scuba Club
366 Sorrento
Manchester, MO 63011

Black River Swamp Angels
Box 302
Poplar Bluff, MO 63901

Aqualunker
7730 Raytown Rd.
Raytown, MO 64133

Seldalia Divers
P.O. Box 1023
Sedalia, MO 65301

Springfield Scuba Club
1247 E. Cambridge
Springfield, MO 65804

Aqua Masters
3013 Clearview Dr.
St. Louis, MO 63121

Y Dolfins
1900 Urban Dr.
St. Louis, MO 63144

NEBRASKA

Aqua Sharks
902 S. Dewey
North Platte, NE 69101

Drifters Diving Club
9211 Sprague St.
Omaha, NE 68134

Knights of Neptune Diving Club
2914 Gold St.
Omaha, NE 68105

Van Winkle Y Divers
5803 N. 30th St.
Omaha, NE 68111

Scubateers, Inc.
c/o Jerry Lemon
Rt. 3
Palmer, NE 68864

York Dolphins
120 West 9th St.
York, NE 68467

NEVADA

Cui Diving Club
YMCA
Reno, NV 89501

NEW HAMPSHIRE

Yankee Trankers
Weirs Blvd.
Laconia, NH 03246

River View Park Divers
415 Cartier St.
Manchester, NH 03102

Lake Sunapee Skin Divers
Star Route
N. Hampton, NH 03256

NEW JERSEY

New Jersey Council of
Diving Clubs
PO Box 175
Highlands, NJ 07732

Underwater Fishermen of
New Jersey
1114 Sunset Ave.
Asbury Park, NJ 08802

Jersey Sea Devils
514 E. Church St.
Blackwood, NJ 08012

Nautilus Divers
1008 Blackhorse Pike
Blenheim, NJ 08012

Sea Hawks
18 Deerfield Pike
Bridgeton, NJ 08302

Clifton Aqua Divers
211 Madison Ave.
Clifton, NJ 07011

Princeton Y Scuba Divers
c/o Maurice Coutts, Applegarth Rd.
Cranbury, NJ 08512

Mask & Fin Divers
15 E. Madison
Cresskill, NJ 07626

The Underwater Sportman
13 Everett St.
East Orange, NJ 07019

City Scuba Divers
311 Spencer St.
Elizabeth, NJ 07202

Scuba Club of New Jersey
37 Gillette RFD
Gillette, NJ 07933

Underwater Fishermen
321 Maolis Ave.
Glen Ridge, NJ 07028

Ridgewood Aqua Splashers
167 Elmwood Ave.
Glen Rock, NJ 07452

Piranhas Diving Club
360 Main St.
Hackensack, NJ 07601

The Manta Ray Diving Club
Box 729
Landing, NJ 07850

Atlantic Underwater Group
48 Sheridan Ave.
Metuchen, NJ 08840

The Metuchen Underwater Divers
c/o Metuchen YMCA
Metuchen, NJ 08840

The New Jersey Skin Diving Club
c/o Montclair YMCA
Montclair, NJ 07042

The Newark Skin Divers
c/o The Newark YMCA
Broad St.
Newark, NJ 07102

Vikings
171 Richelieu Terr.
Newark, NJ 07106

The Raritan Valley Mask & Fin
c/o YMCA
New Brunswick, NJ 08901

Aqua Bats
239 N. 8th St.
Paterson, NJ 07508

Lung & Spear Club
913 Chestnut St.
Paulsboro, NJ 08066

The Piranhas Diving Club
935 Ray Ave.
Ridgefield, NJ 07657

South Jersey Mermen
1045 Mantua Blvd.
Sewell, NJ 08080

Mask & Fin Club
1000 River Rd.
Teaneck, NJ 07666

The Westfins
c/o Westfield YMCA
Westfield, NJ 07090

Passaic Clifton Diving Club
422 Innes Rd.
Woodridge, NJ 17075

NEW MEXICO

Rocky Mtn. Skin Divers
2634 Sierra Dr. NE
Albuerquerque, NM 87110

NEW YORK

Erie Community College Scuba
Club
Main & Youngs Rd.
Amherst, NY 14221

Auburn Skin Divers
12 Metcalf Ave.
Auburn, NY 13021

Aqua Addicts
R.D. 6, 25 Reita St.
Ballston Spa., NY 12020

Explorers of Nadir
1706 Albany Ave.
Brooklyn, NY 11201

Greenpoint Mantas
99 Meserole Ave.
Brooklyn, NY 11201

Highland Divers
570 Jamaica Ave.
Brooklyn, NY 11201

Triboro Aquanauts
1875 Randal Ave.
Bronx, NY 10451

Buffalo Aqua Club
1063 Walden Ave.
Buffalo, NY 14211

Diving Docs
175 Fort Hill Ave.
Canandaigua, NY 14424

Suffolk Submariners
29 Red Bridge Rd.
Center Moriches, NY 11934

Clayton Diving Club
612 Franklin St.
Clayton, NY 13624

Cobleskill Diving Club
8 Grandview Terr.
Cobleskill, NY 12043

Long Island Sea Hunters
5 Pierre Dr.
Commack, NY 11725

Delmariners Scuba Club
111 Dunbarton Dr.
Delmar, NY 12054

Neptune's Intruders
Box 506
Endicott, NY 13760

Posideons Playmates
37 Miles Ave.
Fairport, NY 14450

Frankfort Underwater Diving Team
111 Sheldon Ave.
Frankfort, NY 13440

Ontario Aquanauts
166 W. 5th St., S.
Fulton, NY 13069

Westchester Blackfish
315 Harrison Ave.
Harrison, NY 10528

Central Seals
8925 Parsons Ave.
Jamaica, NY 11431

Kem-ton Mako Sharks
535 Belmont Ave.
Kenmore, NY 14223

Aqua Knights
886 Leeds Ct.
N. Bellmore, NY 11710

Syracuse Skin Divers Club, Inc.
5384 Bear Road
N. Syracuse, NY 13212

Norwich Divers Assn.
Box 387
Norwich, NY 13815

Olean Divers
311 N. 4th St.
Olean, NY 14760

Neversink Divers Club
63 Ponantico Rd.
Ossining, NY 10562

Lake Champlain Wreck Raiders
69 Miller St.
Plattsburgh, NY 12901

Aquatic Explorers
Box 1381
Poughkeepsie, NY 12602

Dutchess Divers Inc.
PO Box 3022
Poughkeepsie, NY 12603

The Aquarians
221 Old Meadow Dr.
Rochester, NY 14626

Rochester Sport Divers
579 Maple St.
Rochester, NY 14611

Tri Aqua Divers
205 Lyndale Dr.
Rome, NY 13440

Scuba Sport Rites Club
PO Box 644
Rye, NY 10580

Southampton Submersibles
Box 4635 Southampton Coll.
Southampton, NY 11968

N.Y. State Diving Club
340 Montgomery St.
Syracuse, NY 13202

Central N.Y. Aqua Knights
1212 Moyes St.
Utica, NY 13502

Hunt Underwater Club
200 E. Main St.
Watertown, NY 13601

Ten Fathom Club
215 Bert Ave.
Westbury, NY 11590

NORTH CAROLINA

North Carolina Skin Diving
Council
11 Summerhill Terr.
Kinston, NC 28501

Asheville YMCA Divers
2 Woodfin St.
Asheville, NC 28801

Barnacle Bumpers
1509 Front St.
Beaufort, NC 28516

Scuba Divers of Isa
611 E. Franklin Ave.
Gastonia, NC 28052

The Deep Six
307 Leftwich St.
Greensboro, NC 27405

Lakewood Lungsters
4412 Cornell Ave.
Greensboro, NC 27407

Snorkel Snorters
Box 395
Nashville, NC 27856

Newport Skin Divers
Box 211
Newport, NC 28570

Shelby Divers
Box 1241
Shelby, NC 28150

Skin Diving Club
Box 202
Wadesboro, NC 28170

Skin Diving Club
Box 788
Wendell, NC 27591

OHIO

Ohio Council of Skin &
Scuba Divers, Inc.
11101 Fallsburg Rd. NE
Frazeysburg, OH 43822

Ridgewood Scuba Club
590 West Dr.
Brunswick, OH 44212

Vikings Scuba Club
7755 Palmyra Rd.
Canfield, OH 44406

Aqua-Mariners, Inc.
2816 11th St. N.W.
Canton, OH 44708

Ross County Y Divers
100 Mill St.
Chillicothe, OH 45601

Y-Nauts Sub Aqua Club
8737 Shagbark Dr.
Cincinnati, OH 45242

Aqua Amigo Scuba Club
PO Box 10073
Cleveland, OH 44110

Aquamasters of Lakewood
Lakewood YM-YWCA
16915 Detroit Ave.
Cleveland, OH 44107

Buckeye Divers
776 Persimmon Ln.
Columbus, OH 43213

Columbus YMCA Sea Nags
40 West Long St.
Columbus, OH 43040

Rubber City Aquanauts, Inc.
723 Roosevelt Ave.
Cuyahoga Falls, OH 44221

Dayton Scuba Divers
3415 Vance Rd.
Dayton, OH 45418

Elyria YMCA Devil Ray Skin
& Scuba Divers Club
265 Washington Ave.
Elyria, OH 44035

Aqua-Amigos
Euclid YMCA
631 Babbitt St.
Euclid, OH 44123

Sandusky Bay Divers
305 E. Buchanan St.
Fremont, OH 43420

Erie Island Diving Club
211 Ashland St.
Huron, OH 44839

Aqua Probes Scuba Club
780 Marilyn Dr.
Kent, OH 44240

Kent State Univ. Scuba Club
Student Activities Center
Kent State University
Kent, OH 44242

Tiki Divers
466 Harvey Ave.
Kent, OH 44240

Dayton Mantish Scuba Club
2432 Vale Dr.
Kettering, OH 45420

Kettering YMCA Scuba Club
4545 Marshall Rd.
Kettering, OH 45429

Buckeye Aquarians
RD. 1
Leetonia, OH 44431

Neptune Imps Diving Club
124 McKinley Ave.
Lisbon, OH 44432

Aqua Masters
16915 Detroit Ave.
Lakewood, OH 44107

Club Cuda
4615 Park Ave. West
RD 12 Box 58
Mansfield, OH 44903

Marion Underwater Explorers
519 Girard Ave.
Marion, OH 43302

Mountaineer Skin Divers, Inc.
PO Box 182
Martins Ferry, OH 43935

Newark YMCA Poseidons
PO Box 96
Newark, OH 43055

Invaders Twelve Scuba Club
123 S. Main St.
New Lexington, OH 43764

Surface Breakers Diving Club
1766 Orkney Rd.
N. Madison, OH 44057

Orrville Divemasters
RD. 2
Orrville, OH 44667

Toledo Submariners
12865 Five Point Rd. #121
Perrysburg, OH 43551

Aquanauts Club
Box 175
Rogers, OH 44455

Alliance Y Tritons
490 S. Lincoln
Salem, OH 44460

Sandusky Scuba Divers
530 46th St.
Sandusky, OH 44870

Springfield Scuba Society
935 N. Limestone St. #4
Springfield, OH 45503

Wadsworth Diving Club
734 Crestwood Ave.
Wadsworth, OH 44281

Zanesville YMCA Aquaniks
1403 Jewett Dr.
Zanesville, OH 43701

OKLAHOMA

Oklahoma Council of Underwater
  Divers, Inc.
PO Box 10376
Midwest City, OK 73110

Southwest Council of Skin
  Diving Clubs
3401 N. Meridian Ct.
Oklahoma City, OK 73122

Sooner State Divers
319 N. 21st St.
Collinsville, OK 74021

Blue Gill Divers, Inc.
821 Vickie Dr.
Del City, OK 73115

Gurglers Diving Club
4612 Bela Ave.
Lawton, OK 73501

Hydronauts Divers, Inc.
I-40 & Sooner Rd.
Midwest City, OK 73110

Thunderbird Divers, Inc.
1008 S. Air Depot
Midwest City, OK 73110

Tinker Divers, Inc.
1416 Oelke
Midwest City, OK 73110

Muskogee Sub Mariners
502 N. 13th
Muskogee, OK 74401

Oklahoma City Barracudas
4313 N. State
Oklahoma City, OK 73122

OREGON

Willamette Divers
YMCA 3311 S. Pacific
Albany, OR 97321

Hydronauts
210 W. 16th
McMinnville, OR 97128

Oregon Divers Club
Box 213
Newport, OR 97365

Salem Reef Rangers
3760 Middlegrove
Salem, OR 97303

PENNSYLVANIA

Abingdon Sub Mariners
YMCA Old York
Abingdon, PA 19001

Allentown Y Divers
c/o Frank Turney
RD 4
Allentown, PA 18103

The Suburban Aquanauts
201 Rolling Rd.
Broomall, PA 19008

Aqualiers
2148 Lee Ln.
Chester, PA 19014

Blue Dolphins
Box 1071
Erie, PA 16512

Capital Area Dauphin Divers
3149 Brookfield Rd.
Harrisburg, PA 17109

Lancaster Divers
412 N. Duke St.
Lancaster, PA 17602

Fathom Phantoms
N. Penn YMCA
Lansdale, PA 19446

Atlantis Diving Club
29 Thimbleberry
Levittown, PA 19054

Main Line Divers
44 War Trophy Ln.
Media, PA 19063

North Penn Fathom Phantoms
406 S. 5th St.
North Wales, PA 19454

Phildelphia Depth Chargers
7900 C Stenton Ave.
Philadelphia, PA 19119

Philadelphia Seahorses
2027 Chestnut St.
Philadelphia, PA 19103

Underwater Explorers
6901 Henley St.
Philadelphia, PA 19119

Gateway Scuba Club
3265 Eastmont Ave.
Pittsburgh, PA 15222

Schuylkill Scuba Divers
402 Mahantongo St.
Pottsville, PA 19464

Sting Ray Divers
3808 Grant St.
Reading, PA 19605

Arlington Submariners
1433 High Ave.
Roslyn, PA 19001

Aqua Knights
811 Quince Ln.
Secame, PA 19019

Keystone Divers Assn.
11 East School Ln.
Yardley, PA 19067

Spearbenders
40 Bedford Place
Yardley, PA 19068

RHODE ISLAND

Narragansett Bay Divers
160 Broad St.
Providence, RI 02903

Newport Underwater Sportsmen
PO Box 643
Newport, RI 02840

Sea Devils
33 Edgewood Ave.
Westerly, RI 02891

SOUTH CAROLINA

Charleston Seafishers
959 S. Shem Dr.
Mt. Pleasant, SC 29464

TENNESSEE

YMCA Smoky Mount Divers
605 W. Clinch Ave.
Knoxville, TN 37902

Rebel Diving Scuba Club
4406 Saunders Ave.
Nashville, TN 37216

TEXAS

Skin Divers Club
2806 Bowie St.
Amarillo, TX 79109

Scuba Divers
Box 196-D, Rt. 1
Carthage, TX 75633

Inland Divers Club
4236 Karne Lane
Ft. Worth, TX 76135

Garland Divers
605 Morris Dr.
Garland, TX 75040

Houston Diving Assn.
5709 Glenmont
Houston, TX 77036

Subaquatics
863 Ramada
Houston, TX 77058

Ten Fathom
5826 Par Four Dr.
Houston, TX 77018

Irving Sea Lions
2601 Douglas St.
Irving, TX 75060

Brazosport Underwater Club
217 Caladium
Lake Jackson, TX 77566

Brazos Valley Divers
Box 195
Peaster, TX 76074

Aquamasters
3305 Flamborough
Pasadena, TX 77503

Alamo Pirahanas
1011 Rayburn Dr.
San Antonio, TX 78221

U.S. VIRGIN ISLANDS

International Dive Club
Cruz Bay
St. Johns, USVI 00830

VERMONT

Green Mountain Marineers
Ed Ball
Poultney, VT 05764

VIRGINIA

Flipper-Dippers
5519 Bouffant Blvd.
Alexandria, VA 22210

Tidewater Scuba Team
PO Box 3272
Hampton, VA 23363

Louisa Skin Divers
General Delivery
Louisa, VA 23093

Lynchburg Underwater Club
3611 Manton Dr.
Lynchburg, VA 24503

Sea Rebels
6228 Wailes Ave.
Norfolk, VA 23502

Pioneer Skin Diving Club
5231 Nutting Dr.
Springfield, VA 22151

Starlit Skin & Scuba Society
9021 Dellwod Dr.
Vienna, VA 22180

The Dolphins
Box 668
Waynesboro, VA 22980

Sand Sharks
c/o William Brandt
Showalter Rd.
Yorktown, VA 2390

WASHINGTON

Whidbey Aquajets
Box 19
Oak Harbor, WA 98277

Bainbridge Divers
Box 186
Pt. Blakely, WA 97110

Pile Drivers
625 Tyler St.
Pt. Townsend, WA 98368

Sea Raiders
115 Veneta Ave.
Bremerton, WA 98310

Cowlita Divers
1212 N. 7th
Kelso, WA 98626

Puget Sound Divers
6420 E. 60th
Seattle, WA 98115

She Urchins
148 NE 156th
Seattle, WA 98155

Kelp Kats
1132 Orchard
Snohomish WA 98290

Inland Empire Divers
E. 3030 15th
Spokane, WA 99203

WISCONSIN

Gillmen
1310 74th St.
Kenasha, WI 53140

Scubaskets
1125 Pierce Ave.
Marinette, WI 54143

Oshkosh Scuba Club
1331 Algoma Blvd.
Oshkosk, WI 54901

Canada

BRITISH COLUMBIA

Campbell River Tide
1410 Evergreen Rd.
Campbell River, B.C.
Canada

Nanaimo Devil Fish
837 Douglas
Nanaimo, B.C.
Canada

Sea Hellions
1106 6th Ave.
New Westminister, B.C.
Canada

Pescaderos
Box 311
North Vancouver, B.C.
Canada

Texaquatics
Box 99
Vananda, B.C.
Canada

MANITOBA

Dauphin Dolphins
Box 374
Dauphin, Manitoba
Canada

Precambrian Aquamasters
c/o Dave Lowe
Flin Flon, Manitoba
Canada

Gimli Cormorants
c/o Barry Waller
Gimli, Manitoba
Canada

Portage Neptunes
112-16th St. NW
Portage la Prairie, Manitoba
Canada

Atikameg Divers
Box 1768
The Pas, Manitoba
Canada R9A 1L5

The Pas Divers
c/o Colin Arfinuk
The Pas, Manitoba
Canada

Goldeyes Diving Club
265 Ubique Crescent
Winnipeg, Manitoba
Canada

ONTARIO

Ontario Underwater Council
559 Jarvis St.
Toronto, Ontario
Canada

Barrie Sub Aquarians
225 Duckworth St.
Barrie, Ontario
Canada

Northern Electric Diving Club
PO Box 3000
Brampton, Ontario
Canada

Deep River Underwater Club
Box 720
Deep River, Ontario
Canada

Orca Divers
c/o M. Bouwmeester
RR A
Dorchester, Ontario
Canada

Aqua Knights of Hamilton
174 Cavell Ave.
Hamilton, Ontario
Canada

Hamilton Barrascuba Club
79 James St. S.
Hamilton, Ontario
Canada

Hamilton Sea Devils
29 Minning Ave.
Hamilton, Ontario
Canada

Hamilton Sub Mariners, Inc.
PO Box 194, Sta. B
Hamilton, Ontario
Canada

Hamilton Tiger Sharks
U/W Diving Club
PO Box 4044, Sta. D
Hamilton, Ontario
Canada

Hawkesbury Otters Diving Club
386 Abbot St.
Hawkesbury, Ontario
Canada

Oakville Sub Aqua Club
1548 Warland Rd.
Oakville, Ontario
Canada

Twin Lake Divers
Box 53
Orillia, Ontario
Canada

Oshawa Diving Club
PO Box 542
Oshawa, Ontario
Canada

C.F.H.O. Sub Aqua Club
PO Box 1347, Sta. B
Ottawa 4, Ontario
Canada

Tridents U/W Club of
Petersborough
Petersborough YMCA
Petersborough, Ontario
Canada

Midland Aqua Divers
Hayes St., Box 213
Port McNicol, Ontario
Canada

Canadian Sub Aqua Club
Box 162
Scarborough, Ontario
Canada

Scarborough Sea Urchins
Underwater Club
6 Wolfe Ave.
Scarborough, Ontario
Canada

Underwater Club of St. Catharines
PO Box 422
St. Catharines, Ontario
Canada

Gem Divers
PO Box 741
Oshawa, Ontario
Canada

Great Lakes Scuba Divers
576 Elm St.
St. Thomas, Ontario
Canada

Peel Diving Club
Box 119
Streetsville, Ontario
Canada

Dolphin Aquatic Club
Box 424
Sudbury, Ontario
Canada

Broadview Y Divers
275 Broadview Ave.
Toronto 8, Ontario
Canada

Devonian Divers of Canada
Box 216 Adelaide St. P.O.
Toronto, Ontario
Canada

Etibicoke Underwater Club
10 Edwalter Ave.
Toronto, Ontario
Canada M8Y 1Z3

Littoral Society of Toronto
Box 1094 Adelaide St. P.O.
Toronto, Ontario
Canada

Underwater Club of Canada
Box 26 Adelaide St. P.O.
Toronto, Ontario
Canada

Quinte Aqua Divers
42 Mobile Village
RR 2
Trenton, Ontario
Canada

Kitchner-Waterloo Dolphins
172 Rodney St.
Waterloo, Ontario
Canada

Fathom Skin Diving Club
4588 Bathurst St.
Willowdale, Ontario
Canada

Metropol Underwater Club
163 Goulding St.
Willowdale, Ontario
Canada

Upper Canada Divers
38 Holmes Ave.
Willowdale, Ontario
Canada

Windsor Y Damsel Divers
958 Eastlawn Blvd.
Windsor, Ontario
Canada

Favorite Dive Sites

One of the great pleasures of the underwater fraternity is sharing information about special dive sites. This chapter contains a compilation of favorite underwater locations from scores of divers all over the world.

The information in each listing is designed to help you determine whether a particular site might be of interest in your travels. Therefore, the listings are grouped geographically. U.S. states are combined in alphabetical order. Other destinations are grouped by area of the world (body of water or, perhaps, island chain) and then by the nearest locale.

Each listing starts by pinpointing the locale of the site in relation to the nearest city. Keep in mind that these locations are approximations, and should be augmented with specific local directions. Under no circumstances should you try to navigate by the directions given here.

We have also tried to include the best season for each location. Since opinions differ, and since "off" seasons vary widely in quality from area to area, these designations should be considered a rough guide and checked out locally.

The remaining information in each listing should help you determine whether that particular site is suitable to your diving tastes and experience level, starting with divers' estimates of depth, visibility, and temperature. These are all subjective observations and should be considered approximations only. Due to the far-flung nature of this material, we have been unable to double-check these observations and cannot vouch for their accuracy.

We have attempted to depict some of the highlights of each area in terms of special features and recommended activities. These are not meant to be full descriptions of everything you can see or do at each site, but a recap of the most memorable experiences reported by the divers who supplied this information.

By the same token, we have listed the most noteworthy restrictions reported for each site (eg: "no spearfishing"). But, since regulations change from year to year or even season to season, you should check on local rules and other restrictions before planning your dive.

Finally, we have indicated whether diving services are available at each site or—barring that—in the nearest city. However, we have not attempted to identify these services. This is a bit of research you should conduct in advance, so you can go into a new area with as much foreknowledge as possible.

If what you read here whets your appetite for a particular area, check the other listings in this book under "Clubs," "Schools," and "Tours and Expeditions," and contact the people with local expertise to help you plan your trip. Also, check the books and periodicals listed in our chapter on "Publications" and read as much as you can about the area you intend to visit. Be sure you know what you're getting into before you pack your gear bag and take off.

No book could possibly present an exhaustive listing of all the world's best dive sites. Our goal in this chapter has been to provide an insight into typical underwater conditions in the nation's and the world's most popular diving locales.

We are extremely grateful to the many divers, shop owners, tour and resort operators, and others who volunteered the following information. If you visit any of these sites, please respect this generosity by taking care not to abuse the life and scenery there. Refer to our Introduction for common sense rules of good diving behavior, and follow them to the best of your ability. That's the best way to repay these people for sharing this information with you. If a favorite site of yours has been overlooked, we will be happy to include it in future editions if you will provide the information in a format as close as possible to the one used here.

Sites

United States

CALIFORNIA

Begg Rock: Nearest city: Avalon, Catalina Island. Location: 8 miles west of San Nicholas Island. Best season: spring. Maximum depth: 200 feet. Visibility: 10-100 feet. Water temperature: 60°-70°F. Bottom: rock pinnacles to sand bottom. Special features: large rock scallops, other invertebrates. Restrictions: reachable by boat only, frequent heavy weather, strong currents, heavy surge. Charter services available in Los Angeles and nearby cities.

Channel Islands: Nearest city: Santa Barbara. Location: Southwest of Santa Barbara. Best season: late spring-late fall. Maximum depth: 100-plus feet. Visibility to 90 feet. Water temperature: 50-68°F. Bottom: rocks, sand. Special features: wrecks, caves, fish, shellfish, vegetation. Recommended for: photography, spearfishing, shellfishing (abalone, lobster). Restrictions: boat access only. Dive services, charters available in Santa Barbara, Ventura, Oxnard.

Scotchman's Cove: Nearest city: Laguna Beach. Location: north approximately 1½ miles on Highway 101. Best season: summer. Maximum depth: 60 feet. Visibility to 70 feet. Water temperature: 50°-60°F. Bottom: sand, rocks. Special features: kelp, halibut, sheepshead, barracuda, abalone, rock scallops, lobster. Recommended for: spearfishing, shellfishing, photography. Restrictions: parking fee, closed seasons on abalone. Full diving services available in Laguna Beach.

Lover's Point: Nearest city: Pacific Grove. Location: beach access, parking just off Lighthouse Blvd. Best season: winter, spring. Maximum depth: 35 feet. Visibility: to 25 feet. Water temperature: 50°-55° F. Special features: thick kelp forest, plentiful tame fish, calmest surf in area. Recommended for: photography, snorkeling, check-outs. Restrictions: marine preserve (no spearfishing, collecting). Full diving services available in Monterey.

Gerstle Cove: Nearest city: Jenner. Location: in Salt Point State Park, 19 miles north of Jenner on Highway 1. Maximum depth: 50 feet. Visibility to 35 feet. Water temperature: 50° F. Bottom: sand, rocks. Special features: kelp, abalone, rock fish. Recommended for: spearfishing, seasonal free diving for abalone (outside cove). Restrictions: cove itself is marine preserve. Limited diving services available at Fort Ross, Jenner.

Timber Cove: Nearest city: Jenner. Location: 8 miles north of Jenner on Highway 1. Best season: May-October. Maximum depth: 100 feet. Visibility to 40 feet. Water temperature: 50°-56° F. Bottom: sand, rock. Special features: giant kelp, rock cod, abalone. Recommended for: spearfishing, seasonal free diving for abalone. Restrictions: license required to take game. Air and some equipment, plus launch facilities available on site.

COLORADO

Grand Lake: Nearest city: Grand Lake. Location: lake borders city limits. Best season: April-July, January-February (ice diving). Maximum depth: 260-plus feet. Visibility: 10-30 feet. Water temperture: to 50° F. Bottom: sand, mud, rocks. Special features: wrecks, ledges, trout, crayfish. Recommended for: spearfishing, photography, ice diving. Restrictions: must use divers flag, muscle-powered guns only. No diving services available at site.

CONNECTICUT

Thimble Islands: Nearest city: Branford. Location: by boat from Branford Harbor. Best season: July-August. Maximum depth: 30 feet. Visibility: 15-20 feet. Water temperature: 65°-70° F. Bottom: sand, rocks. Special features: large rocks, lobsters, mussels, sponges, many fish. Recommended for: spearfishing, lobstering. Diving services available in Branford.

FLORIDA

Amberjack Reef: Nearest city: Destin. Location: by boat from Destin (Gulf of Mexico). Best season: April-October. Maximum depth: 80 feet. Visibility: 5-75 feet. Water temperature: 70°-80° F. Bottom: sand, rock, coral. Special features: wrecks, lobster, dropoff. Recommended for: spearfishing, shell collecting, lobstering, photography. Diving services available in Destin and Ft. Walton Beach.

Ginnie Springs: Nearest city: High Springs. Location: south on Highway 41, west on S-236 6.5 miles, then north one mile on Ginnie Springs Rd. Best season: year round. Maximum depth: 62 feet. Visibility: 100-plus feet. Water temperature: 72° F. Bottom: white sand, lime rock. Special features: cavern and caves, ledges, springs, fish, vegetation, artifacts. Recommended for: cave diving, river diving, photography. Restrictions: steel grid prevents penetration beyond 114 feet, no spearfishing. Diving services available in Ft. White.

Banana Island Spring: Nearest city: Crystal River. Location: 5 minutes by boat. Best season: year round. Maximum depth: 60 feet. Visibility: 100-plus feet. Water temperature: 68°-72° F. Bottom: sand, limestone. Special features: manatees (November-March), cavern, fresh and salt water fish. Recommended for: photography, instruction. Restrictions: no spearfishing, molesting of manatees. Full diving and boat facilities at Plantation Inn Marina, Crystal River.

Wayne's Laughing Place: Riviera Beach. By boat from Riviera Beach. Best season: year round. Maximum depth: 120 feet. Visibility: 30-300 feet. Water temperature: 70°-85° F. Bottom: coral. Special features: abundant tropical fish, lobster, dropoff from 70-120 feet. Recommended for: photography, lobstering. Dive shops, charter boat available in Riviera Beach.

Pompano Area Reefs: Nearest city: Pompano Beach. Location: from 70 yards to three miles offshore. Best season: June-October. Maximum depth: 150 feet. Visibility: 20-80 feet. Water temperature: 65°-90° F. Bottom: sand, rock, coral. Special features: wrecks, tropical and game fish, lobster, shells. Recommended for: lobstering, tropical fish collecting, spearfishing, snorkeling. Restrictions: no spearfishing from beach. Full diving services available in Pompano Beach.

Monomey Wreck: Nearest city: Ft. Lauderdale. Location: one mile off Sunrise Blvd. Best season: May-September. Maximum depth: 65 feet. Visibility: 60 feet. Water temperature: 80° F. Bottom: coral, rocks. Special features: moray eels, rays, sea turtles, barracuda, lobster, reef fish. Recommended for: photography. Full diving services available in Ft. Lauderdale.

Moray Reef: Nearest city: Ft. Lauderdale. Location: head 80° from Pt. Everglades Inlet until water reaches 65 foot depth. Best season: May-September. Maximum depth: 65 feet. Visibility: 50-100 feet. Water temperature: 72°-86° F. Bottom: coral. Special features: caves, 15-foot dropoff, moray eels, lobsters, sea fans, rays, fish. Recommended for: photography. Restrictions: no coral collecting. Full diving services, daily boat tours in Ft. Lauderdale.

Benwood Wreck: Nearest landfall: Pennekamp Park, Key Largo. Location: about 4½ miles southeast of South Sound Creek Marker 2 (marked by red buoy). Best season: year round. Maximum depth: 50 feet. Visibility: to 100 feet. Water temperature: 70°-80° F. Bottom: coral. Special features: wreck of torpedoed freighter, abundant tropical fish, moray eels, groupers. Recommended for: photography. Restrictions: no spearfishing, collecting. Full dive services available in park and in Key Largo.

Elbow Reef: Nearest landfall: Pennekamp Park, Key Largo. Location: about 6 miles at 128° from North Sound Creek Barge. Best season: year round. Maximum depth: 35 feet. Visibility: to 100 feet. Water temperature: 70°-80° F. Bottom: coral. Special features: wrecks, abundant elkhorn coral, porkfish. Recommended for: photography, snorkeling. Restrictions: no spearfishing, collecting. Full dive services available in park and in Key Largo.

French Reef: Nearest landfall: Pennekamp Park, Key Largo. Location: about one mile northeast of Molasses Reef Tower. Best season: year round. Maximum depth: 100 feet. Visibility: to 100 feet. Water temperature: 70°-80° F. Bottom: coral. Special features: canyons, caves, cliffs, gullies, staghorn and elkhorn coral, abundant marine life. Recommended for: photography. Restrictions: no spearfishing, collecting. Full dive services available in park and in Key Largo.

Key Largo Dry Rocks: Nearest landfall: Pennekamp Park, Key Largo. Location: about 5 miles south of North Sound Creek Barge. Best season: year round. Maximum depth: 25 feet. Visibility: to 100 feet. Water temperture: 70°-80° F. Bottom: coral. Special features: 11-foot Christ of Abyss statue, huge brain corals, gullies, steep underwater cliffs. Recommended for photography, snorkeling. Restrictions: no spearfishing or collecting, anchor seaward of marker buoy. Full dive services available in park and in Key Largo.

Molasses Reef: Nearest landfall: Pennekamp Park, Key Largo. Location: about six miles south of South Sound Creek Marker 2. Best season: year round. Maximum depth: 45 feet. Visibility: 40-80 feet. Water temperature: 70°-80° F. Bottom: sand and coral. Special features: 600 varieties of fish, 40 types of coral,

wreck of the schooner Windlass, old cannons and anchors. Recommended for: photography, snorkeling. Restrictions: no spearfishing or collecting, dive boats use southern portion of reef only. Full dive services available in park and in Key Largo.

White Banks: Nearest landfall: Pennekamp Park, Key Largo. Location: about 5 miles southeast of South Sound Creek Marker 2. Best season: year round. Maximum depth: 15 feet. Visibility: to 100 feet (varies widely). Water temperature: 70°-80° F. Bottom: coral. Special features: large brain coral. Recommended for: snorkeling, shallow scuba diving. Restrictions: no spearfishing, collecting. Full dive services available in park and in Key Largo.

Alligator Reef: Nearest city: Islamorada. Location: about 9 miles south of Islamorada. Best season: June-October. Maximum depth: 110 feet. Visibility: 80-120 feet. Water temperature: 70°-80° F. Bottom: sand, coral. Special features: reefs, ravines, canyons, wrecks, kingfish, tropical fish, shells. Recommended for: photography, spearfishing, wreck diving. Full diving services available at Islamorada.

Crocker Reef: Nearest city: Islamorada. Location: 5 miles due east from Islamorada. Best season: July-September. Maximum depth: 80 feet. Visibility: 35-150 feet. Water temperature: 75°-85° F. Bottom: sand, coral. Special features: hard and soft corals, turtles, stingrays, moray eels, tropical fish. Recommended for: photography, lobstering, spearfishing. Restrictions: spearfishing prohibited by some boat operators. Full diving, boat services available in Islamorada.

Sombrero Reef: Nearest city: Marathon. Location: about 8 miles southwest of town, by boat. Best season: year round. Maximum depth: 100 feet. Visibility: 30-100 feet. Water temperature: 70°-85° F. Bottom: sand, coral. Special features: huge coral heads, caves, lobster, grouper, tropical fish. Recommended for: photography, night diving. Restrictions: no coral collecting. Full diving services available at Marathon.

Looe Key: Nearest landfall: Sunshine (Ohio) Key. Location: 9 miles off Big Pine Key. Best season: year round. Maximum depth: 95 feet. Visibility: 60-80 feet. Water temperature: 72°-82° F. Bottom: coral. Special features: large, shallow coral formations, abundant tropical and game fish, 100-foot dropoff into Gulf Stream. Recommended for: photography. Restrictions: no spearfishing, collecting (proposed sanctuary). Full diving, boating services at Sunshine Key Aqua Center.

Sand Key: Nearest city: Key West. Location: 6 miles southwest of Key West. Best season: May-September. Maximum depth: 35 feet. Visibility: 30-100 feet. Water temperature: 70°-80° F. Bottom: sand, coral. Special features: reef ledges, tropical fish. Recommended for: photography, spearfishing, wreck diving, collecting. Full diving, boating services available at Key West.

Seven Mile Reef: Nearest city: Key West. Location: 7 miles south of Key West. Best season: May-August. Maximum depth: 300 feet. Visibility: to 200 feet. Water temperature: 62°-72° F. Bottom: sand, coral. Special features: living coral reef, wrecks, caves, dropoff, 200 species of fish. Recommended for: photography, spearfishing, shell collecting. Restrictions: no coral collecting, must use divers flag. Full dive, boating facilities available at Key West.

GEORGIA

Blackfish Banks: Nearest city: Savannah. Location: 5 miles from Savannah Tower (marked by two red and white buoys). Best season: year round, depending on weather. Maximum depth: 50 feet. Visibility: 20-40 feet. Water temperature: 45°-85° F. Bottom: sand. Special features: sunken barge, loggerhead turtles, abundant fish. Recommended for: photography, spearfishing. Restrictions: boat access only. Diving services available in Savannah.

Firestone Rocks: Nearest city: Savannah. Location: 5.7 miles from Wassaw Seabuoy (103° heading). Best season: spring-summer. Maximum depth: 50 feet. Visibility: 20-75 feet. Water temperature: 47°-86° F. Bottom: sand. Special features: mile-long artifical reef made of tires, small tropical fish, arrow crabs, banded shrimp. Recommended for: photography, spearfishing, collecting. Restrictions: boat access only, best visibility at slack tide. Full diving services, boat charters available in Savannah.

L Buoy Barge Wrecks: Nearest city: Savannah. Location: 11.5 miles from Savannah Tower on a 67° heading. Best season: spring-fall. Maximum depth: 65 feet. Visibility: 40-80 feet. Water temperature: 45°-85° F. Bottom: sand. Special features: two sunken barges with tires, abundant big fish. Recommended for: spearfishing. Restrictions: boat access only. Full diving services available in Savannah.

Liberty Ship: Nearest city: Savannah. Location: From Wassaw Seabuoy, 16.5 miles to J Buoy (147° heading), then 300 yards at 310°. Best season: spring-early summer. Maxium depth: 70 feet. Visibility: 20-75 feet. Water temperature: 47°-86° F. Special features: ship sunk with all compartments sealed, no entry to wreck; large grouper, amberjack. Recommended for photography, spearfishing, collecting fishing lures. Restrictions: boat access only. Full diving facilities, boat charters available in Savannah.

HAWAII

Fantasy Reef: Nearest city: Honolulu, Oahu. Location: one mile by boat from Honolulu. Best season: year round. Maximum depth: 100 feet. Visibility: to 200 feet. Water temperature: 72°-74° F. Bottom: coral. Special features: caves, rock and coral formations, turtles, leopard rays, reef and game fish. Recommended for: photography, spearfishing, collecting. Restrictions: boat access only. Full diving, boat charter facilities available in Honolulu.

Hanauma Bay: Nearest city: Honolulu, Oahu. Location: off Kalanianaole Highway (near Hawaii-Kai). Best season: year round. Maximum depth: 60 feet. Visibility: 30-150 feet. Water temperature: 70°-75° F. Bottom: coral, sand. Special features: shore entry for shallow diving, ledge entry for deeper water, lava tubes, coral reefs, tame fish. Recommended for: photography, fish feeding, snorkeling. Restrictions: no spearfishing, collecting. Diving services available near site and in Honolulu.

100 Foot Hole: Nearest city: Honolulu, Oahu. Location: one mile offshore. Best season: year round. Maximum depth: 85 feet. Visibility: up to 200 feet. Water temperature: 72°-74° F. Bottom: rock. Special features: tunnel through lava rock formation, reef fish, game fish, octopus, lobster, shells. Recommended for: photography, spearfishing, collecting. Full diving, boating facilities available at Honlulu.

Moku Manu: Nearest city: Kailua, Oahu. Location: one mile offshore. Best season: October-April. Maximum depth: 180 feet. Visibility: 150-plus feet. Water temperature: 73°. Bottom: lava, coral. Special features: dropoffs, caves, lava tubes, large and small fish. Recommended for: photography, spearfishing, collecting. Full diving facilities and boat tours available in Kailua.

90-Foot Airplane: Nearest city: Waipahu, Oahu. Location: one mile offshore. Best season: year round. Maximum depth: 90 feet. Visibility: 50-100 feet. Water temperature: 72°-74° F. Bottom: sand. Special features: sunken Corsair fighter lying upright, tropical fish, shells. Recommended for: photography. Restrictions: boat access only. Diving facilities, boat charters at Bojac Dive Shop.

City of Refuge: Nearest city: Kailua-Kona, Hawaii. Location: about seven miles down the coast from Kailua-Kona. Best season: spring and summer. Maximum depth: 40 feet. Visibility: to 100 feet. Water temper-

ature: 71°-80° F. Bottom: lava. Special features: boulders, coral, abundant fish. Recommended for: photography. Restrictions: no spearfishing, collecting. Full diving and boat facilities available in Kailua-Kona.

Koloa Landing: Nearest city: Poipu, Kauai. Location: shore entry from boat landing near Poipu Village Hotel. Best season: year round. Maximum depth: 40 feet. Visibility: 60 feet. Water temperature: 72°-78° F. Bottom: coral, rock. Special features: long reef ledge, tropical fish, shells. Recommended for: photography, spearfishing, lobstering. Restrictions: lobster seasonal. Diving services available near site and in Lihue and Kapaa.

Molokini: Nearest city: Kihei, Maui. Location: five nautical miles southwest of Kihei in Alakakeiki Channel. Best season: year round. Maximum depth: 400 feet. Visibility: 150-200 feet. Water temperature: 70°-76° F. Bottom: rock, coral wall sloping to sand. Special features: dropoff, tame reef fish, shellfish, sharks, rays, small black coral. Recommended for: photography. Restrictions: no spearfishing, collecting. Diving and charter boat services available in Kihei.

MASSACHUSETTS

Cathedral Rocks: Nearest city: Rockport. Location: shore entry within city limits. Best season: summer-fall. Maximum depth: 80 feet. Visibility 15-50 feet. Water temperature: 45°-65° F. Bottom: rock. Special features: fish, starfish, urchins, kelp, weed, lobster, shells, shrimp. Recommended for: photography, spearfishing. Diving services available in Beverly.

Folly Cove: Nearest city: Gloucester. Location: shore entry within city limits. Best season: summer. Maximum depth: 50 feet. Visibility: to 20 feet. Water temperature: 33°-70° F. Bottom: rocks, sand. Special features: hermit crabs, lobster, fish, kelp, seaweed. Recommended for: spearfishing, photography. Diving services available in Beverly.

MICHIGAN

Isle Royale: Nearest city: Grand Portage, MN. Location: 23 miles 100° east of Grand Portage. Best season: June-September. Maximum depth: 130 feet. Visibility: 25-75 feet. Water temperature: 36°-43° F. Bottom: rocky. Special features: lake trout, wrecks (off south, northeast, and northwest ends). Recommended for: photography, night diving. Restrictions: No spearfishing, collecting of marine life or artifacts. Charter boats and air available at Grand Portage.

Lake Superior Shipwrecks: Nearest city: Munising. Location: by boat from Munising. Best season: May-November.

Maximum depth: 110 feet. Visibility: 10-75 feet. Water temperature: 32°-55° F. Bottom: sand, rock. Special features: variety of wrecks, fish, plant life. Recommended for: photography, wreck diving. Restrictions: no collecting of artifacts. Dive services, charter boats available around Munising.

Union Lake: Nearest city: Union Lake Village. Location: public access from Union Lake Rd. south of Cooley Lake Rd. (west side of lake). Best season: winter and spring. Maximum depth: 100 feet. Visibility: to 20 feet. Water temperature: 40°-65° F. Bottom: mud, sand bars. Special features: abundant vegetation, friendly fish, snails, old bottles and other artifacts. Recommended for: macrophotography. Restrictions: divers flag required. Dive services, boat ramp near site.

NEBRASKA

Lake Maloney: Nearest city: Ogallala. Location: North of Ogallala off Highway 61. Best season: May-October. Maximum depth: 147 feet. Visibility: 5-40 feet. Water temperature: 39°-74° F. Bottom: sand, rock, mud. Special features: limestone reefs, dropoffs, dam, game fish, crawdads. Recommended for: spearfishing, collecting. Diving services available on north side of dam.

NEW HAMPSHIRE

"Lady of the Lake" Wreck: Nearest city: Gilford. Location: Glendale Bay, Lake Winnipesaukee. Best season: year round. Maximum depth: 30 feet. Visibility: 20-40 feet. Water temperature: 39°-70° F. Bottom: mud, rocks. Special features: 125-foot wreck with intact superstructure (can be safely entered), different varieties of fish. Recommended for: wreck diving. Restrictions: boat access in summer. Diving services available in Laconia, Wolfeboro.

NEW JERSEY

Shark River Inlet: Nearest city: Neptune City. Location: Under bridge between Avon and Belmar. Best season: May-November. Maximum depth: 40 feet. Visibility: 5-25 plus feet. Water temperature: 28°-74° F. Bottom: rocks, sand. Special features: mussel beds, rock fish, stripers, lobster, bottom fish, crabs. Recommended for: crabbing, photography, night dives. Restrictions: No diving between 8:30 AM-5:30 PM May 1-October 1, some game seasonal. Full diving services available in Neptune City.

Wreck of the "Thistle.": Nearest city: Manasquan. Location: just offshore (beach access). Best season: May-November. Maximum depth: 30 feet. Visibility: up to 20 feet. Water temperature:

34°-75° F. Bottom: sand. Special features: hull of English sailing ship sunk in 1813, lobster, game fish. Recommended for: macro-photography, spearfishing, lobstering, artifact collecting. Full diving services, charter boats available along Jersey shore.

NEW MEXICO

Blue Hole Spring: Nearest city: Santa Rosa. Location: inside city limits. Best season: year round. Maximum depth: 90 feet. Visibility: 10-100 feet. Water temperature: 67°. Bottom: silt and rocks. Special features: catfish, carp, 80-foot diameter natural spring. Recommended for: photography. Restrictions: divers must obtain permit from Santa Rosa Police Department, must be familiar with high altitude diving and be able to use altitude conversion tables. Diving services available in Albequerque.

NEW YORK

Wreck of USS San Diego: Nearest city: Freeport, Long Island. Location: eight miles by boat from Freeport. Best season: July-August. Maximum depth: 120 feet. Visibility: 10-60 feet. Water temperature: 40°-60° F. Special features: hull of 500-foot Navy cruiser which sank in 1918, lobster, blackfish, sea bass, cod. Recommended for: photography, lobstering, artifact collecting. Full diving facilities, boat charters in Freeport area.

Wreck of USS Oregon: Nearest city: Freeport, Long Island. Location: 10 miles by boat from Freeport. Best season: July-August. Maximum depth: 125 feet. Visibility: 20-70 feet. Water temperature: 40°-55° F. Bottom: sand. Special features: hull of 500-foot ocean liner which sank in 1886, lobster, cod. Recommended for: photography, lobstering, artifact collectting. Diving services, charter boats available in Freeport area.

Salt Point (Seneca Lake): Nearest city: Watkins Glen. Location: north off Route 4 (first right turn, then 1½ miles on Salt Point Rd.). Best season: fall. Maximum depth: 90 feet. Visibility: 5-30 feet. Water temperature: 34°-50° F. Bottom: mud, rocks. Special features: sunken railroad boxcars and barges, bass, lake trout. Recommended for: artifact collecting. Restrictions: boat access only (launching site at Watkins Park, south end of lake). Diving services available at Ed's Dive Shop in Elmira Heights.

Coin Pile (Lake Erie): Nearest city: Buffalo. Location: by boat from Buffalo. Best season: May-September. Maximum depth: 17 feet. Visibility: 5-15 feet. Water temperature: 40°-72° F. Bottom: sand, rock. Special features: coins and other artifacts, fresh water fish. Recommended

for: artifact collecting. Restrictions: must use divers flag. Full diving, charter boat services available in Buffalo.

Lake Erie Wrecks: Nearest city: Dunkirk. Location: as close as five minutes by boat. Best season: May-August. Maximum depth: 85 feet. Visibility: 5-35 feet. Water temperature: 35°-60° F. Bottom: sand, slate rock. Special features: artifacts, bass, trout, carp, occasional salmon. Recommended for: photography, artifact collecting. Diving facilities available in Dunkirk, Buffalo.

Niagara River: Nearest city: Buffalo. Location: 10 minutes north by car. Best season: May-September. Maximum depth: 30 feet. Visibility: 5-15 feet. Water temperature: 40°-72° F. Bottom: sand, rocks. Special features: antique bottles and other artifacts, fresh water fish. Recommended for: drift diving, artifact collecting. Restrictions: must use divers flag. Full diving services available in Buffalo.

PENNSYLVANIA

Myerstown Quarry: Nearest city: Richland. Location: off Route 422 east of Route 501 (marked by sign). Best season: summer. Maximum depth: 50 feet. Visibility: to 30 feet. Water temperature: 32°-60° F. Bottom: mud, rocks. Special features: shipwreck, underwater habitat, sunken crane, railroad tracks, switch house. Recommended for: photography, wreck diving. Restrictions: no spearfishing. Some diving services available in Richland area.

RHODE ISLAND

Kings Beach: Nearest city: Newport. Location: right off Ocean Drive. Best season: May-November. Maximum depth: 40 feet. Visibility: 35 feet. Water temperature: 32°-70° F. Bottom: sand, mud, rocks. Special features: easy entry, ample parking, abundant marine life. Recommended for: photography. Diving services available in Newport.

Wreck of U-853: Nearest landfall: Block Island. Location: approximately eight miles northeast of Southeast Light. Best season: June-August. Maximum depth: 130 feet. Visibility: 40-80 feet. Water temperature: 42°-68° F. Bottom: sand. Special features: intact hull of WW II German submarine, large variety of marine life, frequent whale sightings. Recommended for: photography. Diving services available on Block Island, Star Island.

Wreck of the Onondaga: Nearest city: Block Island. Location: 10 miles from Block Island by boat. Best season: August-October. Maximum depth: 60 feet. Visibility: to 60 feet. Water tempera-

ture: 30°-70° F. Special features: popular wreck, various species of fish. Recommended for: photography, wreck diving, spearfishing, bottle collecting. Restrictions: must fly divers flag. Charter boats available in Mystic and Stonington, CT, Jerusalem and Block Island, RI, and Montauk, NY.

SOUTH CAROLINA

Lake Hartwell: Nearest city: Anderson. Location: two miles off Highway I-85. Best season: May-October. Maximum depth: 170 feet. Visibility: 15-60 feet. Water temperature: 40°-85° F. Bottom: sand, mud, rocks. Special features: wrecks, old dam site. Recommended for: spearfishing. Restrictions: some species protected. Diving services available in Anderson.

Hector Wreck: Nearest city: Winyah Bay. Location: 11.7 miles 180° from Winyah Bay (marked by buoy). Best season: summer. Maximum depth: 50 feet. Visibility: 12-150 feet. Water temperature: 45°-75° F. Bottom: sand, rocks. Special features: large bluefish, mackerel, wreck. Recommended for: wreck diving, spearfishing. Diving, boating services available throughout coastal South Carolina.

TEXAS

The Flower Gardens: Nearest city: Galveston: Location: 120 miles offshore. Best season: May-September. Maximum depth: 600 feet. Visibility: 150 feet. Water temperature: 75°-84° F. Bottom: sand, coral. Special features: northernmost coral reef in Western hemisphere, dropoff (60-600 feet), shellfish, reef fish. Recommended for: photography, spearfishing, collecting. Full diving, boating services available in Galveston.

A-76 Oil Rig: Nearest city: Port O'Connor. Location: 35 miles southeast of Port O'Connor. Best season: summer-early fall. Maximum depth: 165 feet. Visibility: 2 feet (at depth)-70 feet (at surface). Water temperature: 75°-85° F. Bottom: mud. Special features: underpinnings of rig are completely encrusted with marine life, abundant bait fish, predators, game fish. Recommended activities: spearfishing, photography. Full diving and boating services available in most coastal cities.

Liberty Ships: Nearest city: Corpus Christi. Location; off Padre Island (north of Corpus Christi). Best season: May-September. Maximum depth: 100 feet. Visibility: 50-100 feet. Water temperature: 75°-85° F. Bottom: sand. Special features: artificial reef formed by three sunken liberty ships, large jewfish, barracuda, ling, spadefish, sheepshead, turtles, octopus. Recommended for: photography, spearfishing, tropical fish collecting. Full diving facilities available on Padre Island.

Scuba Point (Possum Kingdom Lake): Nearest city: Mineral Wells. Location: off Highway 16, north of U.S. 180. Best season: April-June. Maximum depth: 100 feet. Visibility: 20 to 40 feet. Water temperature: 45°-80° F. Special features: shore access, large buffalo fish (early April) best visibility close to Morris Sheppard Dam. Recommended for: spearfishing. Diving facilities available at Scuba Point.

UTAH

Bear Lake: Nearest city: Laketown. Location: approximately 13 miles north on Highway 30 to Cisco Beach. Best season: June-late September. Maximum depth: 210 feet. Visibility: 5-25 feet. Water temperature: 34°-82° F. Bottom: rock, gravel, sand. Special features: dropoff (20-110 feet) approximately 100 yards from shore, crayfish, trash and game fish. Recommended activities: spearfishing, night diving. Restrictions: spearfishing for trash fish only. Diving services available in Ogden or Logan.

Blue Lake: Nearest city: Wendover. Location: 17 miles south of Wendover off US 50 (dirt road marked by small sign). Best season: November-late March. Maximum depth: 65 feet. Visibility: 5-20 feet. Water temperature: 72°-76° F. Bottom: sand and silt. Special features: hot springs keep lake at constant temperature, sponges, long grass, smallmouth bass, bluegill. Recommended for: warm diving any time of year. Restrictions: No spearfishing, minimum 150-yard walk to water with gear. Diving services available at Salt Lake City.

Fishlake: Nearest city: Salina. Location: (take Highway 89 to Route 118). Best season: July-August. Maximum depth: 117 feet. Visibility: 10-40 feet. Water temperature: 37°-58° F. Bottom: rocks. Special features: dropoff, abundant game fish (especially trout and mackinaw). Recommended for: spearfishing, collecting. Restrictions: high altitude location. Diving services available in Salt Lake City.

Lake Powell: Nearest city: Hanksville. Location: southeast along Route 95. Best season: May-October. Maximum depth: varies by specific location. Visibility: 2-20 feet. Water temperature: 45°-85° F. Bottom: sand, slate, mud. Special features: canyons of main channel, underwater cliffs, rock formations, abundant bass, trout, carp. Recommended for: photography, artifact collecting spearfishing. Restrictions: must use divers flag. Air fills available in Page, Arizona (south end of lake).

WASHINGTON

Lake Chelan: Nearest city: Chelan. Location: 12 miles uplake on south side. Best season: April-November. Maximum depth: beyond sport diving range. Visibility: 30 feet. Water temperature: 65° F. Bottom: sand. Special features: stair-like cliffs from 30-130 feet, then gentle dropoff to great depths. Recommended for: artifact collecting (old bottles). Full diving facilities available in Chelan.

Tacoma Narrows: Nearest city: Tacoma. Location: entry ½ mile south of collapsed bridge. Maximum depth: 160 feet. Visibility: 50-100 feet. Water temperature: 39°-64° F. Best season: summer. Bottom: sand, silt. Special features: ledges to 40 feet, octopus, wolf eel, game fish, scallops, Dungeness crabs, mussels. Recommended for: spearfishing, shellfishing, photography. Diving services available in Seattle.

San Juan County Park: Nearest city: Anacortes. Location: 12 miles west of Friday Harbor Ferry Landing. Best season: fall-winter. Maximum depth: beyond sport diving range. Visibility: to 100 feet. Water temperature: 39°-64° F. Bottom: sand, rock. Special features: shore entry, boulders, caves, overhangs, dropoff from 50 feet to great depths, shrimp, rockfish, abalone, free-swimming scallops, octopus, eel grass, bull kelp, anemones, sponges. Recommended for: photography, spearfishing, snorkeling. Air fills at Friday Harbor, other diving services in Anacortes area.

WISCONSIN

Lake Geneva: Nearest city: Lake Geneva City. Location: juncture off Highways 50 and 67. Best season: May-June, September-October, February-March. Maximum depth: 135 feet. Visibility: 10-30 feet. Water temperature: 40°-65° F. Bottom: sand and rocks sloping to mud and silt. Special features: dropoff, artifacts, pike, trout, bass, walleye and other fish. Recommended for: photography, artifact collecting, snorkeling. Restrictions: register with Water Safety Patrol, boat diving only. Diving facilities and boat charters in Lake Geneva area.

Whaleback Shoals: Nearest city: Gills Rock. Location: 7 miles off Gills Rock at northern tip of Door Peninsula. Best season: May-October. Maximum depth: 20 feet. Visibility: 15-40 feet. Water temperature: 50°-70° F. Bottom: sand. Special features: wreck of steamship R.J. Hackett, perch, bass, crayfish. Recommended for: photography, snorkeling, spearfishing. Restrictions: boat access only. Full diving services, charter boat at Gills Rock.

Canada

ALBERTA

Lake Minnewanka: Nearest city: Calgary. Location: 6 miles off Highway 1, past national park gates. Best season: August-October. Maximum depth: 80 feet. Visibility: 30-40 feet. Water temperature: 50° F. Bottom: mud, rocks. Special features: sunken power dam. Restrictions: no collecting, should have experience with high altitude diving. Diving services available in Calgary.

BRITISH COLUMBIA

Kelsey Bay Breakwater: Nearest city: Kelsey Bay. Location: at end of Island Highway, going north. Best season: year round. Maximum depth: 50 feet. Visibility: 30-60 feet. Water temperature: 40°-50° F. Bottom: silt, rocks. Special features: old bottles and fishing lures, rockfish, painted greenlings, urchins, anemones, overhangs (second point west beyond dock), sponges. Recommended for: photography, night diving. Diving and boating facilities available in Campbell River.

The Cut: Nearest city: West Vancouver. Location: 13 miles northwest of West Vancouver in Whytecliff Park. Best season: summer. Maximum depth: 700 feet. Visibility: 30-100 feet. Water temperature: 40°-50° F. Bottom: rock wall. Special features: shore entry, dropoff, octopus, ling cod, rock fish, sea perch, sea pens, urchins, sculpins, sea stars. Recommended for: photography. Restrictions: underwater reserve (no spearfishing, collecting). Full diving services available in Vancouver.

Bamfield Shore: Nearest city: Bamfield, British Columbia. Location: just off shore. Best season: summer. Maximum depth: 60 feet. Visibility: 10-100 feet. Water temperature: 45°-55° F. Bottom: sand, rock. Special features: spectacular rock formations, ling cod, rockfish, abalone, rock scallops, colorful vegetation. Recommended for: spearfishing, shelling. Boat rentals available in Port Alberni.

MANITOBA

Clearwater (Atikameg) Lake: Nearest city: The Pas. Location: 20 miles north of The Pas. Best season: April, June-September. Maximum depth: 135 feet. Visibility: 15-25 feet. Water temperature: 34°-68° F. Bottom: sand, mud, rocks, vegetation. Air available in The Pas.

NOVA SCOTIA

Gooseberry Cove: Nearest city: Sydney. Location: 23 miles southeast from Sydney off route 22 (left turn on

Little Loraine Road for three miles, then left again on small logging road). Best season: May-February. Maximum depth: 70 feet. Visibility: 5-90 feet. Water temperature: 30°-68° F. Bottom: sand, rock, mud. Special features: wreck due south of gap, lobster, crab, sea perch, kelp. Recommended for: photography, spearfishing, night diving. Dive services available in Sydney.

ONTARIO

Tobermory: Nearest city: Owen Sound. Location: approximately 60 miles north off Highway 6. Best season: May-October. Visibility: 10-30 feet. Water temperature: 37°-44° F. Bottom: sand, rock. Special features: wrecks, crayfish. Recommended for: photography. Restrictions: must use diver's flag, some areas restricted, artifacts cannot be removed from wrecks. Full diving services available in Owen Sound.

QUEBEC

Tadoussac: Nearest city: Quebec City. Location: approximately 150 miles northwest of Quebec on Highway 138. Best season: summer. Maximum depth: 100 feet. Visibility: 25 feet. Water temperature: 32°-55° F. Bottom: sand, gravel, rocks. Special features: dropoff, starfish, sea urchins, vegetation. Recommended for: underwater photography. No local diving services.

Bermuda

The Constellation: Nearest city: Hamilton. Best season: May-October. Maximum depth: 30 feet. Visibility: 60-150 feet. Water temperature: 68°-84° F. Bottom: sand, coral. Special features: wreck of a wooden schooner which sank in 1943 with a cargo of drugs (inspiration of "The Deep"). Restrictions: no spearfishing or collecting. Diving services available in Hamilton.

The Le Hermine: Nearest city: Hamilton. Best season: May-October. Maximum depth: 40 feet. Visibility: 60-150 feet. Water temperature: 68°-84° F. Bottom: sand, coral. Special features: wreck of a 60-gun French frigate which sank in 1838; anchor and cannons and other wreck debris visible on reef. Recommended for: photography. Restrictions: no spearfishing or collecting. Diving services available in Hamilton.

The Montana: Nearest city: Hamilton. Best season: May-October. Maximum depth: 30 feet. Visibility: 60-150 feet. Water temperature: 68°-84° F. Bottom: sand, coral. Special features: wreck of iron-hulled paddle wheeler which sunk in 1863; boiler housing and portion of bow still intact. Restrictions: no spearfishing or collecting. Diving services available in Hamilton.

South West Breaker: Nearest city: Hamilton. Best season: May-October. Maximum depth: 40 feet. Visibility: 60-150 feet. Water temperature: 68°-84° F. Bottom: sand, coral. Special features: large natural tunnel running through coral reef, tame fish. Recommended for: fish feeding, photography. Restrictions: no spearfishing or collecting. Diving services available in Hamilton.

Caribbean

BAHAMA ISLANDS

Ginger Bread Grounds: Nearest city: Alice Town, Bimini. Location: 25 miles northeast from Bimini. Best season: summer. Maximum depth: 25 feet. Visibility to 200 feet. Water temperature: 78°-80° F. Bottom: sand, coral. Special features: large shallow reefs, lobster. Recommended for: spearfishing (slings only), photography. Diving services: charter boats (Bimini).

Tuna Alley: Nearest city: Alice Town, Bimini. Location: 14 miles by boat from Alice Town. Best season: spring-summer. Maximum depth: 90-plus feet. Visibility to 200 feet. Water temperature: 85° F. Bottom: coral reef. Special features: giant bluefin tuna, marlin, sailfish, black coral. Recommended for: photography. Diving services: served by Key Largo charter boats.

Benis Wall: Nearest city: Freeport, Grand Bahama. Location: check with Underwater Explorers Society guides. Best season: May-October. Maximum depth: 95 feet. Visibility: to 200 feet. Water temperature: 68°-84° F. Bottom: sand, coral. Special features: big grouper, schools of snapper and grunt, wall approximately ½ mile offshore drops from 30-95 feet. Recommended for: photography (spearfishing, collecting prohibited). Full diving services available.

Deep Reef: Nearest city: Freeport, Grand Bahama. Location: reachable in 10 minutes by charter boat from Scubahamas (Victorian Inn) or Underwater Explorers Society. Best season: April-October. Maximum depth: 90 feet. Visibility: 100-plus feet. Water temperature: 72°-78° F. Bottom: heavy coral, canyon formation. Special features: large fish (eg: grouper), colorful reef fish, wreck at 70 feet. Recommended for: photography. Full diving services available.

The Wall: Nearest city: Freeport, Grand Bahama. Location: reachable by charter boat from Underwater Explorers Society headquarters near Freeport. Best season: April-October. Maximum depth: 3,000 feet. Visibility: 100-plus feet. Water temperature: 72°-76° F. Special features: vertical wall from 175 feet to 3,000 feet. Recommended for: photography, deep diving (must be experienced to 150 feet). Full diving services available.

Plateau: Nearest landfall: Harbour Island. Location: by boat from Harbour Island. Best season: April-January. Maximum depth: 100 feet. Visibility: 100-plus feet. Water temperature: 70°-80° F. Bottom: 2 acre coral plateau rising from sand (100 feet) to 50 feet. Special features: deep coral crevices, abundant fish. Recommended for photography. Air and boat and gear rentals available at Romora Bay Club on Harbour Island.

BELIZE

Blue Hole: Nearest city: Belize City. Directions: 15 minutes off island by boat. Best season: January-April. Maximum depth: 408 feet. Visibility to 200 feet. Water temperature: 70° F. Bottom: sand with coral formations. Special features: corals, sponges, abundant tropical fish, stalactites. Recommended for: spearfishing, shell collecting photography. Full diving services available in Belize.

Dropoff: Nearest city: Belize City. Location: ¼ mile offshore. Best season: January-April. Maximum depth: 1,000 plus feet. Visibility to 200 feet. Water temperature: 80° F. Bottom: sand and coral formations. Special features: dropoff from 30-1,000 feet. Recommended for: spearfishing, shell collecting, photography. Full diving services available onshore.

Lighthouse Reef: Belize City. Location: 55 miles offshore. Best seasons: December-February, May-August. Maximum depth: 200 feet. Visibility: to 200 feet. Water temperature: 80°-85° F. Bottom: reefs dropping off to sand. Special features: steep wall, black coral, large fish. Recommended for: photography, spearfishing (for food only). Restrictions: no coral may be removed. Full diving services available in Belize.

BONAIRE

Karpata: Nearest city: Kralendijik. Location: north on main island road (by car or bus) to Marker 42. Best season: year round. Maximum depth: 130 feet. Visibility: 150 feet. Water temperature: 80° F. Bottom: coral reef. Special features: beach entry, narrow channel with abundant marine life, including huge sea fans. Recommended for: fish feeding, photography. Restrictions: no spearfishing, collecting. Full diving services.

BRITISH VIRGIN ISLANDS

Blonde Rock: Nearest city: Road Town, Tortola. Best season: summer. Maximum depth: 60 feet. Visibility: 150 feet. Water temperature: 75°-80° F. Bottom: coral. Special features: ledges, caves, large fish. Recommended for: photography. Restrictions: no spearfishing. Full diving services available in Road Town.

Box Fish Reef: Nearest city: Road Town, Tortola. Best season: summer. Maximum depth: 80 feet. Visibility: 150 feet. Water temperature: 75°-80° F. Bottom: coral. Special features: abundant trunk fish, angelfish, sharks. Recommended for: photography. Restrictions: no spearfishing. Full diving services available in Road Town.

Wreck of the Rhone: Nearest city: Road Town, Tortola. Location: 5½ miles by boat from Road Town, (near western point of Salt Island). Best season: year round. Maximum depth: 100 feet. Visibility: to 150 feet. Water temperature: 72°-80° F. Bottom: sand, coral. Special features: used as an underwater setting for film "The Deep," fish (grunts and snappers) and soft corals throughout wreck. Recommended for: photography. Resrictions: no spearfishing. Full diving services, charters available throughout Virgin Islands.

CAICOS ISLANDS

Grand Canyon Dropoff: Nearest city: Cockburn Harbor, South Caicos. Location: 10 minutes by boat from shore. Best season: February-November. Maximum depth: 4,200 feet. Visibility: to 150-plus feet. Water temperature: 74°-84° F. Bottom: sand, coral. Special features: vertical wall starting 65 feet below surface, 600 lb. jewfish, rays, sea turtles, sleeping nurse shark, tame reef fish. Recommended for: photography, conch collecting. Restrictions: no spearfishing. Full diving services available at Turk-Cai Watersports.

CAYMAN ISLANDS

Eden Rocks: Nearest city: George Town, Grand Cayman. Location: about one mile south of George Town harbor. Best season: summer. Maximum depth: 40 feet. Visibility: 100-plus feet. Water temperature: 78°-82° F. Bottom: sand with interconnecting coral caverns. Recommended for: photography. Restrictions: no spearfishing, collecting. Full diving services available throughout Grand Cayman.

Grand Cayman: Nearest city: George Town, Grand Cayman. Location: North of George Town by boat. Best season: year round. Maximum depth: 6,000 feet. Visibility: to 200 feet. Water temperature:

about 80° F. Bottom: coral wall. Special features: canyon formed by two great coral buttresses growing perpendicularly away from North Wall, black coral, abundant fish, eagle rays. Recommended for: photography. Full diving services available throughout Grand Cayman.

Waldo's Cave: Nearest city: George Town, Grand Cayman. Location: just off Casa Bertmar resort. Best season: year round. Maximum depth: 35 feet. Visibility: 100 feet. Water temperture: 80° F. Bottom: sand and coral. Special features: tame moray eel may be petted or hand-fed. Recommended for photography. Restrictions: beach access limited to resort guests; no spearfishing, collecting. Full diving services available at Casa Bertmar and throughout Grand Cayman.

Wreck of the Balboa: Nearest city: George Town, Grand Cayman. Location: 10 minutes by boat from George Town. Best season: year round. Maximum depth: 40 feet. Visibility: 100 feet. Water temperature: 80° F. Bottom: sand and coral. Special features: well-preserved wreck, large schools of tame fish. Recommended for: photography, fish-feeding, night dives. Restrictions: No spearfishing, collecting. Full diving and boating services available throughout Grand Cayman.

Trinity Caves: Nearest city: West Bay, Grand Cayman. Best season: summer. Maximum depth: 100 feet. Visibility: to 100 feet. Water temperature: 76°-86° F. Bottom: sand, coral. Special features: huge cave and tunnel formations, 6,000 foot wall, black coral forests, large grouper and rays. Recommended for: photography. Restrictions: access by boat only, must have guide; no spearfishing, collecting. Full diving services available throughout Grand Cayman.

MEXICO

Akumal: Nearest city: Cancun. Location: 103 kilometers south of Cancun. Best season: April-mid-September, November-January. Maximum depth: 130 feet. Visibility: 120 feet. Water temperature: 75°-80° F. Bottom: sand, barrier reef. Special features: Wreck of El Mantancero, Spanish merchantship of 1739. Recommended for: photography. Restrictions: no spearfishing, shell collecting. Full diving services at Hotel-Club Akumal Caribe.

Palancar Reef: Nearest city: Cozumel. Location: ¼ mile offshore, about 1½ hours south of Cozumel by boat. Best season: June-September. Maximum depth: 175 feet. Visibility: 100 plus feet. Water temperature: 74°-76° F. Bottom: sand. Special features: 5 mile long coral reef reaching to within 30 feet of surface, laced with caves. Recommended for: photography. Restrictions: spearfishing, collecting dis-

couraged. Full diving services available on Cozumel.

PANAMA

Isla Grande: Nearest city: Portobelo, Colon. Location: by water taxi from resort near Portobelo. Best season: June-October, December-April. Maximum depth: 47 feet. Visibility: 75-125 feet. Water temperature: 80° F. Bottom: sand, volcanic rock, coral. Special features: 10 different types of living corals, caves on north side of island, wrecks on lee shore. Recommended for: photography, metal detector searches. Restrictions: no spearfishing with scuba, no live samples from in front of resort. Rentals, air, instruction, boats and guides available at Isla Grande Tours.

PUERTO RICO

60 Foot Hole: Nearest city: Esperanza, Vieques Island. Location: 1.5 miles to sea on 280° heading. Maximum depth: 100 feet. Visibility: 25-125 feet. Water temperature: 78°-80° F. Bottom: sand, rocks, coral. Special features: sleeping sharks. Recommended for: photography, spearfishing. Full diving services available on Vieques.

ST. MAARTEN

The Alleys: Nearest city: Philipsburg. Location: south of St. Maarten by boat. Best season: year round. Maximum depth: 50 feet. Visibility: 40-100 plus feet. Water temperature: 75°-82° F. Bottom: sand, coral. Special features: caves, crevices, tunnels in coral, diverse sponges, large fish. Recommended for: photography. Restrictions: no collecting. Tours and diving facilities available at Mullet Bay.

ST. VINCENT

Lapaze Rock: Nearest city: Layou. Location: by boat to left harbor entrance, up coast ¼ mile. Best season: year round. Maximum depth: 140 feet. Visibility: 70-100 feet. Water temperature: 78° F. Bottom: coral-covered rocks. Special features: gradual dropoff from 20-140 feet, abundant shells, fish, and corals. Recommended for photography, shell collecting. Diving services available on St. Vincent.

U.S. VIRGIN ISLANDS

Coki Point: Nearest city: Charlotte Amalie, St. Thomas, U.S.V.I. Location: 7 miles east of city. Best season: year round. Maximum depth: 70 feet. Visibility: 50-100 feet. Water temperature: 76°-80° F. Bottom: sand, coral, eel grass. Special features: easy beach entry, coral reefs. Recommended for: photography. Restrictions: marine preserve. Full diving services available on St. Thomas.

French Cap Cay: Nearest city: Charlotte Amalie, St. Thomas. Location:

5 miles south of St. Thomas (by boat). Best season: May-November. Maximum depth: 90 feet. Visibility: 75-150 feet. Water temperature: 72°-78° F. Bottom: coral. Special features: undersea pinnacle 50-140 feet, abundant reef fish, rays, lobster. Recommended for: photography. Restrictions: no spearfishing, collecting. Full diving services available on St. Thomas.

Indian Ocean

SEYCHELLES

Wreck of the Ennerdale: Nearest city: Port Victoria, Mahe. Location: eight miles northwest (look for leaking oil). Best season: year round (depending on weather). Maximum depth: 80 feet. Visibility: 45 plus feet (best upcurrent of rusting hull). Water temperature: 70°-80° F. Bottom: sand. Special features: dynamited tanker hull, partially intact; batfish, golden snappers, blue-finned jacks, barracuda, reef fish. Recommended for: photography. Restrictions: no spearfishing, collecting. Diving services, boat charters available in Port Victoria.

Pacific

AUSTRALIA

Big Bommie: Nearest city: Gladstone, Queensland. Location: 200 miles offshore. Best season: August-November. Maximum depth: 180 feet. Visibility: 100-200 feet. Water temperature: 74°-76° F. Bottom: sand, large coral pinnacles. Special features: sharks, reef fish, sea snakes. Recommended for: all underwater activity. Full diving services available at Gladstone.

Heron Island: Nearest city: Gladstone, Queensland. Location: 45 miles northeast of town (by boat). Best season: August-November. Water temperature: 70°-80° F. Special features: abundant tame fish, including giant turtles. Restrictions: no spearfishing. Diving services, charter launches and helicopter service available at Gladstone.

Saumerez Reef: Nearest city: Gladstone, Queensland. Location: 220 miles off coast by boat. Best season: August-November. Visibility: up to 200 feet. Water temperature: 70°-80° F. Bottom: giant coral mound. Special features: shipwreck atop mound, deep caverns and crevices. Recommended for: photography. Diving services available at Gladstone, Hamilton, Cairns.

ECUADOR

Galapagos Islands: Nearest city: Guayaquil. Location: 600 miles due west. Best season: March-August. Maximum

depth: 500 feet. Visibility: 40-80 feet. Water temperature: 60°-70° F. Bottom: sand, lava boulders. Special features: unique marine life found nowhere else, caves, dropoffs. Restrictions: no spearfishing, collecting. Diving services available through tour operators, charter companies.

FIJI

Beqa Island: Nearest city: Suva. Location: 22 nautical miles from Suva, on south coast of Viti Levu. Best season: May-October. Visibility: to 200-plus feet. Water temperature: 75°-80° F. Special features: 40 mile Beqa Barrier Reef with abundant fish life in passages (jacks, barracuda, and others). Recommended for: photography. Full diving services available at Scubahire, Suva.

Suva Reef: Nearest city: Suva. Location: 15 minutes by boat from Suva. Best season: May-October. Maximum depth: 1,000 feet. Visibility: to 200 feet. Water temperature: 75°-80° F. Bottom: coral heads to within 10 feet of surface, vertical dropoff to 1,000 feet. Special features: black coral, huge gorgonia, tame reef fish, anchor from square-rigger Woosung. Recommended for: photography, snorkeling, fish feeding. Restrictions: no spearfishing, collecting. Full diving services available in Suva.

Wreck of the Woodburn: Nearest city: Suva. Location: 5 miles by boat from Suva, outside main barrier reef. Best season: May-October. Maximum depth: 100 feet. Visibility: 100-plus feet. Water temperature: 75°-80° F. Special features: wreck of steel-hulled square-rigger covered with many varieties of coral; reef fish, moray eels. Recommended for photography. Full diving services available at Scubahire, Suva.

GUAM

Double Reef: Nearest city: Agana. Location: accessible by charter boat. Maximum depth: 60 feet. Visibility: 100-300 feet. Water temperature: 84° F. Bottom: coral reef. Special features: abundant fish, shellfish, corals. Recommended for: photography, collecting, spearfishing. Full diving services available on Guam.

Blue Hole: Nearest city: Agat. Location: by boat from Agat. Best season: year round. Maximum depth: 250 feet. Visibility: 100-300 feet. Water temperature: 84° F. Bottom: sand, rock. Special features: abundant big fish, shells, corals. Recommended for: photography, collecting. Full diving services available on Guam.

NEW GUINEA

Salamaua: Nearest city: Lae. Location:

south by boat. Best season: year round. Maximum depth: 250 feet. Visibility: 150 feet. Water temperature: 85° F. Bottom: sand and coral. Special features: wrecks, dropoffs, large fish and shells. Recommended for: photography, spearfishing, collecting. Diving services available in Lae.

OKINOWA

Yaeyama Reefs: Nearest city: Ishigaki. Location: by boat from Ishigaki. Best season: May-October. Visibility: to 150 feet. Bottom: sand, coral. Special features: coral caves, dropoffs, tropical fish. Recommended for: photography. Diving services available in Ishigaki.

PHILIPPINES

Culebra Island: Nearest city: Batangas. Location: by boat from Batangas. Best season: October-May. Maximum depth: 100 plus feet. Visibility: 30 plus feet. Water temperature: 72°-74° F. Bottom: coral. Special features: abundant marine life. Recommended for: photography, shelling. Dive boat services available at Quezon City.

Sea of Cortez

MAINLAND MEXICO

San Carlos Bay: Nearest city: Guaymas. Location: 6 miles north of Guaymas on paved road. Best season: year round. Maximum depth: 200 feet. Visibility: 20-150 feet. Water temperature: 69°-85° F. Bottom: rocky, with cliffs and ledges. Special features: good beach entry, large sea bass, lobster, turtles, seals. Recommended for: photography, spearfishing, shell collecting. Charter boats, air available in Guaymas.

Red Sea

ISRAEL

Neviot: Nearest city: Elat. 75 kilometers south of Elat (bus or taxi) then offshore by boat. Best season: year round. Visibility: 150 feet. Water temperature: 70°-75° F. Bottom: coral. Special features: sharks, barracuda, dropoffs. Recommended for: snorkeling, photography. Restrictions: no spearfishing, collecting. Full diving services available at Neviot.

Ras-Um-Sid: Nearest city: Ophira. Location: shore entry due north of city. Best season: year round. Visibility: 50-200 feet. Water temperature: 70°-80° F. Bottom: coral. Special features: 1,000 species of fish, large tuna, sharks, turtles, grouper, moray eels, fan coral. Recommended for: photography. Restrictions: no spearfishing, no collecting. Diving services available within 15 minute drive from site.

Tours and Expeditions

Today hundreds of diving resorts, charter boats, tour operators, and outfitters are catering to traveling divers. In this chapter you will find listings describing some of the better known tours, expeditions, dive boat and resort packages.

We strongly urge you to write for brochures and other up-to-date information before planning any diving vacation. Local conditions can change without warning, so we cannot guarantee the accuracy of this information. If possible, check with another diver who's been to your chosen destination or, if you can, consult a travel agent with diving expertise.

Here are some questions to ask when comparing various packages:

How much diving is involved? Some programs are designed for maximum time in the water, others are not. Determine how many days of the package are actually devoted to diving, as opposed to travel or other out-of-water activities. Only you know which mix is right for you.

What is and isn't included? Some "all-inclusive"

packages actually omit some meals, fees, and other costly items. Get a complete breakdown in advance. You can compare the relative costs of two competitive packages by computing the charges on a "cost-per-dive" basis. If, on your arrival you find you crave more diving than your tour offers, you may be able to find some supplementary half-day or full-day trips by checking with local outfitters, boat harbors, hotels, dive shops, or clubs.

Are the rates quoted for groups or independent travelers, and are accommodations priced on an individual or double occupancy basis? If a package is offered only to groups, determine whether you must form your own minimum-size party or whether you can join an already-formed group.

What equipment should you bring? Local outfitters (and their insurance agents) are insisting on more and more safety gear, such as submersible pressure gauges and buoyancy compensators. The best rule of thumb is to take as much of your own gear as possible (except for heavy tanks and weightbelts which are almost universally provided). You'll be most comfortable with your own equipment, and you'll probably save rental fees, as well.

What sort of paperwork is required? Besides the typical tourist documents, you'll almost definitely need proof of certification. (In fact, you'd be best off avoiding any outfitter that doesn't require certification.) Make sure your certification is acceptable. If not, check into a cross-certification program (as described in our chapter on "Instruction") before going. In some rare cases advance certifications, or log books documenting certain levels of experience, are also required. Check first, and avoid being disappointed once you get there.

Is instruction available? Some resorts offer "quickie" introductory sessions, which may be fine for a few closely-supervised dives in calm, shallow waters. But unless the course offers one of the recognized basic scuba certifications, it will not qualify you for any further diving. It's definitely best to get your basic certification before going. If the diving package offers specialties like cave, wreck, or night diving, find out whether any local instruction is available. If not, see if you can find a course in the specialty you plan to pursue before you leave. Some resorts and tours also offer advanced certifications for those travelers wishing to further their underwater educations.

To compile the following listings, we contacted over 500 tour and expedition outfitters. From the responses, we concentrated on multi-day packages suitable for long diving weekends or vacations. We could not include the vast number of day trips or half-day trips available around the world. If you know of a good tour or expedition that is not represented here, we'd like to include it in future editions. Please send us brochures and any other printed information, plus a description in a format as close as possible to the one used here.

Since quality judgments are highly subjective and personal, we have presented only the facts provided to us by the outfitters themselves. We cannot vouch for the quality of the diving, accommodations or other particulars in any of these packages, and no recomendation is implied. We suggest you use the guidelines in this chapter to fully investigate any of these tours or expeditions which interest you.

Because divers are generally more interested in the body of water than the nation they'll be visiting, we have grouped our overseas listings alphabetically by ocean, sea, or island chain.

North American packages are grouped alphabetically by state and provinces.

As far as possible, we have attempted to provide the information for each package in a uniform manner, with each listing divided into specific subjects. The following definitions of the subject headings may be helpful in reviewing the listings:

Season: Those months in which the package is offered. This may or may not coincide with peak diving or tourism seasons.

Duration: Number of days from departure of tour to return. In some cases, the duration is open, and a daily rate is charged.

Carrier: Airline or vessel used for transportation to the dive destination(s). When the choice of carrier is left open, you can select a carrier and make reservations through any travel agent.

Departure: City or cities from which tour departs. In most cases you are responsible for getting to the departure city on your own. Actual dates and times of departures, as well as other details, must be determined by writing the operator (or contact, as explained below).

Accommodations: Sleeping accommodations (hotel, club, boat, etc.) and a description of other amenities included, such as meals. These listings do not contain definitive ratings of room quality or food service. You should obtain this information from the operator or a knowledgeable travel agent.

Features: Highlights of the diving and other activities scheduled. Features may vary seasonally and with weather conditions, so these listings should not be considered complete.

Requirements: Stipulated by the tour sponsor, these may include necessary personal gear, certification, licenses, or permits. For group tours, we have tried to include minimum and maximum group sizes. Double check to be sure there are no other requirements, such as minimum experience levels.

Cost: Subject to change at any time. May vary with your choice of charter, accommodations, season, or other options. Request full cost details before making reservations.

Sponsor: Type of organization offering the tour. We have divided this category into the following classifications:

tour operator— a firm or institution *not based at the dive destination* offering a package with scheduled departures (usually including travel from U.S. gateways).

resort operator— hotel or club offering accommodations and diving services at or near the dive site(s).

club/organization— local, national or international non-profit group which makes travel packages available to non-members or which you might consider joining to qualify for a particular trip.

carrier— airline or cruise ship offering a package of diving plus accommodations.

dive shop— retailer which packages and promotes its own trips. Some are based at the dive destination, others in various U.S. cities. If the shop is near you, try to visit it and meet the group leader and some other divers who have signed up for the trip you want to take.

dive boat— vessel based at the dive destination, offering overnight accommodations on board or at participating resorts. Some may offer "working" cruises with passengers expected to help operate the vessel, cook, or perform other topside chores.

Contact: Particular firm or organization marketing the tour in North America. The contact may be the sponsor of the tour, a travel agent, a club, or some other organization.

Tours

Atlantic

BERMUDA ISLANDS

Bermuda: Season: May-October. Duration: 7 days. Carrier: not included. Departures: Bermuda. Accommodations: rooms at The Gables Guest House, double occupancy. 20% discount on all food and beverages. Features: 4 days of diving from 25-foot and 28-foot dive boats, many shallow water wrecks, reefs, sea gardens. Requirements: maximum of 20 people, all levels of experience. Cost: $299. Sponsor: resort operator/dive boat. Contact: Skin Diving Adventures, The Gables Guest House, Paget, Bermuda.

Canada

BRITISH COLUMBIA

Vancouver Island: Barclay Sound. Season: year round. Duration: minimum of 1 day. Carrier: 45-foot motor vessel *Rendezvous*. Departures: Port Alberni, B.C. Accommodations: bunks, all meals. Features: wrecks, reefs, marine life. Requirements: bring own equipment, dive vest or BC required, maximum 10 divers. Cost: $200 per day for entire boat and crew, includes unlimited air, minimum 2 dives per day. Sponsor: dive boat. Contact: Rendezvous Dive Ventures, Box 135, Port Alberni, British Columbia, Canada V9Y 7M6.

ONTARIO

Georgian Bay: Season: June and September. Duration: 2 and 3 days. Carrier: personal auto. Departures: Cleveland. Accommodations: cabins with cooking facilities, meals not included. Features: dive the wrecks of Georgian Bay, very clear water. Requirements: C-card, log book. Cost: $45 and $55, includes charter of 46-foot boat. Sponsor: dive shop. Contact: Buckeye Diving Schools, 46 Warrensville Center Rd., Bedford, OH 44146.

Caribbean

BAHAMA ISLANDS

Andros Island. Season: July. Duration: 7 days. Carrier: not included. Departures: Andros Town. Accommodations: Small Hope Bay Lodge, double occupancy, all meals. Features: guided by NAUI instructors, explore the Great Bahama Bank. Requirements: none, for beginners, and experienced divers. Cost: $375, includes 7 dives, all equipment and diving transportation. Sponsor: tour operator. Contact: Fred Calhoun's Underwater Safaris, P.O. Box 291 Back Bay Annex, Boston, MA 02117.

Bahama Islands: cruising islands on boat. Season: year round. Duration: minimum 3 days. Carrier: 75-foot motor vessel *Big Winner*. Departures: Marathon, FL. Accommodations: bunks on board, all meals. Features: wide variety of dive sites. Requirements: C-card, full gear required, maximum of 30 divers, only dive shops and clubs are taken. Cost: $2500 for the boat for 3 days, $500 every day thereafter. Sponsor: dive boat. Contact: Capt. M.L. Winner, 2109-81 Gulf, Marathon, FL 33050.

Bahama Islands: cruising islands on boat. Season: April-May. Duration: 7 days. Carrier: 35-foot ketch *Sora*. Departures: Bahama Islands. Accommodations: bunks, all meals. Features: sailing and diving the Exumas, Cat Island, Little Salvador, Eleuthera, Abaco Cays, skipper is professor of underwater archeology. Requirements: group of 2 to 4 people. Cost: $315. Sponsor: organization. Contact: Oceanic Expeditions, 240 Fort Mason, San Francisco, CA 94123.

Bahama Islands: cruising islands on boat. Season: year round. Duration: open. Carrier: 65-foot motor vessel *Dragon Lady*. Departures: Nassau, Bahamas. Accommodations: cabins with bunks, all meals. Features: exploring Exuma Cays between Ship Channel and Staniel Cay, some nights ashore, blue holes, caves tunnels, superb photography, drift dives. Requirements: maximum of 14 people, minimum of 5 days. Cost: $600 for the boat per day for first 5 days, $500 per day for additional days, includes unlimited air, tanks, backpacks, weightbelts. Sponsor: dive boat. Contact: Out-Island Oceanics, Inc., 800 SE 17th St., Ft. Lauderdale, FL 33316.

Bahama Islands: cruising islands on boat. Season: year round. Duration: 5 to 14 days. Carrier: 65-foot motor vessel. Departures: Freeport, Nassau, Bimini, Chub Cay. Accommodations: double staterooms, all meals. Features: captain with 20 years experience diving the area, reefs, wrecks, walls, night dives. Requirements: maximum of 10 people. Cost: $57 per day, includes unlimited air, tanks, backpacks, weightbelts. Sponsor: dive boat. Contact: Adventure Cruises, Inc., P.O. Box 22284, Ft. Lauderdale, FL 33316.

Grand Bahama Island: Season: April-December. Duration: open. Carrier: not included. Departures: Freeport. Accommodations: deluxe rooms at Victoria Inn, double occupancy, breakfasts and dinners. Features: diving in the area. Requirements: none. Cost: $47 per day, includes 2 single tank dives per day. Sponsor: resort operator. Contact: Victoria Inn/Scubahamas, P.O. Box F1261, Freeport, Grand Bahama Island.

Long Island: Season: year round. Duration: 7 days. Carrier: National Airlines. Departures: Los Angeles, San Francisco. Accommodations: deluxe rooms at Stella Maris Inn, all meals. Features: 6 days of diving with 2-3 tanks per day. Requirements: none. Cost: $740, includes airfare, all diving, special rates available for groups. Sponsor: tour operator. Contact: Bay Travel Diving Adventures, 2435 East Coast Hwy., Corona Del Mar, CA 92625.

North Eleuthera: Season: year round. Duration: 7 days. Carrier: National Airlines. Departures: Los Angeles and San Francisco. Accommodations: rooms at Current Club, all meals. Features: 6 days of diving. Requirements: C-card. Cost: $611 or $710 depending on high or low season, includes airfare, all diving. Sponsor: tour operator. Contact: Bay Travel Diving Adventures, 2435 East Coast Hwy., Corona Del Mar, CA 92625.

North Eleuthera: Season: April-December. Duration: 4 days or 7 days. Carrier: Shawnee from Ft. Lauderdale or Miami, Bahamasair from Nassau. Departures: Ft. Lauderdale, Miami, Nassau. Accommodations: deluxe rooms at Romora Bay Club, all meals. Features: Civil War train wreck, plateau dive. Requirements: none. Cost: $178 or $333, not including airfare, group rates upon request. Sponsor: resort operator. Contact: Romora Bay Club, Box 146, Harbour Island, Bahamas.

San Salvador: Season: May and August. Duration: 8 days. Carrier: not specified. Departures: Ft. Lauderdale, FL. Accommodations: rooms at Riding Rock Inn, double occupancy, all meals. Features: 2 dives daily, total 12 dives, Southampton Reef with wrecks and caves, Conception Island Wall with black coral. Requirements: C-card, personal diving gear including BC and gauge. Cost: $495, includes airfare, boat, guide, air, tanks, backpack, weightbelt. Sponsor: organization. Contact: American Association of Certified Scuba Divers, Inc., 1066 Westover Road, Stamford, CT 06902.

Turks & Caicos Islands: Season: year round. Duration: 7 days. Carrier: Southeast Airlines, Red Carpet Charters. Departures: Miami (SE), Clearwater (RC). Accommodations: standard rooms at Admiral Arms Inn, double occupancy, all meals. Features: all new equipment, within swim of drop-off, dive Grouper Heights, South Point, Admiral's Aquarium, Chimney Rock, Saul's Cave. Requirements: maximum group 24 people, all levels of diving proficiency acceptable. Cost: $369, includes unlimited use of watersports equipment, use of 2 inflatables and 34-foot trimaran. Sponsor: resort operator. Contact: Turk-Cai Watersports, Ltd., 84-C Walnut, Ft. Devens, MA 01433.

BELIZE

Belize: Season: May-August. Duration: 7 days. Carrier: SAHSA, TACA or BAL airlines. Departures: New Orleans, Houston. Accommodations: camping, hammocks, all meals. Features: diving the Great Blue Hole, Lighthouse Reef, West Wall of Half Moon Cave. Requirements: C-card, experience in deep diving (to 180 feet) must bring own gear, group limited to 20. Cost: $495, includes airfare, dive boat, first and last night at hotel. Sponsor: tour operator. Contact: Silver Streak Dive Tours, 4211 Melissa Lane, Dallas, TX 75229.

Belize: Season: year round. Duration: 6 days. Carrier: TAN, SAHSA, TACA, or Air Belize Airlines. Departures: Miami, New Orleans. Accommodations: berths on 50-foot motor vessel, all meals. Features: diving the 190-mile long barrier reef from boat, wide variety of sites, including the Blue Hole, abundant marine life. Requirements: bring personal equipment, maximum 6 persons per boat. Cost: $595, including airfare, including unlimited air, tanks, backpack, weightbelt. Sponsor: tour operator. Contact: Go Diving, Inc., 715 Florida Ave. S., Minneapolis, MN 55426.

Belize: Season: year round. Duration: 8 days. Carrier: 85-foot motor vessel *Belize Sundiver.* Departures: Belize City. Accommodations: berths on board, all meals. Features: diving wide variety of sites along 70 miles of Turneffe banks and Lighthouse Reef, Great Blue Hole. Requirements: acceptance of application form specifying experience and interests. Cost: $600, excludes airfare, includes air, tanks, backpack, weightbelts. Sponsor: tour operator. Contact: See & Sea Travel Service, Inc., 680 Beach St., Suite 340, San Francisco, CA 94109.

Belize City: Season: December-April. Duration: 7 days. Carrier: not included. Departures: Belize City. Accommodations: camp area with cabin tents, all family style meals under thatched cabana. Features: drop-off, Blue Hole, up to 200 feet visibility,

abundant marine life and coral gardens, tour to Mayan ruin, jungle walks, sailing, water skiing. Requirements: C-card. Cost: $475, $25 for each additional day, includes air, tank, tank packs, weightbelts. Sponsor: tour operator. Contact: Lighthouse Reef Expeditions, Inc., P.O. Box 1249, Turlock, CA 95380.

Belize City: Season: April-September. Duration: 7 days. Carrier: Delta Airlines. Departures: most major U.S. cities. Accommodations: rooms at Caye Aquarius Hotel, all meals. Features: island resort within 1 mile of the barrier reef, unlimited diving around area. Requirements: C-card. Cost: $700 to $1041 depending on city of departure, excludes local airfare to island, includes airfare to Belize and return, air, tanks, weightbelts. Sponsor: organization (NASDS). Contact: Club Aquarius Travel, P.O. Box 17067, Long Beach, CA 90807.

Caye Chapel Island: Season: year round. Duration: 7 days. Carrier: TAN, TACA. Departures: New Orleans, Miami. Accommodations: modern motel units, all meals. Features: inside or outside diving of world's 2nd largest barrier reef from 48-foot and 72-foot dive boats, Blue Hole, excellent spearfishing. Requirements: C-card, logbook. Cost: $400, excluding airfare, including air, tanks, boats. Sponsor: dive shop. Contact: Buckeye Diving Schools, 46 Warrensville Center Rd., Bedford, OH 44146.

BRITISH VIRGIN ISLANDS

Tortola: Season: year round. Duration: 8 days. Carrier: 75-foot motor vessel *Eros.* Departures: Road Town, Tortola. Accommodations: cabins on board, all meals. Features: cruise and dive the many islands and reefs, wreck of the Rhone. Requirements: acceptance of application form specifying experience and interests. Cost: $600, excluding airfare, including air, tanks, backpack, weightbelts. Sponsor: tour operator. Contact: See & Sea Travel Service, Inc., 680 Beach St., Suite 340, San Francisco, CA 94109.

Tortola, Road Town: Season: year round. Duration: 4 days and up. Carrier: American and Eastern Airlines. Departures: Boston, New York, Washington. Accommodations: first class rooms at Prospect Reef Resort, meals not included. Features: wreck of the Rhone, other dive sites around the islands, bicycles, tennis. Requirements: bring own diving equipment. Cost: $189 and up, group rates vary according to size, excludes airfare, includes minimum of 5 dives with instructor/guide, dive boat, air, tanks, backpacks, weightbelts. Sponsor: resort operator. Contact: Prospect Leisure, 280 Park Ave., New York, NY 10017.

Tortola: Season: year round. Duration:

minimum 7 days. Carrier: 49-foot sail boat *Bonaventure.* Departures: Road Town. Accommodations: bunks on board, all meals and beverages. Features: reef diving, night diving, wreck diving—the Rhone and others on Aneganda. Requirements: bring your own regulator. Cost: $55 per day, includes tanks and unlimited air. Sponsor: dive boat. Contact: Capt. Manfred Zerbe, Box 325, Road Town, Tortola, British Virgin Islands.

Tortola: Season: year round. Duration: 8 days. Carrier: not included. Departures: Road Town. Accommodations: standard rooms at The Moorings, meals not included. Features: diving around 40 islands, 400 wrecks on Anegada Reef. Requirements: C-card, bring personal diving gear. Cost: $227 April-December, $311 December-April, includes 5 single tank dives with guide, air, tanks, backpack, weightbelts. Sponsor: resort operator. Contact: The Moorings, Ltd., P.O. Box 50059, New Orleans, LA 70150.

Virgin Gorda: Season: year round. Duration: open. Carrier: not included. Departures: Virgin Gorda. Accommodations: choice of 6 hotels and resorts. Features: selection of over 50 different dive sites. Requirements: divers should bring personal diving gear. Cost: $140 package for 5 single tank dives, $180 package for 5 two tank dives, excludes airfaire and accommodations. Sponsor: dive shop. Contact: Kilbrides Underwater Tours, Box 40, Virgin Gorda, British Virgin Islands.

CAYMAN ISLANDS

Cayman Islands: cruising islands on boat. Season: January-June. Duration: 7 days. Carrier: 83-foot motor vessel *Cayman Diver.* Departures: Grand Cayman. Accommodations: berths on board, all meals. Features: cruising and diving the coastline of these 3 islands, gardens, forests, wreck of the *Balboa,* black coral trees. Requirements: acceptance of application form specifying experience and interests. Cost: $600, excluding airfare, including unlimited air, tanks, backpack, weightbelt. Sponsor: tour operator. Contact: See & Sea Travel Service, Inc., 680 Beach St., Suite 340, San Francisco, CA 94109.

Cayman Brac: Season: March. Duration: 5 days. Carrier: not specified. Departures: St. Petersburg, FL. Accommodations: double occupancy, all meals. Features: 8 dives, night dive, Little Cayman Wall with 700 foot drop, coral caves, abundant marine life. Requirements: C-card, personal diving gear including BC and gauge. Cost: $341, includes airfare, boat, guide, air, tanks, backpack, weightbelt. Sponsor: organization. Contact: American Association of Certified Scuba Divers, Inc., 1066 Westover Road, Stamfort, CT 06902.

Grand Cayman: Season: year round. Duration: 7 days. Carrier: National Airlines. Departures: Los Angeles, San Francisco. Accommodations: 6 resort hotels to choose from, breakfasts and dinners. Features: 6 days of diving, dropoffs, wrecks, reefs. Requirements: C-card. Cost: $550 to $650 depending on choice of accommodations, includes airfare, all diving. Sponsor: tour operator. Contact: Bay Travel Diving Adventures, 2435 East Coast Hwy., Corona Del Mar, CA 92625.

Grand Cayman: Season: year round. Duration: 3 or 7 days. Carrier: Eastern Airlines. Departures: any major U.S. city. Accommodations: rooms at Cayman Kai Resort, all meals. Features: 2 dives daily, wrecks, cliffs, black coral, caves, chimneys. Requirements: C-card, minimum group of 10. Cost: $163 or $357 April-December, $196 or $434 December-April, excludes airfare, includes dive boat, guide, air, tanks, backpack, weightbelt. Sponsor: tour operator. Contact: Hotel Plans, Inc., 1301 W. 22nd St., Oak Brook, IL 60521.

Grand Cayman: Season: year round. Duration: 4 days. Carrier: Cayman or Southern Airways. Departures: Miami. Accommodations: standard rooms at Casa Bertmar, meals not included. Features: coral reef and large coral heads less than 100 feet from beach, dive boat *Bertmar Diver* to wrecks, caves, wall. Requirements: C-card, maximum of 40 people. Cost: $114 April-December, $135 December-April, excludes airfare, includes 3 half day boat trips, 2 full tanks, backpack, weightbelt. Sponsor: resort operator/dive boat. Contact: Casa Bertmar, P.O. Box 637, Grand Cayman, British West Indies.

Grand Cayman: Season: year round. Duration: open. Carrier: Southern or Cayman Airlines. Departures: Miami. Accommodations: deluxe rooms at Spanish Bay Reef Resort, double occupancy, all meals. Features: diving via 3 dive boats and beach, 50 sites in area, Wall of Cayman plunges 6000 feet. Requirements: bring personal dive gear, no spearfishing. Cost: $65 per day April-December, $85 per day December-April, excludes airfare, includes unlimited air, dive boat, tanks, backpacks, weightbelts. Sponsor: resort operator. Contact: Spanish Bay Reef Resort, P.O. Box 800, Grand Cayman Island, British West Indies.

Grand Cayman: Season: April and November. Duration: 8 or 10 days. Carrier: open. Departures: Hartford, CT. Accommodations: first class hotel room, double occupancy, all breakfasts and dinners. Features: hotel on beach with 50 feet of diving, boat trips optional. Requirements: C-card, bring own BC vest, pressure gauge. Cost: $515 or $585, includes guide for diving. Sponsor: dive shop. Contact: Jack's

Dive Center, 466 East St., Plainville, CT 06062.

Grand Cayman: Season: May-August. Duration: 7 days. Carrier: Southern Airways. Departures: Houston, Dallas-Ft. Worth. Accommodations: deluxe hotel, double occupancy, meals not included. Features: wreck of 330-foot ship Balboa in 35 feet of water, walls, night dives, visibility up to 200 feet. Requirements: C-card. Cost: $299 to $349 depending on departure and hotel, includes airfare, dive package is extra at 3 dives for $54, 6 for $108, 12 for $192, includes air, tank, backpack, weightbelt. Sponsor: tour operator. Contact: Moore Tours, 5633 W. Lovers Lane, Dallas, TX 75209.

Grand Cayman: Season: October. Duration: 8 days. Carrier: American Airlines. Departures: New York. Accommodations: hotel, 2 meals per day. Features: diving from boat around island. Requirements: C-card with 10 logged dives. Cost: $550, includes airfare, boat, diving equipment. Sponsor: dive shop. Contact: Ski & Scuba, Foot of Broad St., Stratford, CT 06497.

Grand Cayman: Season: year round. Duration: 5 days or 7 days. Carrier: Cayman or Southern Airways. Departures: Miami. Accommodations: private villas with kitchens. Features: 36 foot trimaran dive boat, reefs, wrecks, abundant marine life. Requirements: none. Cost: $250 or $325 April-December, $300 or $365 December-April, minimum 2 people, group rates are $176 or $235 April-December, minimum 10 people, includes airfare, 2 tank boat dives per day. Sponsor: dive shop. Contact: Seasports, P.O. Box 1516, Grand Cayman Island, British West Indies.

CUBA

Isle of Pines or Costa Sur: Season: year round. Duration: 5 or 8 days. Carrier: private charter. Departures: Tampa, FL. Accommodations: deluxe hotel, double occupancy, all meals with beer and wine. Features: last virgin reefs in Western Hemisphere, dropoffs, walls, blue holes. Requirements: 30 days advance booking. Cost: $395 or $595, includes airfare, daily dive trips on 68-foot motor vessel, air, tanks, weightbelts, tennis, horseback riding. Sponsor: tour operator. Contact: Atlantis Divers World, Inc., 500 Ave. of the Americas, New York, NY 10011.

DOMINION REPUBLIC

Santo Domingo: Season: December-May. Duration: 8 days. Carrier: Pan American Airlines. Departures: Boston, MA. Accommodations: deluxe hotel room, double occupancy, breakfasts. Features: entire coast ringed with reefs, dropoffs, blue holes, abundant marine life. Requirements: none.

Cost: $309, includes airfare, tennis, excludes daily dive tours which are $40 from dive boat. Sponsor: dive shop. Contact: Northeast Scuba, Inc., 125 Liberty St., Danvers, MA 01923.

HONDURAS

San Pedro Sula: Season: all year except October, November. Duration: 6 days. Carrier: TAN, SAHSA or Air Belize Airlines. Departures: Miami, New Orleans. Accommodations: cottage units at Anthony's Key Resort, double occupancy, all meals. Features: 30 diving areas within 15 minutes of resort, including Pillar Gardens, Eagle's Perch, Eel Garden, Wreck of the Gwendolyn, Bear's Den. Requirements: bring personal diving equipment. Cost: $359, excluding airfare, including dive boat, one night dive, riding, sailing, deep-sea fishing, beach party, tanks, backpack, weightbelt. Sponsor: tour operator. Contact: Go Diving, Inc., 715 Florida Ave. S., Minneapolis, MN 55426.

MEXICO

Cozumel Island: Season: year round. Duration: 8 days. Carrier: Continental Airlines, Aeromexico. Departures: any major U.S. city. Accommodations: rooms at Cabanas del Caribe, all meals. Features: diving from boat every day, Palancar Reef, drift diving, beach party. Requirements: acceptance of application form specifying experience and interests. Cost: $600, excluding airfare, including air, tanks, backpack, weightbelt, dive boat. Sponsor: tour operator. Contact: Sea & Sea Travel Service, Inc., 680 Beach St., Suite 340, San Francisco, CA 94109.

Cozumel Island: Season: year round. Duration: 7 days. Carrier: Mexicana Airlines. Departures: Los Angeles. Accommodations: selection of 5 hotels, meals not specified. Features: 6 days of diving from boat on Palancar Reef, 2 tanks per day, lunch included. Requirements: C-card. Cost: $420 to $693 depending on choice of hotel, includes airfare, all diving, group rates are available. Sponsor: tour operator. Contact: Bay Travel Diving Adventures, 2435 East Coast Hwy., Corona Del Mar, CA 92625.

Cozumel Island: Season: year round. Duration: 6 days. Carrier: Aeromexico, Mexicana Airlines. Departures: Miami, Houston, Los Angeles. Accommodations: rooms at either El Presidente Hotel with breakfasts and dinners, or Barracuda Hotel with no meals. Features: dive famous Palancar Reef, giant pinnacles, caves, arches, walls. Requirements: bring own personal diving gear. Cost: depends on which hotel and plan you choose, write for details, includes dive boat, tanks, backpack, weightbelt, picnic. Sponsor: tour operator. Contact: Go Diving, Inc., 715 Florida Ave.

S., Minneapolis, MN 55426.

Cozumel Island: Season: November-August. Duration: 8 days. Carrier: not included. Departures: Cozumel. Accommodations: rooms at Galapagos Inn Dive Resort, double occupancy, all meals. Features: certified divemasters and guides, dive famous Palancar Reef, five 2-dive days, trip to Mayan ruins. Requirements: C-card. Cost: $299, includes dive boats, tanks, weightbelts, backpack. Sponsor: resort operator. Contact: Galapagos Inn Dive Resort, Apdo. Postal 289, Cozumel, Q, Roo, Mexico.

Cozumel Island: Season: year round. Duration: 3 to 8 days. Carrier: Aeromexico. Departures: Houston, TX. Accommodations: standard hotel room, double occupancy, some meals. Features: Cozumel rated fifth best diving location in the world by CMAS, English speaking instructors. Requirements: C-card. Cost: $189 to $325, includes airfare, boat diving. Sponsor: dive shop. Contact: Blue Water Diving School, 910 Westheimer, Houston, TX 77006.

NETHERLANDS ANTILLES

Bonaire: Season: year round. Duration: 8 days. Carrier: KLM Airlines. Departures: Miami, FL. Accommodations: standard room at Flamingo Beach Hotel, double occupancy, breakfast and dinner daily. Features: major reef right in front of hotel, over 41 dive sites around island, certification course available. Requirements: bring personal diving gear. Cost: $326, 6 days of diving, round trip transfers airport - hotel. Sponsor: resort operator/dive shop. Contact: Dive Bonaire-Flamingo Beach Hotel, P.O. Box 686, Ithaca, NY 14850.

PANAMA

Isle Grande: Season: year round. Duration: 10 days. Carrier: Pan American. Departures: Miami. Accommodations: deluxe rooms, all meals. Features: 17-foot Whalers to 42-foot Hatteras, new area open for just 2 years, midway between Spanish treasure towns of Portobelo and Nombre de Dios, good treasure diving. Requirements: no excessively deep dives, maximum group of 16 divers plus 20 non-divers. Cost: $569, includes airfare, 2 tanks per day, plus several extras such as Panama Canal tour, casino gambling, boat excursions. Sponsor: Isle Grande Resorte. Contact: Isle Grande Tours, 6003 N. Palafox, Pensacola, FL 32503.

PUERTO RICO

San Juan: Season: June-August, January. Duration: 1-2 weeks. Carrier: Eastern Airlines. Departures: Buffalo, NY. Accommodations: hotel. Features: reefs, the Wall, deep dives, Monkey Island. Requirements: group size 1-15. Cost: $430, includes airfare,

all transportation, dive boat, air, tanks. Sponsor: dive shop. Contact: Great Lakes Divers, Inc., 244 Niagara Falls Blvd., Buffalo, NY 14223.

ST. KITTS

St. Kitts: Season: July. Duration: 8 days. Carrier: not specified. Departures: New York. Accommodations: rooms at Royal St. Kitts Golf and Racquet Club, double occupancy, breakfasts and dinners. Features: 6 dives, 7 wrecks, newer diving area. Requirements: C-card, personal diving gear including BC and gauge. Cost: $499, including airfare, boat, guide, air, tanks, backpack, weightbelt. Sponsor: organization. Contact: American Association of Certified Scuba Divers, Inc., 1066 Westover Road, Stamford, CT 06902.

ST. MAARTEN

St. Maarten: Season: July. Duration 8 days. Carrier: not specified. Departures: New York. Accommodations: rooms at Great Bay Beach Hotel, double occupancy, breakfasts and dinners. Features: 6 dives, Man-O-War reef, H.M.S. Proselyte wreck, Green Cay, Dog Island. Requirements: C-card, personal diving gear including BC and gauge. Cost: $499, includes airfare, boat, guide, air, tanks, backpack, weightbelt. Sponsor: organization. Contact: American Association of Certified Scuba Divers, Inc., 1066 Westover Road, Stamford, CT 06902.

ST. VINCENT

St. Vincent: Season: year round. Duration: 7 or 14 days. Carrier: not included. Departures: St. Vincent. Accommodations: deluxe hotel room, breakfasts and dinners. Features: diving trips along the coast by boat. Requirements: C-card, pressure gauges. Cost: $358 summer, $392 winter, 7 days, includes tanks, backpacks, weightbelts. Sponsor: dive shop. Contact: Dive St. Vincent, Ltd., Box 864, St. Vincent, West Indies.

U.S. VIRGIN ISLANDS

St. Croix: Season: December-March. Duration: 8 or 5 days. Carrier: not included. Departures: Christiansted, St. Croix. Accommodations: first class rooms at King Christian Hotel, double occupancy, meals not included. Features: 10 dives (8 days) or 6 dives (5 days) around the island, Cane Bay Dropoff, Salt River. Requirements: none. Cost: $299 for 8 days, $182 for 5 days, includes all scuba equipment, 1 day use of u/w camera. Sponsor: resort operator/dive shop. Contact: Pressure, Ltd., Box 3612, Christiansted, St. Croix, U.S. Virgin Islands 00820.

St. Croix: Season: year round. Duration: 8 days, escorted or unsupervised. Carrier: not included. Departures: St. Croix. Accommodations: room at hotel, breakfasts. Features: beach diving, Salt River

dropoff, Cane Bay dropoff, Buck Island barrier reef. Requirments: C-card. Cost: $325, includes 6 full days of diving with a minimum of 13 dives from beach and boat with guide, or $225 for unsupervised diving with directions to dive sites and use of rental car. Sponsor: dive shop. Contact: V.I. Divers, Ltd., Pan Am Pavilion, Christiansted, St. Croix, U.S. Virgin Islands 00820.

St. John: Season: year round. Duration: 7 days. Carrier: 42-foot catamaran. Departures: St. John. Accommodations: private staterooms, all meals. Features: diving throughout the U.S. and British Virgin Islands, wreck of the *Rhone,* the Baths of Virgin Gorda, the caves of Treasure Island, Aegada's Horseshoe Reef. Cost: $335, includes unlimited air, group leader complimentary with 7 guests. Sponsor: dive boat. Contact: Charles Smithline, Caneel Bay Plantation, P.O. Box 120, Cruz Bay, St. John, U.S. Virgin Islands 00830.

St. John: Season: April-December. Duration: 7 days. Carrier: not included. Departures: St. John. Accommodations: canvas cottages with planked decks, 4 divers to a cottage, one night aboard 50-foot motor vessel *Caribe Diver,* meals not included. Features: average 2 dives per day from *Caribe Diver,* including one wreck dive and one night dive. Requirements: C-card, 6 divers per group. Cost: $230, includes all diving, air, tanks, backpacks. Sponsor: dive boat. Contact: Maho Bay Camps, Inc., 17 E. 73rd St., New York, NY 10021.

St. Thomas: Season: June. Duration: 10 days. Carrier: Eastern Airlines. Departures: Miami. Accommodations: rooms at Bali Hai Hotel, all meals. Features: 2 boat dives per day guided by underwater naturalist, Cow and Calf Rocks, Thatch Cay, Frenchman's Cap, night dive at Little St. James, first of 3 Virgin Island trips—others to St. Croix and Tortola. Requirements: C-card, bring personal diving gear. Cost: $855, includes airfare, boat, guide, all diving. Sponsor: tour operator. Contact: Sea Life Discovery, Inc., 19915 Oakmont Dr., Los Gatos, CA 95030.

St. Thomas: Season: April-December (off-season). Duration: 7 days: Carrier: not included. Departures: St. Thomas. Accommodations: rooms at beach resort with kitchen facilities. Features: five ½-day dives throughout islands, wreck of the *Rhone,* use of Nikonos camera. Requirements: bring personal diving equipment. Cost: $210, includes air, tanks, weightbelts. Sponsor: dive shop. Contact: Watersports Center, P.O. Box 2432, St. Thomas, U.S. Virgin Islands 00801.

St. Thomas: Season: year round. Duration: 1 to 14 days. Carrier: dive boat. Departures: St. Thomas. Accommodations: not included, can be arranged.

185

Features: a variety of selected diving trips around islands. Requirements: C-card to dive from boat, none from beach. Cost: variable. Sponsor: dive shop. Contact: Virgin Islands Diving Schools, Box 9707, St. Thomas, U.S. Virgin Islands 00801.

St. Thomas: Season: year round. Duration: 8 days. Carrier: American or Eastern Airlines. Departures: St. Thomas. Accommodations: guest house, double occupancy, no meals. Features: 8 different dives, including the 1867 wreck of the *Rhone*, use of club's beach chairs, towels, pool, photography and shell clinics. Requirements: none. Cost: $298 off-season, $320 in-season, excludes airfare, includes all scuba equipment, dive boat. Sponsor: resort operator. Contact: St. Thomas Diving Club, P.O. Box 4976, St. Thomas, U.S. Virgin Islands 00801.

Coral Sea
AUSTRALIA

Great Barrier Reef, The Coral Sea: Season: October. Duration: 17 days. Carrier: 79-foot motor vessel *Coralita*, all meals. Departures: Yeppoon on the Queensland Coast. Accommodations: staterooms on one of the world's finest diving boats, all meals. Features: diving the Swains Group of The Great Barrier Reef, cruising and diving through virgin reefs, atolls and cays of the Coral Sea. Requirements: acceptance of application form specifying experience and interests. Cost: $2300, excluding airfare, including air, tanks, backpack, weightbelt. Sponsor: tour operator. Contact: See and Sea Travel Service, Inc., 680 Beach St., Suite 340, San Francisco, CA 94109.

Heron Island: Season: year round. Duration: 14 days. Carrier: Quantas Airlines. Departures: any major U.S. city. Accommodations: hotel room, all meals. Features: 10 days of diving from boat, 2 dives per day, the Great Barrier Reef, Big Bommey, Wistari Reef. Requirements: C-card, bring personal diving gear, light wet suit recommended. Cost: $595, excluding airfare, includes dive boat, guide, air, tanks, backpack, weightbelt. Sponsor: tour operator. Contact: Bay Travel Diving Adventures, 2435 East Coast Hwy., Corona Del Mar, CA 92625.

Indian Ocean
MALDIVE ISLANDS

Sri Lanka (Ceylon): Season: August. Duration: 14 days. Carrier: 74-foot motor sailer. Departures: New York. Accommodations: berths on board, all meals. Features: cruising and diving the Maldive Islands, "land of a thousand atolls" off the Southwest Coast of India, rich reefs, abundant marine life, visit to tea plantation.

Requirements: acceptance of application form specifying experience and interests. Cost: $1450, excluding airfare, including air, tanks, backpack, weightbelt. Sponsor: tour operator. Contact: See & Sea Travel Service, Inc., 680 Beach St., Suite 340, San Francisco, CA 94109.

Pacific
ECUADOR

Galapagos Islands: Season: January-August. Duration: 20 days. Carrier: one of 4 motor/sailing vessels, 46 to 70 feet long. Departures: Quito, Ecuador. Accommodations: 3 nights at hotel in Quito, balance bunks on board, all meals included except in Quito. Features: primarily a natural history and anthropology expedition, led by naturalists, skin diving and snorkeling are part of activities, no scuba, explore the islands and waters of the Galapagos. Requirements: maximum of 16 people. Cost: $1390, excludes airfare, includes ground transportation, park fees, instruction and leadership. Sponsor: tour operator. Contact: Nature Expeditions International, 599 College Ave., Palo Alto, CA 94306.

Galapagos Islands: Season: March-July. Duration: 18 days. Carrier: 70-foot motor sailer *Encantada*. Departures: Baltra Island, Galapagos. Accommodations: cabins on board, all meals. Features: with local naturalist guide, explore the wide variety of animal and marine life of the several islands in the group, hiking inland, visit Darwin Station. Requirements: acceptance of application form specifying experience and interests. Cost: $2000, excluding airfare, including air, tanks, backpack, weightbelt. Sponsor: tour operator. Contact: See & Sea Travel Service, Inc., 680 Beach St., Suite 340, San Francisco, CA 94109.

FIJIAN ISLANDS

Mana, Taveuni: Season: February-November. Duration: 17 days. Carrier: UTA French Airlines. Departures: most major U.S. cities. Accommodations: rooms at hotel, all meals. Features: 6 full diving days on Taveuni Island exploring virgin 19 mile Rainbow Reef, 5 days diving from Mana Island at a variety of sites. Requirements: acceptance of application form specifying experience and interests. Cost: $1500, excluding airfare, including boats, air, tanks, backpack, weightbelt. Sponsor: tour operator. Contact: See & Sea Travel Service, Inc., 680 Beach St., Suite 340, San Francisco, CA 94109.

Suva: Season: year round. Duration: 14 days. Carrier: Pan American, Quantas, Air New Zealand, UTA. Departures: Los Angeles, San Francisco. Accommodations: rooms at first class hotel, all meals. Features: daily charter boat to various dive

sites, main Suva reef with black coral and greatest wall in South Pacific, Beqa Island considered one of the top 5 dive sites, wreck of sailing barque *Woodburn*, Astrolabe Lagoon, night dives. Requirements: minimum of 4 persons, bring regulator. Cost: $643, excluding airfare, includes dive boat, guide, tanks, backpacks, weightbelts, unlimited air. Sponsor: dive shop. Contact: Scubahire, Ltd., G.P.O. Box 777, Suva, Fijian Islands.

FRENCH POLYNESIA

Marquesas, Tuamottus, Society Islands: Season: year round. Duration: 6, 10 or 18 days. Carrier: 57-foot ketch *Kebir*. Departures: French Polynesia. Accommodations: bunks on board, all meals. Features: organize your own expedition and diving in the Society Islands April-November, or amoung the Marquesas and Tuamotus December-March, skipper and his wife are knowledgeable guides throughout this area. Requirements: grbups of 4 to 6 persons. Cost: $450 for 6 days, $700 for 10 days, $1260 for 18 days. Sponsor: organization. Contact: Oceanic Expeditions, 240 Fort Mason, San Francisco, CA 94123.

Tahiti: Season: June. Duration: 14 days. Carrier: 58-foot auxillary ketch *Danae III*. Departures: Huahine Island. Accommodations: berths on board, all meals. Features: sailing and diving the remote islands of French Polynesia, Huahine, Raiatea, Bora Bora, Rangiroa, excursions to Polynesian villages. Requirements: acceptance of application form specifying experience and interests. Cost: $2000, excluding airfare, including air, tanks, backpack, weightbelt. Sponsor: tour operator. Contact: See & Sea Travel Service, Inc., 680 Beach St., Suite 340, San Francisco, CA 94109.

Tahiti, Bora Bora, Moorea: Season: June. Duration: 12 days. Carrier: not specified. Departures: Los Angeles. Accommodations: first class hotel rooms, double occupancy, all meals. Features: 2 days in Tahiti, 4 in Bora Bora, 4 in Moorea, 8 days diving, 16 dives total, abundant marine life, WW II wrecks, corals, sponges. Requirements: C-card, personal diving gear including BC and gauge. Cost: $1339, includes airfare, boat, guide, air, tanks, backpack, weightbelt. Sponsor: organization. Contact: American Association of Certified Scuba Divers, Inc., 1066 Westover Road, Stamford, CT 06902.

Tuamotos Islands, Rangiroa: Season: year round. Duration: 8 or 12 days. Carrier: not included. Departures: Rangiroa. Accommodations: small house in the village of Avatara, all meals. Features: land based research expedition with marine biologist specializing in the study of sharks and their behavior, plus other marine life around island, day trips on 40-foot ketch *S.E.A.*

Quest. Requirements: C-card, 4 to 6 people. Cost: $480 for 8 days, $660 for 12 days. Sponsor: organization. Contact: Oceanic Expeditions, 240 Fort Mason, San Francisco, CA 94123.

MELANESIA

Melanesia: Season: June-November. Duration: 15, 22 or 24 days. Carrier: 50-foot ketch *Heart of Edna.* Departures: various ports in Melanesia. Accommodations: bunks on board, all meals. Features: sail and dive throughout the Loyalty Islands, New Hebrides, Solomon Islands, New Guinea, explore the islands, skipper and his wife are knowledgeable guides throughout this area. Requirements: group of 6 people. Cost: $675 for 15 days, $900 for 22 days, $1125 for 24 days. Sponsor: organization. Contact: Oceanic Expeditions, 240 Fort Mason, San Francisco, CA 94123.

New Guinea, Papua, Lae: Season: year round. Duration: day, weekend, week. Carrier: not included. Accommodations: private house, all meals. Features: dropoffs, reefs, wrecks, sunken aircraft, spearfishing, photography. Requirements: C-card, approximately 6 divers. Cost: $100 per day, includes air, all equipment, use of 23-foot boat. Sponsor: dive shop. Contact: New Guinea Diving, Box 320, Lae, Papua, New Guinea.

MEXICO

Baja California: Season: June-July. Duration: 5 days. Carrier: 70-foot motor vessel *Sand Dollar.* Departures: San Diego. Accommodations: bunks on board, all meals. Features: reefs, abundant marine life, dive master gives bio-marine seminar during trip. Requirements: group of 20 people. Cost: $335 to $360. Sponsor: organization. Contact: Oceanic Expeditions, 240 Fort Mason, San Francisco, CA 94123.

Jalisco: Season: November. Duration: 8 days. Carrier: Aeromexico. Departures: Houston and other major cities. Accommodations: deluxe rooms at Mexican Hacienda Club Med location, all meals. Features: diving along the coast. Requirements: must pass test in scuba proficiency maximum of 20 people. Cost: $650, includes airfare from Houston, transfers, all diving equipment. Sponsor: tour operator. Contact: Kirk Anders Travel, P.O. Box 1418, Ft. Lauderdale, FL 33302.

Puerto Vallarta: Season: November. Duration: 8 days. Carrier: not specified. Departures: Los Angeles. Accommodations: rooms at Hotel Playa de Oro, double occupancy, breakfasts and dinners. Features: 10 dives along the coast, large marine life at Vahia de Banderas and Punta Mita. Requirements: C-card, personal diving gear including BC and gauge. Cost:

$429, including airfare, boat, guide, air, tanks, backpack, weightbelt. Sponsor: organization. Contact: American Association of Certified Scuba Divers, Inc., 1066 Westover Road, Stamford, CT 06902.

Zihautanejo, Ixtapa: Season: year round. Duration: 4 days or 8 days. Carrier: not included. Departures: Acapulco by car, Mexico City by airlines. Accommodations: palm thatched bungalows with showers, two meals per day. Features: diving along the coast. Requirements: C-card, must be a minimum group of 10. Cost: summer rates are $127 for 4 days with up to 6 dives, $273 for 8 days with up to 12 dives, winter rates are $156 and $340 respectively. Sponsor: resort operator. Contact: Hotel Plans, Inc., Oak Brook, IL 60521.

MICRONESIA

E.C.I., Moen: Season: year round. Duration: 5 days. Carrier: Continental Airlines. Departures: Agana, Guam. Accommodations: first class hotel rooms, double occupancy, no meals included. Features: shipwrecks from WW II. Requirements: C-card, must have 15 in group to obtain group rates, bring all diving equipment except tanks. Cost: $375, includes airfare, diving and boat expenses. Sponsor: dive shop. Contact: International Divers Association, P.O. Box 6657, Tamuning, Guam 96911.

Guam, Ponape, Saipan, Palan, Truk Lagoon: Season: year round. Duration: 14 days. Carrier: Continental Airlines, Air Micronesia. Departures: Los Angeles. Accommodations: rooms at deluxe hotel, breakfast or dinner. Features: explore 2-3 islands, 18 to 35-foot boats, experienced local guides, reefs on Ponape and Palan, sightseeing cultural aspects of islands. Requirements: minimum of 10 people, maximum of 20, bring all personal diving gear except weights, no decompression diving. Cost: $750-850, excludes airfare, includes 2 tanks per day. Sponsor: dive shop. Contact: Coral Reef Marine Center, Box 2792, Agana, Guam 96910.

Guam, Mariana Islands: Season: year round. Duration: open. Carrier: Continental or Pan American Airlines. Departures: San Francisco. Accommodations: write for details. Features: reef diving, wrecks from WW I and WW II, blue hole. Requirements: C-card, bring all diving equipment except tanks. Cost: depends on stay, write for details. Sponsor: dive shop. Contact: Breakaway Travel, 1021 Center St., Santa Cruz, CA 95064.

Saipan, Mariana Islands: Season: year round. Duration: 4 days. Carrier: Continental Airlines. Departures: Agana, Guam. Accommodations: first class hotel rooms, double occupancy, no meals included. Features: reef diving, blue grotto, a few

wrecks. Requirements: C-card, must have 15 in group to obtain group rates, bring all diving equipment except tanks. Cost: $180, excludes airfare, includes diving and boat expenses. Sponsor: dive shop. Contact: International Divers Association, P.O. Box 6657, Tamuning, Guam 96911.

Truk Lagoon: Season: March-September. Duration: 12 days. Carrier: Continental Airlines. Departures: any major U.S. city. Accommodations: rooms at Truk Continental Hotel, lunches. Features: diving from newly redesigned landing craft on the 64 sunken Japanese warships in Truk lagoon, Zuckerman Reef. Requirements: acceptance of application form specifying experience and interests. Cost: $800, excluding airfare, including air, tanks, backpack, weightbelt. Sponsor: tour operator. Contact: See & Sea Travel Service, Inc., 680 Beach St., Suite 340, San Francisco, CA 94109.

Truk Lagoon, Palau: Season: July. Duration: 21 days. Carrier: Continental Airlines. Departures: Los Angeles. Accommodations: rooms, double occupancy, at Breakers Hotel in Hawaii, Continental Hotels in Guam, Truk and Palau, breakfasts and lunches. Features: diving Japanese ship wrecks in Truk Lagoon, reefs of Palau, guided by diving medical officer and underwater naturalist. Requirements: C-card, bring personal diving gear. Cost: $2500, includes airfare, boat, guide, all diving. Sponsor: tour operator. Contact: Sea Life Discovery, Inc., 19915 Oakmont Dr., Los Gatos, CA 95030.

Truk Lagoon: Season: year round. Duration: based on wishes of the group, individually planned tours. Carrier: Continental's Air Micronesia. Departures: any major U.S. city. Accommodations: arranged upon request. Features: wreck diving, more than 40 WW II ships (declared an underwater museum—unlawful to remove objects). Requirements: C-card, must obtain Truk Diving Permit. Cost: depends on group's wishes, prices available on request, includes 2 tanks with air, pack, weightbelts, boat and diving guide. Sponsor: dive shop. Contact: Micronesia Aquatics, P.O. Box 57, Truk Lagoon, E.C.I. 96942.

PALAU ISLANDS

West Carolines, Korkor: Season: year round. Duration: 5 days. Carrier: Continental Airlines. Departures: Agana, Guam. Accommodations: first class hotel rooms, double occupancy, no meals included. Features: reef diving. Requirements: C-card, must have 15 in group to obtain group rates, bring all diving equipment except tanks. Cost: $450, includes airfare, diving and boat expenses. Sponsor: dive shop. Contact: International Divers Association, P.O. Box 6657, Tamuning, Guam 96911.

PHILIPPINE ISLANDS

Cebu, Apo Reef: Season: year round. Duration: 8 days maximum. Carrier: 57-foot motor vessel *Tadpole*. Departures: Manila. Accommodations: bunks, all meals. Features: diving around the 7100 islands of the Philippines, route is flexible so alternative sites can be included, two major routes are Cebu area and Apo Reef. Requirements: C-card, BC's, pressure gauges. Cost: $300, includes inter-island airfare, dive boat guide, air, tanks, backpack, weightbelts. Sponsor: dive boat/dive shop. Contact: Marine Sports Center, Inc., Lawyers' Inn Bldg., 25 Caliraya St., Quezon City, Metro-Manila, Philippines 3008.

Semirara Islands: Season: February-July. Duration: 16 days. Carrier: 102-foot motor vessel *Seaquest*. Departures: San Jose, Mindoro Island. Accommodations: cabin on boat, all meals. Features: 1 day in Manila, tour Corregidor, 5 days of diving the primitive Semirara Islands, the Calaiman group, visit Indian villages. Requirements: acceptance of application form specifying experience and interests. Cost: $1800, excluding airfare, including air, tanks, backpack, weightbelt. Sponsor: tour operator. Contact: See & Sea Travel Service, Inc., 680 Beach St., Suite 340, San Francisco CA 94109.

SOUTH SEAS

South Seas Tour:, Fiji, Australia, Heron Island, The Great Barrier Reef, Tahiti: Season: October. Duration: 21 days. Carrier: UTA French Airlines. Departures: Los Angeles. Accommodations: hotel rooms, double occupancy, some meals included. Features: 4 days of diving in Fiji, 4 nights in Sydney, over night at Heron Island to dive the Marine National Park, 7 days diving the Great Barrier Reef, 2 nights at Tahiti. Requirements: C-card, personal diving gear. Cost: $2229, including airfare, dive boats. Sponsor: tour operator. Contact: World Wide Divers, Inc., 155 East 55th St., New York, NY 10022.

Red Sea

ISRAEL

Eilat, Sharm El Sheikh: Season: May-February. Duration: 6 days. Carrier: El Al Israel Airlines. Departures: any major U.S. city. Accommodations: Holiday Villages, half board basis. Features: Moses Rock, "Nueiba Oasis," Ras-um Sid, Ras Muhamed, Robino Bay, Gardens at Naama Bay, "Canyon," the undersea haven. Requirements: C-card, does not have to be group. Cost: $381, includes all equipment, air, diving guide. Sponsor: tour operator. Contact: Daphna Knassium, Ltd., 444 Madison Ave., New York, NY 10022.

Eilat, Ras Muhamed: Season: year round.

Duration: 2 or more days. Carrier: not included. Departures: Eilat. Accommodations: camping or hotel as requested, all meals. Features: scuba safaris by jeep, canyon and blue hole at Dahab, dropoffs at Ras Muhamed, giant fan coral at Ras-um Sid. Requirements: C-card, minimum group of 10 people. Cost: $35 per day for camping with gear furnished, $26 per day for hotel with hotel extra, includes vehicles, trailers, guide. Sponsor: dive shop. Contact: Aqua Sport Red Sea Diving Centre, P.O. Box 300, Eilat, Israel.

Mssada, Jericho, Jerusalem, Tel Aviv, Sharm El Sheikh: Season: September-October. Duration: 14 days. Carrier: El Al Israel Airlines. Departures: New York. Accommodations: first class hotels, double occupancy, breakfasts and dinners. Features: tours of cities, 8 days of diving including Sharm El Sheikh, Mara-El-Et, Ras Muhamed, Ras-um Sid, Shark Point, Amphorae, Masa Burka, Gardens. Requirements: C-card, group size 15-20. Cost: $1799, includes airfare, flights within Israel, all diving. Sponsor: tour operator. Contact: Atlantis Safaris, P.O. Box 530303, Miami Shores, FL 33153.

Neviot: Season: year round. Duration: 7 days. Carrier: not included. Departures: Elat. Accommodations: 3 nights at hotel, 4 nights camping out on safari, 2 meals per day at hotel, all meals camping. Features: diving safaris to Dahab, Sharm El Sheikh, Ras Muhamed. Requirements: diving license, no minimum group. Cost: $305, includes air, tanks, weightbelt. Sponsor: dive shop. Contact: Neviot Diving Centre, Neviot, Post Elat, Israel.

Sharm El Sheikh: Season: October. Duration: 16 days. Carrier: Trans World Airlines. Departures: New York. Accommodations: rooms at Sharm Hotel, double occupancy, breakfasts and dinners. Features: 11 days of diving, 2 dives per day, guided by underwater naturalist, diving by boat from Sharm El Sheikh to Ras Muhamed, tours of Tel Aviv and Jerusalem. Requirements: C-card, bring personal diving gear. Cost: $2325, includes airfare, boat, guide, all diving, city tours. Sponsor: tour operator. Contact: Sea Life Discovery, Inc., 19915 Oakmont Dr., Los Gatos, CA 95030.

JORDAN

Aqaba: Season: May and October. Duration: 15 days. Carrier: Trans World Airlines. Departures: any major U.S. city. Accommodations: room at hotel in Aqaba, all meals. Features: daily dive trips by native boats along coast, 2 inland excursions including Lawrence of Arabia's desert fortress Wadi Rum. Requirements: acceptance of application form specifying experience and interests. Cost: $2000,

excluding airfare, including boats, air, tanks, backpack, weightbelt. Sponsor: tour operator. Contact: See & Sea Travel Service, Inc., 680 Beach St., Suite 340, San Francisco, CA 94109.

SUDAN

Port Sudan: Season: year round. Duration: 16 days. Carrier: Sudan Airways. Departures: London, England. Accommodations: partly at Port Sudan camp headquarters on camp beds, partly on Cambridge Coral Starfish Research Group's reef platform, partly in open camps on islands, all meals included. Features: diving from reef platform situated on edge of Towarfit Reef, 4 kilometers offshore, boat trips to other reefs and islands. Requirements: deep diving requires doctor's certificate of health. Cost: $905, includes airfare, all diving equipment and instruction. Sponsor: tour operator. Contact: World Expeditionary Association, Graybar Bldg., Suite 354, 420 Lexington Ave., New York, NY 10017.

Port Sudan: Season: year round. Duration: 9, 16 or 23 days. Carrier: Sudan Airways. Departures: London, England. Accommodations: base camp with camp beds, bathroom, showers, all meals provided. Features: expedition-type tour led by marine biologists, abundant marine life, wrecks, average 2 dives per day. Requirements: group size 6 to 20. Cost: $781, $1096, or $1303, includes airfare. Sponsor: tour operator. Contact: Explore Beyond, Ltd., 1 Ludgate Circus Buildings, London EC4M 7LQ, England.

Sea of Cortez

MEXICO

Baja Californian: Season: February-March. Duration: 10 days. Carrier: 75-foot motor vessel *Poseidon*. Departures: San Diego, CA. Accommodations: cabins with bunks, hotel rooms for 3 nights en route, all meals. Features: primarily a natural history and anthropology expedition led by marine biologists, skin diving and snorkeling are part of activities, no scuba, explore the coast, islands and waters of Baja from Bahia de Los Angeles to Loreto. Requirements: maximum of 18 people. Cost: $650, includes air charter from San Diego to Bahia de Los Angeles, fishing license, instruction and leadership. Sponsor: tour operator. Contact: Nature Expeditions International, 599 College Ave., Palo Alto, CA 94306.

United States

CALIFORNIA

Channel Islands, Pt. Hueneme: Season: year round. Duration: 1 day to 1 week. Carrier: 55-foot motor vessel. Departures: Pt. Hueneme. Accommodations: bunks, food and drink extra. Features: dive around the islands of Anacapa, Santa Cruz, Santa Rosa and San Miguel. Requirements: BC's and C-cards required unless class situation, limited to 32 on day trips, 24 if more than 1 day. Cost: $20 per day, includes trip fare only. Sponsor: dive boat. Contact: Sea Ventures, 2805 Palma Dr., Ventura, CA 93003.

Santa Barbara, Channel Islands: Season: year round. Duration: mini vacations are 1 to 5 days. Carrier: 65-foot motor vessel *Truth*. Departures: Santa Barbara. Accommodations: berth, all meals and soft drinks. Features: diving, spearfishing, lobstering around 8 islands. Requirements: must bring all diving gear. Cost: $57.50 per day for individuals, group rates available, includes air. Sponsor: dive boat. Contact: Truth Aquatics, Inc. Sea Landing, Santa Barbara Harbor, Santa Barbara, CA 93109.

FLORIDA

Florida Caves: Season: May and June. Duration: 7 days. Carrier: not specified. Departures: Jacksonville or Orlando, FL. Accommodations: first class hotel rooms, double occupancy, breakfasts and dinners. Features: cave diving at Itchticknee River, The Pot Holes, Orange Grove, Peacock Spring, Blue Spring, perhaps seeing the rare Manatee. Requirements: C-card, personal diving gear including BC and gauge. Cost: $200-$250, includes transportation from departure city, guide, air, tanks, backpack, weightbelt. Sponsor: organization. Contact: American Association of Certified Scuba Divers, Inc., 1066 Westover Road, Stamford, CT 06902.

Florida Keys: Season: April-June, September-December, excluding holiday weekends. Duration: minimum 3 nights. Carrier: not included. Departures: Islamorada, FL. Accommodations: efficiency units with a minimum double occupancy. Features: 4 hour trips on day boat to Florida Keys. Requirements: minimum 4, maximum 10 persons. Cost: $26 per day, includes all air, tanks, weightbelt. Sponsor: resort operator. Contact: Coral Reef Resort, Inc., P.O. Box 575, Islamorada, FL 33036.

Florida Keys, Bimini: Season: April-October for the Bahamas, October-March for the Florida Keys. Duration: 3 to 7 days. Carrier: 40-foot motor vessel *Sea Fever*. Departures: Bimini or Key Largo, FL. Accommodations: bunk beds, all meals. Features: wreck, deep wall and night diving. Requirements: C-card, minimum of 4 people. Cost: $60 per day, includes unlimited air, tanks, weightbelts. Sponsor: dive boat. Contact: Capt. Tom Guarino, Sea Fever Cruises, P.O. Box 1335, Key Largo, FL 33037.

Florida Keys, Bahama Islands: Season: year round. Duration: 3 to 7 days. Carrier:

64-foot motor vessel. Departures: Sunshine Key, FL. Accommodations: bunk beds, all meals. Features: for all levels of experience, diving Cay Cal and Dry Tortugas Islands. Requirements: group of 25. Cost: $40 per day. Sponsor: dive boat/dive shop. Contact: Sunshine Key Aqua Center, RR L Box 790-L, Holiday Inn Travel Park, Sunshine Key, FL 33043.

Florida Keys, Cay Sal Bank Area. Season: April-October. Duration: 3, 4 or 5 days. Carrier: 50-foot motor vessel *Plus Ultra*. Departures: Key Largo, FL. Accommodations: bunks, breakfast and dinner. Features: unlimited diving, a great black hole, 5 blue holes, night dives, wrecks, lobstering, fish. Requirements: minimum of 7, maximum of 10 people, divers supply their own equipment. Cost: $75 for 3 days. Sponsor: dive boat. Contact: Capt. Bob Klein, Holiday Inn Scuba Shop, MM100, Key Largo, FL 33037.

HAWAII

Kona Coast: Season: year round. Duration: 7 days. Carrier: Continental and Hawaiian Airlines. Departures: most major U.S. cities. Accommodations: selection of hotels and condominiums available, meals not included. Features: 6 days of diving, 14 tanks total. Requirements: C-card. Cost: $391 and up depending on choice of accommodations, excludes airfare, includes all diving, boat, guide. Sponsor: tour operator. Contact: Bay Travel Diving Adventures, 2435 East Coast Hwy., Corona Del Mar, CA 92625.

Kailua-Kona: Season: year round. Duration: 6 days. Carrier: several. Departures: most major U.S. cities. Accommodations:

apartments at Hale Kona Kai Condominiums, double occupancy, buffet lunch. Features: diving along the Kona Coast, coral gardens, abundant marine life, circle tour of island. Requirements: bring personal diving equipment. Cost: $349, excludes airfare, includes dive boats, guides, tanks, backpacks, weightbelts. Sponsor: tour operator. Contact: Go Diving, Inc., 715 Florida Ave. S., Minneapolis, MN 55426.

Hawaiian Islands: Season: year round. Duration: minimum 2 days up to several weeks. Carrier: 90-foot aluminum motor vessel especially built and equipped for diving cruises. Departures: Lahaina, Maui or Kailua-Kona, Hawaii. Accommodations: 14 air-conditioned staterooms, all meals. Features: cruising and diving throughout the islands on luxurious and comfortable boat. Requirements: C-card for use of scuba equipment. Cost: $299 and up, includes everything except beverages between meals. Sponsor: dive boat. Contact: Pacific Sportdiving Co., 4104 Anaheim St., Long Beach, CA 90804.

MICHIGAN

Lake Superior, Isle Royale: Season: June-September. Duration: minimum of 2 days. Carrier: 36-foot motor vessel. Departures: Grand Portage, MN. Accommodations: bunks, all meals. Features: diving, photography Isle Royale National Park. Requirements: C-card, bring personal diving equipment, maximum of 6 people. Cost: $30 per day, unlimited air, tanks, weightbelt. Sponsor: dive boat/dive shop. Contact: Inter-Space U/W Photos and Dive Tours, 6060 5th St. NE, Minneapolis, MN 55432.

NEW YORK

Long Island, Freeport: Season: not specified. Duration: open. Carrier: 42-foot motor vessel *Sea Hunter*. Departures: Freeport. Accommodations: not included. Features: wrecks along coasts of Long Island and New Jersey where over 4000 ships have been lost, specializing in diving the USS San Diego and SS Oregon. Requirements: maximum of 14 people, bring own equipment or rent. Cost: $25 per day. Sponsor: dive boat. Contact: Capt. John Lachenmeyer, phone (516) 499-9107.

WISCONSIN

Lake Michigan, Green Bay: Season: May-October. Duration: 3 days. Carrier: provide own transportation to Gills Rock. Accommodations: housekeeping A-frame cottages, prepare own meals. Features: tours by reservation, a variety of dive sites for all experience levels. Requirements: best suited for dive clubs and groups. Cost: $68, including unlimited air, boat trips. Sponsor: resort operator. Contact: On the Rocks, Rt. 1 Box 297, Ellison Bay, WI 54210.

Appendix A

Recommended Exposure Protection

Temperature Zone (Farenheit)	Minimum Recommended/Protection
85° +	Wet suit not necessary
75° - 85°	⅛" to 3/16" wet suit (hood may not be necessary)
60° - 70°	Full 3/16" suit
50° - 60°	Full ¼" wet suit
45° - 50°	Full ⅜" wet suit, dry suit, or inflatable suit
below 45°	Special thermal suit

Appendix B

Pressure Increases with Depth

Pressure, atmospheres, absolute	Depth, feet
1	surface
2	33
3	66
4	99
5	132
6	165
10	297
	and so on

Appendix C

Tank Markings

All scuba tanks must carry cylinder identification markings like these:

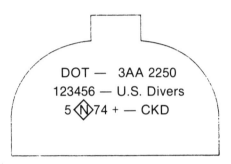

Definitions

DOT: Department of Transportation, agency which sets safety standards for high-pressure vessels. Tanks manufactured before 1970 may be stamped ICC for Interstate Commerce Commission, which performed those functions at that time.

3AA: type of steel (chrome molybednum) used in tank. Aluminum tanks bear the designation SP6498 (Alcon Aluminum).

2250: rated working pressure of the tank, in pounds per square inch. Can range from 1800 to 6,000.

123456: the tank's serial number. It may be preceded by a letter.

U.S. Divers: Name of company marketing the tank.

5⬦74: hydrostatic testing information. This line tells you the tank was tested in May (5th month) of 1974. The ⬦ is the symbol of the hydrostatic testing agency. The + indicates that the tank may be filled to 10% over its working pressure. Subsequent tests should be documented with similar date markings.

CKD: the manufacturer's symbol.

Appendix D

Diving Physics

A number of physical laws govern man's ability to operate in a submarine environment. Here is a brief description of those laws most important to sport divers. All scuba divers should be thoroughly familiar with the effects of these laws, and the methods of preventing or treating problems they may create. This material is intended as an introduction, and should be augmented with further reading.

Archimedes' Principle

"Any object wholly or partially immersed in a liquid is buoyed up by a force equal to the weight of the liquid displaced."

Effects: the displacement of a diver — and of many pieces of his equipment — can be calculated and adjusted for positive, negative, or neutral buoyancy.

Boyle's Law

"If the temperature of a gas is kept constant, the volume varies inversely with the absolute pressure while the density varies directly in proportion to the absolute pressure."

Formula: $PV=C$ where P = absolute pressure
V = volume
C = a constant

Effects: External water pressure can cause "squeeze" of the sinuses, stomach, intestines, eyes, teeth, and even lungs (on breathhold dives)(. Air spaces in equipment such as masks and wet suits can also be squeezed.

Air breathed under pressure and not allowed to escape normally (through regular exhalations) can cause embolisms of the lungs or other tissues, various types of emphysema, or pneumothorax (lung collapse).

Emergency cartridges in some flotation equipment may not generate enough pressure to inflate to lifting capacity at great depths. Vests and compensators must be vented on ascent to avoid ruptures.

Boyle's Law can help calculate the bottom time of a tankful of air. Assuming the breathing rate stays the same, a tank that lasts an hour on the surface would last a half hour at two atmospheres (33 feet), since doubling the absolute pressure halves the bottom time. At three atm you'd have 1/3 as long, as 4 atm, ¼ as long.

Charles' Law

"At a constant pressure the volume of a gas increases when the temperature increases."

Formula: $PV = RT$ or $\dfrac{PV + R}{T}$ where P = absolute pressure
V = volume
T = absolute pressure
R = a universal constant
for all gases

Effects: Since the air trapped in a scuba tank cannot expand in volume, the pressure inside the tank varies with the absolute temperature. A tank filled hot can lose up to 200 psi in cooling. Leaving a full tank in the hot sun could cause the pressure to exceed the D.O.T. rating.

Dalton's Law

"The total pressure exerted by a mixture of gases is the sum of the pressure that would be exerted by each of the gases if it alone were present and occupied the total volume."

Formula: $P_{Total} = PP_A + PP_B + PP_C \ldots$
and

$$PP_A = P_{Total} \times \frac{\% \, Vol._A}{100\%}$$

Where P_{Total} = Total absolute pressure of gas mixture

PP_A = Partial pressure of gas A
PP_B = Partial pressure of gas B
PP_C = Partial pressure of gas C

Effects: When compressed air is inhaled, abnormally high mounts of oxygen, nitrogen, and other gases enter the lungs and bloodstream. The *partial pressure* of oxygen (21% of the total volume of compressed air inhaled) would cause oxygen poisoning at 297 feet. Similarly, an "overdose" of nitrogen at depth can cause nitrogen narcosis ("rapture of the deep").

Carbon dioxide is also produced in greater quantities when breathing under pressure. If it is not properly exhaled, it can lead to CO_2 poisoning, which causes blackouts.

Henry's Law

"With temperature constant, the quantity of a gas that goes into solution of any given liquid is in direct proportion to the partial pressure of the gas."

Effects: The diver's blood stream becomes saturated with air at the ambient pressure. A sudden decrease in pressure (as in a too-rapid ascent) can cause the super-saturated nitrogen to bubble out of solution in the blood, which could cause decompression sickness ("the bends"). This potentially fatal malady can be avoided by making staged asents from deep dives (Appendix F) and is treated by recompressing the diver in a hyperbaric chamber and decompressing him in stages.

Newton's Third Law of Motion

"Every action is opposed by an equal and opposite reaction."

Effect: In kicking with fins, the diver is actually pushing against the water, and the water pushes back, providing the desired propulsion.

Appendix E

"No-Decompression" Limits

Most sport divers never dive deep enough for long enough periods to necessitate decompression. The following table shows that, for instance, a diver reaching 100 feet in a dive must begin his descent within 25 minutes of leaving the surface to avoid decompression.

However, since nitrogen can remain in solution in the blood for several hours, "bottom time" must be accumulated for all dives within any 12-hour period. Tables for computing repetitive dive decompression appear in Appendix F. Any diver contemplating a deep dive or multiple dives should carry waterproof tables or a decompression meter with him to help him calculate his decompression time and stops underwater.

Depth (Ft.)	Bottom Time (min.)
(less than 33)	(no limit)
35	310
40	200
50	100
60	60
70	50
80	40
90	30
100	25
110	20
120	15
130	10
140	10
150 to 190	5

Appendix F

U.S. Navy Standard Air Decompression Table

To prevent the development of decompression sickness, special decompression tables have been established. These tables take into consideration the amount of nitrogen absorbed by the body at various depths for given time periods. They also consider allowable pressure gradients which can exist without excessive bubble formation, and the different gas elimination rates associated with various body tissues.

Stage decompression, requiring stops of specific durations at given depths, is used for air diving because of its operational simplicity. It will be found that the decompression tables require longer stops at more frequent intervals as the surface is approached due to the higher gas expansion ratios which occur at shallow depths.

The USN decompression tables are the result of years of scientific study, calculation, animal and human experimentation, and extensive field experience. They represent the best overall information available, but as depth and time increases, they tend to be less accurate and require careful application.

This appendix is not designed to provide a full education in the use of these tables, but to act as an introduction and reference source. It is strongly recommended that you take an advanced diver training course for a thorough understanding of decompression and how to avoid and treat it.

The following tables present a series of decompression schedules which must be rigidly followed during an ascent following an air dive:

> Standard Air Decompression Table
> No Decompression Limits and
> Repetive Dive Table

The Residual Nitrogen Timetable for Repetive Air Dives provides information relating to the planning of repetive dives.

Selection of Decompression Schedule: The decompression schedules of all the tables are given in 10 or 20-foot depth increments and, usually, 10-minute bottom time increments. Depth and bottom time combinations from actual dives, however, rarely exactly match one of the decompression schedules listed in the table being used. As assurance that the selected decompression schedule is always conservative — (A) always select the schedule depth to be equal to or the next depth greater than the actual depth to which the dive was conducted, and (B) always select the schedule bottom time to be equal to or the next longer bottom time than the actual bottom time of the dive.

If the Standard Air Decompression Table, for example, was being used to select the correct schedule for a dive to 97 feet for 31 minutes, decompression would be carried out in accordance with the 100/40 schedule.

NEVER ATTEMPT TO INTERPOLATE BETWEEN DECOMPRESSION SCHEDULES

If the diver was exceptionally cold during the dive, or if his work load was relatively strenuous, the next longer decompression schedule than the one he would normally follow should be selected. For example, the normal schedule for a dive to 90 feet for 34 minutes would be the 90/40 schedule. If the diver were exceptionally cold or fatigued, he should decompress, according to the 90/50 schedule.

Rules During Ascent: After the correct decompression schedule has been selected, it is imperative that it be exactly followed. Without exception, decompression must be completed according to the selected schedule unless the directions to alter the schedule are given by a diving medical officer.

Ascend at a rate of 60 feet per minute. The diver's chest should be located as close as possible to the stop depth.

The decompression stop times, as specified in each decompression schedule, begin as soon as the diver reaches the stop depth. Upon completion of the specified stop time, the diver ascends to the next stop, or to the surface, at the proper ascent rate. DO NOT INCLUDE ASCENT TIME AS PART OF STOP TIME.

The Standard Air Decompression Table shows bottom times and depths considered safe for sport divers. The diver who exceeds these limits subjects himself to what the Navy calls "exceptional exposure," a danger zone that should only be entered by expert divers under the supervision of a trained diving medical officer.

Repetitive Dives: During the 12-hour period after an air dive, the quantity of residual nitrogen in a diver's body will gradually reduce to its normal level. If, within this period, the diver is to make a second dive — called a repetitive dive — he must consider his present residual nitrogen level when planning for the dive.

Upon completing his first dive, the diver will have a Repetitive Group Designation assigned to him by either the Standard Air Table or the No-Decompression Table. The Table permits this designation to be determined at any time during the surface interval.

Just prior to beginning the repetitive dive time should be determined using the Residual Nitrogen Table. This time is added to the actual bottom time of the equivalent single dive. decompression from the repetitive dive is conducted using the depth and bottom time of the equivalent single dive to select the appropriate decompression schedule. Equivalent single dives which require the use of exceptional exposure decompression schedules should, whenever possible, be avoided.

To assist in determining the decompression schedule for a repetitive dive, a systematic repetitive dive worksheet should always be used.

If still another dive is to follow the repetitive dive, the depth and bottom time of the first equivalent single dive should be inserted in part 1 of the second repetitive dive worksheet.

No-Decompression Limits and Repetitive Group Designation Table for No-Decompression Air Dives: The No-Decompression Table serves two purposes. First it sum-
(continued on page 200)

U. S. NAVY STANDARD AIR DECOMPRESSION TABLE

Depth (feet)	Bottom time (min)	Time first stop (min:sec)	Decompression stops (feet) 50	40	30	20	10	Total ascent (min:sec)	Repetitive group
40	200						0	0:40	*
	210	0:30					2	2:40	N
	230	0:30					7	7:40	N
	250	0:30					11	11:40	O
	270	0:30					15	15:40	O
	300	0:30					19	19:40	Z
50	100						0	0:50	*
	110	0:40					3	3:50	L
	120	0:40					5	5:50	M
	140	0:40					10	10:50	M
	160	0:40					21	21:50	N
	180	0:40					29	29:50	O
	200	0:40					35	35:50	O
	220	0:40					40	40:50	Z
	240	0:40					47	47:50	Z
60	60						0	1:00	*
	70	0:50					2	3:00	K
	80	0:50					7	8:00	L
	100	0:50					14	15:00	M
	120	0:50					26	27:00	N
	140	0:50					39	40:00	O
	160	0:50					48	49:00	Z
	180	0:50					56	57:00	Z
	200	0:40				1	69	71:00	Z
70	50						0	1:10	*
	60	1:00					8	9:10	K
	70	1:00					14	15:10	L
	80	1:00					18	19:10	M
	90	1:00					23	24:10	N
	100	1:00					33	34:10	N
	110	0:50				2	41	44:10	O
	120	0:50				4	47	52:10	O
	130	0:50				6	52	59:10	O
	140	0:50				8	56	65:10	Z
	150	0:50				9	61	71:10	Z
	160	0:50				13	72	86:10	Z
	170	0:50				19	79	99:10	Z

* See No Decompression Table for repetitive groups

Courtesy of U.S. Navy

U.S NAVY STANDARD AIR DECOMPRESSION TABLE

Depth (feet)	Bottom time (min)	Time first stop (min:sec)	Decompression stops (feet) 50	40	30	20	10	Total ascent (min:sec)	Repetitive group
80	40						0	1:20	*
	50	1:10					10	11:20	K
	60	1:10					17	18:20	L
	70	1:10					23	24:20	M
	80	1:00				2	31	34:20	N
	90	1:00				7	39	47:20	N
	100	1:00				11	46	58:20	O
	110	1:00				13	53	67:20	O
	120	1:00				17	56	74:20	Z
	130	1:00				19	63	83:20	Z
	140	1:00				26	69	96:20	Z
	150	1:00				32	77	110:20	Z
90	30						0	1:30	*
	40	1:20					7	8:30	J
	50	1:20					18	19:30	L
	60	1:20					25	26:30	M
	70	1:10				7	30	38:30	N
	80	1:10				13	40	54:30	N
	90	1:10				18	48	67:30	O
	100	1:10				21	54	76:30	Z
	110	1:10				24	61	86:30	Z
	120	1:10				32	68	101:30	Z
	130	1:00			5	36	74	116:30	Z
100	25						0	1:40	*
	30	1:30					3	4:40	I
	40	1:30					15	16:40	K
	50	1:20				2	24	27:40	L
	60	1:20				9	28	38:40	N
	70	1:20				17	39	57:40	O
	80	1:20				23	48	72:40	O
	90	1:10			3	23	57	84:40	Z
	100	1:10			7	23	66	97:40	Z
	110	1:10			10	34	72	117:40	Z
	120	1:10			12	41	78	132:40	Z
110	20						0	1:50	*
	25	1:40					3	4:50	H
	30	1:40					7	8:50	J
	40	1:30				2	21	24:50	L
	50	1:30				8	26	35:50	M
	60	1:30				18	36	55:50	N
	70	1:20			1	23	48	73:50	O
	80	1:20			7	23	57	88:50	Z
	90	1:20			12	30	64	107:50	Z
	100	1:20			15	37	72	125:50	Z

* See No Decompression Table for repetitive groups

Courtesy of U.S. Navy

U. S. NAVY STANDARD AIR DECOMPRESSION TABLE

Depth (feet)	Bottom time (min)	Time to first stop (min:sec)	Decompression stops (feet) 70	60	50	40	30	20	10	Total ascent (min:sec)	Repetitive group
120	15								0	2:00	*
	20	1:50							2	4:00	H
	25	1:50							6	8:00	I
	30	1:50							14	16:00	J
	40	1:40						5	25	32:00	L
	50	1:40						15	31	48:00	N
	60	1:30					2	22	45	71:00	O
	70	1:30					9	23	55	89:00	O
	80	1:30					15	27	63	107:00	Z
	90	1:30					19	37	74	132:00	Z
	100	1:30					23	45	80	150:00	Z
130	10								0	2:10	*
	15	2:00							1	3:10	F
	20	2:00							4	6:10	H
	25	2:00							10	12:10	J
	30	1:50						3	18	23:10	M
	40	1:50						10	25	37:10	N
	50	1:40					3	21	37	63:10	O
	60	1:40					9	23	52	86:10	Z
	70	1:40					16	24	61	103:10	Z
	80	1:30				3	19	35	72	131:10	Z
	90	1:30				8	19	45	80	154:10	Z

Depth (feet)	Bottom time (min)	Time to first stop (min:sec)	Decompression stops (feet) 90	80	70	60	50	40	30	20	10	Total ascent (min:sec)	Repetitive group
140	10										0	2:20	*
	15	2:10									2	4:20	G
	20	2:10									6	8:20	I
	25	2:00								2	14	18:20	J
	30	2:00								5	21	28:20	K
	40	1:50							2	16	26	46:20	N
	50	1:50							6	24	44	76:20	O
	60	1:50							16	23	56	97:20	Z
	70	1:40						4	19	32	68	125:20	Z
	80	1:40						10	23	41	79	155:20	Z

* **See No Decompression Table for repetitive groups**

Courtesy of U.S. Navy

U.S. NAVY STANDARD AIR DECOMPRESSION TABLE

Depth (feet)	Bottom time (min)	Time to first stop (min:sec)	90	80	70	60	50	40	30	20	10	Total ascent (min:sec)	Repetitive group
150	5										0	2:30	C
	10	2:20									1	3:30	E
	15	2:20									3	5:30	G
	20	2:10								2	7	11:30	H
	25	2:10								4	17	23:30	K
	30	2:10								8	24	34:30	L
	40	2:00							5	19	33	59:30	N
	50	2:00							12	23	51	88:30	O
	60	1:50						3	19	26	62	112:30	Z
	70	1:50						11	19	39	75	146:30	Z
	80	1:40					1	17	19	50	84	173:30	Z
160	5										0	2:40	D
	10	2:30									1	3:40	F
	15	2:20								1	4	7:40	H
	20	2:20								3	11	16:40	J
	25	2:20								7	20	29:40	K
	30	2:10							2	11	25	40:40	M
	40	2:10							7	23	39	71:40	N
	50	2:00						2	16	23	55	98:40	Z
	60	2:00						9	19	33	69	132:40	Z

Depth (feet)	Bottom time (min)	Time to first stop (min:sec)	110	100	90	80	70	60	50	40	30	20	10	Total ascent (min:sec)	Repetitive group
170	5												0	2:50	D
	10	2:40											2	4:50	F
	15	2:30										2	5	9:50	H
	20	2:30										4	15	21:50	J
	25	2:20									2	7	23	34:50	L
	30	2:20									4	13	26	45:50	M
	40	2:10								1	10	23	45	81:50	O
	50	2:10								5	18	23	61	109:50	Z
	60	2:00							2	15	22	37	74	152:50	Z
180	5												0	3:00	D
	10	2:50											3	6:00	F
	15	2:40										3	6	12:00	I
	20	2:30									1	5	17	26:00	K
	25	2:30									3	10	24	40:00	L
	30	2:30									6	17	27	53:00	N
	40	2:20								3	14	23	50	93:00	O
	50	2:10							2	9	19	30	65	128:00	Z
	60	2:10							5	16	19	44	81	168:00	Z
190	5												0	3:10	D
	10	2:50										1	3	7:10	G
	15	2:50										4	7	14:10	I
	20	2:40									2	6	20	31:10	K
	25	2:40									5	11	25	44:10	M
	30	2:30								1	8	19	32	63:10	N
	40	2:30								8	14	23	55	103:10	O

* See No Decompression Table for repetitive groups
Courtesy of U.S. Navy

RESIDUAL NITROGEN TIMETABLE FOR REPETITIVE AIR DIVES

*Dives following surface intervals of more than 12 hours are not repetitive dives. Use actual bottom times in the Standard Air Decompression Tables to compute decompression for such dives.

Repetitive group at the beginning of the surface interval

Surface interval times (given as earliest time / latest time) by repetitive group at the beginning of the surface interval (row) and NEW GROUP DESIGNATION (column):

Beginning group	Z	O	N	M	L	K	J	I	H	G	F	E	D	C	B	A
A																0:10 / 12:00*
B															0:10 / 2:10	2:11 / 12:00*
C														0:10 / 1:39	1:40 / 2:49	2:50 / 12:00*
D													0:10 / 1:09	1:10 / 2:38	2:39 / 5:48	5:49 / 12:00*
E												0:10 / 0:54	0:55 / 1:57	1:58 / 3:22	3:23 / 6:32	6:33 / 12:00*
F											0:10 / 0:45	0:46 / 1:29	1:30 / 2:28	2:29 / 3:57	3:58 / 7:05	7:06 / 12:00*
G										0:10 / 0:40	0:41 / 1:15	1:16 / 1:59	2:00 / 2:58	2:59 / 4:25	4:26 / 7:35	7:36 / 12:00*
H									0:10 / 0:36	0:37 / 1:06	1:07 / 1:41	1:42 / 2:23	2:24 / 3:20	3:21 / 4:49	4:50 / 7:59	8:00 / 12:00*
I								0:10 / 0:33	0:34 / 0:59	1:00 / 1:29	1:30 / 2:02	2:03 / 2:44	2:45 / 3:43	3:44 / 5:12	5:13 / 8:21	8:22 / 12:00*
J							0:10 / 0:31	0:32 / 0:54	0:55 / 1:19	1:20 / 1:47	1:48 / 2:20	2:21 / 3:04	3:05 / 4:02	4:03 / 5:40	5:41 / 8:40	8:41 / 12:00*
K						0:10 / 0:28	0:29 / 0:49	0:50 / 1:11	1:12 / 1:35	1:36 / 2:03	2:04 / 2:38	2:39 / 3:21	3:22 / 4:19	4:20 / 5:48	5:49 / 8:58	8:59 / 12:00*
L					0:10 / 0:26	0:27 / 0:45	0:46 / 1:04	1:05 / 1:25	1:26 / 1:49	1:50 / 2:19	2:20 / 2:53	2:54 / 3:36	3:37 / 4:35	4:36 / 6:02	6:03 / 9:12	9:13 / 12:00*
M				0:10 / 0:25	0:26 / 0:42	0:43 / 0:59	1:00 / 1:18	1:19 / 1:39	1:40 / 2:05	2:06 / 2:34	2:35 / 3:08	3:09 / 3:52	3:53 / 4:49	4:50 / 6:18	6:19 / 9:28	9:29 / 12:00*
N			0:10 / 0:24	0:25 / 0:39	0:40 / 0:54	0:55 / 1:11	1:12 / 1:30	1:31 / 1:53	1:54 / 2:18	2:19 / 2:47	2:48 / 3:22	3:23 / 4:04	4:05 / 5:03	5:04 / 6:32	6:33 / 9:43	9:44 / 12:00*
O		0:10 / 0:23	0:24 / 0:36	0:37 / 0:51	0:52 / 1:07	1:08 / 1:24	1:25 / 1:43	1:44 / 2:04	2:05 / 2:29	2:30 / 2:59	3:00 / 3:33	3:34 / 4:17	4:18 / 5:16	5:17 / 6:44	6:45 / 9:54	9:55 / 12:00*
(Z)	0:10 / 0:22	0:23 / 0:34	0:35 / 0:48	0:49 / 1:02	1:03 / 1:18	1:19 / 1:36	1:37 / 1:55	1:56 / 2:17	2:18 / 2:42	2:43 / 3:10	3:11 / 3:45	3:46 / 4:29	4:30 / 5:27	5:28 / 6:56	6:57 / 10:05	10:06 / 12:00*
NEW → GROUP DESIGNATION	Z	O	N	M	L	K	J	I	H	G	F	E	D	C	B	A

RESIDUAL NITROGEN TIMES (MINUTES)

REPETITIVE DIVE DEPTH	Z	O	N	M	L	K	J	I	H	G	F	E	D	C	B	A
40	257	241	213	187	161	138	116	101	87	73	61	49	37	25	17	7
50	169	160	142	124	111	99	87	76	66	56	47	38	29	21	13	6
60	122	117	107	97	88	79	70	61	52	44	36	30	24	17	11	5
70	100	96	87	80	72	64	57	50	43	37	31	26	20	15	9	4
80	84	80	73	68	61	54	48	43	38	32	28	23	18	13	8	4
90	73	70	64	58	53	47	43	38	33	29	24	20	16	11	7	3
100	64	62	57	52	48	43	38	34	30	26	22	18	14	10	7	3
110	57	55	51	47	42	38	34	31	27	24	20	16	13	10	6	3
120	52	50	46	43	39	35	32	28	25	21	18	15	12	9	6	3
130	46	44	40	38	35	31	28	25	22	19	16	13	11	8	6	3
140	42	40	38	35	32	29	26	23	20	18	15	12	10	7	5	2
150	40	38	35	32	30	27	24	22	19	17	14	12	9	7	5	2
160	37	36	33	31	28	26	23	20	18	16	13	11	9	6	4	2
170	35	34	31	29	26	24	22	19	17	15	13	10	8	6	4	2
180	32	31	29	27	25	22	20	18	16	14	12	10	8	6	4	2
190	31	30	28	26	24	21	19	17	15	13	11	10	8	6	4	2

RESIDUAL NITROGEN TIMES (MINUTES)

Courtesy of U.S. Navy

NO-DECOMPRESSION LIMITS AND REPETITIVE GROUP DESIGNATION TABLE FOR NO-DECOMPRESSION AIR DIVES

Depth (feet)	No-decom- pression limits (min)	A	B	C	D	E	F	G	H	I	J	K	L	M	N	O
10		60	120	210	300											
15		35	70	110	160	225	350									
20		25	50	75	100	135	180	240	325							
25		20	35	55	75	100	125	160	195	245	315					
30		15	30	45	60	75	95	120	145	170	205	250	310			
35	310	5	15	25	40	50	60	80	100	120	140	160	190	220	270	310
40	200	5	15	25	30	40	50	70	80	100	110	130	150	170	200	
50	100		10	15	25	30	40	50	60	70	80	90	100			
60	60		10	15	20	25	30	40	50	55	60					
70	50		5	10	15	20	30	35	40	45	50					
80	40		5	10	15	20	25	30	35	40						
90	30		5	10	12	15	20	25	30							
100	25		5	7	10	15	20	22	25							
110	20			5	10	13	15	20								
120	15			5	10	12	15									
130	10			5	8	10										
140	10			5	7	10										
150	5			5												
160	5					5										
170	5					5										
180	5					5										
190	5					5										

Courtesy of U.S. Navy

marizes all the depth and bottom time combinations for which no decompression is required. Secondly, it provides the repetitive group designation for each no-decompression dive. Even though decompression is not required, an amount of nitrogen remains in the diver's tissues after every dive. If he dives again within a 12 hour period, the diver must consider this residual nitrogen when calculating his decompression.

Each depth listed in the No-Decompression Table has a corresponding no-decompression limit given in minutes. This limit is the maximum bottom time that a diver may spend at that depth without requiring decompression. The columns to the right of the no-decompression limits column are used to determine the repetitive group designation which must be assigned to a diver subsequent to every dive. To find the repetitive group designation enter the table at the depth equal to or next greater than the actual depth of the dive. Follow that row to the right to the bottom time equal to or next greater than the actual bottom time of the dive. Follow that column upward to the repetitive group designation.

Depths above 35 feet do not have a specific no-decompression limit. They are, however, restricted in that they only provide repetitive group designations for bottom times up to between 5 and 6 hours. These bottom times are considered the limitations of the No-Decompression Table and no field requirement for diving should extend beyond them.

Any dive below 35 feet which has a bottom time greater than the no-decompression limit given in this table is a decompression dive and should be conducted in accordance with the Standard Air Table.

Residual Nitrogen Timetable for Repetitive Air Dives:

The quantity of residual nitrogen in a diver's body immediately after a dive is expressed by the repetitive group designation assigned to him by either the Standard Air Table or the No-Decompression Table. The upper portion of the Residual Nitrogen Table is composed of various intervals between 10 minutes and 12 hours, expressed in hours: minutes (2:21 = 2

hours 21 minutes). Each interval has two limits; a minimum time (top limit) and a maximum time (bottom limit).

Residual nitrogen times, corresponding to the depth of the repetitive dive, are given in the body of the lower portion of the table. To determine the residual nitrogen time for a repetitive dive, locate the diver's repetitive group designation from his previous dive along the diagonal line above the table. Read horizontally to the interval in which the diver's surface interval lies. The time spent on the surface must be between or equal to the limits of the selected interval.

Next, read vertically downwards to the new repetitive group designation. This designation corresponds to the present quantity of residual nitrogen in the diver's body. Continue downward in this same column to the row which represents the depth of the repetitive dive. The time given at the intersection is the residual nitrogen time, in minutes, to be applied to the repetitive dive.

If the surface interval is less than 10 minutes, the residual nitrogen time is the bottom time of the previous dive. All of the residual nitrogen will be passed out of the diver's body after 12 hours, so a dive conducted after a 12 hour surface interval is not a repetitive dive.

There is one exception to this table. In some instances, when the repetitive dive is to the same or greater depth than the previous dive, the residual nitrogen time may be longer than the actual bottom time of the previous dive. In this event, add the actual bottom line time of the previous dive to the actual bottom time of the repetitive dive to obtain the equivalent single dive time.

Example—
Problem — A repetitive dive is to be made to 98 fsw for an estimated bottom time of 15 minutes. The previous dive was to a depth of 102 fsw and had a 48 minute bottom time. The diver's surface interval is 6 hours 28 minutes (6:28). What decompression schedule should be used for the repetitive dive?

Solution — Using the repetitive dive worksheet —

REPETITIVE DIVE WORKSHEET

I. PREVIOUS DIVE:
48 minutes   ☑ Standard Air Table

102 feet   ☐ No-Decompression Table

M repetitive group designation

II. SURFACE INTERVAL:
6 hours **28** minutes on surface.

Repetitive group from I **M**

New repetitive group from surface

Residual Nitrogen Timetable **B**

III. RESIDUAL NITROGEN TIME:
98 feet (depth of repetitive dive)

New repetitive group from II. **B**

Residual nitrogen time from

Residual Nitrogen Timetable **7**

IV. EQUIVALENT SINGLE DIVE TIME:
7 minutes, residual nitrogen time from III.

+ **15** minutes, actual bottom time of repetitive dive.

= **22** minutes, equivalent single dive time.

V. DECOMPRESSION FOR REPETITIVE DIVE:
22 minutes, equivalent single dive time from IV.

98 feet, depth of repetitive dive

Decompression from (check one):
☐ Standard Air Table ☐ No-Decompression Table
☐ Surface Table Using Oxygen ☐ Surface Table Using Air
☑ No decompression required

Decompression Stops: _____ feet _____ minutes

     _____ feet _____ minutes

     _____ feet _____ minutes

Schedule used _____   _____ feet _____ minutes

Repetitive group _____   _____ feet _____ minutes

Courtesy of U.S. Navy

Appendix G

Dive Planning

In a well-planned dive, the divers always return to the boat or shore with plenty of air left. Here are some general rules of proper air planning:

1. Plan to complete your dive with a minimum of 300 psig in your tank (500 psig is recommended).
2. The first diver to reach the turnaround point dictates the air planning for the entire group.
3. On decompression dives, always plan to have at least a third of your air supply left when you begin your decompression.
4. Always hold enough air in reserve to cover any unusual situations that might come up, regardless of your other planning.

Use the following formula to determine your air consumption rate at the surface or any given depth:

$$\frac{PSI \div t}{33/33 + d/33}$$

PSI = PSI consumed in timed swim at a constant depth
t = Duration of timed swim
d = Depth of timed swim

To calculate the actual volume of a partially charged cylinder, use:

$$\frac{P^2 \times V^1}{P^1} = V^2$$

where P^1 = pressure of fully charged cylinder

P^2 = pressure gauge reading

V^1 = rated volume of cylinder at P^1

V^2 = volume of cylinder at P^2

Once you know your air consumption rate and the amount of air to be consumed, you can figure how much time may be spent a given depth this way:

$$\frac{t = Ac}{S.A.C.} \bullet \frac{33}{d + 33} \quad \text{where } t = \text{time (minutes)}$$

Ac = air consumed (psi)
S.A.C. = surface air consumption rate
d = depth (feet)

Remember that changes in your breathing rate due to increased activity or cold will alter all of these calculations so they should be considered *maximums*. For safety's sake, stay well within the limits you calculate for yourself.

Appendix H

Manufacturer Addresses

The following listing contains the name and address of each manufacturer represented in our "Equipment" and "Accessories" chapters:

AMF Voit*
3801 S. Harbor Blvd.
Santa Ana, CA 92704

Andreassen Enterprises
PO Box 2431
Rancho Palos Verdes,
CA 90274

Aquatic Research
Engineering, Inc.
205 Chester Ave.
Moorestown, NJ 08057

Aquatic Specialties
PO Box 65
Berwick, PA 18603

A.S. Newton, O.D.
575 W. 6th St.
San Pedro, CA 90731

Avon/Seagull Marine
1851 McGaw Ave.
Irvine, CA 92714

Bayleysuit, Inc.
900 S. Fortuna Blvd.
Fortuna, CA 95540

Belcher Industries, Inc.
PO Box 557412
Miami, FL 33155

Benson Optical
Company, Inc.

1812 Park Ave.
Minneapolis, MN 55440

Berkey Marketing
Companies
25-20 Brooklyn-Queens
Expwy. West
Woodside, NY 11377

Bonair Boats, Inc.
15501 W. 109th St.
Lenexa, KS 66219

Camp-Ways Inflatable
Boats
12915 S. Spring St.
Los Angeles, CA 90061

Carter Bag Company
29500 Green River
Gorge Rd.
Enumclaw, WA 98022

Catalina Marine
PO Box 983
San Pedro, CA 90733

Chronosport, Inc.
119 Rowayton Ave.
Rowayton, CT 06853

Cressi-Sub
Flagler Station
P.O. Box 014420
Miami, FL 33101

C-Slate Company
7904 W. 100th St.
Palos Hills, IL 60465

Dacor Corporation*
161 Northfield Rd.
Northfield, IL 60093

Del Mar Supplies
427 W. Palmyra St.
Orange, CA 92666

Divex
2245 Breaux Ave.
Harvey, LA 70059

Diving & Fishing Boats

1455 N. Hayworth Ave.
Los Angeles, CA 90046

Dolfino Division
Aqua-Leisure
  Industries, Inc.
PO Box 25
Avon, MA 02322

Elmo Manufacturing
  Corp.
32-10 57th St.
Woodside, NY 11377

fmRoberts Enterprises
Box 608
Dana Point, CA 92629

Fuji Photo USA, Inc.
350 Fifth Ave.
New York, NY 10001

Healthways*
Subsid. of Eldon
  Industries, Inc.
5340 W. 102nd St.
Los Angeles, CA 90045

Helle Engineering, Inc.
7198 Convoy Ct.
San Diego, CA 92111

Henderson Aquatics
Buck & Sassafras Sts.
Millville, NJ 08332

Hydro-Fairing
425 29th St.
Hermosa Beach,
  CA 90254

Hydro Photo
3909 13th Ave. S
Seattle, WA 98108

Ikelite Underwater
  Systems
3303 N. Illnois St.
Indianapolis, IN 46208

Image Devices, Inc.
1825 NE 149th St.
Miami, FL 33181

Imperial Manufacturing
  Company*
PO Box 4119
Bremerton, WA 98310

J.K. Gilbert Company
PO Box 95
Leesville, TX 78122

J.W. Fishers
  Manufacturing
  Company
Anthony St.
Tauton, MA 02780

Kent Corporation
1147 Greenridge Rd.
Jacksonville, FL 32207

Kitteredge Industries,
  Inc.
U.S. Rt. 1
Warren, ME 04864

L.A. Screw Products,

8401 Loch Lomond Dr.
Pico Rivera, CA 90660

Leonard Maggiore,
  Optician
69-03 Fresh Pond Rd.
Ridgewood, Queens, NY
  11227

Lord Byron, Ltd.
PO Box 6385
San Rafael, CA 94903

Nash Industries
6768 Crooked Palm Terr.
Miami Lakes, FL 33014

Nikonos/Ehrenreich
  Photo-Optical
  Industries, Inc.
623 Stewart Ave.
Garden City, NY 11530

Oceanic/Farallon*
1333 Old Country Rd.
Belmont, CA 94002

O'Neill
1071 41st Ave.
Santa Cruz, CA 95060

Orange Coast
  International
1537-C E. McFadden Pl.
Santa Ana, CA 92705

Parkway Fabricators*
241 Raritan St.
S. Amboy, NJ 08879

Pelican Products
23763 Madison St.
Torrance, CA 90505

Pennform Plastic
  Products, Inc.
365 Mulberry
Wyandotte, MI 48192

Princeton Tectonics
P.O. Box 764
Hightstown, NJ 08520

Proko International
12511 Beatrice St.
Los Angeles, CA 90066

Recta S.A.
Rue du Viaduc 3
CH-2501 Bienne
Switzerland

Rolex
665 5th Ave.
New York, NY 10022

Royak, Inc.
3510 La Grande Blvd.
Sacramento, CA 95823

Scubapro*
3105 Harcourt
Compton, CA 90221

Seaboard Products
PO Box 4275
Malibu, CA 90265

Seaquest, Inc.*
722 Genevieve St.,
  Suite N
Solano Beach, CA 92705

Sea Research/Bosco
PO Box 589
Bartow, FL 33830

Sea Sonics, Inc.
1224 E. Algonquin Rd.
Schaumburg, IL 60195

Sea Sports
10 Buckingham Pl.
Norwalk, CT 06851

Seatec*
425 W. Palmyra Ave.
Orange, CA 92666

Seatech Corporation
985 NW 95th St.
Miami, FL 33150

Serl Underwater
  Products
110 Glenn Way
Belmont, CA 94002

Sevylor USA, Inc.
6279 E. Slauson Ave.
Los Angeles, CA 90040

Shakespeare Products
241 E. Kalamazoo Ave.
Kalamazoo, MI 49007

Sherwood Selpac
  Corporation*
120 Church St.
Lockport, NY 14094

Sonic Research
5111 Santa Fe St.,
  Suite H
San Diego, CA 92109

Sound Wave Systems,
  Inc.
3001 Red Hill, Bldg. 1
Suite 102
Costa Mesa, CA 92626

Sportsways*
2050 Laura Ave.
Huntington Park, CA
  90255

Subsalve Industries
PO Box 9287
Providence, RI 02940

Tekna*
3549 Haven Ave.
Menlo Park, CA 94025

Undersea
  Environmentals, Inc.
131 E. Redwood St.,
Suite 300
Baltimore, MD 21202

Undersea Systems
112 W. Main St.
Bay Shore, NY 11706

Underwater Kinetics
7052 Convoy Ct.
San Diego, CA 92111

U.S. Cavalero*
3186 Airway Ave.,
  Suite F
Costa Mesa, CA 92626

U.S. Divers Company*
3323 W. Warner Ave.
Santa Ana, CA 92702

U.S. Laboratory
PO Box 317
Port Royal, SC 29935

U.S. Nemrod, Inc.
2315 Whitney Ave.
Hamden, CT 06518

Vectronic Instruments
568-A Alger Drive
Palo Alto, CA 94306

Watergill
18030 S. Euclid St.
Fountain Valley, CA
  92708

Wenoka Cutlery
85 North Ave.
Natick, MA 01760

White's Electronics, Inc.
1011 Pleasant Valley Rd.
Sweet Home, OR 97386

White Stag Water
  Sports* Division
  363 W. Victoria St.
Carson, CA 90749

World Below
Box 20622 SW Station
St. Louis, MO 63139

Zodiac of North
  America, Inc.
  11 Lee St.
Annapolis, MD 21401

*Members of Diving Equipment Manufacturers Association, which was formed in 1970 to set equipment performance standards, watchdog diving legislation, and sponsor a yearly trade show/convention for dive store dealers. The DEMA trade show is the world's largest preview of every major line of diving equipment.

Glossary

ABS: Acrylonitril-butadiene-styrene. High impact plastic material used in a number of underwater products. Cycolac is the brand name of a particular grade of ABS.

Absolute Pressure: The total pressure exerted underwater. To find the absolute pressure, add the surface air pressure (usually 14.7 lbs. per sq. in. to the gauge pressure, also expressed as PSIA (pounds per square inch absolute).

Air Embolism: Blockage of blood vessels by gas bubbles in bloodstream. Usually occurs in lungs due to holding pressurized air in lungs on ascent. Can be fatal.

Ambient Pressure: The surrounding water pressure at any given depth, expressed as absolute pressure.

Arbalete: From the French word for "crossbow." Describes a type of speargun powered by one or more rubber slings.

Atmosphere: Unit of pressure equivalent to the pressure of air at sea level (14.7 psi). Water pressure increases by one atmosphere every 33 feet. Abbreviated as atm or ATM.

Bathyscaphe: Greek for "light boat." A navigable submersible with a watertight compartment beneath a buoyancy chamber.

Bathysphere: Tethered pressureproof diving sphere.

Bends: See "Decompression Sickness."

Bottom Time: Total elapsed time from moment diver leaves surface in descent to next full minute he begins ascent, measured in minutes.

Breathhold: See "Free Diving," "Skin Diving."

Bug: Diver's slang for lobster.

C-Card: Certification card. Documentation that diver has completed a course of instruction. Generally required for renting or buying life-support apparatus, having scuba tanks filled, or diving with most clubs or charter operations.

Caisson Disease: See "Decompression Sickness."

Check-Out: Dive made during training to determine how well students have mastered skills learned in pool or classroom. Should always be conducted in open water.

Closed Circuit: Type of scuba in which exhalations are re-circulated. Also called a rebreather.

Closed Dress: Type of helmet diving dress in which diver is fully sealed off from water.

Decompression Sickness: Illness or injury caused by gas dissolved in blood stream or body tissues under pressure forming bubbles as ambient pressure decreases. Caused by ascending too fast from certain depths and not following decompression tables. May be prevented by proper "staged ascent" or treated in a decompression chamber (see "Hyperbaric Chamber").

Demand Regulator: Automatic mechanical device that reduces cylinder pressure to ambient water pressure and feeds it to diver on demand.

Equalizing: Adjusting air pressure on each side of a membrane to relieve pressure from one side. See "Eustachian Tubes."

Eustachian Tube: Bony tube from middle ear to nasopharynx. Letting pressurized air into the eustachian tubes (by swallowing or holding the nose and blowing) will equalize water pressure on the eardrum.

Exposure Suit: Body covering designed to keep the diver warm underwater. May be "wet" (with water allowed to seep into an insulating neoprene foam) or "dry" (with water kept away from contact with diver's skin).

Fathom: Measurement of the depth of water equal to 6 feet.

Free Diving: Vague term sometimes applied to both skin and scuba diving as opposed to surface-connected diving, but used most frequently (and exclusively in this book) as a synonym for "Skin Diving."

Free Flow: Unchecked escape of compressed air. In regulators, free flow can be caused by a malfunction or by a differential in pressure which opens second stage valve allowing a steady stream of air to escape.

Frogman: Misnomer for underwater swimmer first applied to early U.S. Underwater Demolition Teams in WW II because of the resemblance of their fins to the webbed hind feet of a frog.

Hard Hat: Slang description of helmet used with traditional closed diving dress. The term "hard hat diving" differentiates the helmeted, tethered bottom-walker from the free swimming skin and scuba diver.

Hydroplane: Rudder on horizontal axis designed to obtain reaction from water it moves through. Commonly used on submersibles.

Hydrostatic Pressure: The pressure a liquid exerts or transmits. In this book, hydrostatic pressure is used as a synonym for water pressure.

Hydrostatic Testing: Measuring scuba tank's ability to withstand its rated (working) pressure. Tank is placed in sealed, waterfilled container and pressurized with water to 5/3 of its working pressure. Expansion and contaction of the tank are measured through water displacement. By law, high-pressure tanks must be hydrostated every five years. Each tank must carry the date of each hydrostatic test.

Hyperbaric Chamber: Pressurized chamber used in treating decompression sickness. Pressure is increased until inert gases are dissolved back into blood stream, then gradually reduced to allow them to come out of solution normally. Also called a recompression or decompression chamber.

Ichthyologist: Zoologist specializing in fishes.

Nitrogen Narcosis: Reversible disoriented state resembling intoxication and caused by overexposure to nitrogen. Occurs when breathing compressed air at great depths.

Oceanography: Study of extent and depth of oceans, including the physics and chemistry of their waters, exploitation of their resources, and marine biology.

Octopus Second Stage: Spare second stage, complete with demand mechanism and mouthpiece, which connects to low pressure port of regulator to allow two people to breathe from one tank without sharing a mouthpiece.

Open Circuit Scuba: Breathing apparatus which expels exhalations into water instead of re-circulating them.

Open Dress: Old-fashioned helmet-diving rig with helmet open to water at bottom. Air pressure inside helmet kept water away from diver's face as long as he remained in straight upright position.

O-Ring: Ring of rubber or other soft compound that forms a watertight seal between two surfaces. Most commonly seen in scuba tank valve where regulator first stage attaches to tank. Also used in camera cases and other waterproof coverings.

Oxygen Poisoning: Condition that occurs when breathing O_2 in pressures greater than one atm. Can occur when breathing pure oxygen or oxygen in combination with other gases (eg: nitrogen, helium). Symptons include convulsions, nausea, vertigo, tunnel vision. Can be fatal.

Partial Pressure: Pressure exerted by each gas in a mixture, proportionate to percentage it represents of total volume. Since air contains 21% oxygen, oxygen exerts 21% of the partial pressure of air.

Physiology: Study of functions and activities of living matter and physical and chemical phenomena involved.

Pony Tank: Spare tank carried by diver as reserve air supply.

PSIG: Pounds per square inch gauge. Measure of water pressure regardless of surface air pressure. Since most depth gauges are calibrated starting with 0 at sea level, their measurements must be converted from psig to absolute pressure when diving at altitudes where surface pressures are lower than 14.7 psi.

Purge Valve: One-way valve designed to let air or water pass in one direction. Most commonly seen in the diving mask, where it lets exhalations or water out without letting more water in.

Self-Contained Underwater Breathing Apparatus: Device in which breathing gas supply is carried with diver, so he can swim with no connection to surface. Includes both open circuit and closed circuit scuba.

Skin Diving: Diving without artificial breathing aids other than a snorkel. See "Breathhold" and "Free Diving."

Sport Diving: Catchall phrase encompassing both skin and scuba diving.

Staged Ascent: Stopping on ascent to allow gas to be eliminated normally from tissues and blood stream, thus avoiding decompression sickness. Decompression tables spell out the number and duration of stops necessary for various bottom times at various depths.

Venturi Effect: Increase in flow of a liquid or gas as it is forced into a constricted passage. Some regulator second stages employ venturi tubes to increase air flow. Vented fins utilize venturi action to add velocity in power phase of kick.

Visual Inspection Program: Interior inspection of scuba tank, to detect signs of rust or pitting (steel cylinders) or aluminum oxide (aluminum cylinders). Should be conducted annually.

Notes

A NOTICE TO THE READER

The prices of all products listed in this book have been omitted primarily because they are subject to frequent change. This would make the book outdated before the next edition could be printed. The publisher does, however, maintain a printed list of current prices. This may be obtained by sending two (2) first class stamps along with your name and address to: The Great Outdoors Trading Company, 24759 Shoreline Highway, Marshall, California 94940

WE NEED YOUR HELP

It is the intention of the publisher to stay abreast of the developments in this sport by printing new editions of this book on a regular basis. We ask, then, that all readers, organizations, dealers and manufacturers join in the effort to keep this book up-to-date by sending us any corrections, additions, revisions or deletions they may have. This information, concerning any of the subjects covered herein, will be gratefully appreciated. We ask that this data follow the general format of our present listings and be mailed to: The Great Outdoors Trading Company, 24759 Shoreline Highway, Marshall, CA 94940.